EXPLORING GEOGRAPHY

3 The Global Community

Vincent Bunce

Series editor Simon Ross

Addison Wesley Longman Limited
Edinburgh Gate, Harlow, Essex, CM20 2JE, England
and Associated Companies throughout the World.

First published 1992
Fifth impression 1998
ISBN 0 582 06796 0

Set in 12/13 pt Palatino (Lasercomp)

Produced by Addison Wesley Longman China Limited, Hong Kong.
GCC/05

Member of BPCC Ltd
Illustrations by Kathy Baxendale, Peter Edwards, Hardlines and
Lynn Williams

British Library Cataloguing in Publication Data

Bunce Vincent
Exploring Geography 3. The Global Community.
I. Title
910
ISBN 0-582-067960

We are grateful to the following for permission to reproduce photographs and other copyright material;

Baltimore Sun/Today/Kevin Kallangher (print from Centre for Study of Cartoons, University of Kent), page 47; BBC, 8.4 fig 1 *left*; Michael Bussell, 9.3 fig 1 and 11.2 fig 5 *above*; J. Allen Cash Photolibrary, 2.1 fig 3, 3.1 fig 1 *above left*, 3.2 fig 2 (tundra), 4.1 fig 1 *below right*, 7.2 fig 3 *right*, 9.5 fig 8 and 10.1 fig 3; DAS Photo, 7.4 fig 2 *above right*; Environmental Picture Library 8.1 fig 2 *below* (Bob Martin); Greg Evans Picture Library, 9.2 fig 1 *left*, 10.2 fig 1 *left*, 10.5 fig 3, 11.1 fig 6 *below*, 11.2 fig 4, 12.1 fig 1 *left* and 12.2 fig 1; Ffotograff, 4.5 fig 2 (Charles Aithie); Leslie Garland Picture Library, 12.3 fig 1; Sally and Richard Greenhill, 6.2 fig 1 *above centre*; Greenpeace Communications, 11.3 fig 3 *below left* (Midgeley) and 12.4 fig 5 (Ferraris); Robert Harding Picture Library, 2.3 fig 2, 2.4 fig 1 *right*, 3.5 fig 8 *above left*, 5.4 fig 2 *below right* (Gavin Hellier), 7.3 fig 1, 10.2 fig 1 *above right*, 11.1 fig 6 *above* and 11.2 fig 1 *above right*; Holt Studios International, 9.5 fig 4 *above right* and *below right* (Nigel Cattlin); Hutchison Library, 10.3 fig 6 (Jordai); ICCE Photo Library, 3.5 fig 8 *above centre*; Image Bank, 3.2 fig 2 (rainforest/J. Carmichael), 6.1 fig 1 (Hildago), 6.1 fig 3 (Nancy Brown), 6.2 fig 1 *above left* (Scmid Langsfield); 9.1 fig 2 *above right* (Rossi), 9.1 fig 2 *below* (Grafton M. Smith) and 10.2 fig 1 *below right* (Sobel McOnsky); London Docklands Development Corporation, 10.5 fig 4; Lonrho PLC, 10.4 fig 1 (3); Orion Press, Tokyo, 8.1 fig 5; Christine Osborne Pictures, 2.4 fig 6 and 8.4 fig 1 *right*; Panos Pictures, 3.4 fig 11 *above* (Tryeve Bolstad) and 7.2 fig 3 *left* (Bruce Paton); Photofusion, 3.5 fig 8 *above right* (Bob Watkins) and 3.5 fig 8 *below* (Janis Austin); Photo Researchers Inc, 6.2 fig 1 *above right*; Picturepoint, 5.2 figs 3 and 5, 5.3 fig 3 (3) and 5.4 fig 2 *below left*; Planet Earth Pictures, 1.1 fig 1 *below* (D. Barrett), 11.2 fig 5 *below* (A and M Shah), 12.1 fig 3 *right* (Lythgoe), 12.1 fig 3 *left* (Gasson) and 12.4 fig 1 (Amsler); Russia and Republics Photo Library, 8.1 fig 2 *above left* (Mark Wadlow); Sealand Aerial Photography, 7.1 fig 1; Select Photo Agency, 6.6 fig 1 (Alain Evrard) and 6.6 fig 3 (Ron Haviv/Saba); Science Photo Library, 1.1 fig 1 *above* (NASA), 2.1 fig 6 (David Parker), 4.2 fig 1 (Lawrence Livermore Laboratory), 6.4 fig 2 (Martin Dohrn), 7.1 fig 2 (Earth Satellite Corporation), 7.4 fig 2 *below right* (David Parker), 8.3 fig 5 (A and H Michler), 8.4 fig 2 (Sheila Terry) and 12.2 fig 5 (NASA); Skyscan Balloon Photography, 11.5 fig 1; South American Pictures, 8.1 fig 2 *above right* and 9.2 fig 1 *right* (Tony Morrison); Frank Spooner Pictures, 4.4 fig 2 (Gamma Liaison/Nickelsnerg), 8.2 fig 2 (E. Sander/Liaison) and 10.4 fig 4 (Gamma/Lochon); Still Pictures, 3.2 fig 2 (grassland/M. Edwards), 9.1 fig 2 *above left* (M. Edwards), 9.2 fig 1 *centre left* (M. Edwards) and 12.1 fig 1 right (Daniel Dancer); Tony Stone Worldwide, 5.4 fig 4 (Le Garsmeur) and 7.4 fig 2 *centre right* (M. Edwards); Swift Pictures, 2.3 fig 9 (Mike Read); Telegraph Colour Library, 1.3 fig 3 (SF NRSC), 3.1 fig 1 *above right* (International Stock Photolibrary), 4.1 fig 1 *above right* (VCL), 7.4 fig 3 (VCL) and 9.1 fig 1 (A. Low); Toyota UK, 10.2 fig 4; Tropix, 2.4 fig 8 (Martin Birley), 3.1 fig 1 *below* (D. Stewart), 3.4 fig 11 *below* (R. Cansdale), 4.1 fig 1 *below* (M and V Birley) and 9.5 fig 4 *left* (M and V Birley); Tony Waltham, 2.4 fig 2 *left*, 2.4 fig 5 *left* and *below right* and 9.2 fig 1 *centre right*.

The Ordnance Survey map on page 159 is reproduced by permission of her Majesty's Stationery Office, Crown ©.

All other photographs were supplied by the author.

The author would like to acknowledge material provided by: Dave Barlow, F. Basley (3.3 Fig 5), and John Hughes.

Thanks to all my former colleagues, the staff and students, of St Mary and St Joseph's School, Sidcup, Kent, especially Ron Hesketh and Brian McLaughlin.

Contents

1 Understanding maps 1

1.1 Maps in geography 1
1.2 Knowing where places are 4
1.3 Why are places different? 6
1.4 A world of difference 8

2 Landscapes and processes 11

2.1 Violent earth 11
2.2 Drifting continents 15
2.3 Battered coasts 18
2.4 Growing deserts 22
2.5 Contrasting landscapes in Iceland 26

3 Weather and climate 30

3.1 The world of weather 30
3.2 Looking at climate 32
3.3 Climatic hazards 34
3.4 Climate change 38

4 Resources and energy 42

4.1 A world full of energy? 42
4.2 A nuclear world? 44
4.3 Renewable energy – the only alternative? 47
4.4 Earthly riches – minerals in Brazil 49
4.5 Opening up Siberia 52

5 Places in the wider world 55

5.1 The superpowers compared 55
5.2 Industry, energy and environment in Japan 56
5.3 China: The giant of Asia 59
5.4 Is China and economically developing country? 62

6 People and quality of life 65

6.1 Worlds apart; the 'north-south' divide 65
6.2 Measuring development 68
6.3 Growing population 71
6.4 Health for all? 73
6.5 Aid debt and closing the gap 76
6.6 Refugees 77

7 Settlement 81

7.1 People patterns 81
7.2 Expanding cities 84
7.3 World metropolis 88
7.4 City present ... city future 91

8 Transport, communications and trade 96

8.1 Growing networks 96
8.2 Types of transport 99
8.3 International trade 102
8.4 Information flows 107

9 Farming 111

9.1 Feeding the world 111
9.2 World farming systems 115
9.3 Farming in the developing world 118
9.4 Developed world farming 120
9.5 Important issues in farming today 123

10 Industry 129

10.1 Patterns of work 129
10.2 Large or small – which is best? 132
10.3 Changing industry 136
10.4 Transnational companies and newly industrialising countries 139
10.5 Expanding services 142

11 Leisure and recreation 146

11.1 Time on our hands 146
11.2 Visiting the great outdoors 149
11.3 Cyprus – an island of tourists 152
11.4 Tourism in the developing world 155
11.5 People, leisure and the environment 158

12 Ecosystems and environment 161

12.1 Ecosystems, environment and people 161
12.2 Tropical rainforest – a fragile ecosystem 163
12.3 Fouling the nest – a dirty planet 166
12.4 Polluting the seas 169

Acknowledgements

We are grateful to the following for permission to reproduce copyright material:

Basic Books *World Resources* 1988–89 6.1 Fig 5, 6.3 Fig 1, 6.4 Fig 1, 6.5 Fig 2, 9.1 Fig 3; Berkhamsted School. Members of 4B (1990) 1.1 Fig 2; BP Statistical Review of World Energy 1989 4.1 Fig 2, 1990 8.3 Fig 6; *Brazil Trade & Industry* May 1985 p. 32 4.4 Fig 1; Centre for World Development Education *Tourism Development* 11.4 Fig 6; *Cyprus Weekly* June 2–8 1989 Edition 500 "Government moves to limit development" 11.3 Fig 5; *Daily Mail* 26.6.90 8.2 Fig 1; Dept of Transport *Transport and the environment* p. 7 8.2 Fig 4; *Development Forum* vol. 18 (2) March-April 1990 (UN Dept of Public Information) 6.2 Fig 3; Development and Cooperation 1/82 p. 32 4.3 Fig 3, 6/89 6.4 Fig 3, No 2 1990 10.4 Fig 4; East Anglian, London Regional and University of London Schools Exam Council Joint O-level/CSE Geog Syll. A (954) 1987 2.3 Fig 9; East Midland Regional Exam Board/ Cambridge local exam syndicate joint GCE/CSE paper 14–18 Project paper 1080/1 Summer 1984 7.3 Fig 2; *The Economist* 23.9.89, World Bank UNCTAD 8.3 Fig 4; *Evening Standard* Company Ltd 19.2.88 "The cliff-top village that is fighting the sea" 2.3 Fig 1; *Financial Times* 8.6.90 8.4 Fig 3, 27.1.89 p. 42 10.5 Fig 1; Geodaetsk Institute 1:100 000 Iceland, sheet 59 Dyrholaey Landmaelingar Islands/Iceland Geodetic Survey 2.5 Fig 3; Greenpeace *Greenhouse Effect* leaflet 3.4 Fig 3; Worldwide *Guardian* "25 000 die in Iranian earthquake" 22.4.90 2.1 Fig 8, 19.9.91 3.1 Fig 2, "Hot summer, mild winter" 21.6.89 3.2 Fig 3, "The world's oil lifeline" 6.8.90 8.3 Fig 5, 2.11.90 "For years we resisted but there is no reaction" 12.2 Fig 6, 15.7.88 12.3 Fig 4; HMSO *Regional Trends* 1990 p. 189 10.5 Fig 4 reproduced with the permission of the controller of HMSO; Hobsons Publishing Plc *Finding out about conservation and development* p. 5 12.4 Fig 6; Hodder & Stoughton Ltd extract from *Quest for Adventure* Chris Bonnington p. 186 1.1 Fig 1; *Independent* 22.11.89 p. 5 4.2 Fig 4, "Gold diggers bring ecological tragedy to Brazil" 3.8.89 p. 10 4.4 Fig 3, 18.12.89 p. 18 6.5 Fig 2, 8.5.90 12.3 Fig 3; *Independent on Sunday* 26.5.91 1.4 Fig 1; *Japan Education Journal* No 39 1989 p. 4 article by M. Carr 9.4 Fig 2, No 40 article by M. Carr 10.2 Fig 5; Japan National Tourist Organisation 7.3 Fig 4; LEAG GCSE paper 2 June 1988 8.1 Fig 3; Lonrho Plc Annual Report & Accounts 1989 10.4 Fig 1; Simon & Schuster Young Books *Natural Hazards* J. Flatt 3.3 Fig 3; Marie Stopes International 6.3 Fig 3; Mary Glasgow Publications *Geoactive 3* 1989 p. 2 3.3 Fig 4, *Geoactive 12* "Rainforest destruction, Brazil" Spring 1990 12.2 Fig 2; Midland Examining Group Syll. M GCSE paper 2 1989 2.4 Fig 7; *National Geographic* Magazine June 1968 2.2 Fig 3, Special Energy supplement Feb 1981 p. 69 4.3 Fig 2 (part); Thomas Nelson & Sons Ltd *The World* D. Waugh (1987) 9.2 Fig 1; New English Library *The Greenhouse Effect* S. Boyle & J. Ardill 3.4 Fig 4; *New Internationalist* Nov 1988 "Sweetness and plight" P. Cox 9.3 Fig 5; *New Scientist* 22.10.88 3.4 Fig 1 "Trees for Africa" P. Harrison 14.5.87 4.3 Fig 1, 15.9.88 9.5 Fig 8; *New Society* 17.8.78 "A world without oil" D. Jackson 8.3 Fig 5; Nippon Steel 10.3 Fig 5; ODA *British Overseas Development* June 1989 No 7 6.6 Fig 7, 8.4 Fig 3; *OECD Observer* No 155 Dec 1988–Jan 1989 p. 24 4.5 Fig 3; Oliver & Boyd *Worldscapes* ed. T. H. Masterton p. 13 2.2 Fig 2. *North America* Tweed et al. 10.3 Fig 4; Ordnance Survey 1:50 000 sheet 188 Maidstone, reproduced with the permission of the controller of Her Majesty's Stationery Office 11.5 Fig 3; Worldwide Oxford University Press *Landforms: Introduction to Geomorphology* Wiegard & Galbraith 2.4 Fig 5, *Resources, Energy and Development* Punnett 4.3 Fig 2 (part), *Sense of Place Alternative Workbook 3* Beddis 5.3 Fig 4, figures from *Global Report on Human Settlement* 1986 7.2 Fig 1; Pan Books *Gaia Atlas of Planet Management* ed. N. Myers reproduced with the permission of Gaia Books Ltd pp. 84–85 12.4 Fig 2; Penguin *Among the Cities* Jan Morris pp. 183–4 2.5 Fig. 2a, *Inside Japan* P. Tasker pp. 2–4 7.3 Fig 3; The Refugee Council 1991 6.6 Fig 5; *Refugees* Feb 1989 p. 21 6.6 Fig 3; Routledge Ltd "Industry, energy and transport" in M. Howard *Geography of Contemporary China* eds. Cannon & Jenkins 5.4 Fig 3; Adapted from 'Strategies for Energy Use', John H. Gibbons, Peter D. Blair, Holly L. Guin, Copyright © 1989 by Scientific American, Inc. All rights reserved. p. 91 4.3 Fig 4; *South* Magazine July 1989 p. 18 Fig 1, pp. 12–16 "Going for the fast lane" M. K. George 8.3 Fig 1, 10.4 Fig 5, August 1989 p. 16 "Riding the tourist boom" 11.1 Fig 4; *Soviet Union* No 3 (480) 1990 10.3 Fig 7; Worldwide *Sunday Times* John Lawson 12.2.89 3.3 Fig 1, Phil Green 2.4.89 12.4 Fig 3; *Teaching Geography* "Environments, pollution and Japan" Heppell & Wiltshire April 1990 5.2 Fig 6; Thomson Worldwide 11.2 Fig 3; Stanley Thornes (Publishers) Ltd *Steps in Geography Book 1* R. Bateman & F. Martin 2.4 Fig 2, *Decision-making Geography* Law & Smith 7.2 Fig 3; *Time* Magazine "Colombia's mortal agony" 25.11.85 2.1 Fig 5, 17.4.89 "The two Alaskas" 12.4 Fig 4; *Today* "Our global hothouse" 26.5.90 3.4 Fig 2; Tokyo Subway 8.1 Fig 1; Copyright, United Nations 4.1 Fig 3; UNDP Human Development Report 1991 5.1 Fig. 4, 5.3 Fig. 1, 5.4 Fig 5; UNESCO Courier No 122 July–August 1990 11.1 Fig 3; UNFPA State of the World Report 1990 5.4 Fig 5, estimates for 1991 7.1 Fig 4; UNICEF *State of the world's children* 1989 6.2 Fig 4; UNHCR Magazine Feb 1989 6.6 Fig 4; World Bank *World Development Report* 1989 6.2 Fig 4, *World Bank Atlas* 1989 9.1 Fig 4; Worldwatch Institute *State of the world* 1990 9.5 Fig 6; Kevin Kallaugher, Today, Centre of Cartoon Study, University of Kent 4.2 Fig 5

Every effort has been made to contact copyright holders but if any have been overlooked, the publishers would welcome information enabling them to rectify this.

1 Understanding maps

1.1 Maps in geography

The study of geography is concerned with people, places and environments. These vary greatly from one part of the world to another. Evidence to show what places are like, and how they differ can take different forms:

- statistics - facts and figures;
- written descriptions;
- visual images - drawings, photographs, and images gathered by **remote sensing** devices like satellites.

Each method reveals something different about a place. Figure 1 shows how Mount Everest can be described using the methods listed.

Figure 1
Mount Everest – what is it like?

Mount Everest: What is it like?

Expeditions now discouraged due to environmental damage

Height: 8848 metres (29 028 feet)

Mountain range: Himalayas

Latitude: 27.59°N

Longitude: 86.56°E

Lowest recorded temperature: −47°C

From the south, Mount Everest resembles a medieval fortress – its triangular summit, the keep, guarded by the turreted walls of the outer bailey; Lhotse, fourth highest mountain in the world, is a massive corner tower linking the high curtain wall of Nuptse. The gateway to this fortress is the Khumbu Icefall, portcullised with séracs, moated with crevasses. Few mountain peaks are better guarded or have resisted so many assaults. There was no doubt concerning the whereabouts of the mountain or even of how to approach it from the south, as there had been in the case of Annapurna and Dhaulagiri, but there was a great deal of doubt as to whether it could be climbed from this direction.

from *Quest for Adventure* by Chris Bonington

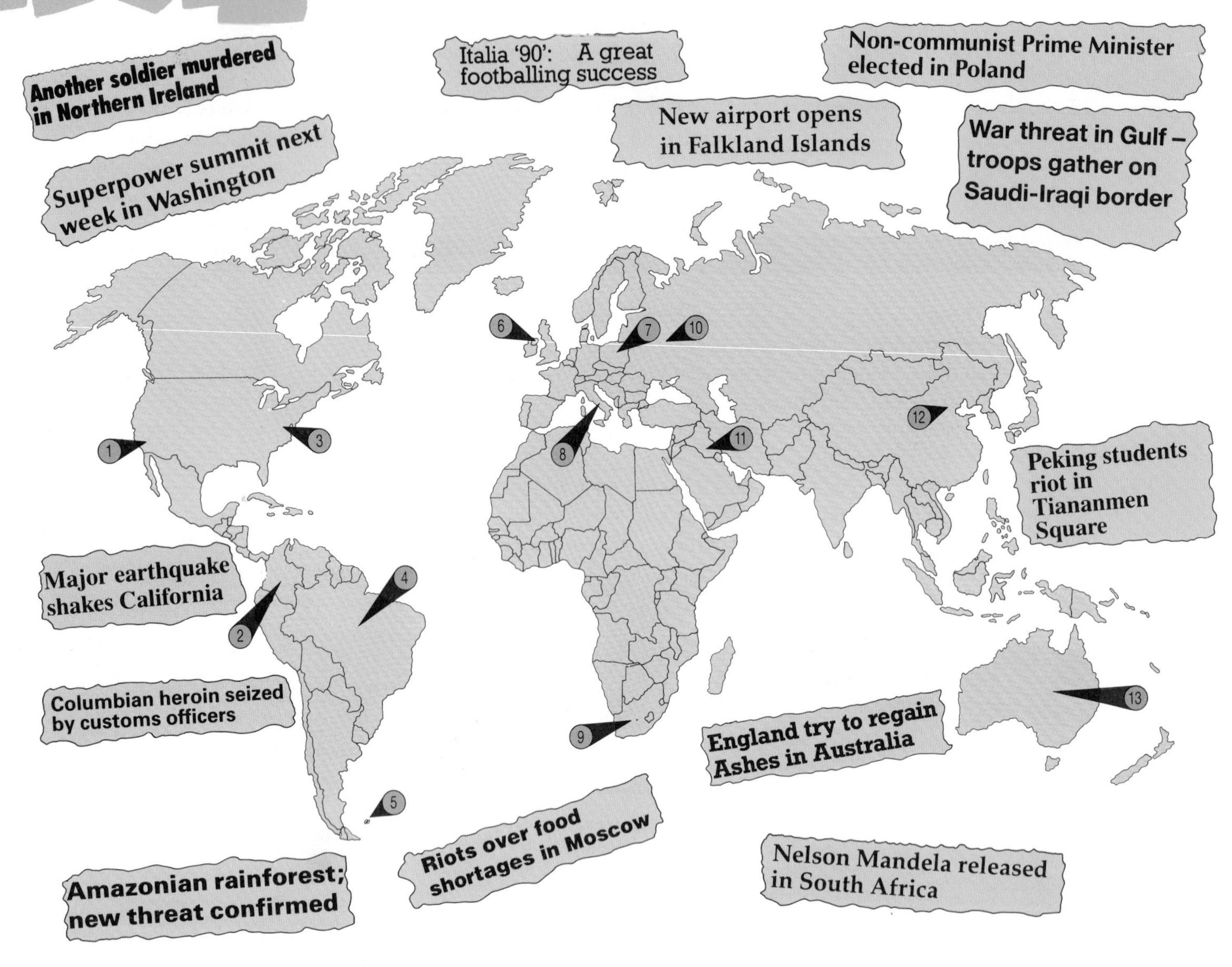

Figure 2 Geography in the news

One of the most useful ways that geographers have of looking at the world is by using **maps**. Maps are scale drawings which show what a landscape, or a particular aspect of it, is like. They take a birds-eye or plan view. Maps are used in different ways in everyday life: they appear in newspapers and on the television news; they tell us what the weather will be like; they help us find our way around, and also to make sense of what is going on around us (Figure 2). There are different uses for maps, and many different kinds of maps (Figure 3).

Maps have two important functions. They indicate where places are, and also what they are like. Both functions are important. A casual look through any newspaper will reveal news from all over the world. Today, communities world-wide are more dependent on each other than ever before - international trade has reached new levels, many of our raw materials come from overseas; people migrate huge distances to new homes; and more people are enjoying overseas holidays.

Figure 3 Different types of maps

topographical map	a map showing an area's detailed surface features e.g. ordnance survey maps
topological map	map in which scale & direction have been distorted. Often used for transport networks
mental map	map which shows one person's ideas about where places are located. Not usually drawn to scale
thematic map	map which shows the distribution of a particular aspect of geography e.g. climate maps, landuse maps
choropleth map	map using colours or shading to represent regions which are different from one another in a particular way
isoline map	map using lines to join together places which have something in common e.g. contour lines, or pressure lines (isobars) on a weather map.

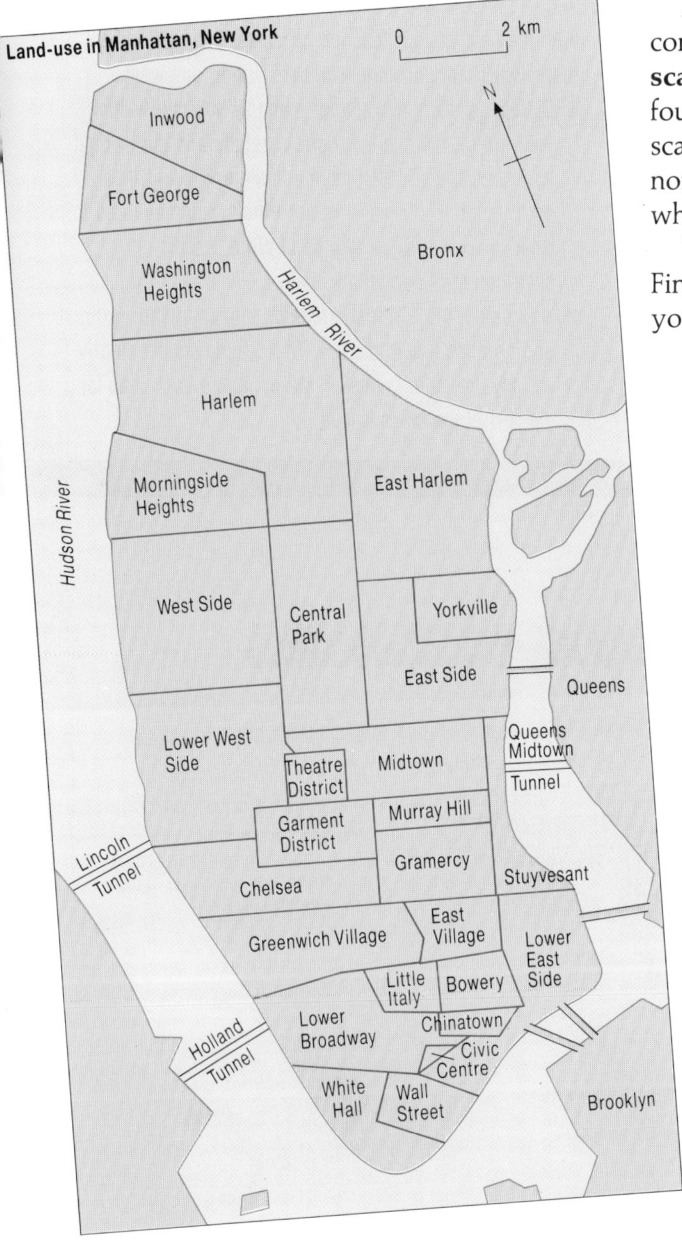

Although maps may have different purposes, they should all contain certain elements. Take Figure 4 as an example. It has a title, **scale**, **north point**, a **key**, and a border. These elements should be found on all maps. The map's title describes its purpose, while the scale tells you how much smaller or larger than real-life it is. The north point allows you to **orientate** the map, and the key explains which symbols have been used to depict particular features.

Try to be aware of maps, wherever and whenever they are used. Find out what their purpose is, and look at them carefully to see if you can 'read' or interpret them.

Area	Land use	Area	Land use
Inwood	RH	Murray Hill	RH
Fort George	RH	Gramercy	RH
Washington Heights	RL	Chelsea	RH
Harlem	RL	Stuyvesant	RH
East Harlem	RL	Greenwich Village	S
Morningside Heights	RH	East Village	RH
West Side	RH	Lower East Side	RL
Central Park	OS	Lower Broadway	S
East Side	RH	Little Italy	S
Yorkville	RH	Bowery	RL
Lower West Side	RL	Chinatown	S
Theatre District	S	White Hall	CF
Midtown	CBD	Wall Street	CF
Garment District	S	Civic Centre	CF

Key

CBD	Central Business District
OS	Open space
CF	City, government and financial area
RH	Residential (high quality)
RL	Residential (low quality)
S	Specialist (education, arts, retail and industry)

Figure 4

Activities

1 Study the information about Mount Everest contained in Figure 1.

a Each of the items shown tells you different things. Which two **types** of information do you think are the most useful? Explain your answer.

b What additional resource would you need to explain to someone where Mount Everest was located?

c Produce a diagram of your own similar to that in Figure 1. It can be about a place or area of your choice, e.g. a town, a forest, an ocean.

2 Maps are an important method used by the media to convey information about the location of places. A quick survey of newspaper headlines in 1990 (Figure 2) shows thirteen events occurring in different parts of the world.

a Match each headline with the correct numbered location on the map. You may need an atlas to help you with this activity.

b Organise your own media survey. Choose a newspaper or a TV news broadcast. One day list between 10-15 important news stories taking place around the world. Plot the locations of stories on a blank world map. Draw a small symbol or sketch by each location to indicate the type of news story. Include a key with brief details of the news event shown.

3 This book contains different types of maps. Look through it to find **one** example of each of the map types listed in Figure 3. Write down the number of the page on which each type appears.

4 You will need a copy of the map in Figure 4 for this activity.
  a Choose 6 colours or shades. Then complete your map by colouring (or shading) each neighbourhood marked on the map. Include your chosen colours or shades in the key.
  b Now answer these questions using your completed land-use map:
    i Where is the most important city, government and financial area in Manhattan?
    ii Is the CBD well-located in Manhattan? Explain why.
    iii What sort of housing mainly surrounds the open space of Central Park?
    iv Approximately what area of Manhattan is covered by residential landuse? (Use the method of estimating areas you learnt in Exploring Geography 2).

5 You will need to work in groups of 3 or 4 for this activity. With the help of your teacher, organise a survey of the maps which appear in newspapers during one week.
  a Collect as many newspaper maps as you can within your group. Look at each one carefully and think about how good it is. Does it have a scale and a key, or a north point? Is it clear and accurate? (You may need to refer to your atlas to help you.) Write a short assessment of each map.
  b Now select the 10 most interesting maps in your group, and produce a wall display. The display should clearly identify the main points of interest about each map for the rest of the class to see.

1.2 Knowing where places are

When a number of maps are collected together in book form, they are called an atlas. It is important for all of us to be able to use an atlas quickly and efficiently to find the particular information we want.

Using an atlas

There are two ways of finding the correct map in any atlas. At the front there will be a contents page. This lists the main maps and gives brief information about what type they are. The majority of maps in most atlases will be of two types:

1 Physical maps: (or relief maps): these show the main highland and lowland areas as well as rivers, lakes, deserts and other physical features;
2 Political maps: these show the main countries, towns and cities, as well as economic features like transport routes.

There may in addition be some special thematic maps, which show the distribution pattern of a particular feature like climate or population. The contents page is a good way of quickly finding out which pages the map of a particular country or area you want to look at are on. If you want to find the location of a specific place though, you will need to look at the index at the back of the atlas.

Figure 1

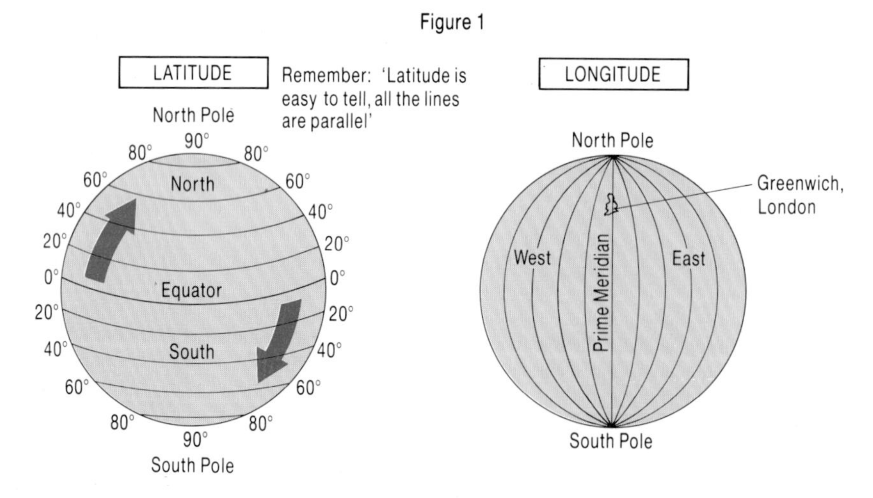

Figure 2
Key lines of latitude and longitude

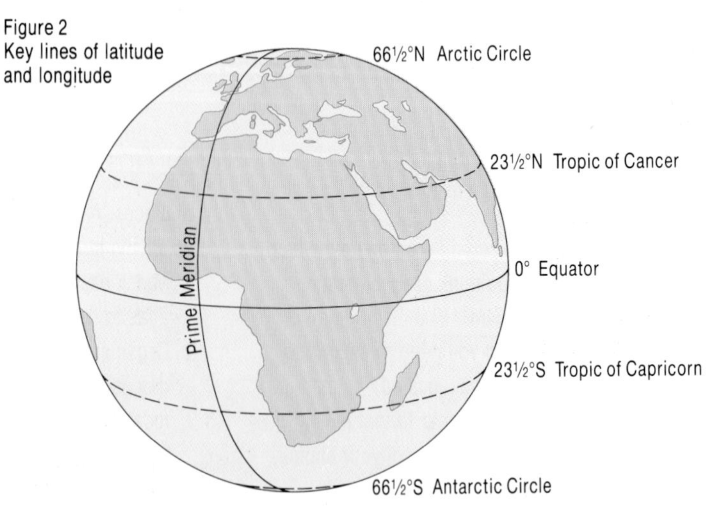

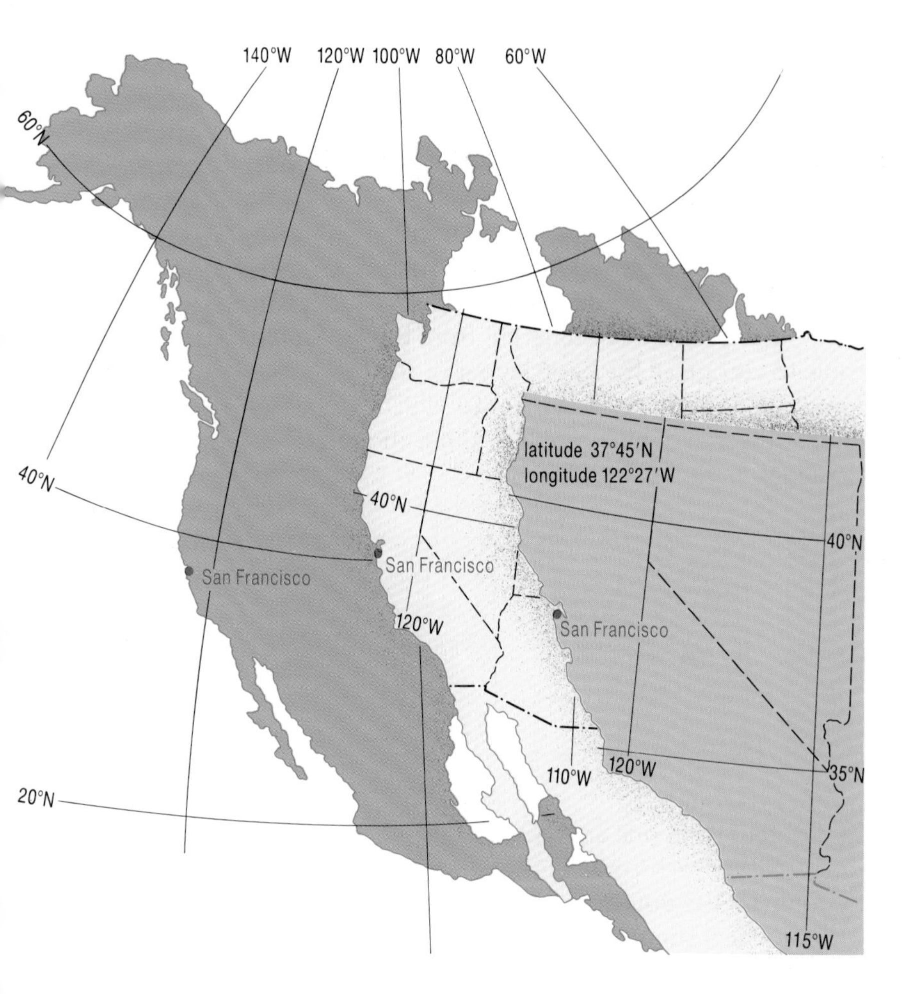

Latitude and Longitude

The index, as you have now seen, tells you which page to look on to find a specific place, and uses a grid system to help you locate that place precisely. The grid is based on lines of **latitude** and **longitude**. Lines of latitude run around the world, parallel to the equator. Lines of longitude pass through the north and south poles (Figure 1).

There are five key lines of latitude and one key line of longitude (Figure 2). Towns and cities can be located by measuring, in degrees, how far they are north or south of the equator, and east or west of the **Prime Meridian** or Greenwich Meridian. The latitude and longitude measurements form a pair of co-ordinates, which describe the location of a place precisely (Figure 3). The latitude and longitude of every location on the earth's surface is unique.

Figure 3
Locating San Francisco

Activities

1 You will need an atlas for this activity.
   a Write down the atlas page numbers for the following:
      i A physical map of the world;
      ii A political map of Asia;
      iii Maps of the British Isles;
      iv The most detailed map of California;
      v A map of Japan.
   b What type of map shows towns and cities?
   c How many world maps does your atlas have? What do they show ?

2 Use your atlas index to find out all you can about the 4 places listed below. (*Hint:* you may need to refer to the abbreviations to find out what some things mean).
   a Indus; *c* Cotopaxi;
   b Gozo; *d* Ontario.

3 Study Figure 1 carefully. Write down at least two differences you notice between lines of latitude and lines of longitude.

4 Draw a circle (diameter about 5 cms) to represent the earth. Figure 2 may help.
   a Mark on the five key lines of latitude and name them.
   b Mark on the Prime Meridian.
   c Mark on the British Isles in the correct position.
   d Look up the correct latitude and longitude for London in the index and make a note of it.

5 The following list of clues should help you to locate some of the most important features on the earth's surface. Use your atlas to help you solve the clues and name each feature.
   a A great river with its mouth on the Equator;
   b a desert in Africa through which the Tropic of Cancer passes;
   c the largest country in the world through which latitude 60°N passes;
   d large port at the mouth of the Yangtze River (31°N);
   e the Prime Meridian passes through this African capital city;
   f the 'Windy City' beside Lake Michigan (42°N) in the USA;
   g the European sea (40°N, 10°E) where many of us holiday;

6 Use your atlas to locate the towns and cities which lie at the following latitude and longitude positions:

a	51°N	0°	*d*	34°S	18°E	*g*	12°S	77°W	*j*	19°N	99°W
b	5°N	0°	*e*	56°N	38°E	*h*	19°N	73°E			
c	7°N	80°E	*f*	34°S	151°E	*i*	42°N	12°E			

1.3 Why are places different?

In the last unit we learnt that every place has a unique location, and that this location can be described using latitude and longitude. Each of the seven major **continents** (Europe, Asia, North America, South America, Africa, Australasia and Antarctica) is very different from the next. You should by now be able to recognise the basic layout of the world on an atlas map. See if you can identify the continent to which each of the land masses in Figure 1 belongs. Think carefully about the differences between these continents.

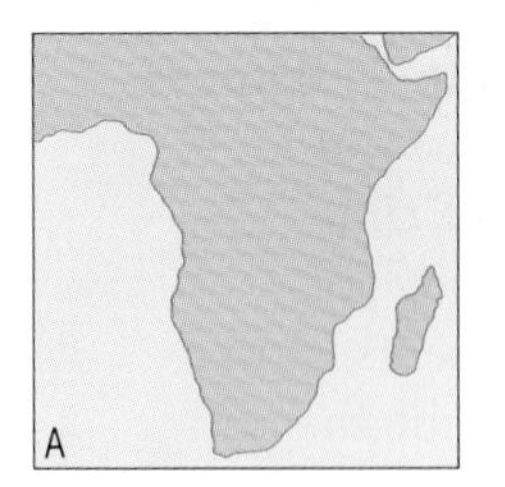

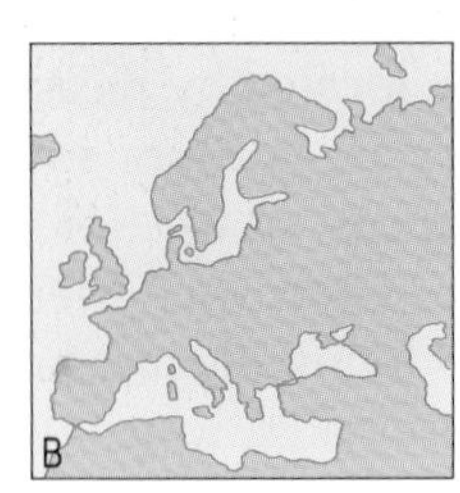

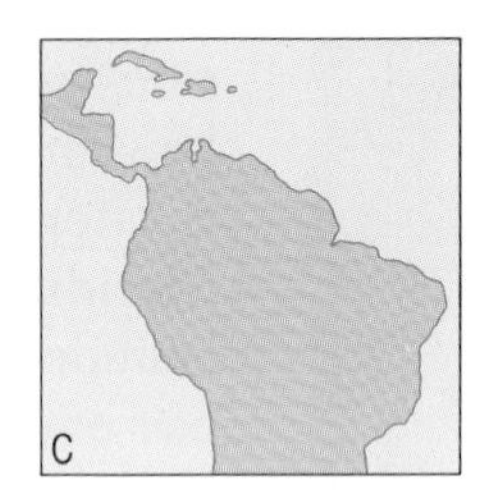

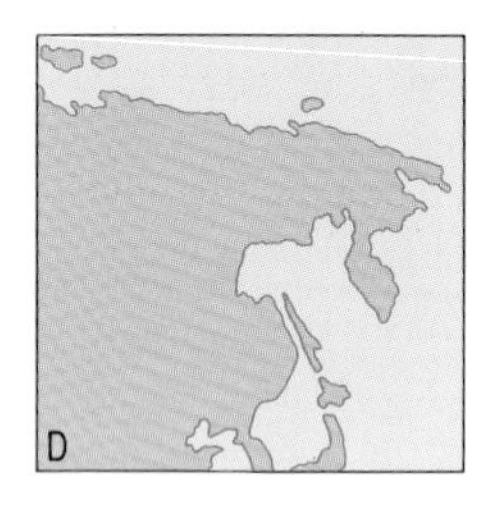

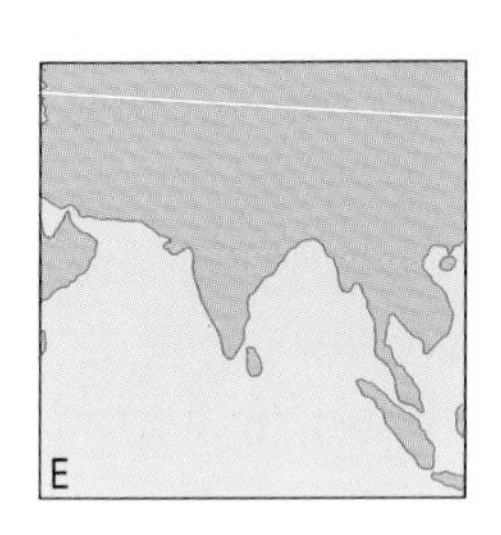

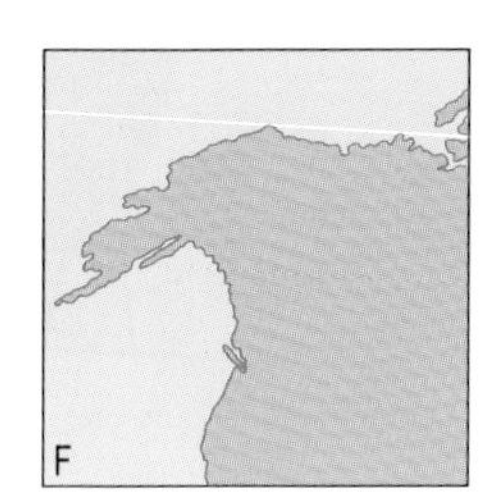

Figure 1
Global land masses

As well as continents being different from one another, it is also true that there are many contrasts within each continent. The earth's surface has many different environments as you can see in Figure 2.

Photographs often contain clues which suggest to us where they were taken: it might be the appearance of the landscape, or the type of vegetation or wildlife found there. Human activities also provide good clues e.g. the sort of crops growing or the type of industries. The appearance of people and their clothing also varies, and may suggest a location.

Figure 2
The world's temperature zones

Planet Earth (Figure 3), despite having a large and growing population, vast industries, and massive environmental problems still contains some landscapes of great beauty, such as the tropical rainforests or the unspoilt scenery of Antarctica. If the planet is to survive, then we must all take an interest in protecting these landscapes because, although they are distant, they help to maintain many of the planet's life-support systems.

Figure 3 Planet Earth

Factors which help to make places different from one another

There are several factors which combine to give a place a distinctive look and feel. These include the **latitude** or location; the **climate** (which is largely responsible for vegetation) and **resources**, which often determine where people live.

a Latitude

One reason that places vary in their characteristics is that they may be located at different distances from the equator. This has an effect on the temperature of the place, and on what will grow there. Places like Lagos in Nigeria, which is near the equator, are generally hotter than other locations further away, because the sun is stronger there. The latitude of a place and its location relative to the equator also help to control the timing and length of the seasons that it has.

b Climate

Temperature, rainfall and other aspects of climate also help to determine what a place is like. They influence the sort of vegetation that can grow, and the sort of crops that can be cultivated. Climate may also affect people's behaviour. In most Mediterranean countries there is little activity in the afternoons ('siesta time') because it is simply too hot. There are some ways in which climate limits the sort of activities that people can do in a place, but technology is enabling these limitations to be overcome. For example, parts of some deserts are now being settled and farmed with the aid of irrigation water; and minerals are being extracted in sub-zero temperatures in both Siberia and Alaska.

c Resources

The distribution of natural resources has had a major effect on the patterns of population and industrial activity. Often a deposit of coal or iron-ore leads to population growth and the development of industry and transport. The effect of resources on human patterns is most dramatically seen when a new resource is discovered, such as gold in California in the last century, or in Brazil today (Unit 4.4), and, more recently, oil in Alaska.

Activities

1 a Study the land masses in Figure 1 carefully and identify which continent each one belongs to. Refer to your atlas if you need to.

b Each of the following is a description of one of the continents. Identify the continent correctly. Use your atlas if it will help.

i. Two-thirds of this almost uninhabited continent is hot desert. The Murray-Darling river is found here.

ii. This continent contains the world's largest desert. There are over 40 countries. It is separated from the continent to the east by the Suez canal.

iii. 30% of the earth's surface is covered by this continent. Its principal mountain range, the Himalayas, contains the world's highest peak. Two huge countries dominate most of the land area.

c Using your atlas, write brief descriptions for two other continents. Each should contain clues. See if your neighbour can identify the continents you have chosen after hearing your description.

2 Choose pictures of two different landscapes from a magazine, newspaper or holiday brochure and stick them into your notes.
   a Write a brief description of each landscape.
   b List some of the main contrasts between the landscapes.

3 You will need a copy of the world map in Figure 2 for this activity. The map shows the contrasts in temperature between places which are different distances from the equator. Complete the map by shading each zone correctly. Remember to complete the key with the colours or shading you have used.

4 The following is a list of 24 geographical features (rivers, mountains, deserts, cities etc.) which you should know.

   Alps, Amazon, Andes, Athens, Berlin, Danube, Himalayas, Jakarta, Japan, Mississippi, New York, Nigeria, Nile, Peru, Rhine, Rockies, Rome, Sahara, São Paulo, Saudi Arabia, St Lawrence, Thames, Toronto, Zambezi

   a Divide the features into these categories: rivers, deserts, mountains, cities and countries. Write out each of these as a list. You may need to use your atlas index to help you.
   b Mark and label each feature on a world outline map.
   c The following lists of features each contain one feature that is an odd-one out. Find this, and explain why it is odd. You may need the help of your atlas.
      i Berlin, Paris, Shanghai, Rome, Dublin.
      ii Rockies, Andes, Himalayas, Sahara, Pennines.
      iii Johannesburg, Severn, Lagos, Zambezi, Cairo, Kenya.
      iv Arctic Circle, Equator, Tropic of Cancer, Prime Meridian, Tropic of Capricorn.
      v Tokyo, Leningrad, Beijing, Bombay, Calcutta.
      vi Yangtze, Colorado, Congo, Danube, Delhi.

5 Planet earth looks quite different to most other planets when seen from space. Figure 3 was taken from space.
   a Imagine what a space traveller might think when seeing earth like this for the first time. Write a short description.
   b If a spacecraft landed on earth it could encounter some very different landscapes. Imagine a spacecraft landing in or near your school grounds. How might the scene be described? (You may choose to write or to draw what the aliens might see.)
   c Why do you think the earth is sometimes referred to as a 'spaceship'?

1.4 A world of difference

Maps are often used in newspapers (see, for example Figure 1) to explain where places are located, but they are not often the subject of major news stories. This did happen a few years ago, when a new way of drawing the world was suggested by a German mathematician – **Arno Peters**. It led to a major controversy and arguments, with geographers and others split over the best way to draw a map of the world (Figure 2).

You will probably have used a globe in your geography lessons at school and may even have one at home. Globes are spherical like the world itself, and so they are accurate. However, when you come to draw a map on a flat surface like a piece of paper, accuracy is much more difficult to achieve. Some distortion of the earth's features is bound to occur.

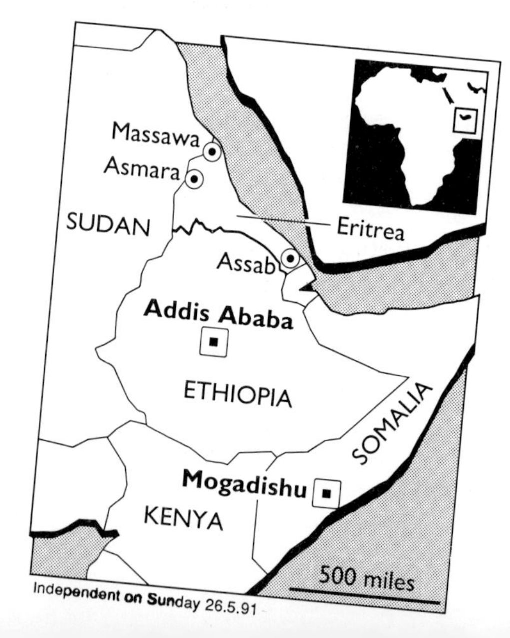

Figure 1 Newspaper map

There are various ways of turning the globe into a flat map – each of these methods is called a **map projection**. Projections are usually named after the people who first worked them out. The projection which has perhaps been used the most is called the **Mercator** projection (Figure 3). It was devised in 1569 by a Flemish **cartographer**. This map was really devised for navigators. It had to provide true directions so that compasses could be set using the map. However, in order to achieve this, Mercator had to place the lines of latitude further apart towards the poles. This distorted the size (area) of land masses, and made Greenland and the other northern hemisphere countries much larger than they really are. Compare the sizes of the land masses on the Mercator projection (Figure 3) with those on the globe. Africa is really about 15 times larger than Greenland, but on the map they appear the same size! It doesn't distort the shape of land masses, but Europe appears at the centre of the world.

There are many projections which have tried to improve on Mercator – look in your atlas to see some of them. One such projection is the **Winkelsche** projection (Figure 4), which uses a rounded grid. This means that directions are distorted, as are the shapes of countries on the edge of the map. However the areas are much truer. Compare the size of Greenland and Africa with the Mercator projection.

This brings us to the **Peters** projection. Peters decided that he wanted a map which showed countries according to their true area, and which showed directions accurately. To achieve these two things, the shapes of many countries appear rather distorted. Africa, on the Peters map looks twice as long (north-south) as it is wide (east-west). In fact the distances are about the same. Countries near the poles also appear rather flattened.

Drawing maps on flat surfaces is all about making compromises. No one projection can be entirely accurate. When you are looking at and using world maps, try to ensure you have some idea which projection has been used, and what its limitations are.

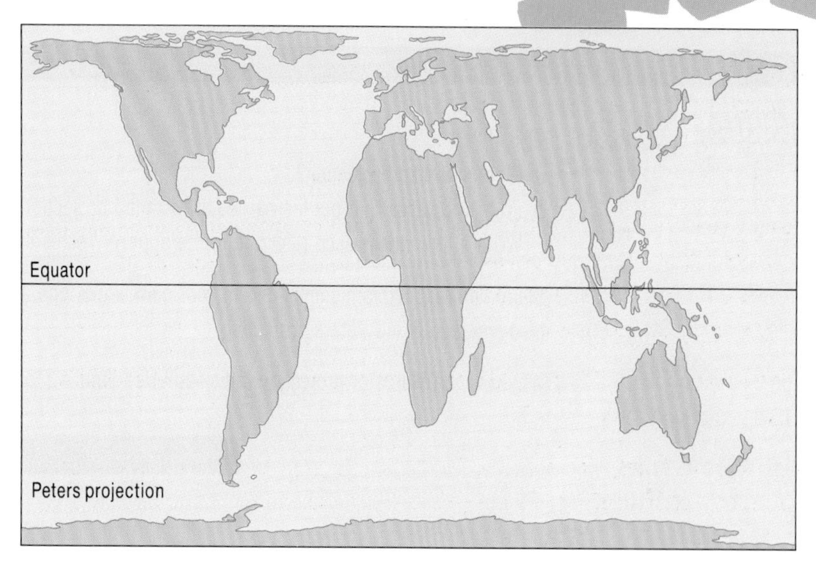

Figure 2 Peters projection

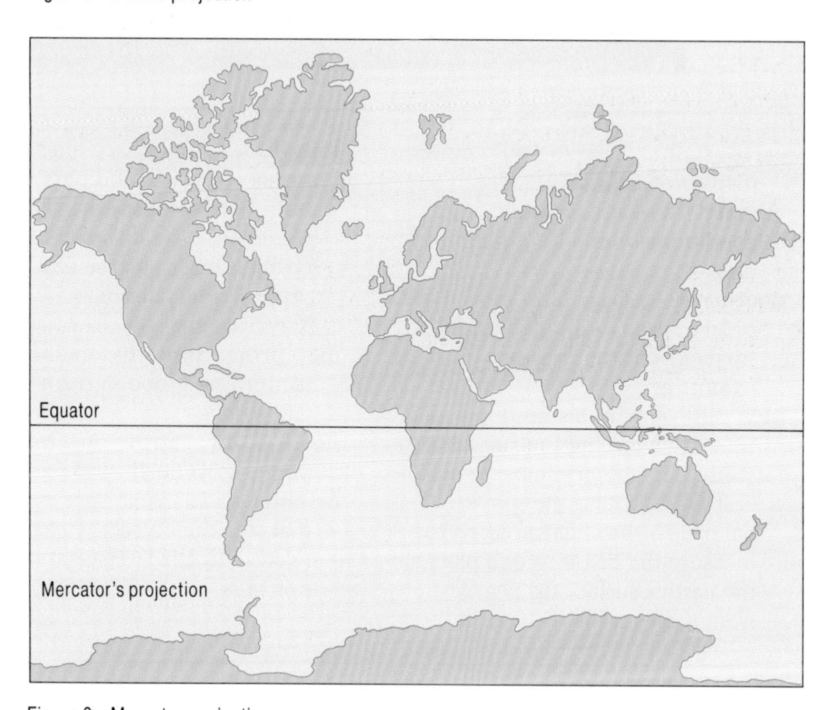

Figure 3 Mercator projection

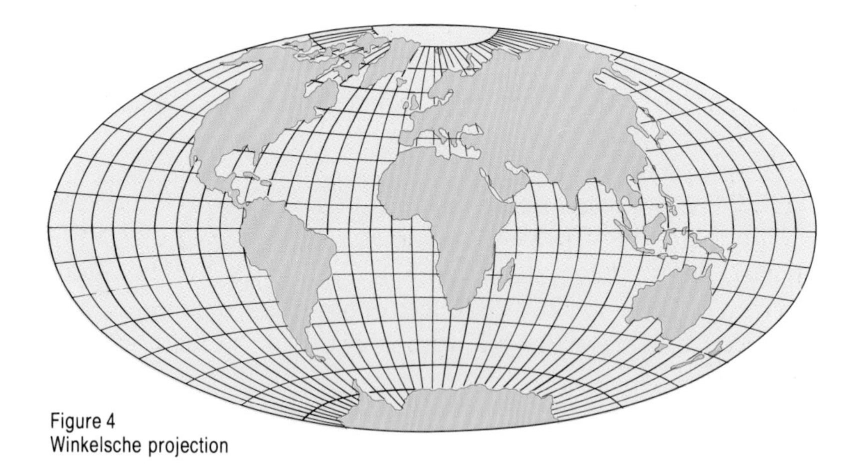

Figure 4
Winkelsche projection

Activities

1 a What is a map projection?
  b From your atlas find out the names of two map projections not mentioned in this unit. Write a little about each referring to the apparent sizes of Africa and Greenland.

2 Study Figure 2. Explain simply and in your own words one advantage and one disadvantage of the Peters projection.

3 Why was the Mercator projection criticised? Use Figure 3 to help you answer this question.

Dictionary

cartographer person who draws maps professionally
climate average weather conditions over a long period of time
continent a large, unbroken mass of land, usually divided into smaller political divisions (countries)
key list of symbols used in a map, to show what they mean
latitude imaginary lines running east-west around the globe, parallel to the equator. Used to measure the distance of a place on the earth's surface (in degrees) from the equator
longitude imaginary lines which run north-south and pass through both north and south poles. Used to measure the distance of places on the earth's surface east or west of the Prime Meridian (Greenwich)
map projection the method used to turn the globe into a map on a flat surface
north point arrow on a map pointing to north
orientate to organise a map so that it is the correct way up relative to the landscape it portrays
Prime Meridian the 0° line of longitude which runs through Greenwich, and is sometimes known as the Greenwich Meridian
remote-sensing looking at the earth from outer-space and collecting photographic images
resources things like energy and minerals which are provided by nature and which people need in order to survive
scale information on a map (a line or a fraction) which shows how much smaller or larger than real life the map is

2 Landscape and processes

2.1 Violent earth

The earth's surface, where we all live, is constantly changing. New houses, roads, shops and offices are continually being built. These alter the appearance of the **built environment**. The same thing is happening to the earth's surface itself. The **natural environment** either changes gradually and over a long period through the action of rivers, glaciers and the sea, or violently and quickly through the action of earthquakes and volcanoes.

The violent actions of earthquakes and volcanoes are no more important than the more gradual changes which are occurring all the time, but they do attract great interest (Figure 1), because they can cause considerable damage in a very short period of time.

22,000 killed in violent eruption

The blast that moved a mountain

Round the clock effort to divert lava flow away from hospital

Figure 1

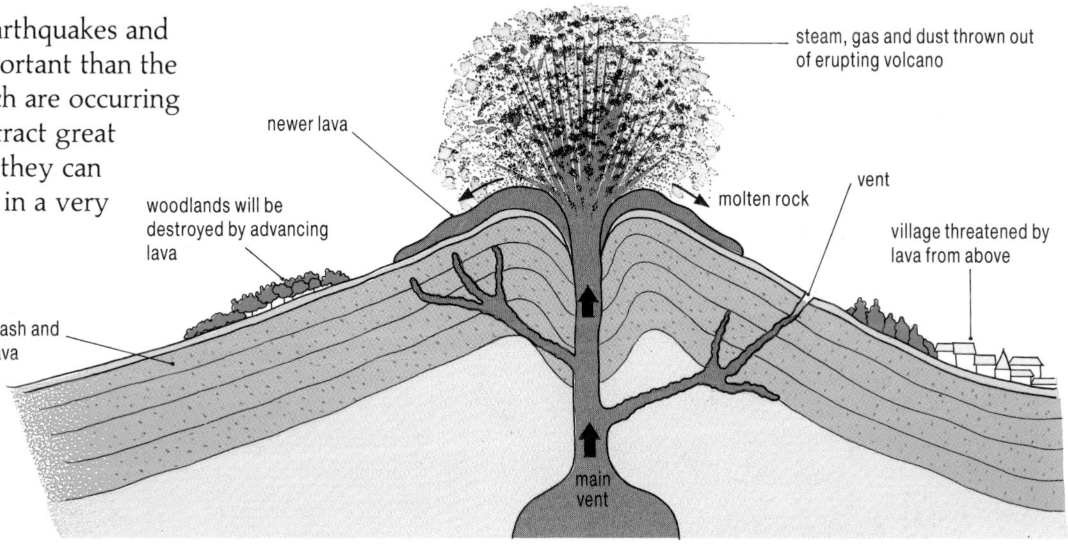

steam, gas and dust thrown out of erupting volcano
newer lava
molten rock
vent
woodlands will be destroyed by advancing lava
village threatened by lava from above
layers of ash and cooled lava
main vent

Figure 2
Cross-section of a volcano

Volcanoes

Deep inside the earth, hundreds of kilometres beneath the **crust**, temperatures are much hotter than on the surface. They are so hot that the rock is in a liquid or molten form called **magma**. In locations where there are cracks or weak spots in the earth's crust this magma is able to escape to the surface where it moves across the land in **lava flows** before cooling. This escape is often under pressure and results in volcanic explosions or **eruptions** with steam, gas and dust being thrown high into the air and molten rock pouring down the mountain-side (Figures 2 and 3).

Figure 3 Erupting volcano

Most volcanoes are located around the Pacific 'Ring of Fire'. Others are found in the middle of the Atlantic or Pacific Ocean and there are some in other locations in Southern Europe and Africa (Figures 4a and b). They fall into 3 main categories: active, dormant or extinct. **Active volcanoes** are those which still erupt (there are 530-540 of these). Thousands of others have not erupted for many years and are said to be **dormant**, while the remainder, which have been lifeless for so long that they are not expected to erupt again, are called **extinct**.

Apart from causing loss of life and damaging trees, farmland and property, volcanic eruptions may have serious long-term effects. The dust which is thrown into the atmosphere can partly block out the sun's heat and help to increase rainfall. There are also some positive effects. Underground water in volcanic areas is often very hot and can be used to generate electricity or for heating. This is common in Iceland. Some lavas weather to form fertile soils, and many volcanic areas are even becoming popular spots for tourists to visit !

Volcano	Country	Location*
Mount Hekla	Iceland	
Nevado del Ruiz	Colombia	
Stromboli	Italy	
Paricutin	Mexico	
Mauna Loa	Hawaii	
Mount St Helens	USA	
Etna	Italy	
Tristan da Cunha	Tristan da Cunha	
Cotopaxi	Ecuador	
Krakatoa	Indonesia	
Kilimanjaro	Tanzania	
Mount Pelée	Martinique	
Katmai, Alaska	USA	
Popocatépetl	Mexico	
Mount Shasta	USA	
Surtsey	Iceland	
Vesuvius	Italy	

*Key
RF Ring of Fire
AP Atlantic or Pacific Ocean
O other (including South Europe and Africa)

Figure 4a Major volcanoes of the world

Figure 4b Volcanic areas

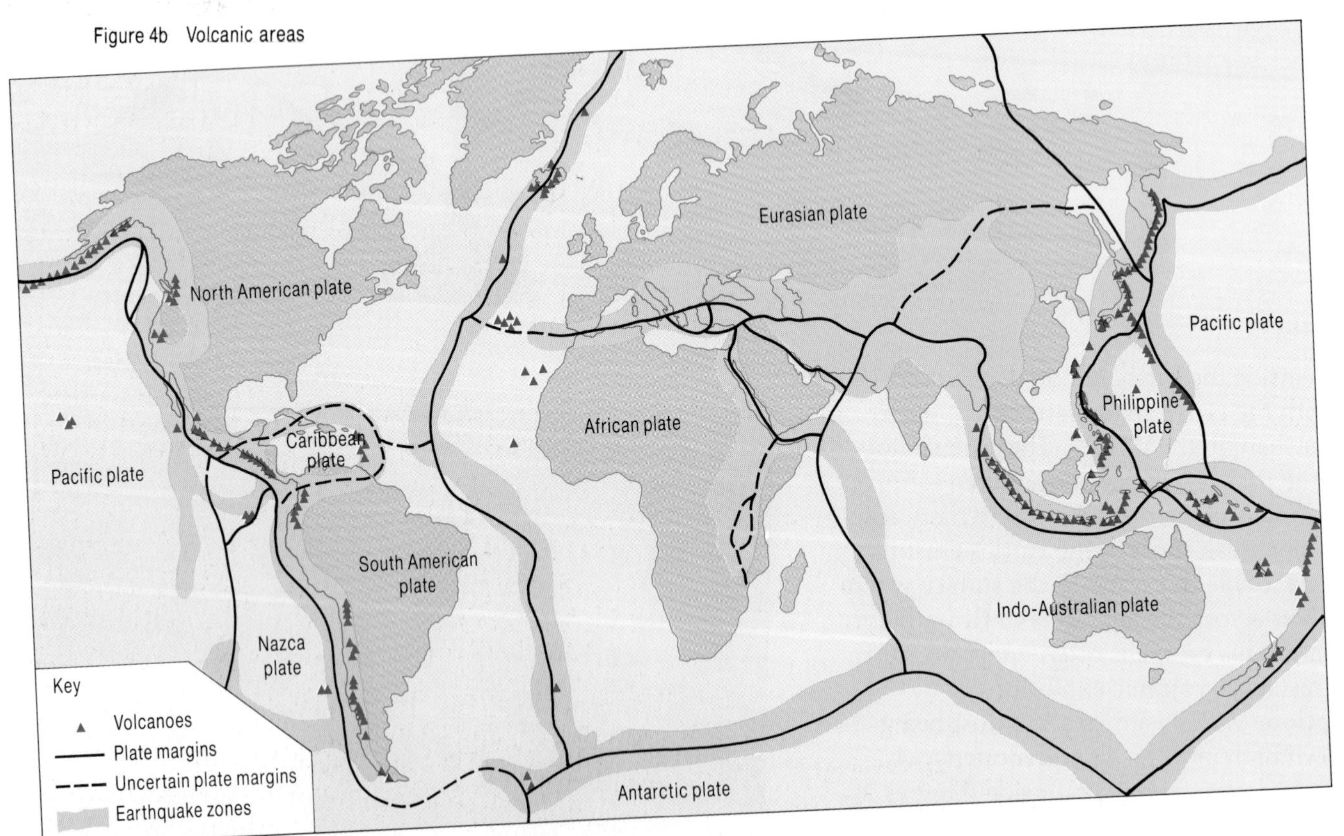

DISASTERS

Colombia's Mortal Agony

A volcano unleashes its fury, leaving at least 20,000 dead or missing

It was shortly after 9 p.m. Wednesday, and Pilot Manuel Cervero was nearly home. Cervero was flying a DC-8 cargo jet from Miami to the Colombian capital, Bogota, a sprawling city of 5 million in the Andes. The plane was cruising at 24,000 ft , ten minutes from El Dorado International Airport. Then, without warning, Cervero and his aircraft ran afoul of one of nature's most destructive phenomena.

"First came a reddish illumination that shot up to about 26,000 ft ," the pilot recalled. "Then came a shower of ash that covered us and left me without visibility. The cockpit filled with smoke and heat and the smell of sulfur." The blast charred the nose of the DC-8 and turned the aircraft's windows white. Flying only on instruments, Cervero diverted the plane to the city of Cali, 20 minutes from Bogota. Making his final approach, the pilot said, he had to push open one of the cockpit's side windows in order to catch a glimpse of the airport's runway lights. He landed safely.

Cervero did not at first know that he had been flying 7,000 ft. above a 17 716-ft - high, long-dormant volcano known as Nevado del Ruiz at the exact moment when it came thunderously alive. Within hours, that rebirth had left upwards of 20,000 people dead or missing in a steaming, milewide avalanche of gray ash and mud. Thousands more were injured, orphaned and homeless. The Colombian town of Armero (pop. about 22,500) had virtually disappeared. At week's end a huge cloud of ash, rising as high as 45,000 ft , hung dramatically over the area. The pall obscured the sun and caused the normal afternoon temperature of 77°F to drop to about 55°F. As rescuers hunted frantically amid the devastation for mud-covered survivors, it was soon clear that Nevado del Ruiz would rate as one of the deadliest volcanic eruptions in recorded history, roughly equivalent to the A.D. 79 explosion of Mount Vesuvious, which destroyed the cities of Pompeii and Herculaneum.

Source : Time Magazine : 15.11.1985

Figure 5

Figure 6 San Andreas fault

There have been many famous volcanic eruptions throughout history including the eruption of Vesuvius in AD 79 which buried the cities of Herculaneum and Pompeii; the huge explosion which accompanied the eruption of Krakatoa near Java in 1883 killing 36 000 people; the Mount St Helens disaster in the USA in 1980, and more recently the eruption of Nevado del Ruiz in Colombia in 1985 which killed over 22 000 people in a few minutes (Figure 5).

Earthquakes

As important as volcanoes, but potentially more dangerous, are earthquakes. They occur near the cracks or faults which exist in the earth's crust (Figure 6). During an earthquake the ground shakes violently. This happens because rocks on either side of these faults are trying to move in different directions. Tension gradually builds up until the pressure is enormous. Suddenly a huge amount of energy is released as the slabs of rock jerk past each other. The point inside the earth from which energy is released is called the **focus**. Directly above the focus on the earth's surface is the earthquake's **epicentre**. The energy takes the form of **seismic waves** which travel through the earth's crust towards the surface where they can cause great damage (Figure 7). Earthquake magnitude or intensity is measured on the **Richter Scale**.

Earthquakes, like volcanoes, are found in particular locations, and these form a distinctive pattern on a map. Every year there seems to be one particularly tragic earthquake. In 1988 the town of Spitak in Armenia virtually ceased to exist at 11.44 am on Wednesday 7th December when it was hit by an earthquake measuring 6.9 on the Richter scale. 25 000 people were killed. In 1989, 270 people died, including many who were crushed in their cars, in California when, at 17.04 on October 17th, the ground shook for 15 seconds. In 1990 between 25 000 and 50 000 people lost their lives in the Zanjan province of northern Iran. Here, at 2.50 am on June 21st, a tremor lasting over one minute (7.3 on the Richter scale) wrought havoc and caused most buildings to collapse, burying their inhabitants as they slept.

Volcanic eruptions and earthquakes cause as much damage and loss of life today as they have done for centuries. Much remains to be learnt about:

- the processes which cause them;
- predicting when they are going to occur.

However, these events are much better understood now than in the past, as more has been learnt about the internal structure of the earth.

Figure 7 Earthquake effects

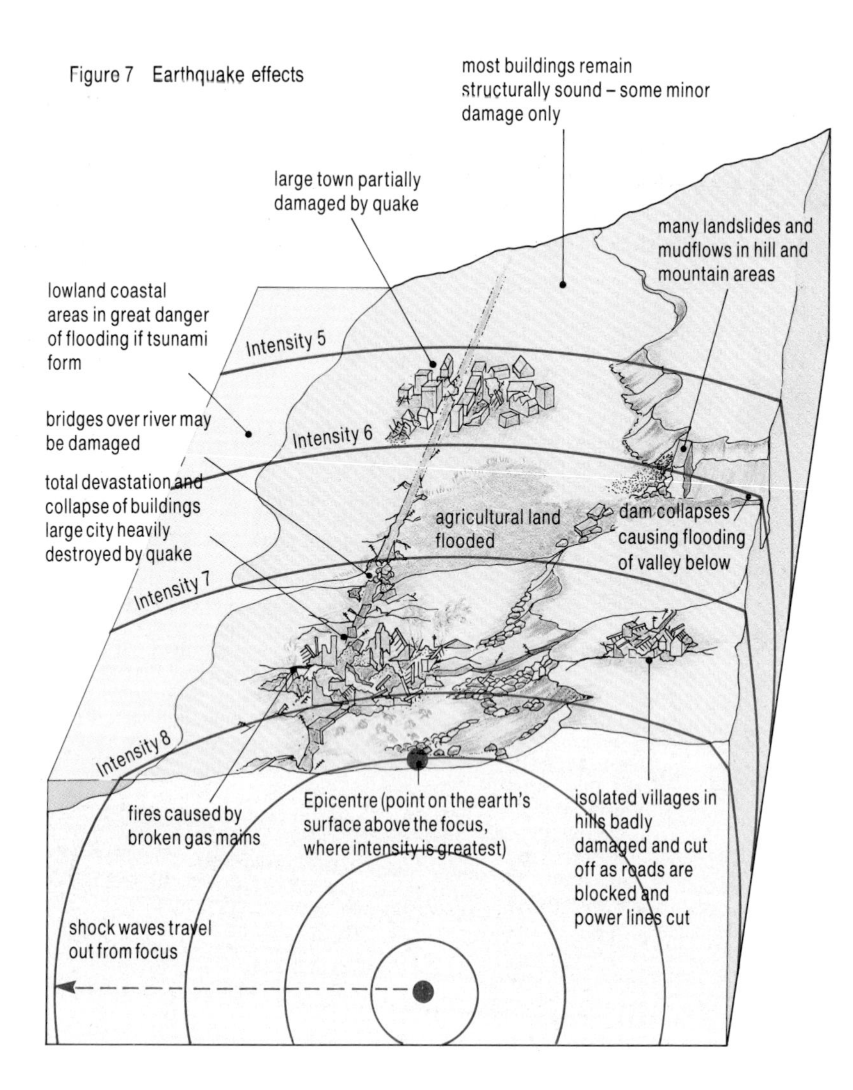

Activities

1 a List some of the damaging effects that volcanoes can have on their surroundings when they erupt.

b Choose one of the newspaper headlines in Figure 1 and write an article about 250 words long for the next edition of the paper. Your article can be entirely imaginary, or based on a real eruption which you have looked at in class or researched yourself.

2 a Heading: 'Inside a Volcano.'
Make your own copy of the cross-section of a volcano shown in Figure 2. Colour and label the diagram carefully.

b Copy and complete the following passage. All the answers are in the text or the illustrations.

Volcanoes are part of the .... environment. When a volcano erupts, molten rock called .... pours through its main .... before reaching the surface. Steam, ... and .... are also often thrown into the air. The molten rock runs down the side of the mountain and cools to form ....

3 Read the account of the eruption of Nevado del Ruiz (Figure 5), especially the comments of the pilot of a cargo jet caught in the blast. Imagine the pilot was able to land the plane and that he and his crew were the first people on the scene.

i In groups of 3 or 4 try to decide what you would be able to do to help in the first 24-hour period;

ii What would need to be done by rescue workers during the week or two after the eruption?

iii What would the country's government need to do in the year after the disaster?

4 On a copy of Figure 7 mark:
  a the focus of the earthquake.
  b shade the zones according to the intensity of the earthquake:
  - shade red the areas where intensity >7 was recorded;
  - shade orange the areas where intensity of 5-7 was recorded;
  - shade yellow areas where intensity <5 was recorded;

  c What is the difference between the focus of an earthquake and its epicentre?
  d List the different types of damage which occurred in each of these three zones.

5 *a* What problems will Iran have in recovering from the serious earthquake of June 1990 which is reported in Figure 8?
  b From what you have learnt about earthquake damage, suggest:
    i which land uses you would allow in an earthquake zone;
    ii which land uses you would disallow in an earthquake zone.

Figure 8

25,000 die in Iranian earthquake

Reuter and AP in Tehran

AT LEAST 25,000 people were reported dead last night after a huge earthquake devastated the Caspian region of Iran, reducing more than a hundred towns and villages to rubble. 25,000 were killed and tens of thousands injured.

With all but air communications destroyed by landslides across much of the farming region close to the border with Soviet Azerbaijan, it could be days before a clear estimate of the total damage can be reached.

The quake, measuring 7.3 on the Richter Scale, struck at 2.50 am local time, with its epicentre in the Caspian Sea about 125 miles north-west of Tehran. It lasted one minute. A second earthquake, measuring 6.5 degrees, hit just after midday.

An estimated four million people live in Zanjan and Gilan provinces. With a combined area of 20,000 square miles they form the country's bread basket, producing wheat, rice, tobacco, tea and fruit.

Guardian 22.6.90

2.2 Drifting continents

When Jules Verne wrote his famous story 'Journey to the Centre of the Earth' in 1864, little was known about what such a journey would have been like. If such a trip could be made it would certainly be interesting. The voyage of over 6 700 kilometres (Figure 1) would be very hot, and would have to pass through solid and molten rocks!

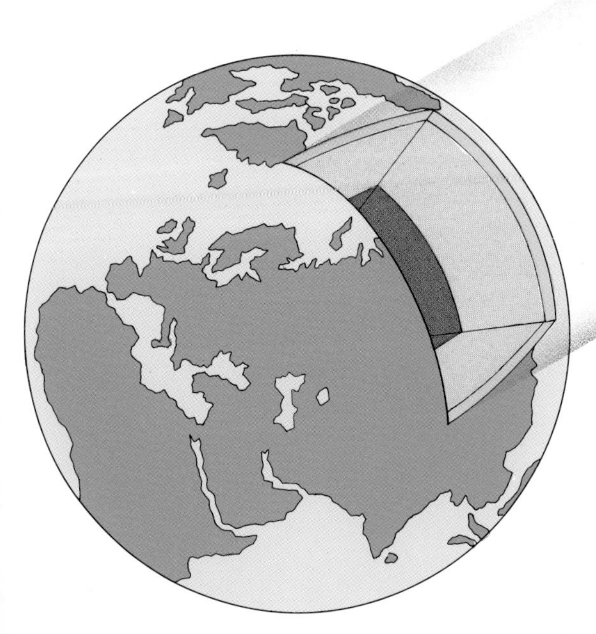

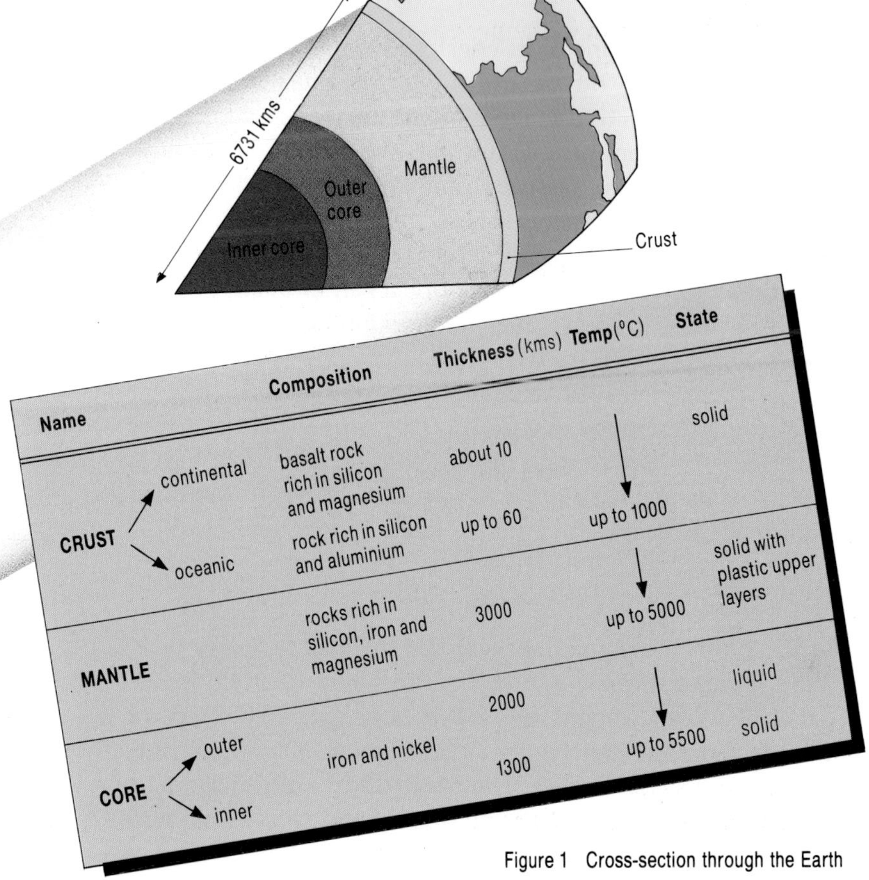

Name		Composition	Thickness (kms)	Temp(°C)	State
CRUST	continental	basalt rock rich in silicon and magnesium	about 10		solid
	oceanic	rock rich in silicon and aluminium	up to 60	up to 1000	
MANTLE		rocks rich in silicon, iron and magnesium	3000	up to 5000	solid with plastic upper layers
CORE	outer	iron and nickel	2000		liquid
	inner		1300	up to 5500	solid

Figure 1 Cross-section through the Earth

Scientific exploration and measurements have allowed the development of new ideas which help to explain some of the landforms on the earth's surface, as well as the processes operating underneath it.

These new ideas are known as **plate tectonics**. The earth's surface is like a jigsaw puzzle, with the top layer or **crust**, being split into a number of large pieces called **plates.** The edges or boundaries of the plates are where most earthquake, volcanic and mountain-building activity goes on and are known as **active zones**.

Continental drift

Scientists believed that the continents had once formed a kind of supercontinent which they called Pangaea. It was suggested that the supercontinent then split up. This idea is known as **continental drift**.

There is a much evidence for this theory. For example, rocks which are similar in type, age and structure are found on opposite sides of oceans, as are identical fossils. The idea of drifting continents is now part of plate tectonic theory.

The earth is made up of seven major plates each composed of continental and oceanic crust. They move very slowly around the earth's surface by 'floating' on the top plastic layer of the mantle. This movement is caused by warm **convection currents** in the mantle carrying magma to the surface, forming a new crust on the ocean floors at the **mid-ocean ridges**, and forcing plates apart. This location is a **constructive margin**, and is one of three types of plate boundary (Figure 2a).

If a plate is growing at its constructive margin, then, unless the earth is expanding, other parts of the plate must be disappearing ! Along the **destructive margin** or **subduction zone**, oceanic crust is forced beneath continental crust into the mantle, where it melts and is absorbed (Figure 2b). Destructive margins are usually found around the edges of the continents. These are the active zones referred to earlier where volcanoes, earthquake activity and fold mountains are commonly found. When two continents are moving towards each other on collision course, then fold mountains are formed on the edges of their plates.

Elsewhere, plates just slide past one another with crust neither created nor destroyed (Figure 2c). This happens at the **conservative margin**. Even here though there is considerable friction as one land mass runs up against another, and earthquakes are common, as in California along the San Andreas fault.

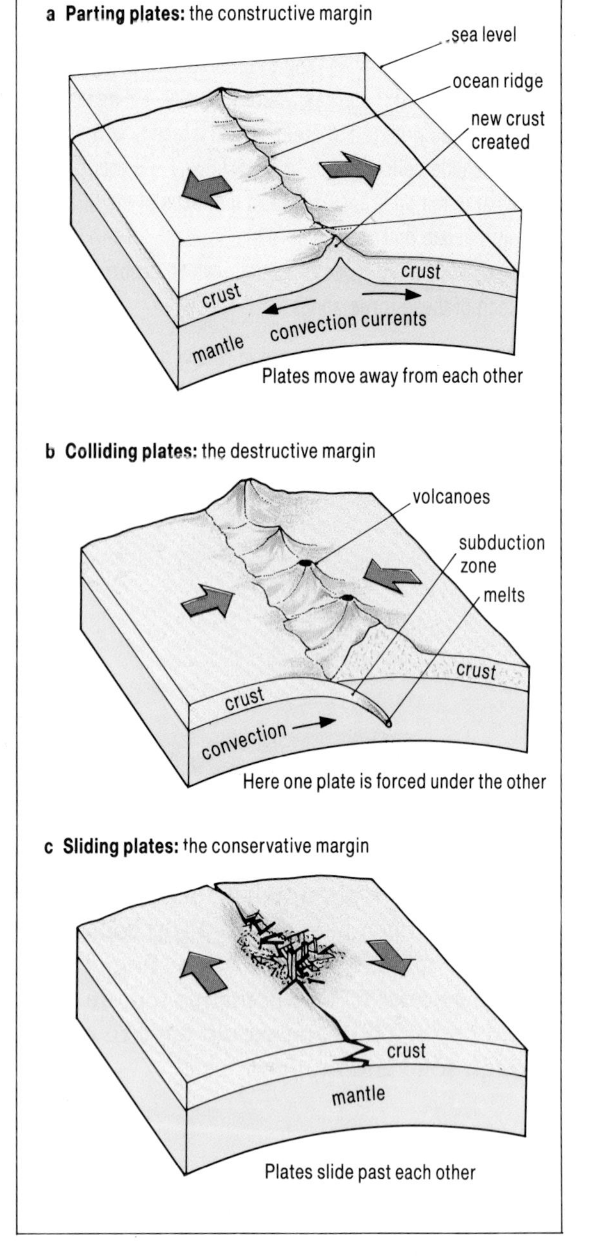

Figure 2
Three types of plate boundary

Ocean floor

In the 1960s the ocean floor was first mapped properly on a large scale. It was a surprise to find that the major ocean floors were not flat as had been thought, but that they housed vast chains of submarine mountains (Figure 3). Some were even higher than those on the earth's land surface. The ocean floor is also made up of moving plates. At the edge, the oceanic and continental plates collide and form deep trenches.

Figure 3 Atlantic ocean floor

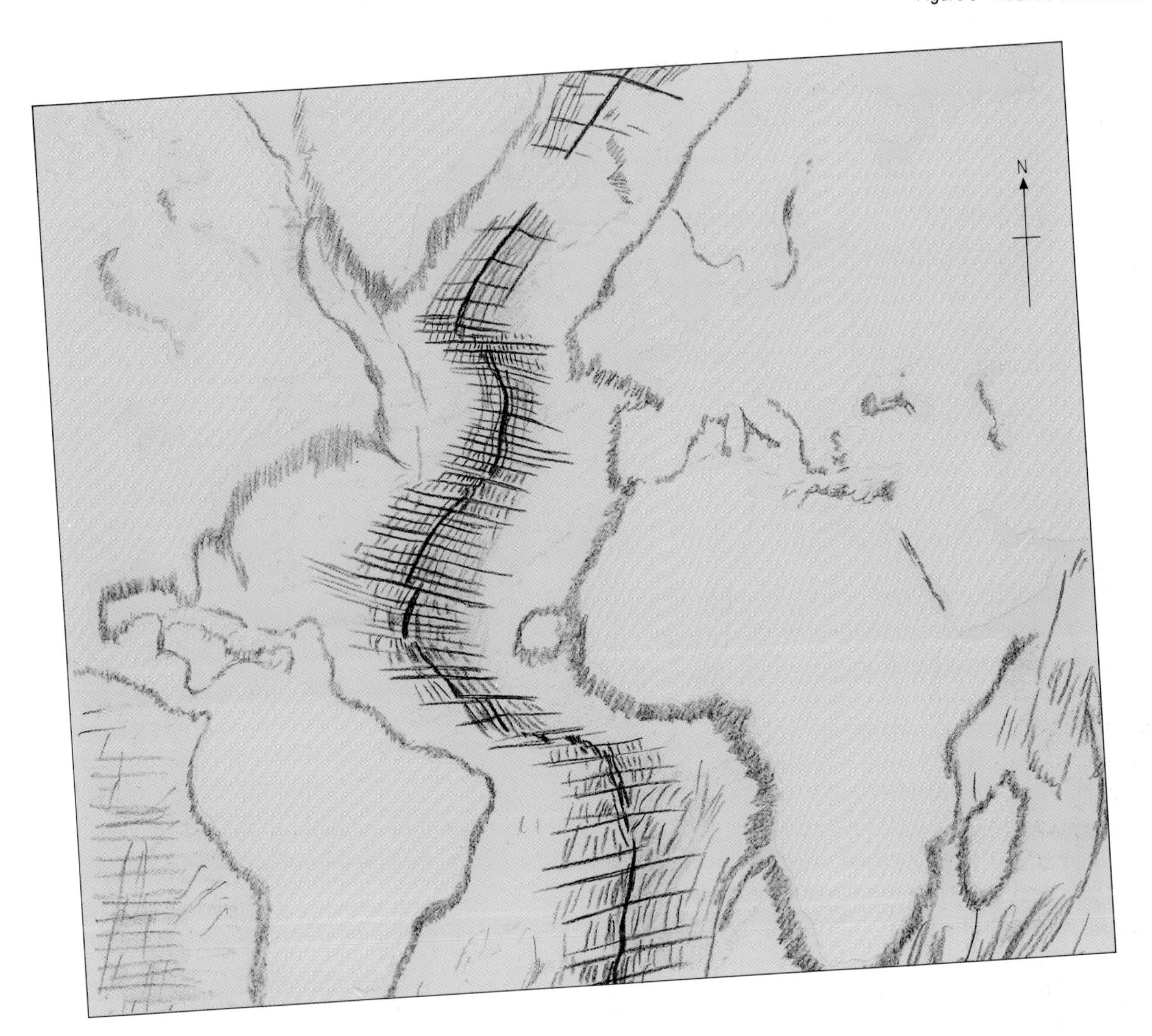

Activities

1 List the difficulties you think would be encountered in trying to reach the centre of the earth. The Channel Tunnel project might give you a few ideas.

2 a Explain how the earth's core, mantle and crust are different from one another . Use Figure 1 to help you.

b Work out the diameter of the earth from the radius which is given.

c How long would it take to reach the centre of the earth assuming you could make progress at a constant 1 kilometre per day?

d Does the earth's radius vary from place to place?

3 a What do you notice about the distribution of volcanoes and plate boundaries shown in Figure 4?

b Now look back to Figure 4b in Unit 2.1. How does the distribution of earthquakes compare with the pattern you noticed in *a*?

c You will need an atlas as well as Figure 4 for this activity. Name the mountains which are located:

i where the Pacific plate meets the North American plate;

ii where the African plate meets the Eurasian plate (in Southern Europe);

iii where the Indo-Australian plate meets the Eurasian plate in Northern India.

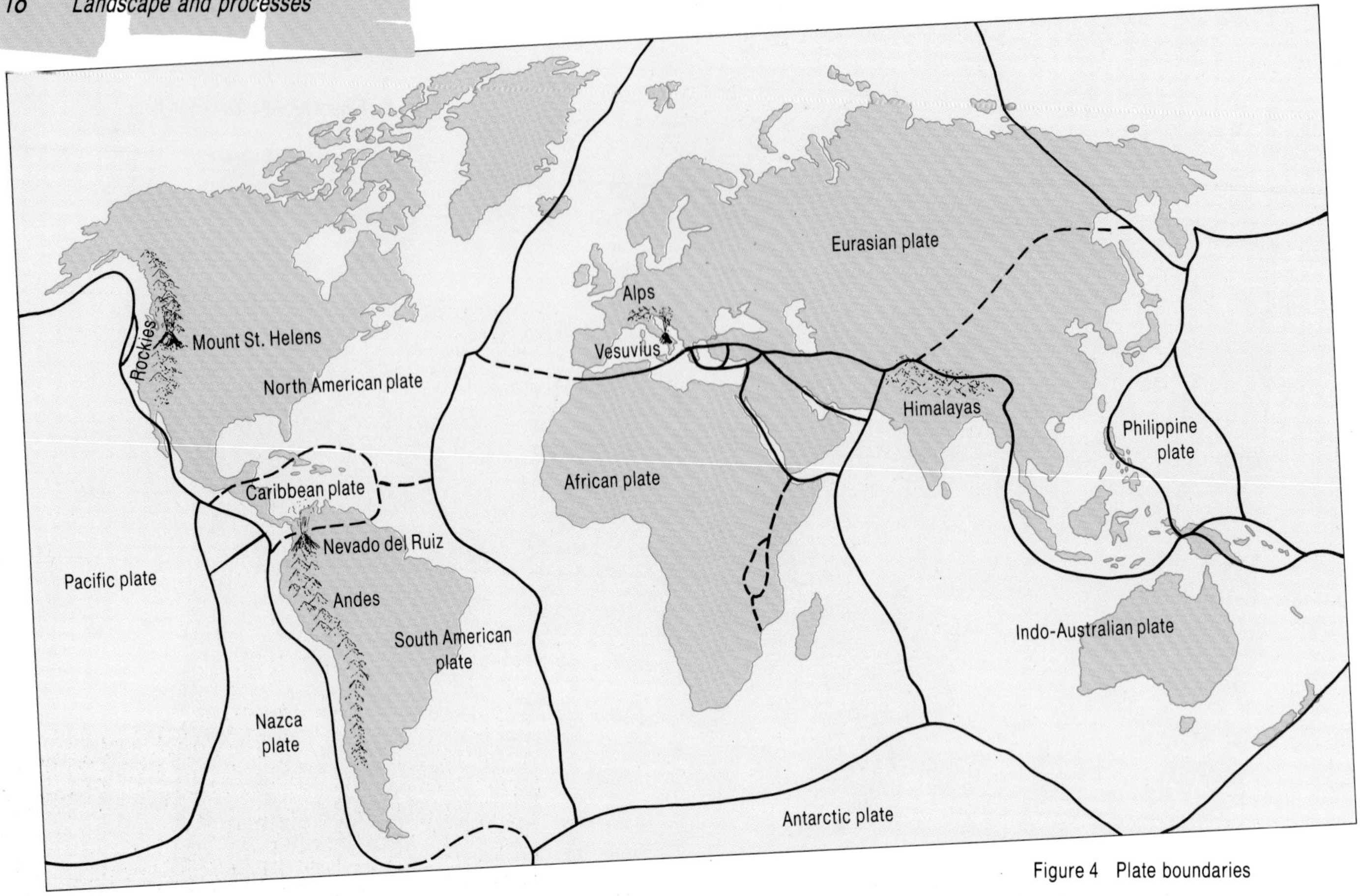

Figure 4 Plate boundaries

4 *a* What are 'active zones' and where would you expect to find them?
b Describe the locations of the two active zones nearest to the United Kingdom.
c Copy and complete these 2 sentences by adding a suitable ending:
i A **constructive** margin is ....
ii A **destructive** margin is ....

5 Draw and label your own sketches from Figure 2 to show the three different types of plate margin or boundary.

6 *a* At which type of plate margin or boundary would you find:
- fold mountains;
- submarine volcanic eruptions;
- new oceanic crust;
- severe earthquakes;
- crust being destroyed.

b Use your atlas to help you locate Iceland. What sort of plate boundary is it located near?

2.3 Battered coasts

Most people, apart from those who live there, only come into contact with the coast when going on holiday or beginning a sea journey. For holidaymakers, the coast is a calm and tranquil place. The main attraction is often a wide sandy beach with waves gently breaking. However, most of the year round the reality is a little different.

The cliff-top village that is fighting the sea

by Bill Davey

A COMMUNITY in danger of vanishing into the sea is calling for urgent Government action.

Some houses in Fairlight, East Sussex, are now standing on the brink of 100-foot cliffs.

Five years ago Squadron Leader John Lutman left the RAF to enjoy what he thought would be a peaceful retirement growing roses.

Today, as Chairman of the parish council, and the area representative on Rother District Council, he is at the forefront of a battle to save the village from extinction.

Watching the waves pound the shoreline near Hastings, Mr. Lutman said: "Less than 10 years ago, district council officials told us erosion would be minimal.

"Now the road along the coast has been closed and many houses are in danger of falling into the sea.

"To add insult to injury, the council has just issued instructions to householders on what they can do about the situation.

"The so-called helpful suggestions include advice about getting your gas, electricity and water supply cut off."

At the root of the problem is the fact that the sandstone cliffs are based on clay which is crumbling into the sea at an alarming rate.

Evening Standard 19.12.88

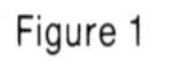

Figure 1

Figure 2

Our coasts are actually a battle-zone (Figure 1) which is the scene of an almost continual fight for supremacy. Here the sea, with its enormous erosive power and capacity to transport material, comes face to face with a solid land barrier (Figure 2). This battle results in a series of landforms being created. Some are caused by **erosion** and some by **deposition**.

Waves

We all know what waves look like, but not everybody realises that they are caused by friction between sea and air. Waves seem to move in the same direction as the wind, but only the wave shape actually moves, not the water. In shallow water, however, friction against the sea-bed prevents the water at the bottom of the wave moving as quickly as that at the top, so the wave breaks. There are two main types of wave action (Figure 3).

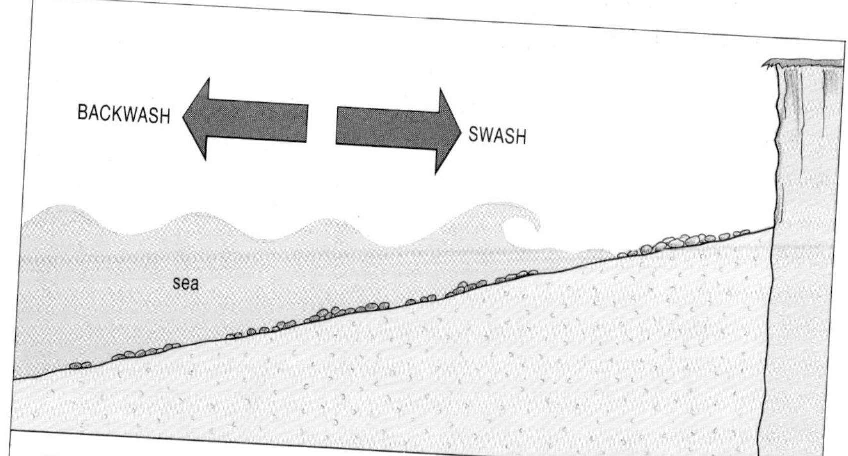

There are two types of wave:

1 **Destructive waves** – these are steep waves, quite close together, which break quickly and have a weak swash and a strong backwash. They remove beach material and are thus destructive.

2 **Constructive waves** – these are shallow and there is a gap between successive waves. The swash is strong and the backwash less powerful. This causes material to be carried up the beach.

Figure 3 Waves

Coastal Erosion

Destructive waves are responsible for many coastal landforms. Among the most spectacular are cliffs like those at Seven Sisters in Sussex. See if you can work out from Figure 4 how cliffs are actually formed. Notice how they retreat leaving a flat rocky surface called a **wave-cut platform**.

Powerful wave-action leads to various types of **erosion** (Figure 5). Rubble from collapsed cliffs is gradually worn down into pebbles and then sand-sized particles, which, of course, form beaches. Where the rocks are weak or faulted, erosion is more rapid and **bays** are formed. Harder rocks stand out as **headlands**, the sides of which are eroded forming sea-caves. Eventually the sea breaks through a headland producing an **arch.** The top of this may collapse leaving a column called a **stack** separated from the headland by the sea (Figure 6).

Diagram a

land

sea

high tide level

sea level

low tide

area attacked by wave action

Diagram b

cliff

notch

undercut by waves

wave-cut platform

material eroded from cliffs

Figure 4 The formation of cliffs

Figure 5 Types of coastal erosion

Corrasion: the wearing away of coastal rock by fragments carried by waves.

Hydraulic Action: air is forced into joints and cracks in coastal rocks and compressed under enormous pressure from breaking waves.

Attrition: the wearing down and smoothing of material being carried by waves into pebbles, shingle and finally sand.

Chemical Solution: sea-water sometimes has a chemical action with minerals contained in rocks. This can lead to rocks being dissolved in solution.

Figure 6 Landforms of coastal erosion

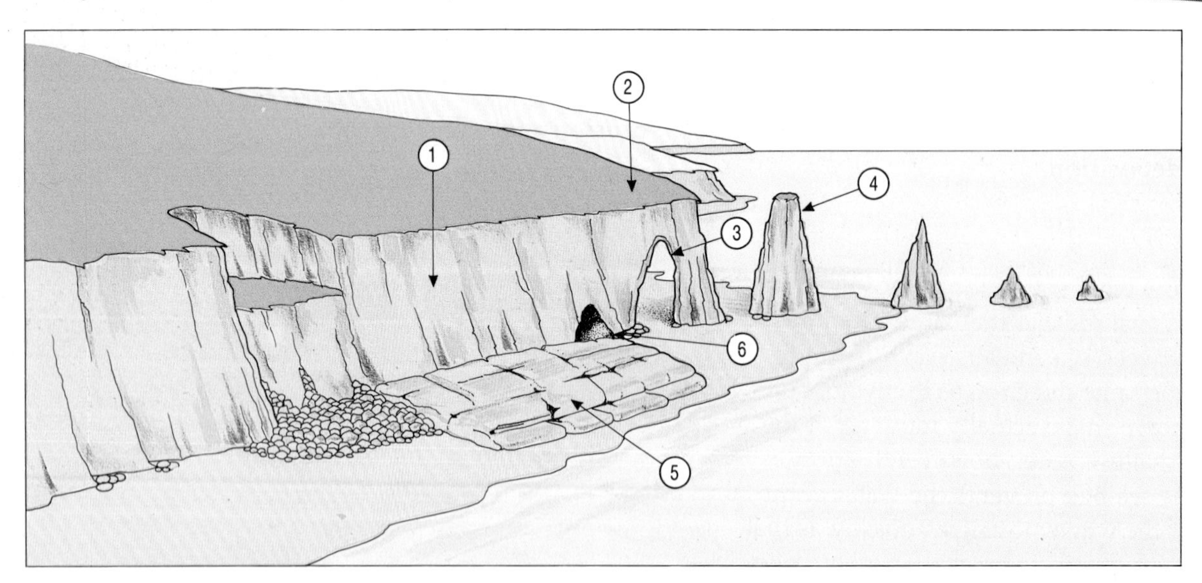

a)

b)

c)

Coastal Deposition

As well as being **destructive** and causing erosion, waves may be **constructive**. They can transport and deposit material, so building new landforms. The beach is a depositional feature. Many such features are formed because of a process called **longshore drift** (Figure 7). The diagram shows how material is moved from left to right because the waves break at an angle to the beach. A combination of swash and backwash produce a zig-zag movement carrying sand along the coast.

When the coastline changes direction, for example near a headland or a bay, or when a river enters the sea, sand continues to move in the direction of longshore drift. The mouth of a river in this situation may be blocked by a finger-shaped deposit of sand and shingle called a **sand-spit**, causing it to be diverted (Figure 8). Occasionally the build-up of material continues from one headland to another, or across an estuary. When a sand or shingle ridge connects two headlands it is called a **bar**.

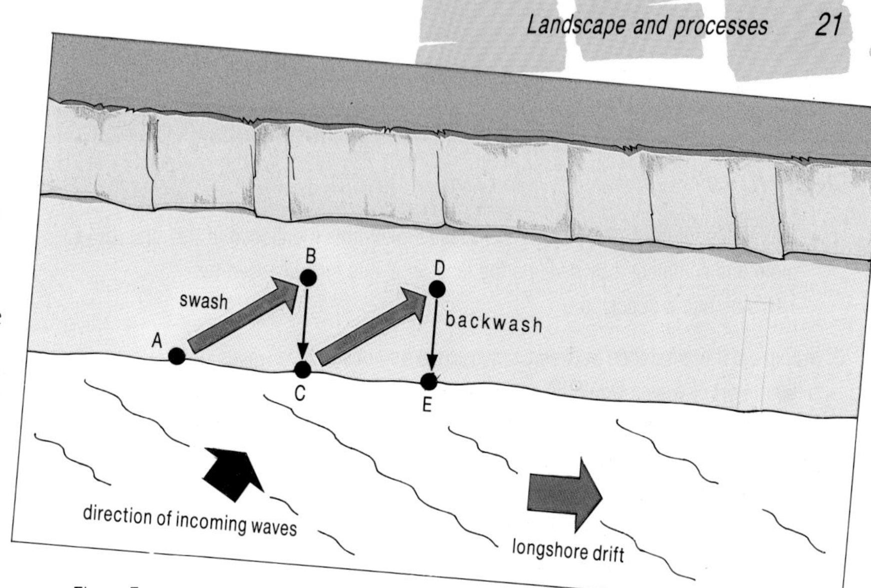

Figure 7

Figure 8
Mudeford spit, Dorset

People and Coasts

Many people like to visit coasts, especially in summer, and many different types of development occur there. Stretches of coastline with good beaches may have a pier, marina and hotels. There may be a coastal path along the cliff-top, a railway line and a harbour. However, as well as having amenities for visitors and residents, coasts must also be protected. This can be done in various ways (Figure 9). It is important to remember that the coastline is an important boundary in geography, where the land meets the sea. It is constantly changing as a result of the actions of people, the sea and the weather.

Figure 9

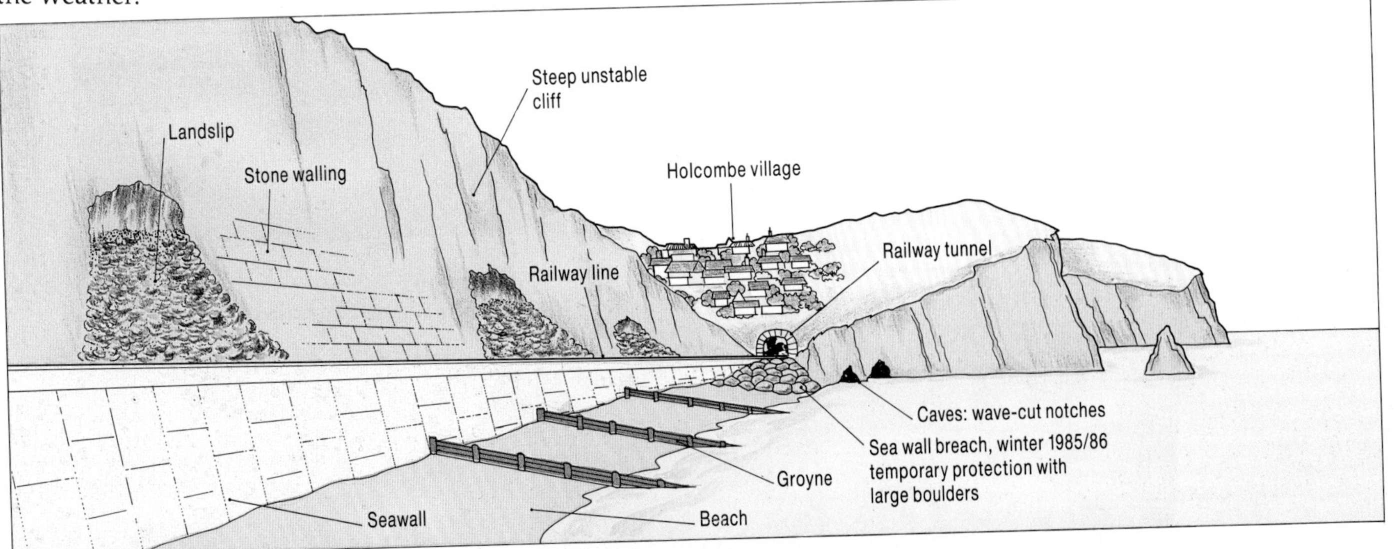

Activities

1 *a* Make a list of most of the important coastal landforms mentioned in this unit. Draw up a table and complete it by dividing the landforms into those caused by:
i erosion and *ii* deposition.

2 *a* Explain the difference between constructive and destructive waves (Figure 3).
b What sort of waves would be required to produce the following landforms: (*i*) a beach; (*ii*) a cliff?
c Study Figure 4, then explain briefly how cliffs are actually formed. Make a copy of Figure 4, and add a third sketch showing what happens next (*Hint:* look at the area around the notch!).

3 Make a table of the information in Figure 5 showing the different types of coastal erosion. Complete it by drawing a sketch to illustrate each type of erosion.

4 Landforms produced by coastal erosion take a variety of different forms. Most are shown in the sketch (Figure 6). Study it carefully and re-read the two paragraphs about coastal erosion in this unit.
a Name the features numbered from 1-6.
b Identify some of the landforms from photographs. List the landform(s) in each.

5 You might like to work in small groups for this activity. Look through some holiday brochures featuring beach holidays in this country or abroad.
a Try to find pictures of as many coastal landforms (erosional and depositional) as you can.
b Cut out the best example of each one and label it.
c Produce an informative brochure about a particular stretch of coastline. Use diagrams, sketches and maps to describe and explain the various coastal features.

6 Examine Figure 9 closely.
a What evidence is there of erosion here?
b Why might people visit a stretch of coastline like this one?
c How have people affected the coastline in this area?
d Why do you think a sea-wall has been constructed?

2.4 Growing deserts

About one-third of the earth's land area is made up of areas known as deserts. These are frequently thought of as extremely hot, dry and sandy places. While this description may correctly refer to some **deserts,** there are occasions when it does not apply. Overall, less than 1% of the world's deserts are made up of sand dunes. The surfaces are mostly rocky (Figure 1). In addition, deserts may not always be as hot and dry as we usually think.

Figure 1 Desert landscapes are very varied

Most of the world's deserts have less than 250mm rain each year. High daytime temperatures mean that moisture is quickly evaporated. This lack of rain means that plants cannot easily grow. Soil cannot easily be formed because there is little **decaying organic matter**. This leaves huge land surfaces exposed to the elements. Sun, wind and frost help to weaken the rocks by various types of **weathering**, and so sand is produced (Figure 2).

The world's hot deserts are found in different continents, but occupy the same types of location as the map in Figure 3 shows. Many deserts contain areas which are close to a coastline, where there is plenty of moisture. In these locations night-time fogs are common and frosts form when temperatures drop below freezing-point (Figure 4). Freeze-thaw action and other types of **mechanical** and **chemical weathering** weaken the rocks, making them more prone to erosion.

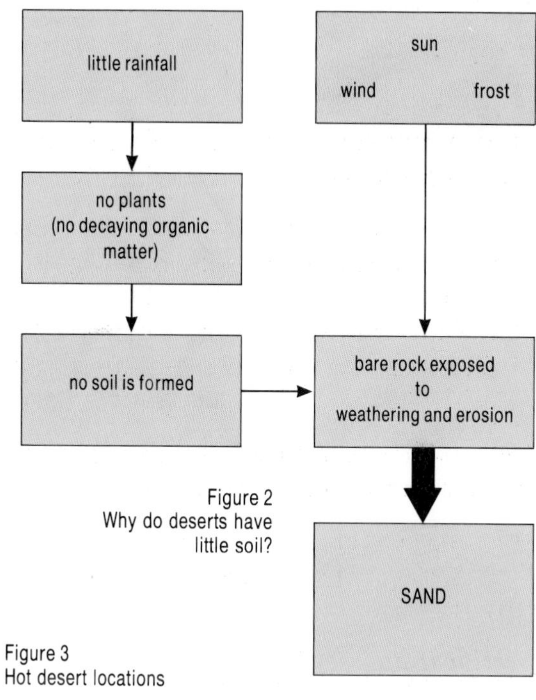

Figure 2
Why do deserts have little soil?

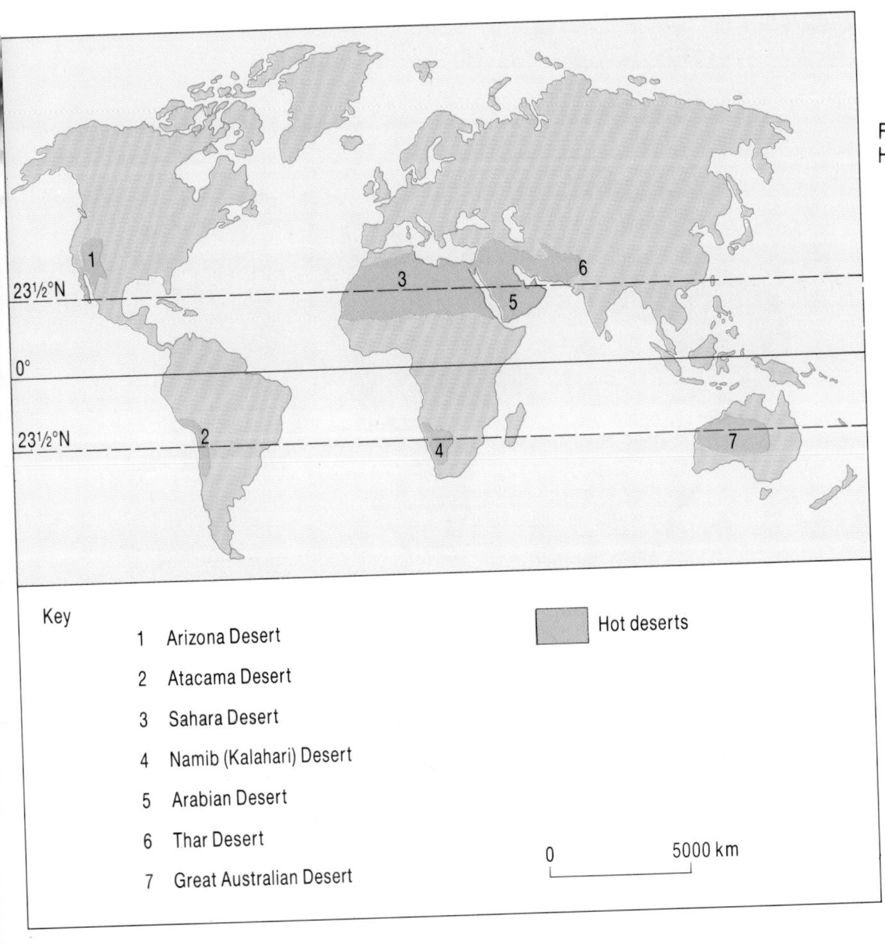

Figure 3
Hot desert locations

Figure 4 Extremes of temperature

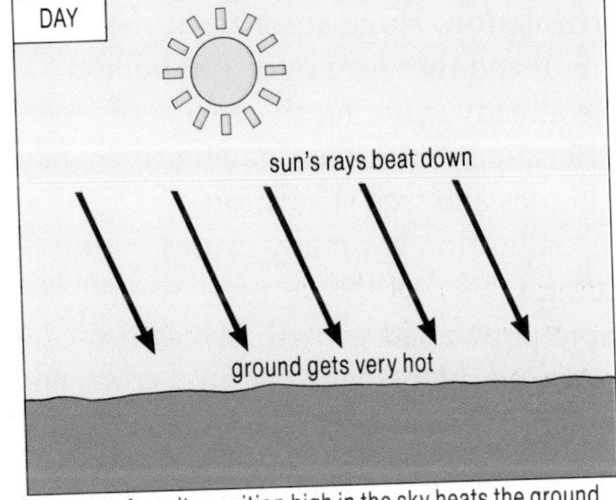

i The sun from its position high in the sky heats the ground well. No heat is absorbed by the atmosphere as the skies are cloudless.

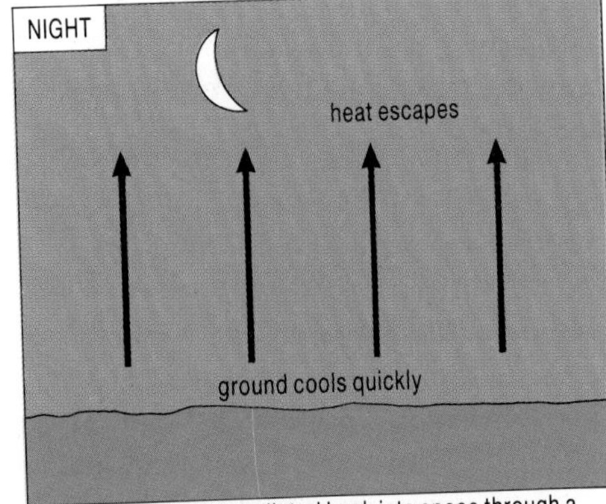

ii All the sun's heat is radiated back into space through a cloudless sky.

Many landforms are actually formed by the action of water, despite the low rainfall. When it does rain, it pours! The dry river beds and valleys or **wadis** rapidly fill with water. Huge boulders are moved in these storms, and a great deal of erosion takes place, to give desert surfaces their unique appearance (Figure 5). It is also important to remember that without water, much of the weathering mentioned earlier would not occur.

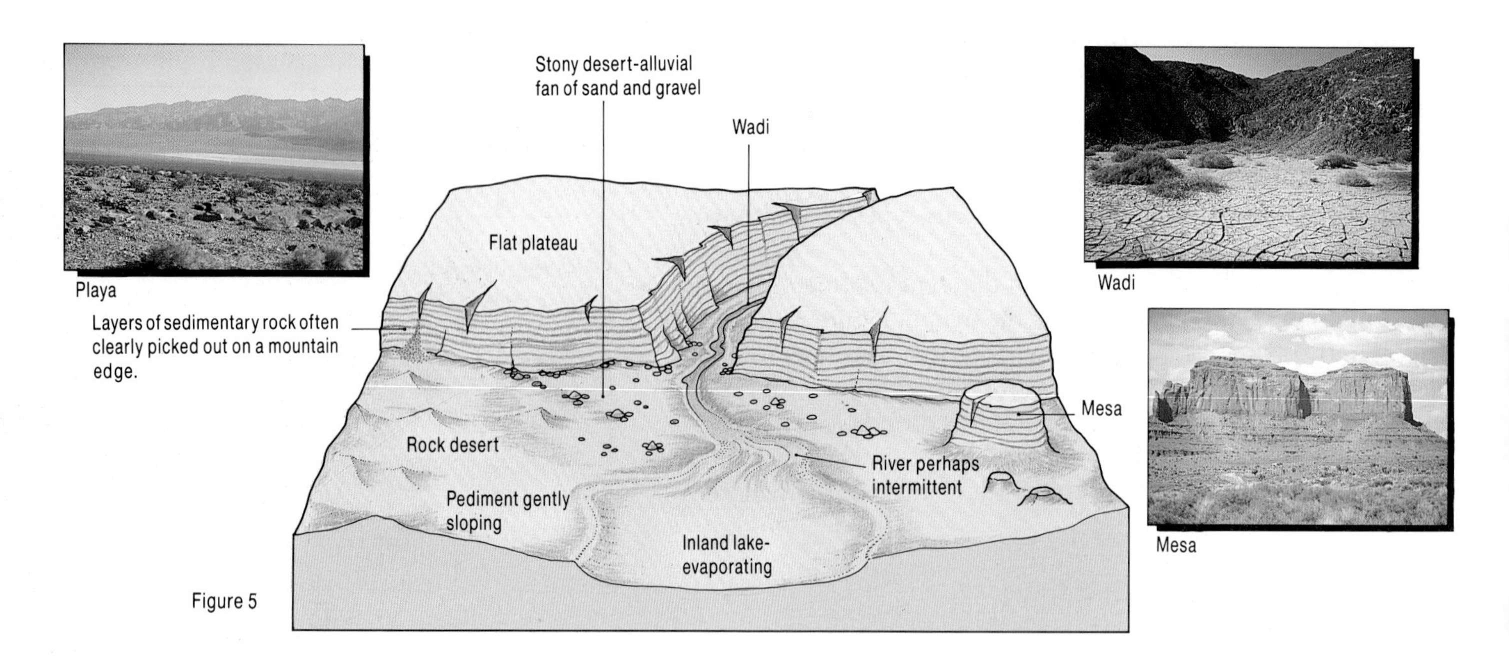

Figure 5

Desertification

Only about one in seven of the world's population lives in desert areas. However, there is concern that deserts are expanding into neighbouring areas, a process known as **desertification.** Huge areas are at risk (Figure 6) and there are over 100 million people already suffering the effects of desertification – including having to abandon their homes and face starvation.

Desertification has many causes (Figure 7), including:

- rapid population growth, which has increased the demand for food crops and required the use of land that would not previously have been used;
- overcultivation and overgrazing of existing arable land and pasture;
- the cutting down of rainforests, particularly for fuelwood;
- poor irrigation practices and recurrent droughts.

The consequences of desertification can be severe. Mauritania has been more seriously affected than any other country in the Sahel region of Africa. Here, drought has killed plants and left the land surface open to erosion – the desert has slowly but surely advanced. Over 30% of the nation's cattle and 20% of the sheep and goats have died. The country's population, which has traditionally been nomadic, began heading for the cities. The capital city of Nouakchott (look this up in your atlas), which was built for 30 000 people, now has over 500 000 inhabitants.

Figure 6 Deserts and risk areas

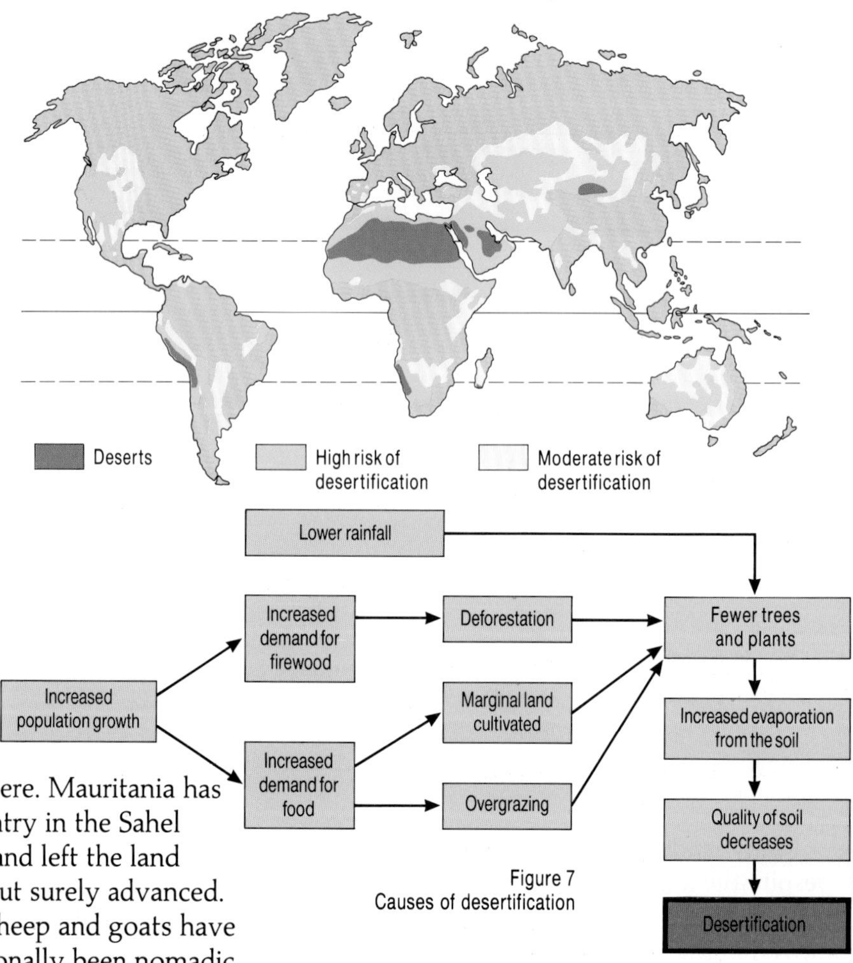

Figure 7
Causes of desertification

However, attempts are being made to halt the advance of the sand (see Figure 8). In the past villagers tried to anchor the dunes in position by piling branches on top of them. Now they are being anchored naturally by the new types of tree which are being planted. These drought–resistant varieties need watering only once just as they are planted. This allows their tap roots enough moisture to burrow down and take advantage of the moisture deep in the ground. In one area, over 700 hectares of arable land was saved along with 65 hectares of date palm plantations. Four villages which were abandoned as the sand came ever nearer have been reoccupied. However, the scientists in one area actually had to leave the research post where they were doing their research because of desertification!

Figure 8 Afforestation

Activities

1 With a classmate, 'brainstorm' as many words as you can in one minute, which come into your mind when you think of deserts. When the time is up, reduce your list to 10 words which remind you most of deserts.

2 Explain in your own words why soil is such a rare sight in desert areas. (*Hint:* Figure 2 might help).

3 Three of the following sentences are true and three are false. Copy only the three correct sentences into your notebook:

a Hot deserts are found only in the northern hemisphere.
b The Tropics of Cancer or Capricorn pass through most of the desert areas.
c The deserts lie between 30°-50° North or South of the equator.
d The world's largest desert is in the United States of America.
e Deserts are mostly found on the western sides of continents.
f Deserts lie between 15°-35° North and South of the equator.

4 Look carefully at Figure 4.

a Why do deserts have such extreme temperatures?
b Why is this information likely to be important to drivers taking part in a car rally across the Sahara Desert?
c Calculate the diurnal (daily) temperature range for a desert location which has a maximum of 34°C. during the day and experiences a low of −17°C. at night.

5 *a* Why is water important in deserts for:
i people; and *ii* landforms?
b Draw a simple line sketch of a wadi (from Figure 5), and explain how it differs from a river valley in the United Kingdom.
c Explain the difference between mechanical and chemical weathering.

6 *a* What is desertification?
b If desertification affects areas which are currently used for growing arable crops or grazing animals, why must it be slowed down or halted?

2.5 Contrasting landscapes in Iceland

The earth's landscape has evolved over many thousands of years. While most landscape changes have occurred gradually, others have been rapid and violent. The processes of **weathering** and **erosion** have gently worked over long periods to shape the mountains and valleys. More violent events such as **earthquakes** and **volcanic eruptions** have also shaped landscapes, but more powerfully and quickly.

Glaciers, rivers, the wind and the power of the sea have worked in various combinations round the world to produce many landforms – drumlins, mesas, levées, spits, U-shaped valleys, sand dunes, stacks and a host of others (see Figure 1). Rocks are also being slowly weathered. This weakens them and allows them to be eroded more easily. Elsewhere, the power of internal earth forces manifests itself in the form of volcanoes and earthquakes.

Figure 1 Variety of landscapes in Iceland

Case-study of Iceland: 'Land of ice and fire'

Although only a small island, Iceland's landscape is full of contrast and variety (Figure 2a). It contains features resulting from rapid and violent landscape processes as well as many produced by slow and gradual evolution. The physical environment of Iceland presents both enormous benefits to Icelanders as well as posing serious threats.

Iceland is known as the 'land of ice and fire' because of its **glaciers** and volcanoes. However, the power of its rivers and the surrounding ocean have also shaped the land surface. Geologically it is a young country which is, literally, in the process of being created. A volcanic eruption in 1963 created the island of Surtsey in the Westman group off the southern coast (look this up in your atlas). In 1973 the island of Heimay was enlarged by a volcanic eruption. Moreover the mid-Atlantic ocean ridge passes through Iceland – almost the only time it surfaces above sea-level.

After visiting Iceland in 1970, travel writer Jan Morris wrote:

Iceland is a large island almost in the middle of the North Atlantic, poised between Europe and America. The island is not so cold as it looks or sounds. The Arctic Circle passes just to the north of the Icelandic mainland, and the Gulf Stream warms its shores. It is, though, a violent country. A thousand volcanoes have pitted its landscapes with craters, jagged lava lumps, wildernesses of grey basalt. The ferocious winds of the north have kept it almost treeless, only a few scraggy thickets or cosseted garden rowans pathetically surviving the blast. About an eighth of the island is one vast snowfield, the Vatnajökull, which is itself about the size of Corsica, and sweeps away in grand sterile silence from the peak of Hekla.

In summer this colossal landscape is clothed in fragile green, speckled with wild flowers. In the winter the snow falls like a clamp upon the island, closing the rough roads of the interior and filling, like saucepans, the shallow craters of extinct volcanoes. Summer or winter the weather is startlingly changeable. Through it all, heatwave or snowstorm, the geysers and hot springs of Iceland bubble and fume away – some in the middle of Reykjavik itself, so that citizens bathe in open-air pools all the year round, and heat their homes with subterranean steam.

Among the cities Jan Morris

Figure 2a

Over 11% of the land surface is covered by glaciers. Four massive ice-caps dominate the island (Figure 2b). Although they are retreating, they are powerful agents of change and are responsible for landforms of both erosion and deposition. The largest is Vatnajökull. It is over 1000 metres thick in places and covers an area of 8 400 kilometres². This equals the combined size of all the glaciers on mainland Europe. Huge rivers called **meltwater streams** carry meltwater away from these glaciers. They swell to many times their normal size in spring and summer as the ice begins to melt. With temperatures near zero for several months each year, **freeze-thaw weathering** is common. Even in early June, snow and ice can be seen in shady pockets on mountain-sides and north-facing slopes. Screes are formed through frost-action, and collect at the base of steep slopes giving a characteristic **scree slope** .

Figure 2b Iceland

Apart from meltwater streams, Iceland has many **freshwater rivers** due to the heavy rainfall. These can easily be distinguished from meltwater streams because they contain clear water. The water in meltwater streams is very cloudy because of the volume of sediment and debris being carried. Most rivers are fast-flowing and so are not navigable. They often pass over huge waterfalls as they carve their way to the sea. Some rivers have been used to produce hydro-electricity (HEP). However, only about 10% of the island's potential HEP has been harnessed. **Waterfalls** have been formed by the powerful rivers, and some like Gullfoss and Skógafoss have become important tourist attractions.

The main reason that geologists are interested in Iceland is because the boundary between the Eurasian and the North American plate passes through the island. Nowhere is a boundary between two plates more apparent than in the huge valley at Thingvellir, east of Reykjavik. Here in 1789 the valley-bottom sank by 50cm in just 10 days during a huge earthquake. On the western side of the valley is the American continent, and on the east side is Europe. The area is criss-crossed by ravines and fault lines, perhaps the most famous being Almannagjá.

As a result of being on a major plate boundary, there is much volcanic activity in Iceland. In total there are over 200 volcanoes. Perhaps the most famous is Hekla, which has erupted 17 times. In 1947 the eruption lasted 13 months and the resulting lava covered an area of over 25 square miles. Later eruptions occurred in 1970, 1980 and 1981. About 10% of the land surface is composed of lavafields, which so resemble the moon surface that they were actually used for training by American astronauts.

There are more hot springs and **geysers,** (about 800) in Iceland than anywhere else in the world. The thin crust means that water can be heated naturally. One of the best known is 'Strokkur', which spouts boiling water several metres into the air every few minutes. The largest hot spring produces 150 litres (40 gallons) of boiling hot water per second. In Reykjavik, hot spring water is piped to most houses giving a cheap and reliable form of energy that has no harmful effects on the environment.

Activities

1 Identify whether the 18 landforms listed below (some of which are pictured in Figure 1) are associated with coasts, deserts, ice or rivers. Rewrite the list in four clearly headed columns:

drumlins, ox-bow lakes, mesas, levées, spits, saltmarshes, U-shaped valleys, sand dunes, inselbergs, deltas, erratics, waterfalls, arches, stacks, rias, eskers, moraines and buttes

2 *a* Write a sentence to explain the difference between weathering and erosion.
b Why is Iceland known as the 'land of ice and fire'?
c How would you tell the difference between a freshwater river and a meltwater stream?

3 *a* Using the photographs in this unit, list 10 words which best describe the landscape, scenery and features of Iceland.
b Read Jan Morris's description of Iceland in Figure 2(a). Is this the sort of place you would like to visit? Explain your answer.
c Imagine you could visit the Vatnajökull glacier. What features of glacial erosion would you expect to see? What equipment would make your visit comfortable and safe?

4 Use the map in Figure 2b to calculate the following distances. Assume you can travel in straight lines:
a from the volcano Hekla to Akureyri;
b from the town of Hofn to the waterfall at Skógafoss;
c from Lake Myvatn to the International airport at Keflavik;
d from the capital city Reykjavik to the island of Surtsey.
e Work out and give a compass bearing for each journey.

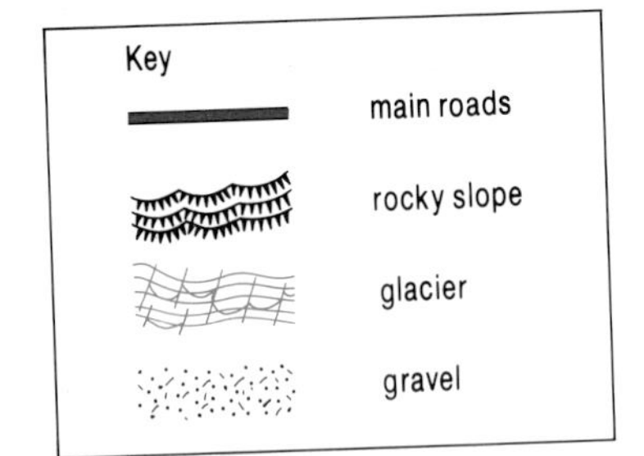

Figure 3 1:100 000 Iceland

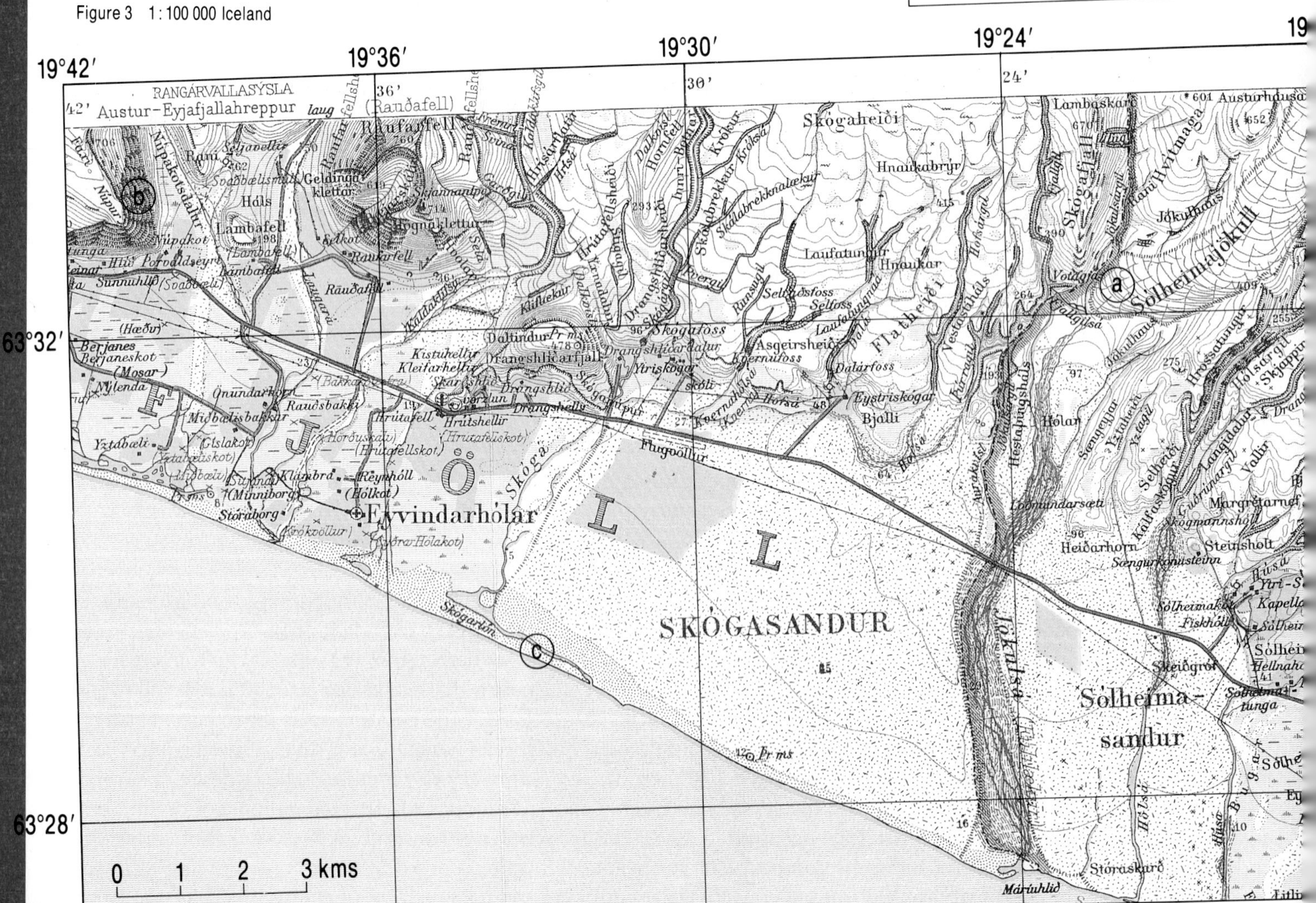

5 Study the map in Figure 3 carefully then answer the following questions:

a *i* Identify the features marked **a**, **b** and **c** on the map;

ii Explain in your own words (with diagrams) how Feature **c** might have been formed.

b How does landuse near the coast west of 19°36′W. differ from that to the east of 19°33′W.?

c Find Skógafoss on the map and state its location accurately. In which direction is the River Skoga flowing? How do you know?

d Describe the route you would give to a tourist who asked how to get from the church at Eyvindarhólar (near 19°36′W.) to the front of the Solheimajökull glacier at Point 'A' on the map. The journey must be made by road as far as possible.

i Calculate the distance covered by your route.

ii In what direction would the tourist travel?

iii Draw a simple sketch map to show the route.

6 Work in pairs for this activity to design and produce a brochure aimed at school geography groups visiting Iceland.

First decide which features are likely to be of most interest to such a group. The brochure should be no more than four sides of A4, including maps and a climate graph. You should also indicate how to get to Iceland. Some library research will be needed. You could draw sketches of some of the features visiting groups could expect to see. Make your brochure as interesting to look at as possible!

Dictionary

active zones volcanic and seismically active areas near plate margins

chemical weathering the break up or decomposition of rocks

conservative margin where two plates slide past each other

constructive margin where two plates are separating and new crust is being created. Usually a mid-ocean ridge location

constructive wave a wave which helps to construct a beach

continental drift the process of continents changing their relative locations which was suggested by coastal similarities

convection currents flows of molten material in the earth's mantle

desertification the process by which deserts are spreading into neighbouring areas

destructive margin where two plates are moving towards one another and one of them is being destroyed

destructive wave wave causing a net loss of beach material

epicentre the point on the earth's surface which is directly above the focus of an earthquake

freeze-thaw action a type of weathering which weakens rock as a result of alternate heating and cooling

freshwater rivers rivers which originate from underground springs, fed by rainwater

focus the point inside the earth's crust from which the energy in an earthquake is released

lava flow molten rock or magma which moves across the land surface

longshore drift the process causing beach material to move along the coast by wave-action

magma molten rock originating inside the earth

mechanical weathering the breakdown (physical disintegration) of rock into smaller fragments

meltwater streams streams which carry water away from melting glaciers

mid-ocean ridges mountainous areas, located mostly underwater, which mark the constructive margin between two plates

plates large sections of the earth's crust (continental and oceanic)

plate tectonics a group of ideas that help explain volcanic and seismic activity, as well as many features of the earth's surface

Richter scale a scale which measures the power of an earthquake

subduction zone the zone of friction where one plate is drawn down under another into the mantle and begins to melt

wadi valley found in a desert area which is usually dry

3 Weather and climate

3.1 The world of weather

If you have been on holiday abroad recently, the weather was probably one of the main attractions. Each summer millions of us head south to take advantage of the sun, especially to Spain, southern France and other parts of the Mediterranean. In the winter months, skiing holidays in the cold and snowy conditions of the Alps and Pyrenees mountains are popular.

You would encounter different types of weather (Figure 1) if you were to travel outside Europe – to the cold, empty expanses of the Gobi Desert or Patagonia, or to the humid tropical forests of Malaysia for example.

The most important components of the weather are **temperature**, **precipitation** and **atmospheric pressure** (which controls the wind pattern). These vary from place to place and determine the **weather** conditions in each particular location.

Figure 1

Figure 2 Newspaper weather

Around the World

(Yesterday's lunch-time reports)

		C	F
Ajaccio	S	26	79
Algiers	S	29	84
Amsterdam	R	19	66
Athens	S	29	84
Bahrain	S	32	90
Barcelona	F	26	79
Beirut	C	28	82
Belgrade	F	21	70
Berlin	S	24	75
*Bermuda	F	28	82
Biarritz	S	25	77
Bombay	F	29	84
Bordeaux	S	26	79
Brussels	C	20	68
Budapest	R	22	72
*B Aires	F	12	54
Cairo	S	32	90
Cape Town	R	14	57
Casablanca	S	25	77
Cologne	R	22	72
Copenhagen	F	19	66
Corfu	S	30	86
*Dallas	F	29	84
*Denver	S	23	73
Dublin	F	17	63
Dubrovnik	C	27	81
Edinburgh	F	18	64
Faro	S	28	82
Florence	F	25	77
Frankfurt	S	24	75
Funchal	F	27	81
Geneva	S	22	72
Gibraltar	S	25	77
Helsinki	S	16	61
Hong Kong	S	29	84
Innsbruck	F	20	68
Inverness	F	17	63
Istanbul	S	24	75
Jersey	S	19	66
Jo'burg	S	22	72
Karachi	F	29	84
Larnaca	S	35	95
Las Palmas	S	27	81
Lisbon	S	28	82
Locarno	S	24	75
London	C	19	66
Luxembourg	C	21	70
Madrid	S	27	81
Majorca	S	29	84
Malaga	S	28	82
Malta	S	30	86
Melbourne	C	17	63
*Mexico City	S	20	68
*Miami	Th	25	77
Montreal	S	19	66
Moscow	F	12	54
Munich	C	19	66
Naples	Th	23	73
New Delhi	F	30	86
*New York	C	22	72
Nice	S	25	77
Oporto	S	29	84
Oslo	S	19	66
Paris	F	25	77
Peking	R	15	59
Perth	F	12	54
Prague	F	22	72
Reykjavik	S	7	45
Rhodes	S	27	81
*Rio De Jan	S	24	75
Riyadh	S	41	106
Rome	Th	19	66
Salzburg	S	19	66
Seoul	S	27	81
Singapore	S	31	88
Stockholm	R	16	61
Strasbourg	S	24	75
Sydney	S	26	79
Tangier	F	31	88
Tel Aviv	F	29	84
Tenerife	F	28	82
Tokyo	C	22	72
Tunis	F	28	82
Valencia	S	28	82
Venice	Th	23	73
Vienna	F	21	70
Warsaw	S	23	73
*Washington	C	30	86
Wellington	R	13	55
Zurich	C	20	68

C, cloudy; Dr, drizzle; F, fair; Fg, fog; H, hail; R, rain; Sl, sleet; Sn, snow; S, sunny; Th, thunder.

*(Previous day's readings)

Guardian 19.9.91

Ocean currents also affect temperature. They can, as Figure 3 shows, be divided into two groups – warm and cold currents. Winds which pass over warm currents raise the temperatures on nearby land, while winds which pass over cold currents decrease temperatures.

Newspapers provide an excellent source of information about the world's weather. Figure 2 shows that on one day in September, the conditions in many locations around the world were very different from those in London.

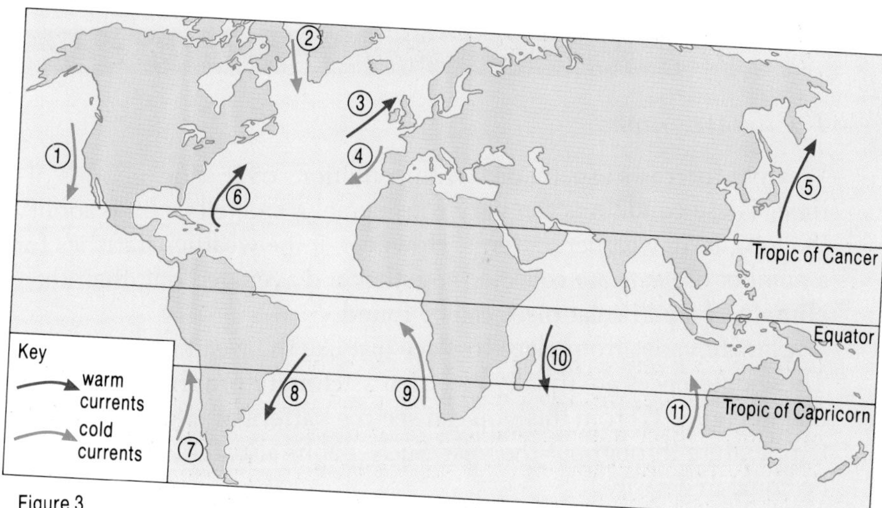

Figure 3

Activities

1 Look carefully at the photographs in Figure 1. They show what the weather can be like in different parts of the world.

a Write a sentence or two to describe the weather conditions in each place.

b What effect do you think each type of weather has on people?

c Choose one type of weather shown. Describe what precautions people might take to protect themselves if they lived in the area.

d In small groups discuss which type of weather you would least like to experience, and why.

2 You will need an atlas to help you with this activity. Figure 2 indicates the temperatures reached on one day in September in a variety of locations around the world.

a Which locations experienced the hottest and coldest conditions listed? In which countries are these locations?

b Choose 20 locations from the list. Try to include at least some places in each continent. On an outline map of the world, and using an atlas, mark the position of each location carefully. Clearly mark the temperature at each location. Can you see any pattern?

c With a partner find Melbourne and Cape Town in your atlas and discuss why these two towns have relatively low temperatures.

3 ***Project:*** *Recording the world's weather*

You can monitor the world's weather by keeping a close watch on the weather summary in the daily newspaper.

First make a **weather log** like the one shown in Figure 4. You may need extra columns if the summary in the newspaper you use has extra information. Next, choose one location in each continent (in addition to London). Fill in the column headings in your log. Now keep a record of weather conditions at each location every day for one month. Record all the details accurately, using the same daily newspaper for the whole month.

Figure 4

WEATHER LOG

LOCATION / DAY	1		2		3	
	Conditions	Temp	Conditions	Temp	Conditions	Temp

At the end of the month look carefully at the log that you have made. What do you notice? Have overall conditions changed? How do the weather conditions elsewhere compare with those in London? Calculate the weekly average temperatures. Do they change during the month?

Write a report summarising the observations you have made.

3.2 Looking at climate

1 Climate graphs

Weather forecasts usually deal with conditions over short periods of time. These conditions can vary considerably, and tell us little about the long-term weather patterns. However, if the weather statistics for a number of years are collected together and averaged out, then the **climate** of a particular place can be found.

Climate varies from place to place just like the weather conditions. These differences are usually recorded as **climate graphs**, like the one in Figure 1. From this you can see the pattern of rainfall and temperature throughout the year. Such graphs also allow climates to be compared easily.

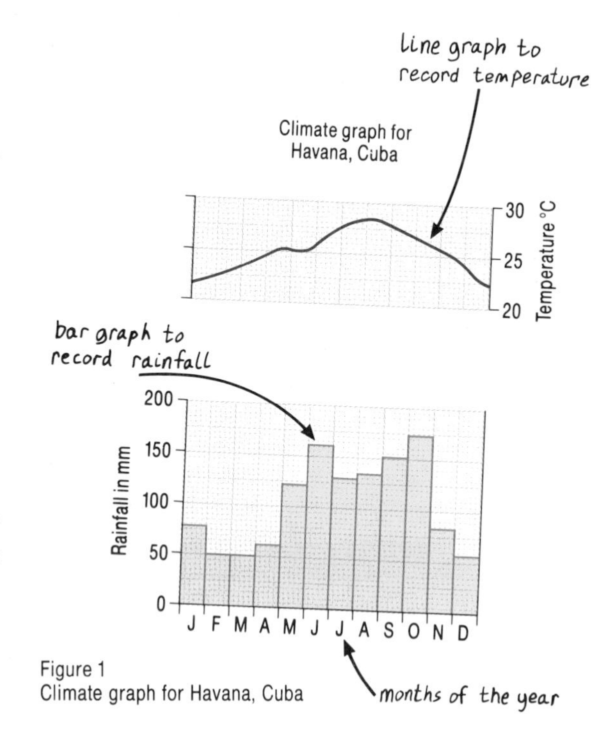

Figure 1
Climate graph for Havana, Cuba

2 Climate patterns

Although the climate of every location is almost unique, it is possible to recognise patterns across the earth's surface (Figure 2). The climate of any place, like its weather, is influenced by its location relative to the equator and the sea, as well as its position on the land mass. Generally, those places which are the same distance from the equator and on the same side of a continent, have a similar climate.

Figure 2
World climatic environments

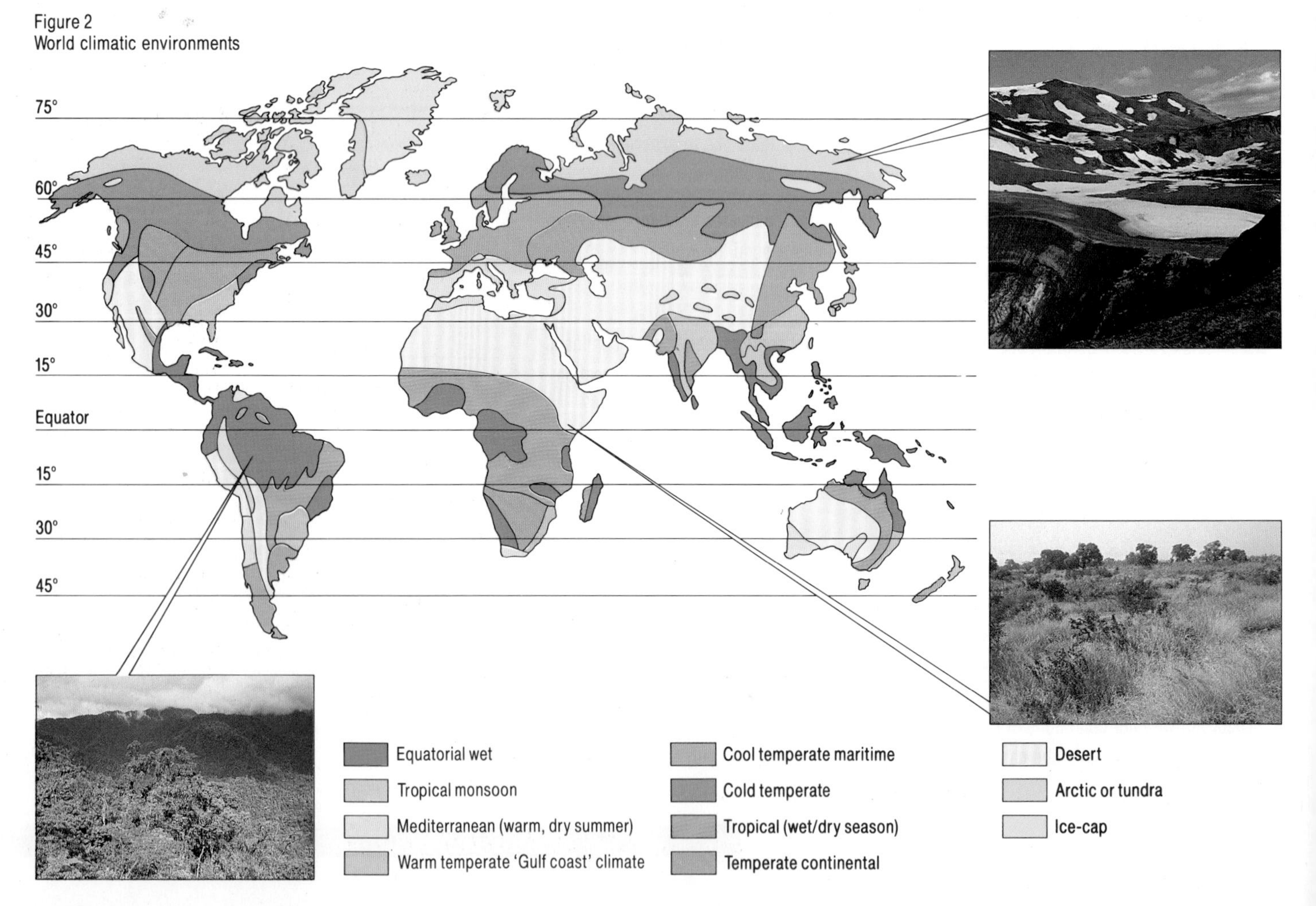

Climate is important because it affects what a place looks like and what grows there, as well as influencing the sort of human activity that can take place. The earth contains such varied climates that a range of different environments exists. Each climatic environment is unique in several ways – it may have distinctive vegetation which has become specially adapted to the climatic conditions, or wildlife unique to the area.

Activities

1 Figure 1 shows the climate of Havana, Look up Cuba in your atlas and find Havana the capital city. Now copy and complete the following:

Havana's climate is hot and wet. The average temperature is .... °C and the yearly rainfall is .... mm. Havana's coolest months are .... and ...., and the temperature range is .... °C. Every month experiences some rainfall, but the wettest months are .... and ....

2 Hong Kong's weather is described in Figure 3. Read the description very carefully and make a list of at least six differences from the climatic conditions in Britain that you are used to.

3 Construct a climate graph for Hong Kong (like the one in Figure 1). The rainfall figures are below, and the temperature statistics are in Figure 3. Remember that temperature is shown as a line graph.

Month	J	F	M	A	M	J	J	A	S	O	N	D
Rainfall (mm)	28	45	70	130	301	375	361	352	253	113	41	27

4 Look carefully at the map of world climatic environments (Figure 2). Now copy and complete the table below:

Position (latitude and location in continent)	*Climatic environment*
a located on the 0° line of latitude	....
b found on the east side of a continent between 25-35°	....
c	*Hot desert*
d located between about 60°N and 75°N	....
e	*Mediterranean*

5 The photographs in Figure 2 show what the landscape and vegetation of some of the climatic environments actually look like.

a Choose one environment that you would like to live in and explain why.

b Choose one environment which you would not like to live in. Explain the reasons for your choice.

c Pay special attention to newspapers, television and radio programmes while you are studying this unit. Are any of these environments mentioned? Why?

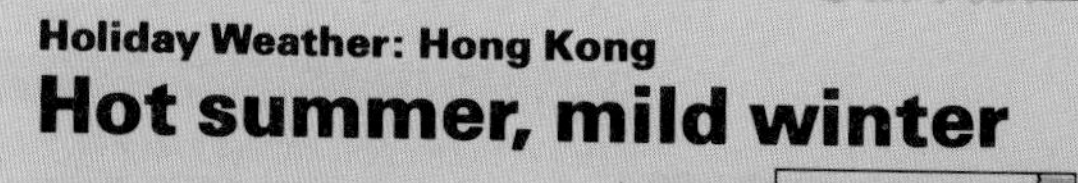

Holiday Weather: Hong Kong

Hot summer, mild winter

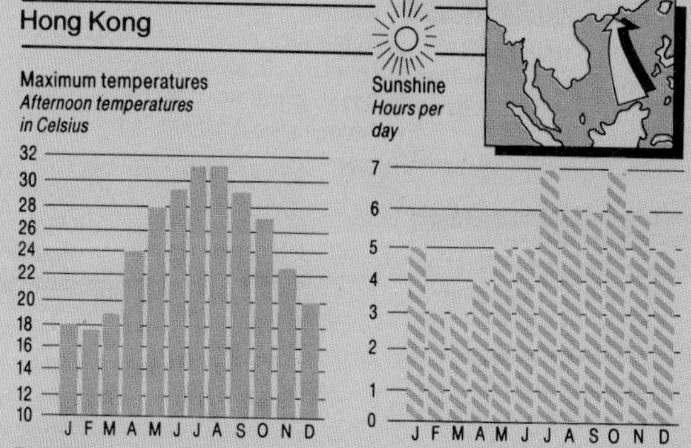

Dick File
London Weather Centre

HONG KONG island is only a few miles across and separated from Kowloon on the Asiatic mainland by the narrow harbour area. To the north of Boundary Road in Kowloon lie the New Territories with hills as well as rice-paddies.

Hong Kong lies just inside the Tropic of Cancer at latitude 22° North, so in June and July the sun is virtually overhead at midday. The summer is tropical with hot and unsettled weather but the winter is more typical of the subtropics being cooler, drier and sunnier. Hong Kong is much affected by the monsoon season.

Temperatures rise quickly during late March with daytime values similar to Britain in mid-summer and broadly equivalent chance of drizzle or showery rain. April is quite hot but can still be rather cloudy. By May the average daytime maximum temperature is up to 28C (82F) with high humidities. Rainfall is around 300 millimetres (12 inches) in the month and although this is five times that of lowland Britain there is still some sunshine between the downpours. June, July, August and early September have even higher rainfall totals though two days in five are virtually dry. This is the season of the southwest monsoon with winds blowing in from the South China Sea. Night-time temperatures typically stay around 26C. The accompanying humidity means that short-stay tourists will have difficulty in sleeping without air conditioning. Late summer is also the typhoon season with July to October the main months at risk.

By October, the typhoon risk is starting to recede, afternoon temperatures are down to 27C (81F) and significant rainfall occurs on only six days in the month.

November is usually a magnificent month as the dry north easterly wind becomes established and only brief unsettled interruptions occur.

December to February, although officially winter, brings good sight-seeing conditions. There will be some cooler days in January when northerly winds blow out from the Chinese mainland. February is rather more prone to grey skies but overall winter is sunny.

Guardian 21.6.89

Figure 3

3.3 Climatic hazards

1 *Extremes of climate and weather*

There has been much speculation recently that the world's climate is changing. This is partly because we have experienced many extremes of weather in quite a short period of time. We will be looking more fully at climate change in the next unit, but for now, let's consider some of the unusual recent weather occurrences. In Britain we had a 'hurricane' in 1987 and unusually dry and hot summers in 1989 and 1990. Elsewhere in the world records have been broken by unusual conditions (Figure 1).

Figure 1

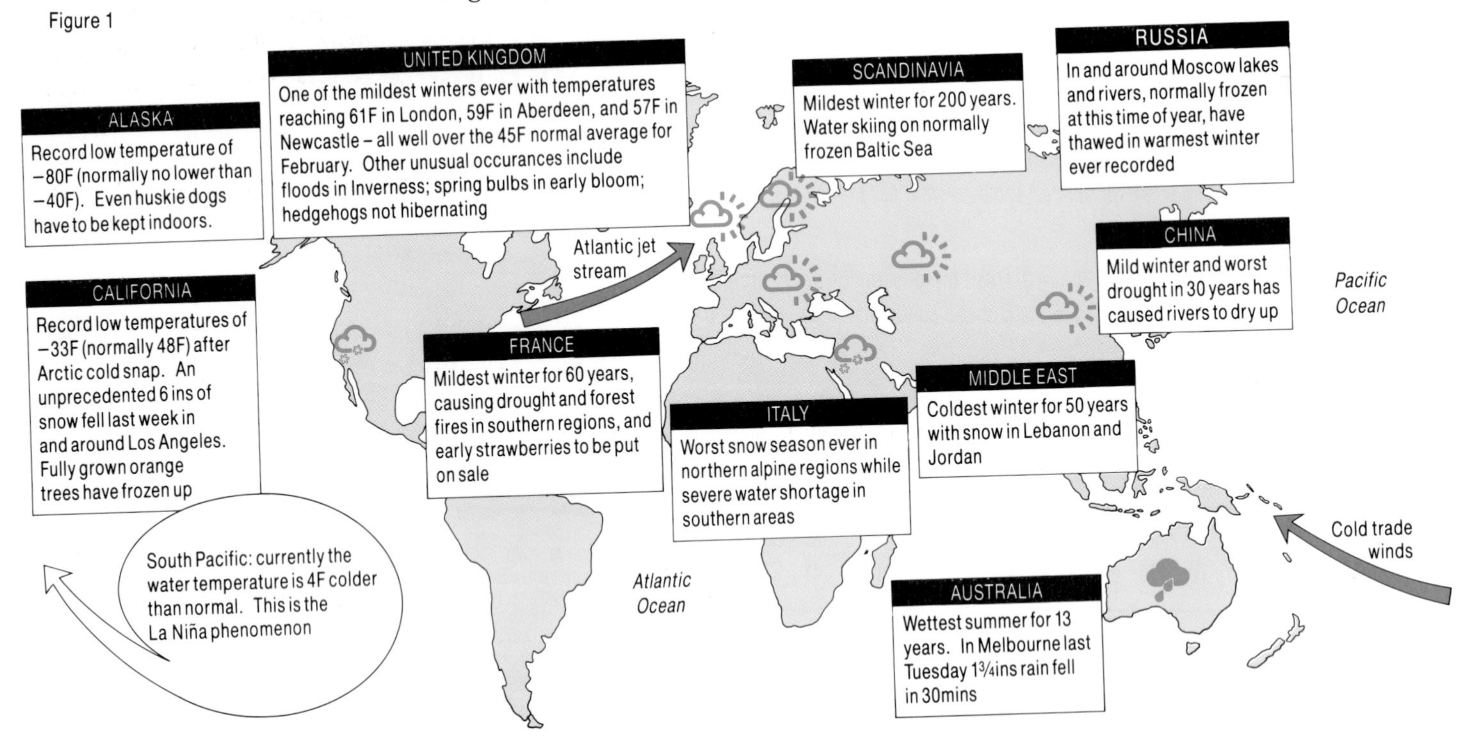

The American drought of 1988

Extreme conditions like hurricanes, floods or severe snow only occur rarely. They are not just uncomfortable, but also disrupt services and affect many people's way of life. A good example of this is the 1988 American Drought, claimed by many people to be the worst **drought** to hit the USA's farming areas since the 1930s.

The drought occurred because 1987 was drier than average. In early 1988, rainfall was only 30% of the normal amount. Temperatures of over 40°C evaporated the little rain that fell, and by the end of June a drought emergency had been declared in 18 states by the US Department of Agriculture.

Figure 2
Area affected by 1988 American drought

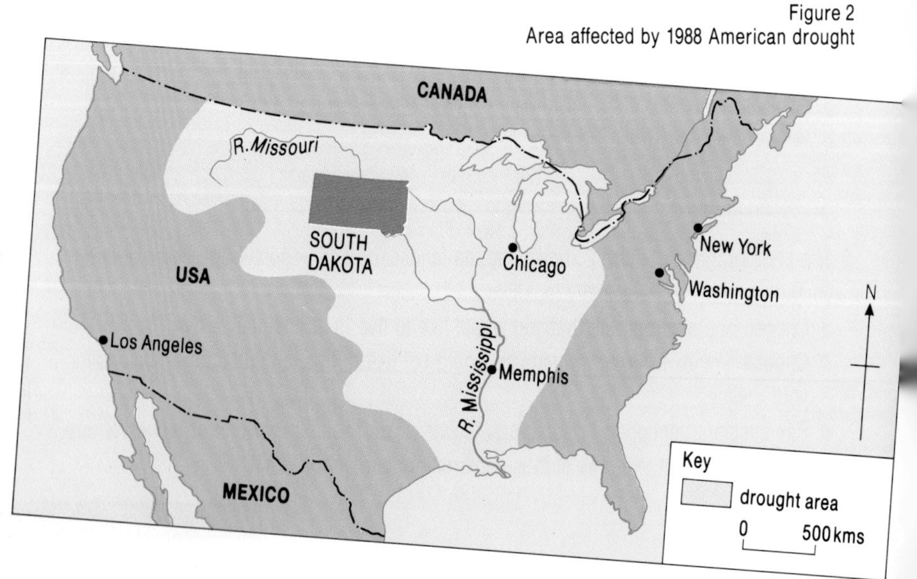

The worst affected areas included the Great Plains and the farming areas of the Midwest, south of the Great Lakes (see Figure 2). The community of Eureka in South Dakota, like hundreds of other small towns across the USA's farmbelt, was affected by the drought. By the middle of 1988 the reservoirs which supplied local people and farmers with water were empty, and the farmers saw their crops threatened.

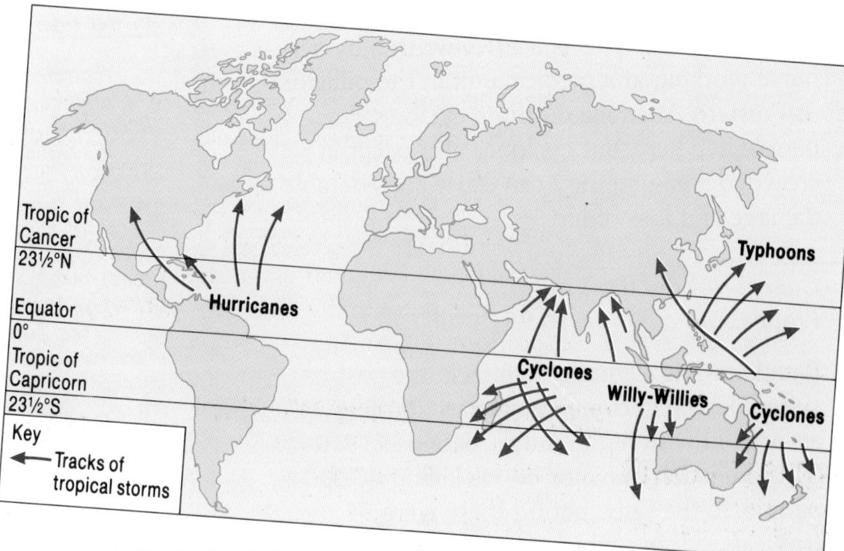

Figure 3 Tracks of tropical storms

2 Tropical Storms

Many people in the world live in areas affected by tropical storms. These hazards still cannot always be predicted accurately despite the birds-eye view given by modern satellite pictures. Tropical storms are known by different names around the world (see Figure 3).

Tropical storms, or **cyclones**, begin developing over warm tropical seas, usually in late summer. Warm air rises and draws in cool air to replace it. As it rises it begins to spin and gains energy. The air cools and clouds form, leading to heavy rain (see Figure 4). Cool air from the upper atmosphere is sucked into the centre or **eye** of the storm. Ground-level conditions here are calm.

The tracks taken by cyclones are not easy to predict because they can change direction suddenly. Once the cyclone moves over land, it loses its energy supply and so the storm fades and dies. Before this happens, however, terrible damage is often caused.

Figure 4 Section through a cyclone

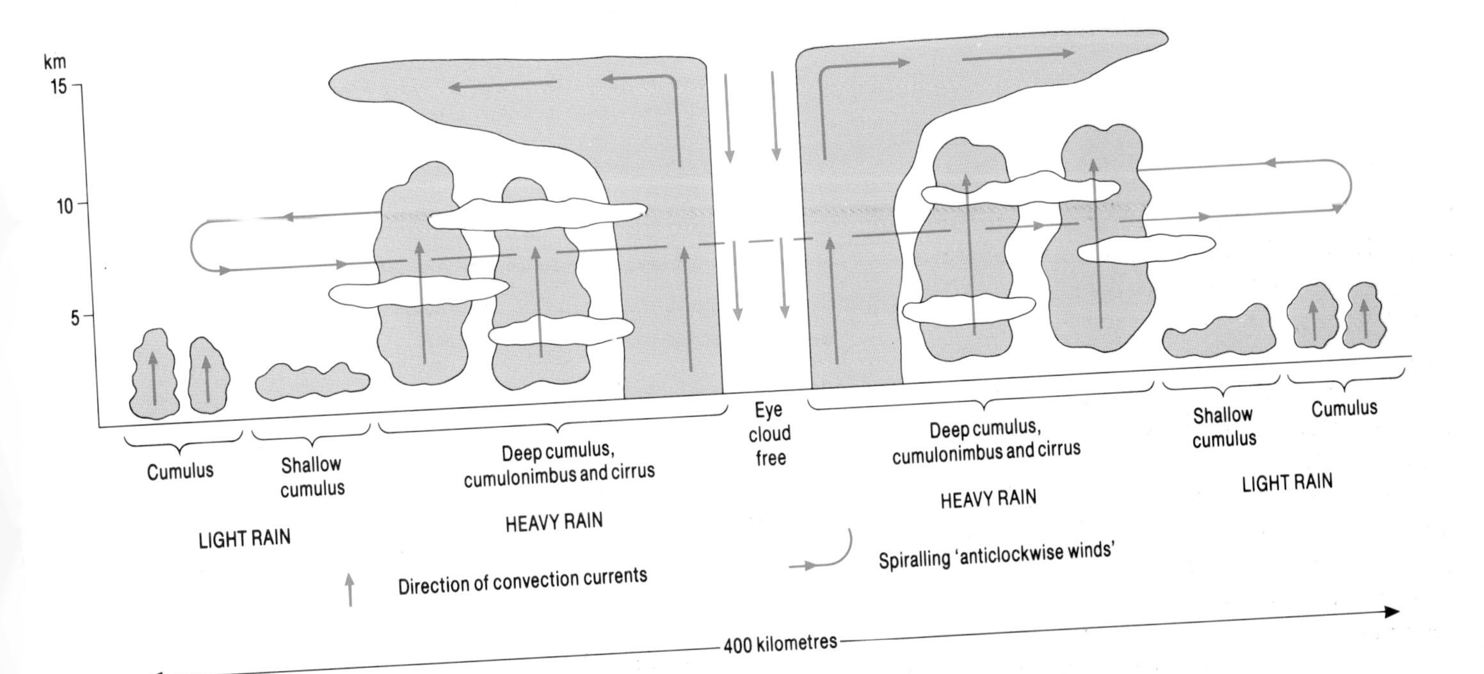

For those unlucky enough to be caught in a cyclone, conditions can be frightening, as Figure 5 shows. This is a letter written by a nurse working at a medical unit in the oilfields of Western Australia during a cyclone. Few people live here, but cyclones also occur in crowded areas, so they can cause considerable damage and loss of life.

Case-Study – Bangladesh
Floods and cyclones: 1987 and 1991

Bangladesh is a country which in the past has suffered from cyclones as well as flooding associated with high rainfall. Between 1960-81 there were 17 major floods killing 40 000 people. In the same period there were 37 tropical cyclones which resulted in over 330 000 deaths.

In 1987, flooding caused serious damage (Figures 6 and 7). It resulted from a combination of heavy rainfall, a tidal wave two metres above normal sea-level and a cyclone. Floods are particularly serious in Bangladesh because much of the country is low-lying, and most of the population live on flat land close to the many rivers. The cyclone

A letter from Karratha. W. Australia. 29.2.84

As from 1 p.m. today we are on a 'red' cyclone alert. Yesterday we were on a 'blue' alert which is to let everyone know there is one in the area. It was a hot sunny day - you'd not credit it!

It's raining hard - winds are strong - the local radio station is putting out half-hourly bulletins. Everyone has gone home to wait it out. We should expect the worst to hit us at 1a.m. tomorrow, winds of 140 km/h! It's a very bad one. The centre of the cyclone has winds up to 220km/h. We have been advised to batten down. I took my hanging baskets, anything that could move, garden hoses, garbage cans, etc. and put them in the out-house. I've got torches and batteries - cold drink, milk etc. in the house. Filled washing machine and bath with water. Everyone has put their car in the best place with hand-brake on and in reverse gear as instructed. People in caravans have moved to the schools. I'll sleep on a mattress in the corridor away from the windows (cyclone screens are on). This cyclone is called 'Chloe'. Poor guys out on the oil rig. I'll write this as things happen I think. It will make it interesting.

February 29th 1984

5 p.m. News: cyclone expected to cross the coast at 12 midnight. Now at Karratha. Winds in the centre of the storm up to 225km/h. Coming at 13km/h. following coastline. I've packed a small case (passport / jewels / knickers / hairdryer / etc.) Bloody cold! Wrapped myself up in a blanket. Warm wind outside, the strength of which is bending the tall slender gum trees nearly in half.

8 p.m. News: Cyclone expected at 10 p.m. 30 km. north of us. Winds still at 225 km/h. at centre. Radio off the air at 8.05 p.m. Charming! Electricity varying at times. Phoned Security Woodside for check of weather as above.

9.15 p.m. Made my bed up on the diningroom floor (shades of war time!) not near any windows. Wind getting very strong now.

10.45 p.m. Power failure. Eye of the cyclone 30km. away according to radio - back on now! Winds very strong. Feel the house and the windows shaking.

March 1st 1984

9 p.m. Well! Everything's over now. We didn't get the full force of the storm, thank heavens. It was bad enough, the wind. Lots of trees uprooted. A huge tree from next door landed outside my back door squashing the washing line. The power came on at 4 p.m. I did a mass clean up, like everyone else. The air conditioner will still not work.....

Figure 5
A letter from Karratha, W. Australia

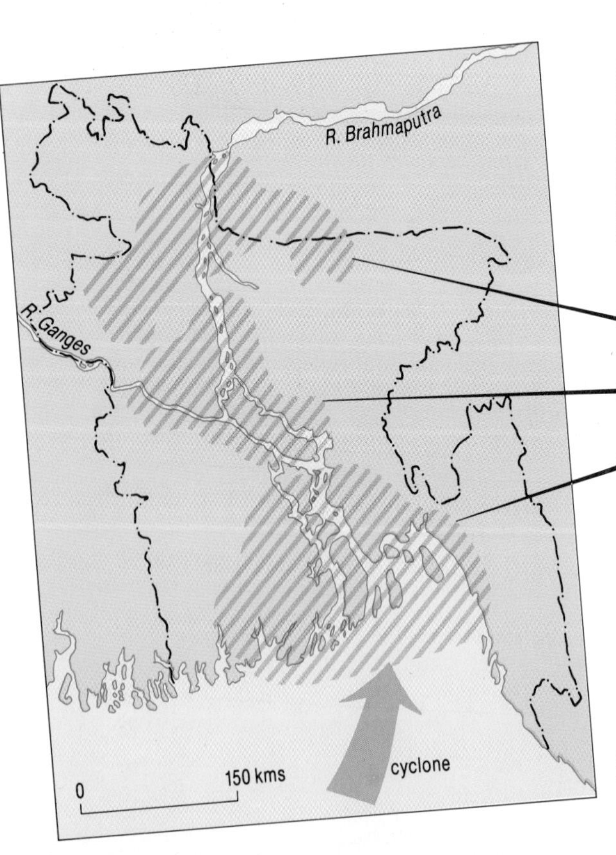

Ⓐ By mid-August flooding of areas around the confluence of the Ganges and Brahmaputra had taken place

Ⓑ Heavy rains in early August cause the level of the Upper Ganges and Brahmaputra to rise and burst their banks

Ⓒ Delta area flooded 6 June by tidal wave following a tropical storm (cyclone) in the Bay of Bengal

Figure 6
1987 flooding in Bangladesh

left 34% of the country under water and killed 800 people. Three million tonnes of grain were destroyed as every river burst its banks. About 25 million people were affected in some way by the disaster.

Some scientists believe that **deforestation** in the mountains to the north of Bangladesh helped to bring about the 1987 floods. This removed an important storage area for the heavy rain which occurs over the mountains. If this was the case, and deforestation continues, then Bangladesh could suffer worse flooding in the future. Various solutions have been suggested to help reduce the risk of flooding, such as planting new trees on the slopes of the mountains.

Disaster struck again in early May 1991. A cyclone travelling over the Bay of Bengal crossed the coastline of Bangladesh at 233 kms per hour. It brought with it tidal waves over 6 metres high, and deluged huge areas of the low lying coast south of Dhaka. Chittagong, the country's second city, with 3 million inhabitants, was swamped. 1 million tons of rice was swept into the sea, and the local shrimp farming industry was destroyed. Some 125 000 lives were lost and estimated $1 billion of damage was caused.

Figure 7 1991 flooding

Activities

1 In pairs, list any unusual or extreme weather conditions which have occurred recently. Keep a special watch on television and radio news programmes and on the newspapers to discover if there are weather problems anywhere in the world now. Your class could produce a wall display charting any unusual or extreme weather conditions that occur during the weeks you are studying 'Weather and Climate'.

2 *a* Using an atlas and Figure 2, make a list of all the states which were affected by the 1988 drought in the USA.
b Estimate the size of the drought-affected area.
c Find out where the heaviest rain normally falls in the USA. From what you have learnt already in this chapter, why do you think this is so?

3 Look carefully at the section through a cyclone (Figure 4).
a What are the conditions like in the eye of the cyclone?
b How high are the tallest clouds, and what type are they?
c Where is the heaviest rainfall?
d In which direction is air moving in the cyclone?
e From what you have read and from the diagram, explain in your own words how and where cyclones are formed

4 Read the letter written by a nurse in Western Australia during a cyclone (Figure 5). What precautions did she take before and during the cyclone? Can you think of any more she could have done?

5 a What caused the flooding in each of the three shaded areas on the map (Figure 6)?

b Look at the photographs in Figure 7. What problems has the flooding caused?

c In small groups discuss what should be done by the government and relief agencies like Oxfam and Save the Children Fund after such a disaster. Try to decide a list of priorities for:

- the first two weeks after the floods;
- 6 months to 1 year after the floods.

6 You will need an atlas and an outline map of Bangladesh for this activity.

a Complete the map of Bangladesh by including these features:

- name Dhaka and Chittagong;
- shade and name the two rivers;
- label the Bay of Bengal;
- show the track taken by cyclones (see Figure 3).

b Why are more people becoming concerned that future flooding will be more serious? What can be done to prevent this occurring?

3.4 Climate change

Changes in the earth's climate have been occurring for thousands of years. We know for example that there have been several **ice-ages** in the earth's history, when temperatures were considerably lower than they are now. However, in the last few years, scientists have become increasingly worried that significant new changes in our climate may be occurring. There is growing evidence of an increase in the earth's temperature (see Figure 1). This has become known as **global warming**. Even in the United Kingdom temperatures are higher than would normally be expected, and are on an upward trend. The earth will soon be at its warmest for over 100 000 years (see Figure 2). This is said to be due to the **greenhouse effect**.

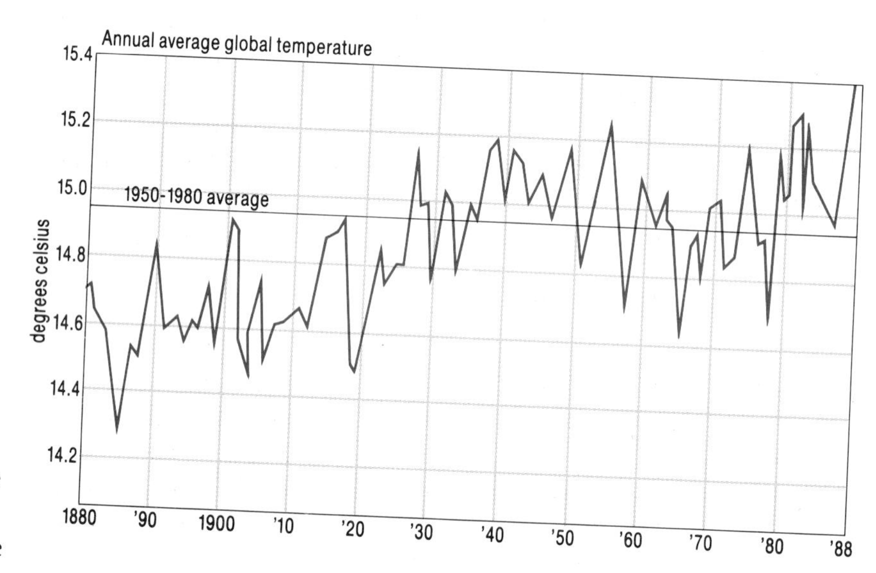

Figure 1 Annual average global temperatures

1 What is the greenhouse effect?

The process of global warming is very like that which goes on in a greenhouse. Here, the sun's heat is trapped by the glass roof and sides of the greenhouse. As a result the temperatures inside begin to rise, making it an ideal place for growing tropical plants, fruits and vegetables.

The earth is behaving as if it were a greenhouse, and temperatures are rising as a result of the so-called **greenhouse effect**. This is because the sun's heat is not able to escape into space through the atmosphere.

Figure 2

OUR GLOBAL HOTHOUSE

by DAVID JONES, Environmental Editor

THE EARTH will soon be at its hottest for 100,000 years, and only emergency action can save mankind from the world's biggest natural disaster.

That was the grim message from 100 of the world's top climate experts last night as they pronounced the greenhouse effect official.

Scientists are now certain that gases from cars, power stations and industry will send temperatures soaring by 3° C by the end of next century, turning the earth into a global hothouse.

The drastic change will spark massive floods as sea levels rise by 2ft and also cause widespread disease, famine and drought.

Met Office chief Dr John Houghton, who chaired the panel of experts, warned: "We are moving into a rate of change in the climate and atmosphere temperature which is outside the range of historic or pre-historic experience over the last 100,000 years. If we continue with business as usual, the rate of the rise will be greater than the Earth has known in man's history.

Western leaders now face the greatest challenge to mankind, to solve the problems of carbon emissions and minimise their effects before it is too late.

The governments must also provide massive aid to Third World countries to help them develop cleaner technology.

Firm decisions are expected to be taken at a World Climate Conference this autumn and they will mean major changes to everyone's life. Luxuries, such as big, fast cars, must be replaced by fuel-efficient models and families will have to make huge energy savings in the home.

Today Newspaper 26.5.90

The atmosphere actually keeps the earth's temperature high enough to be habitable. Without it, temperatures would be up to 35°C. lower than they are. However, its composition is changing and some gases like methane, carbon-dioxide, **chlorofluorocarbons (CFCs)** and nitrous oxide have collected in the upper atmosphere. These absorb the heat which the earth is trying to re-radiate into space (Figure 3), are called **greenhouse gases**, and are thought to be responsible for global warming. They are found in several household objects and are being produced in huge quantities by seemingly harmless human activities (Figure 4).

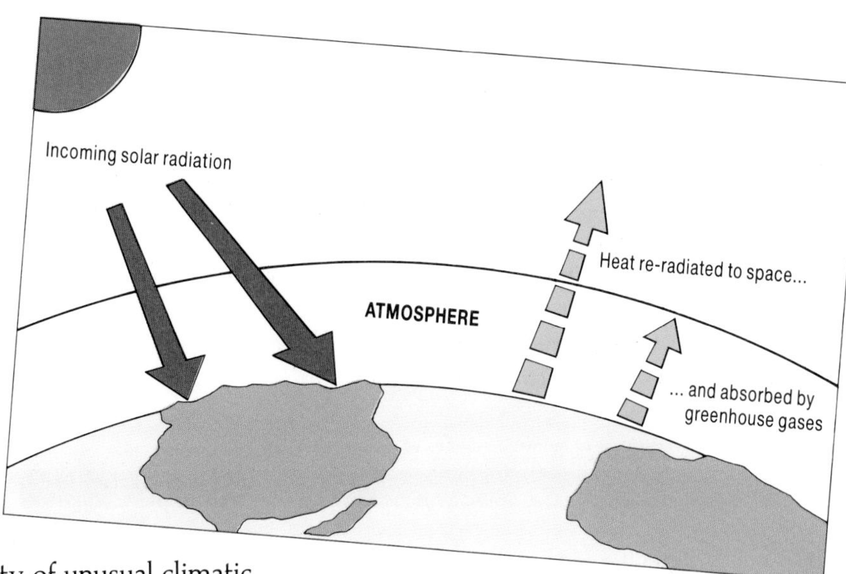

Figure 3 The greenhouse effect

Evidence for global warming includes a variety of unusual climatic events in the last two decades. We have already looked at the American Drought of 1988 (Unit 3.3), and desertification in Mauritania (Unit 2.4). Across Africa more generally, there has been recurrent drought over the last two decades in the area known as the Sahel. There is also evidence around the world of rising sea-level and of ice-sheets going into retreat and melting.

It looks likely that global warming is due to larger quantities of greenhouse gases being released into the atmosphere today than in the past. The most important of these are carbon-dioxide and methane, although some other gases have similar effects.

2 How might global warming affect life on earth?

The consequences of long-term climatic change caused by the greenhouse effect are only just beginning to be realised. A recent United Nations report warned that in just 60 years, major changes will already have occurred. Climate patterns, the shape and position of coastlines as well as people's ways of life will all have been altered significantly. These changes will occur in every country of the world, and not only those where greenhouse gases are released. For this reason it is important for international action to be taken to deal with the problem.

Figure 4 The greenhouse gases

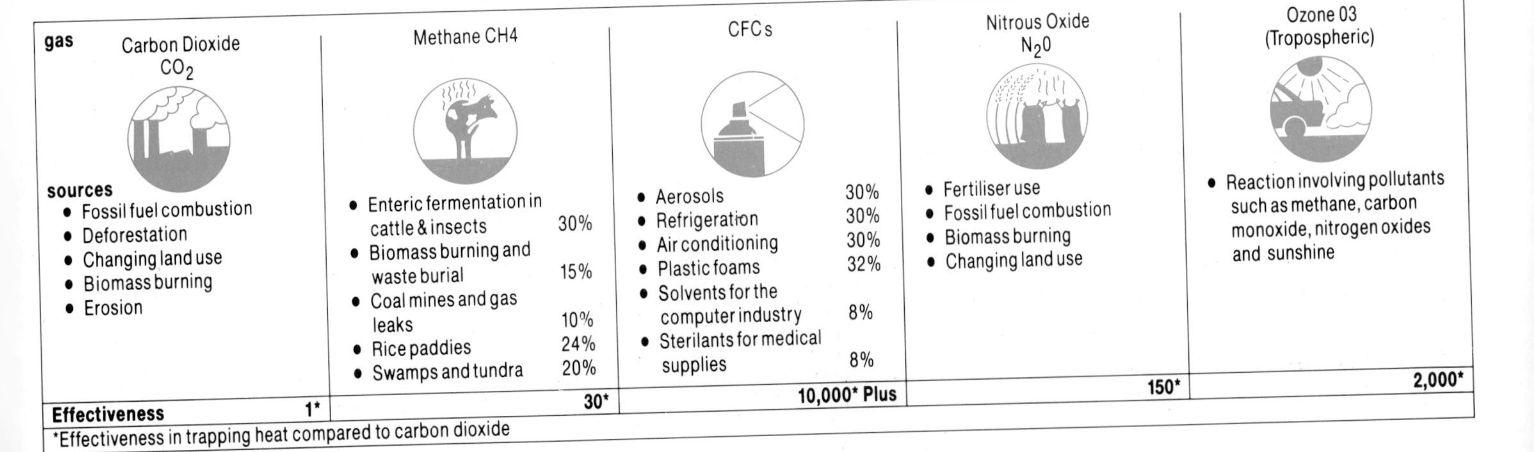

gas	Carbon Dioxide CO_2	Methane CH4	CFCs	Nitrous Oxide N_2O	Ozone 03 (Tropospheric)
sources	• Fossil fuel combustion • Deforestation • Changing land use • Biomass burning • Erosion	• Enteric fermentation in cattle & insects 30% • Biomass burning and waste burial 15% • Coal mines and gas leaks 10% • Rice paddies 24% • Swamps and tundra 20%	• Aerosols 30% • Refrigeration 30% • Air conditioning 30% • Plastic foams 32% • Solvents for the computer industry 8% • Sterilants for medical supplies 8%	• Fertiliser use • Fossil fuel combustion • Biomass burning • Changing land use	• Reaction involving pollutants such as methane, carbon monoxide, nitrogen oxides and sunshine
Effectiveness	1*	30*	10,000* Plus	150*	2,000*

*Effectiveness in trapping heat compared to carbon dioxide

3 What can be done?

Many of these changes are already beginning to occur, so urgent action is required to slow-down or stop the continued release of greenhouse gases. Much of the attention so far has focussed on carbon-dioxide and chlorofluorocarbons (CFCs). If we stop burning fossil fuels such as coal and oil in our power stations, and put a halt to burning the rainforests, then the amount of carbon-dioxide being released could be reduced. The phasing out of CFCs in the manufacture of aerosol cans, refrigerators and polystyrene packaging would also help.

Activities

1 *a* Use the graph in Figure 1 to calculate and then list the average global temperature for every tenth year starting in 1880.

b What do you notice about the list of figures you have collected? What is the trend?

2 What is the greenhouse effect? Explain what is occurring in your own words. Use the diagram in Figure 3 to help you.

a List the main five greenhouse gases.

b Using the information in this unit, identify which greenhouse gas is shown in each of the photographs in Figure 5.

c Look around your own home. Can you find evidence of any of these greenhouse gases?

d Which of the greenhouse gases is the most damaging (the most effective in trapping heat in Figure 4)?

Figure 5 Where do greenhouse gases come from?

3 What evidence is mentioned in this unit for global warming?

4 The figures below show which countries are contributing most to the greenhouse effect in terms of their output of carbon-dioxide, the most important greenhouse gas. Decide on an appropriate type of graph or diagram to show these figures, then draw it. Remember to add a title and key (if required).

Region or country	*% contribution to global warming (Carbon-dioxide) in 1980*
United States of America	21
USSR*	14
EC (European Community)	14
China	7
Brazil	4
India	4
Rest of the world	36

*Independent states from 1992

5 Read the account in Figure 6 of a day in the life of Julia. She is 14 years old and goes to a school just outside Coventry in the West Midlands.
When you have read it work with a partner to make a list of all the ways in which Julia is inadvertently contributing to the greenhouse effect.
(*Hint:* this may be because of some of the things which Julia does, or the products which she uses).

Figure 6

7.45 am	Fall out of bed, then wash and shower.
8.00 am	Take the milk out of the fridge for my breakfast - I usually have cereal, toast and tea.
8.15 am	Put my uniform on.
8.25 am	Dad takes me to school in the car - we often get caught in traffic jams.
9.00 am	School begins - the buildings are nice and new. This is good in the summer because they are air-conditioned. Classrooms are well-equipped. Most have computer terminals which we can use with all our subjects.
12.30 pm	Lunch at last! Most of us go down the road to the new fast-food shop where we can buy hamburgers and chips. We usually walk back to school before eating them - they keep warm because of the foam packaging.
2.00 pm	We are doing some work on energy at the moment. I am looking at the school's oil-fired heating, to see if it can be made more efficient.
4.15 pm	School finishes and I catch a bus home. I always do my homework straightaway before tea. Mum and Dad bought a lovely teak desk for me to work at for my last birthday.
7.00 pm	I watched some television. There was a good programme about the greenhouse effect. It is quite a serious problem, but I can't see what it has to do with me. Can you???

Dictionary

altitude the height of a place above sea-level

atmospheric pressure force exerted by the air, measured in millibars

chlorofluorocarbons (CFCs) gases which are used in the manufacture of refrigerators, aerosols etc. which contribute to global warming

convectional rainfall type of rainfall associated with hot areas. Rain is caused by clouds rising on convection currents

cyclone a tropical storm accompanied by high winds and heavy rain

deforestation the process of removing trees

eye the calm, cloudless area at the centre of a cyclone

frontal rainfall type of rainfall associated with air fronts

ice-ages long periods during geological history when global temperatures were significantly lower than today, causing large parts of the earth's surface to be covered by ice-sheets

ocean current water in the oceans follows particular patterns of movement, mostly circular. These currents can be mapped and have an impact on weather and climate patterns

temperature range the difference between the hottest and coldest temperature during a year (annual range) or a single day (diurnal range)

4 Resources and energy

4.1 A world full of energy?

As the world's population increases and living standards continue to rise, ever-increasing quantities of its energy resources are being used up. Energy is needed to heat and light our homes and workplaces, to provide fuel for our transport, as well as to manufacture goods and to grow food.

There are many different types of energy (Figure 1). Some are called **renewable** because they will not run out. Other types come from stocks which are limited and will eventually become exhausted. These are called **non-renewable** types of energy.

Global energy consumption now stands at record levels. In 1988, the world consumed over 8000 million tonnes of oil equivalent. Since 1970 the figure has increased in almost every year (Figure 2). This constant increase in energy use cannot continue for ever. Only a small proportion of energy used is of the renewable type, and there are serious concerns that other types of energy may run out before long.

1970	5173
1973	5915
1976	6298
1979	6973
1982	6814
1985	7372
1988	8073

Figure 2
Global energy consumption

Figure 1
Types of energy

Some parts of the world use more energy than others. Energy consumption per capita in North and Central America is ten times higher than in Asia, and sixteen times higher than in Africa (Figure 3). Much of the world's population, especially in Asia and Africa, relies on traditional types of energy such as fuelwood (Figure 5), as well as vegetable and animal waste. Coal, oil and gas are still the world's main sources of commercial energy (Figure 4), although the pattern of consumption varies enormously from place to place. China, for example, relies mostly on coal to meet its needs, whereas Japan depends on oil. In France, nuclear power produces over half the electricity generated.

As the earth's population grows, the demand for energy looks set to continue rising. There is now a real **energy crisis** in some places, and this is affecting our environment: in parts of Africa and Asia flooding has resulted partly from deforestation (Figure 5) caused by people seeking fuelwood; the burning of fossil fuels like coal and oil is now known to be contributing to the greenhouse effect by releasing carbon-dioxide into the atmosphere; nuclear power has serious risks associated with it, as accidents at Three Mile Island in the USA (1979) and Chernobyl in the Ukraine (1986) have shown.

If the world is to have sufficient energy to meet its requirements in the 21st century a number of things have to be done:

- alternative 'renewable' sources of energy must be developed, like solar, wave and wind power
- we must reduce our demand for energy by learning to conserve it more effectively
- new deposits of conventional energy need to be developed, and ways found of reducing the damage being done to the environment by its use

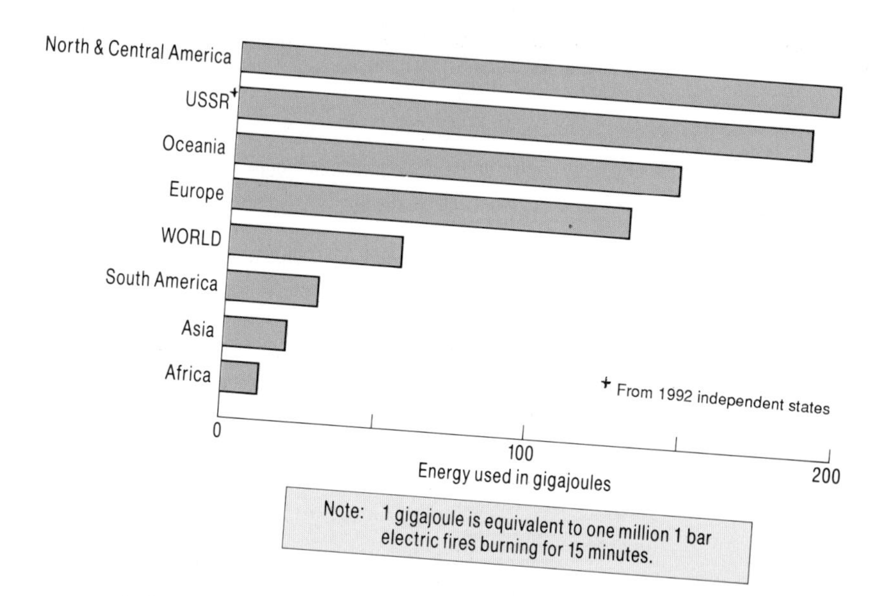

Figure 3 Primary energy consumption per capita, 1986

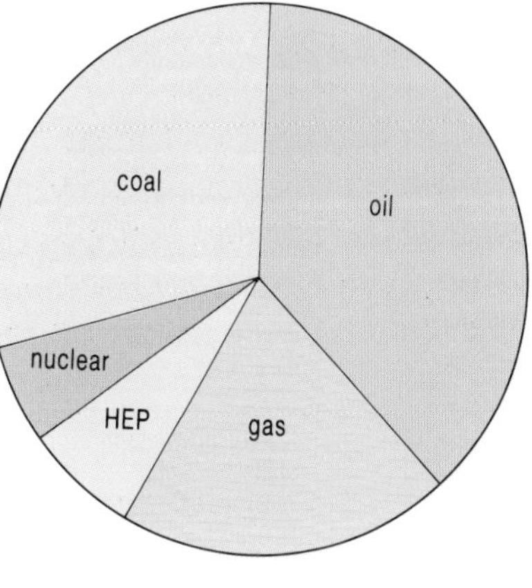

%	Japan	W.Europe	LDCs
oil	55.6	45.3	50.0
gas	9.8	15.2	15.5
coal	19.0	20.1	21.5
nuclear	10.9	11.2	2.0
HEP	4.7	8.2	11.0

Figure 4 World energy consumption 1988

Fuelwood Crisis!

by Jack Freeman in Lusaka

Women and children are having to trek further and further to gather scarce supplies of fuelwood over large parts of Africa and Asia. In the developing countries about 80% of the total timber cut is used by local people for cooking and heating.

The results of this loss of tree-cover have been serious. The topsoil is left unprotected and is easily washed away. Soil nutrients are also lost as heavy rain filters them out of the soil completely. The flooding risk is also increased because there is no longer sufficient soil or vegetation to hold up the flow of heavy rain when it occurs.

Figure 5
Collecting fuelwood

Activities

1 a List the types of energy shown in the photographs in Figure 1.
b Which of these are renewable and which are non-renewable?

2 Copy and complete the table below. Try to fit *one* advantage and *one* disadvantage into each of the blank spaces from the list provided.

Energy Type	Advantage	Disadvantage
COAL		Noise and dust; burning releases CO and CO_2
OIL	Easily transported by pipeline; can be burnt or used to generate electricity	
HEP		
WIND/SOLAR POWER		High production costs at present
ELECTRICITY	Versatile form of energy with many applications	

CHOOSE FROM
Gas emissions; water used for cooling may be returned warm to rivers
No pollution and abundant supplies
Changes natural river flow by dam construction
Cheap and clean to produce
Can be burnt or used to generate electricity
Risk of blowouts or spills; burning releases CO_2 and SO_2

3 a Using Figure 2, describe how world energy consumption has changed since 1970.
b What do you think the energy consumption will be in *i* 1991? *ii* 1994?

4 Explain the world pattern of energy consumption shown in Figure 3. Why are some areas larger energy users than others?

5 a From the pie chart of world energy consumption in Figure 4, rank the five types of energy in order of importance.
b Draw pie-charts for *i* Japan; *ii* Western Europe; and *iii* the Less Developed Countries (LDCs) using the data in Figure 4.
c In which area of the world, of the three shown, is: *i* HEP best developed? *ii* nuclear power most important?
d Write a few sentences to describe the differences between energy consumption in Japan and the LDCs.

6 Fuelwood is used in many parts of Asia and Africa. Read the newspaper article (Figure 5) then use your own words to describe some of the problems it causes.

4.2 A nuclear world?

In 1986, the world was shaken by news of a major accident in the Number 4 reactor of the Chernobyl nuclear power plant. A leak of hydrogen gas caused an explosion and a fire. Some 33 people were killed. More than 130 000 people had to be evacuated as a radioactive cloud was released which drifted across Northwest Europe (see Figures 1 and 2)

Nuclear power is a relatively new source of energy. Up until the last forty years, our energy requirements were met largely from **primary energy** sources like coal, peat and charcoal. Today a variety of newer sources are also used including gas and oil. Both are often burnt in power stations to produce **electricity**, which is a form of **secondary energy**.

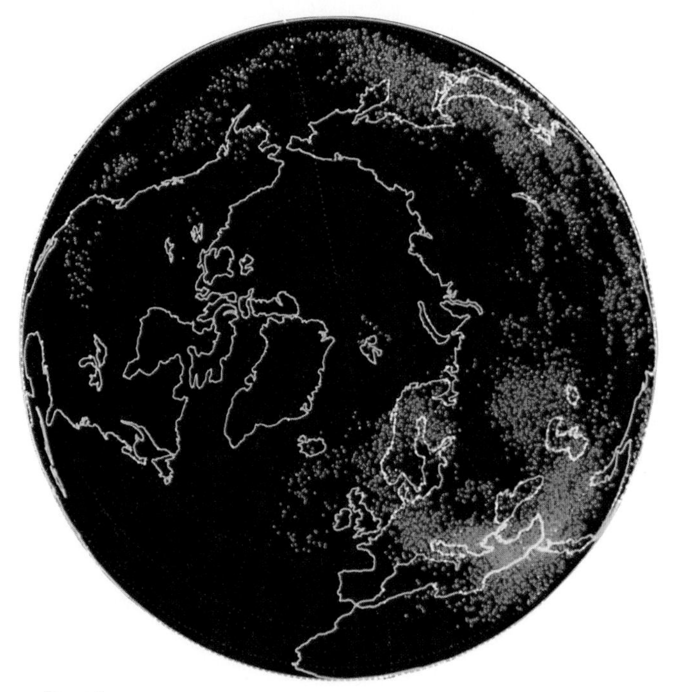

Figure 1
Distribution of radioactivity, ten days after the accident

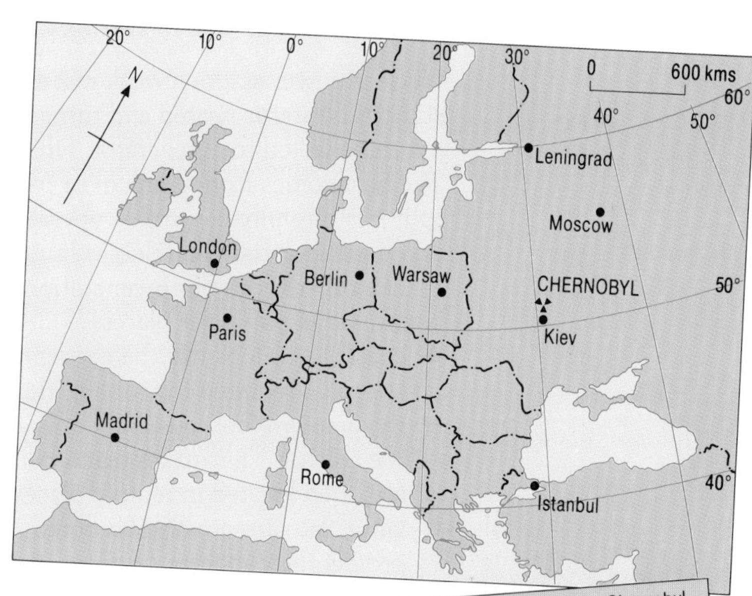

Estimated positions of centre of radioactive cloud from Chernobyl							
Sat. 26	April	51°N	31°W	Sat. 3	May	56°N	5°E
Sun. 27	April	53°N	28°W	Sun. 4	May	56°N	17°E
Mon. 28	April	54°N	20°W	Mon. 5	May	48°N	16°E
Tue. 29	April	49°N	13°W	Tue. 6	May	47°N	10°E
Wed. 30	April	45°N	9°W	Wed. 7	May	52°N	4°E
Thu. 1	May	47°N	6°W	Thu. 8	May	57°N	1°W
Fri. 2	May	51°N	2°W	Fri. 9	May	60°N	6°W

Figure 2 Tracking the radioactive cloud

Nuclear power has only been available since the late 1950s. Scientists then predicted that by 1990 the world would be dominated by nuclear power. Today, however, only about 5% of the world's energy is produced in this way, and nuclear energy is very controversial (Figure 3). Accidents like the one at Chernobyl in the Ukraine, as well as others at Three Mile Island in the USA and Windscale (Sellafield) in the UK have caused concern about the safety of nuclear power stations. It is now believed that less electricity will be generated by nuclear power in the year 2000 than is produced today. Despite the controversy, many countries still depend on nuclear power to generate huge amounts of electricity (Figure 4).

Figure 3 Views about nuclear power

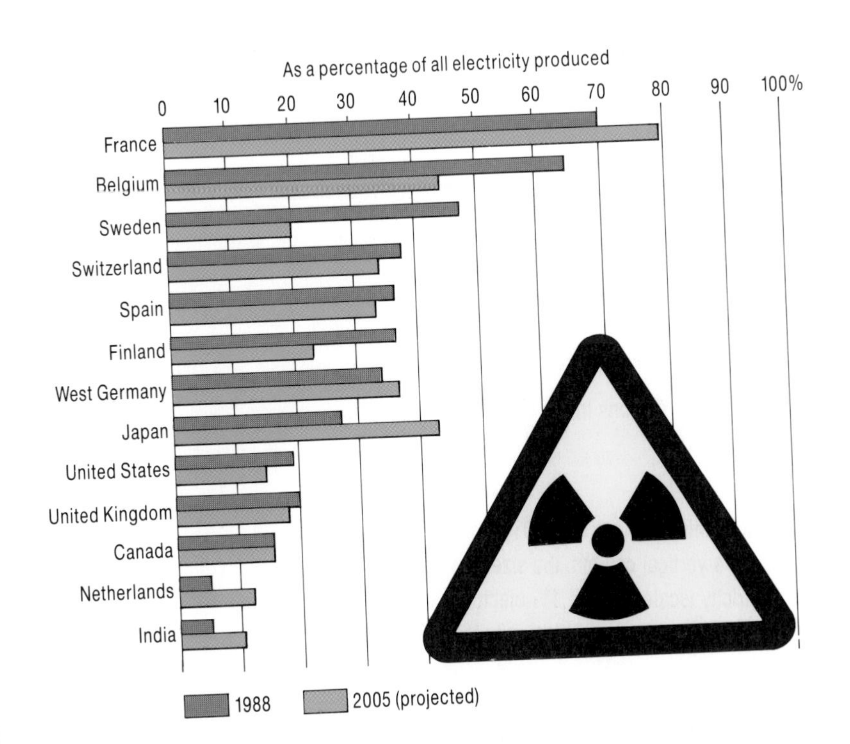

Figure 4 Nuclear electricity generation

How do nuclear power stations work?

Nuclear power stations work in a similar way to conventional power stations. Water is heated and turned to steam, which is used to drive a turbine linked to a generator, which in turn produces electricity. The heat comes from uranium or plutonium atoms when they are split in a carefully controlled operation in a **reactor**. This process, called **nuclear fission**, releases huge amounts of heat.

Like other types of power station, nuclear stations ideally need to be located in particular places:

- coastal locations may be chosen because large amounts of water are often required for cooling the reactors
- the uranium fuel rods are highly radioactive when removed from the reactor. This makes reactor sites dangerous, so nuclear stations are often located in remote places
- large, flat sites are also favoured, in areas of stable geology to protect the dangerous reactor core.

These locations have been favoured in Britain but elsewhere there have been some differences. In California, several nuclear reactors have been built on or near fault lines. In the area formerly known as the USSR, most nuclear power stations have inland locations close to towns, like Chernobyl near Kiev.

We are a long way from living in a nuclear world, though some countries like France, Japan and Belgium which already rely heavily on nuclear energy, have decided that they want to develop this source further. Whether nuclear power remains important in the future will depend on how safe the reactors prove to be in the next few years, and how quickly other types of energy are developed.

Activities

1 *a* On a copy of Figure 2, carefully plot the progress of the radioactive cloud from Chernobyl.
b Make a list of the large towns and cities that the cloud seems to have passed close to.
c Why do nuclear accidents in one country concern neighbouring countries?

2 *a* Why are so many people concerned about the development of nuclear power? The headlines in Figure 3 might help you.
b What benefits are associated with nuclear power compared with fossil fuels?

3 Look in an atlas to discover where the nuclear power stations in the UK are located. Mark them on a map and suggest reasons for their locations.

4 Study Figure 4 carefully.
a On an outline map of the world mark those countries where over 10% of electricity in 1988 was generated by nuclear power. Draw a vertical column, the size of which is proportional to the amount of nuclear electricity (scale 1mm = 1% electricity).
b Which three nations relied most heavily on nuclear generated electricity in 1988? Will they be the same in 2005?

5 The cartoon in Figure 5 suggests that people generally are quite worried about nuclear power.
  a Why do you think this is the case?
  b What do *you* think about nuclear power? Do you think the risks are so great that no more nuclear stations should be developed, or do you believe that nuclear power is important for the future?

Figure 5
Public confidence is not very high

4.3 Renewable energy – the only alternative?

People are becoming worried about the damage that traditional types of energy are doing to the world's environment. The dangers of nuclear power, damage to wildlife caused by oil tanker spills, devastation caused by opencast mining, and the effects of burning fossil fuels are all well-known. It is not surprising then that safer sources of energy are being researched.

The majority of the world's population, around 2.5 billion people, depends on **biomass** fuels such as fuelwood, crop residues and dung. Surveys have shown that fuelwood plays a significant role in most developing countries. In most countries in Africa it accounts for over 75% of energy requirements. There are, however, severe shortages of this type of energy (see Figure 1). As a result, the development of energy sources which are both environmentally safe and **renewable** is even more vital.

In many parts of the world renewable sources of energy are well developed: in Southern Japan, Hungary, Iceland and Italy **geothermal** power is used for heating homes and factories; in parts of the USA, the Mediterranean and Japan **solar power** is used extensively, and there are **wind farms** producing electricity in Denmark and in California in the USA.

One of the most exciting renewable sources is solar power. The sun radiates huge amounts of energy. The amount of solar energy striking the earth at any given moment is equivalent to 40 000 one-bar electric fires burning for every single person on earth! If we are able to trap a small amount of this, we will go a long way to solving the world's energy problems. The sun's energy can be captured in a

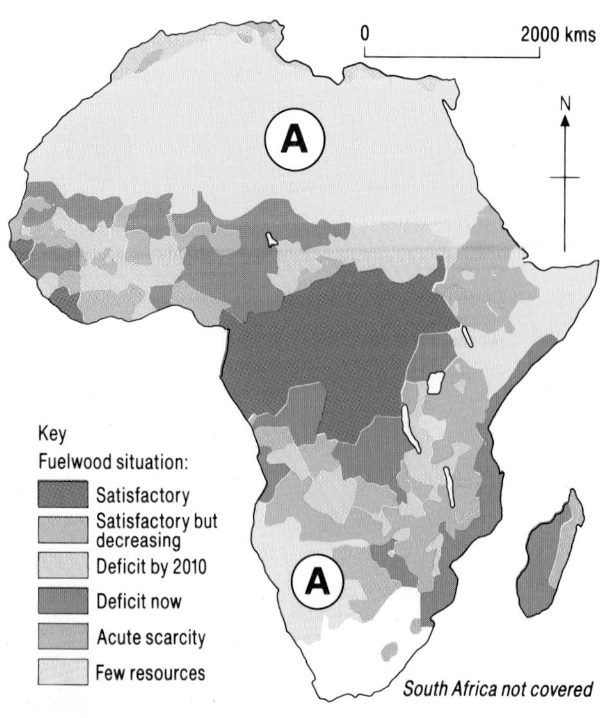

Figure 1 The fuelwood crisis in Africa

variety of ways (Figure 2). It is already being used to provide hot water for houses in Japan, to power spacecraft circling the earth and to light the streets in India's capital city, New Delhi. However, electricity produced in this way is about ten times more expensive than that produced in more conventional ways.

About one-fifth of the energy consumed in the world today is from renewable sources; in particular solar, wind, tidal, geothermal and hydro-electric-power. Often these are best developed in the poorer countries of the 'South', where the lack of **fossil fuels** or the cost of importing them has required the development of alternatives. There is much to be learnt from countries like China where techniques for using energy from the sun, wind, rivers and manure are quite advanced (Figure 3).

Elsewhere, more advanced technology is likely to lead to the development of some exciting schemes. There are plans to construct **barrages** across tidal inlets like the Mersey and Severn estuaries on the western side of Britain, and across the Wash on the east coast. These schemes are only in their planning stage, but they are creating a lot of interest.

Figure 2
Three ways of collecting the sun's energy

1 Flat plate collectors
These contain tubes filled with water or air which can be pumped through the solar collector. These normally sit on south-facing roofs in the northern hemisphere and may be used to heat household water.

2 Tracking concentrators
These comprise a large reflective dish which concentrates solar radiation on a small area to produce sufficient heat to boil water and create steam and so can generate electricity. They track the sun continually.

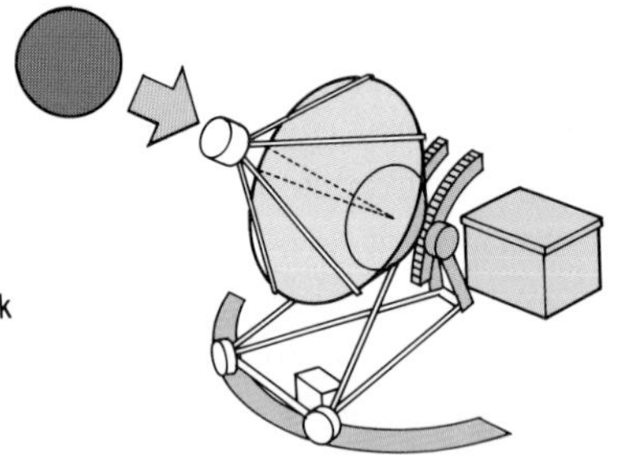

3 Solar-electric cells
These contain banks of photovoltaic cells which convert the sun's energy into electricity, which in turn can be stored in batteries.

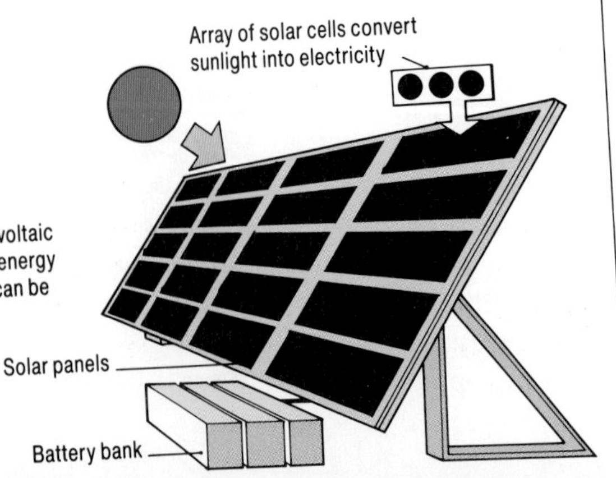

Alternative sources of energy provide more than one quarter of China's needs.

Solar energy is important. There are over 2000 locally manufactured solar cookers in use. China also has some 100 000 square metres of flat plate solar collectors which heat water for hospitals and offices.

The Chinese are developing advanced silicon solar cells. These are used to convert sunlight directly into electricity, which is then used for powering railway signals, electric fences and other things.

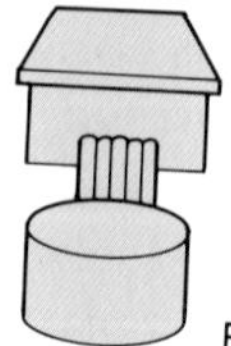

Biogas digesters are widely used to convert human, animal and crop waste into methane gas which can be used for heating, cooking and powering machines.

There are wind turbines producing electricity in remote regions like Inner Mongolia. Wind energy is still relied on by many junks (China's sail boats) which moved 600 000 tons of cargo in 1979.

Figure 3
Alternative energy developments in China

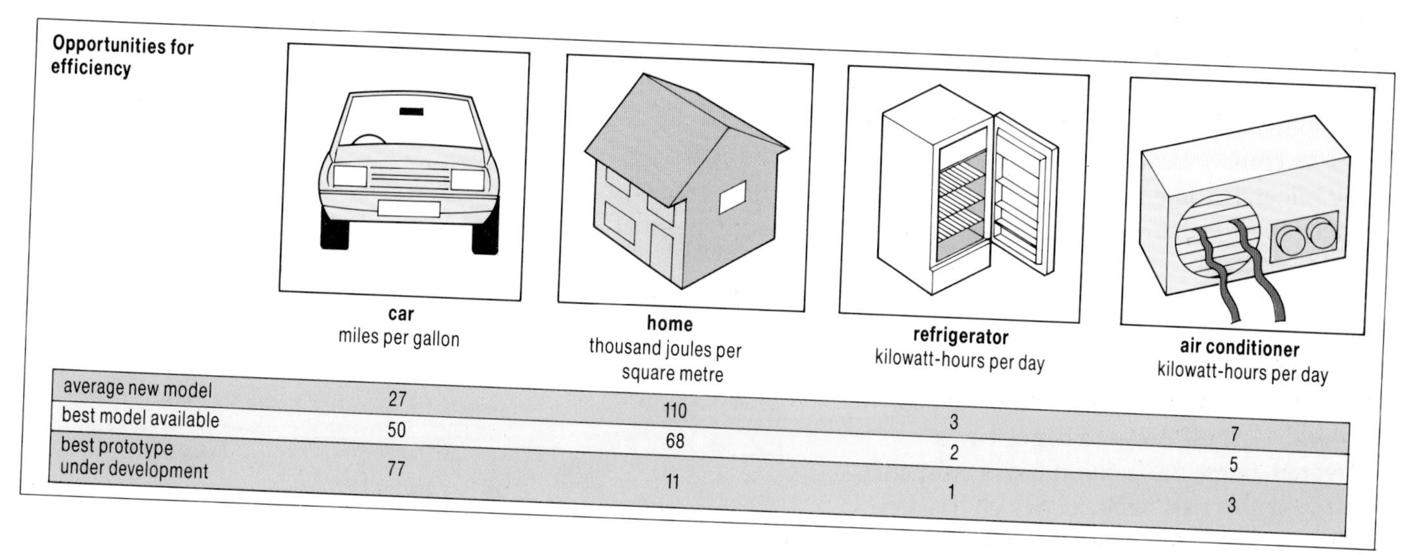

	car miles per gallon	home thousand joules per square metre	refrigerator kilowatt-hours per day	air conditioner kilowatt-hours per day
average new model	27	110	3	7
best model available	50	68	2	5
best prototype under development	77	11	1	3

Figure 4 Methods of increasing energy efficiency

There are, however, other ways in which the world's energy crisis can be solved. Individuals and organisations can reduce their use of non-renewable energy. We should each use every opportunity to conserve energy, and to develop technology (Figure 4), making the world more energy-efficient.

Activities

1 Study the map showing the fuelwood crisis in Africa (Figure 1).
- *a* Name three countries where there is an acute fuelwood scarcity.
- *b* Briefly describe the fuelwood situation in Nigeria.
- *c* Why is there no fuelwood in the two areas marked A?
- *d* In which country will the deficit of fuelwood increase most between now and the year 2010?
- *e* Study a map of rainfall in Africa in your atlas. Is there any relationship between this and Figure 1?

2 What general advantages do the sun, wind and sea have as potential sources of energy compared with coal or oil?

3 Figure 4 shows some ways we may be more efficient in the future.
- *a* How much more efficient are ● cars and ● homes of the future likely to be than those of today?
- *b* Do the statistics in Figure 4 give you hope for the future? Explain your answer.

4.4 Earthly riches – minerals in Brazil

Most countries depend on mineral resources just as much as they depend on energy resources. Metallic minerals like iron-ore, lead, zinc, bauxite and copper are used by industries to manufacture many of the things we use everyday. Others like diamonds and precious stones may be made into expensive jewellery, or might have industrial applications.

Some countries have richer deposits than others. Brazil has mineral resources of great variety and value. It is a major producer of aluminium, iron-ore and tin, and the output of gold is becoming increasingly important. Many minerals come from Amazonia in northern Brazil, where mining is giving great cause for concern.

In the 1980s the biggest development was in the Serra dos Carajas (see Figure 1), where in an area of tropical rainforest southwest of Belem, the city at the mouth of the Amazon, the world's largest iron-ore deposit was discovered. Some $62 million has been spent developing this part of Brazil, which has an area larger than Britain and France combined. To export iron-ore from Carajas a 900-kilometre long railway line had to be built to the coast near Sao Luis, where a new deepwater port was constructed.

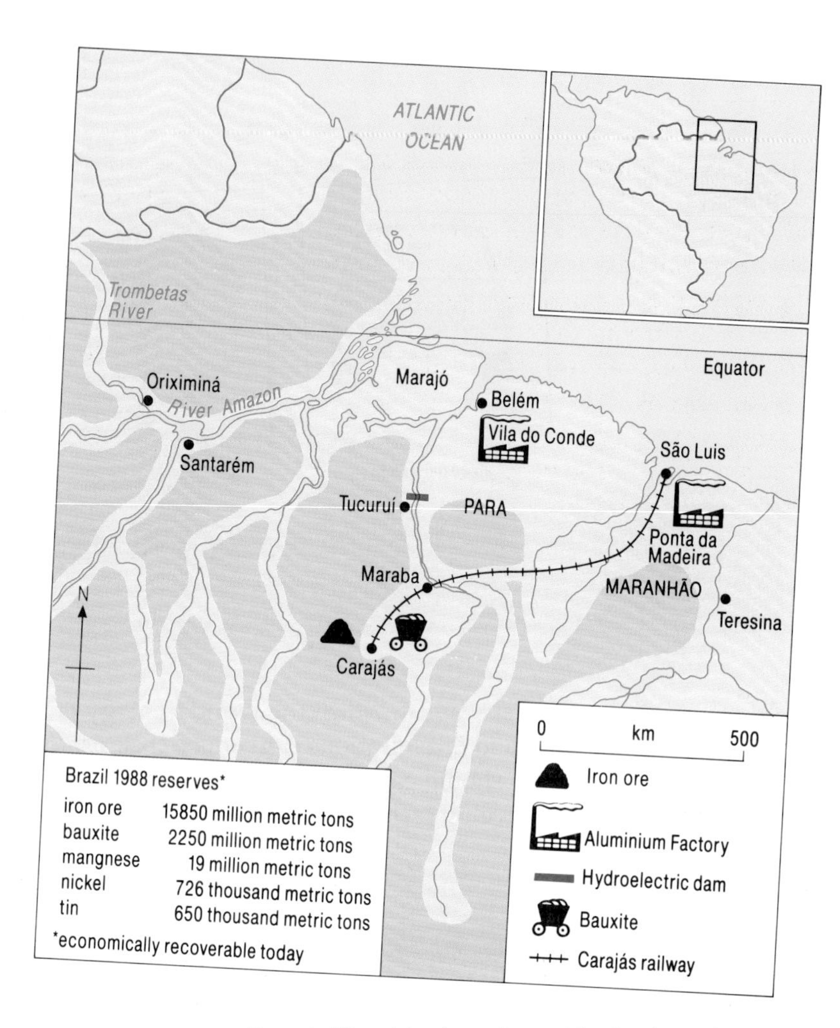

Figure 1 Mineral development around Carajas, Amazonia

Figure 2
Gold mining

In addition to an estimated 18 billion tons of iron-ore, there are large deposits of bauxite, manganese, tin, nickel and copper. Already smelters, hydro-electric-power schemes and large industries are being drawn to the area. Thousands of Indians belonging to tribes who had lived undisturbed in the forest for centuries have been uprooted from their lands and moved on. The mineral discovery will change the area's environment and the way of life of its people for ever.

In the 1990s gold output will become one of Brazil's major mineral products. Already over 600 000 garimpeiros (miners) are looking for it all over Brazil. The search is concentrated on Serra Pelada in the state of Para where gold was first discovered in 1981 (see Figure 2). Almost 80 000 people flocked to what was then just a hole in the ground.

The hole is now over 1600 metres deep and produces more than 10 million tons of gold a year. Its sides are almost vertical, and the workers toil here for more than 12 hours a day carrying 30 kilogram sacks of soil from the bottom of the pit to the surface. More than 100 000 people work in the mine, which covers an area of about 1 square kilometre. Here too, mining is having a real impact on people and the environment as the newspaper report (Figure 3) shows.

Gold-diggers bring ecological tragedy to Brazil

There are 600,000 gold prospectors mining on the Amazon. Their massive use of mercury is poisoning the region and its people, writes Richard House.

THE FORESTS and rivers of the Brazilian Amazon are suffering an ecological tragedy of global proportions, caused by almost 2,000 tons of mercury that gold miners have released into the environment.

To purify gold extracted from rivers and shallow mines, 600,000 prospectors working deep in the forest use a primitive technique involving burning of the metal with a mercury amalgam. Each gram of gold requires almost twice as much mercury. Mining Ministry figures show 1,026 tons of gold have been extracted since 1973, so more than 1,800 tons of mercury were used. Last year gold production – and mercury pollution – leapt 23 per cent to 103 tons.

Metallic mercury enters the food chain and the diet of fish-eating riverside dwellers, but may also break down into poisonous chlorates, fatal even in tiny quantities.

"We calculate that if all the mercury accumulated in the Amazon region due to past gold mining were transformed into toxic compounds, there would be enough to kill the world population six times over," said Gerobal Guimaraes, the assistant director of the mining ministry's minerals production department.

Independent 3.11.89

Figure 3

Activities

1 a Use an atlas to find out where Brazil is and what it is like. Work in pairs. Each of you should list five things you have found out from the atlas. Swap lists and check your partner's work.

b Which minerals seem to be the most important in Brazil? Where are they found?

c Draw a sketch-map to show Brazil's main cities. Shade the main mining centres on your map.

2 What would the conditions at Serra Pelada be like? Write a diary entry describing your impression of what a day's work here would be like.

3 Imagine that your teacher is preparing a set of slides for local schools. You have been given the six stages in Figure 4, which show how aluminium is manufactured, and asked to help.

a Write a script to link the frames. It should tell the story of how aluminium is made from bauxite in a simple and clear way.

b List some of the uses to which aluminium is put. Why do you think its popularity is growing?

Figure 4 Making aluminium from bauxite

Bauxite is the ore from which aluminium is made. It is found in Australia, Guinea and Jamaica. Recently huge bauxite deposits have been found in the Trombetas River area of northern Brazil.

The process by which aluminium is made from bauxite is over one hundred years old, and involves a series of stages:

1. Surface vegetation cleared by bulldozer, then bauxite is exposed by removing topsoil.
2. The bauxite is drilled and blasted, loaded into trucks and brought to the alumina plant.
3. The ore is crushed and mixed with hot caustic soda to remove impurites. A solution of aluminium oxide (alumina) is produced.
4. Alumina is taken to a reduction plant where an electric current is passed through it. This separates the mixture into oxygen and molten aluminium which is siphoned off.
5. It is poured into casts. Then the slabs are hot-rolled into aluminium sheets or coils.
6. Aluminium can be used to make a variety of products from pans to cans, cars to spacecraft.

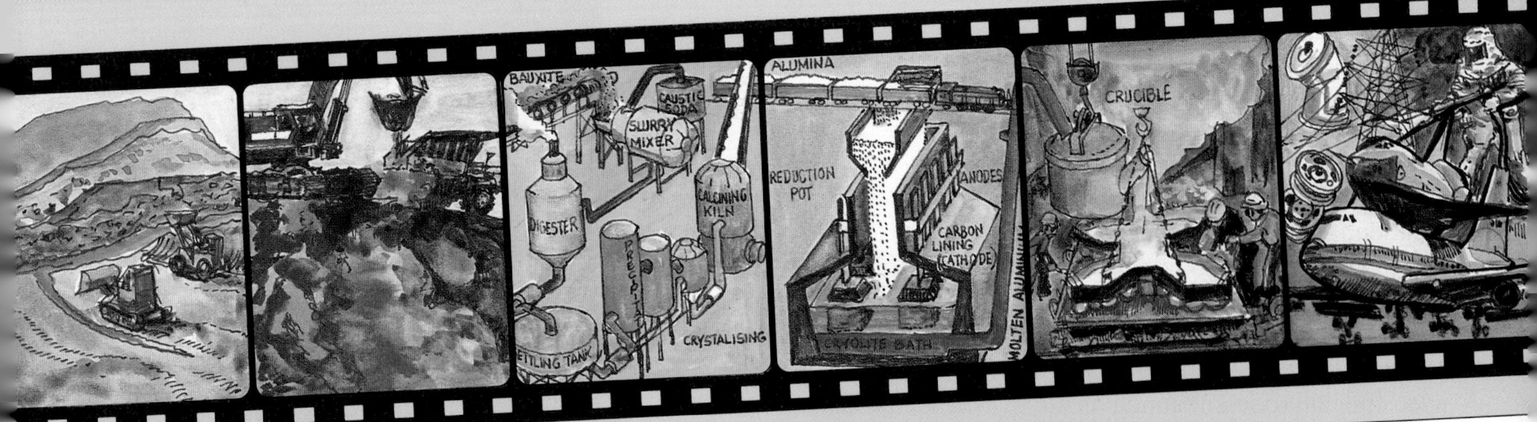

4.5 Opening up Siberia

One of the wealthiest places in the world is Siberia. This is not because its people are particularly rich, but because the ground under Siberia contains huge deposits of minerals and other resources. Use an atlas to find out about Siberia. Where is it located? How large is the area, and what is it like there?

Figure 1
Comparing climates

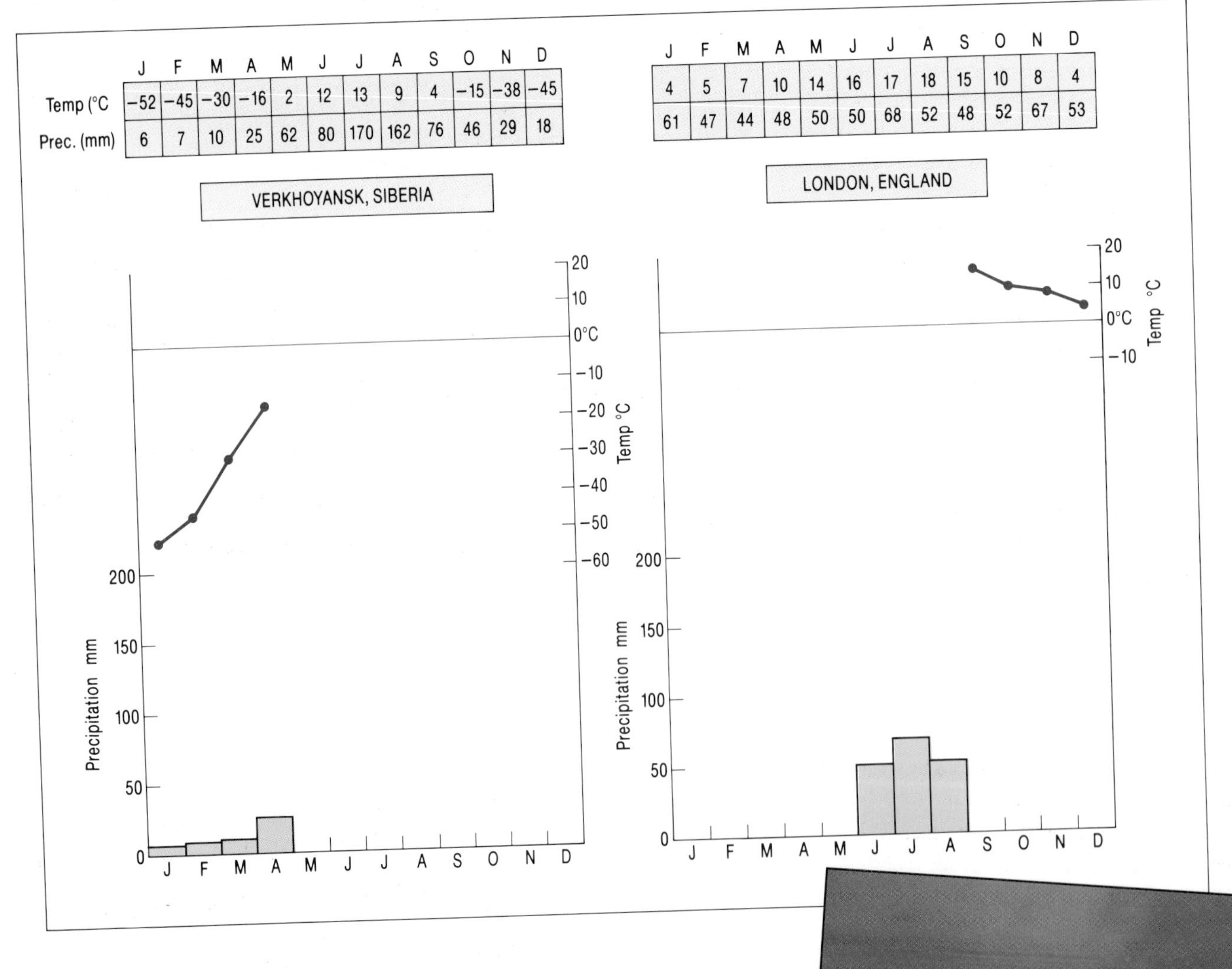

VERKHOYANSK, SIBERIA

	J	F	M	A	M	J	J	A	S	O	N	D
Temp (°C	−52	−45	−30	−16	2	12	13	9	4	−15	−38	−45
Prec. (mm)	6	7	10	25	62	80	170	162	76	46	29	18

LONDON, ENGLAND

J	F	M	A	M	J	J	A	S	O	N	D
4	5	7	10	14	16	17	18	15	10	8	4
61	47	44	48	50	50	68	52	48	52	67	53

Many important resources are located in inaccessible and remote regions of the world like Siberia. Brazil has huge energy and mineral deposits in Amazonia and most of Canada's minerals are found in the ancient hard 'Shield' lands of the frozen north.

With an area of some 10 million square kilometres, Siberia makes up about 40% of the land area of what was the USSR, yet contains less than 10% of the population. Vast tracts of this area are deserted, with most of the small population living in cities. Few people actually choose to live there because conditions are difficult and the climate is so hostile (Figures 1 and 2). The temperatures are usually below zero, and often fall to less than minus 40° C. The area is distant from the main population centres, and permafrost makes house construction and mining difficult.

Figure 2 Siberia's hostile environment

Many of the region's mineral and energy resources are found in Siberia (Figure 3). The last ten years have seen a gradual development of these resources, after a period of exploration which was expensive. Siberia is one of the most important resource rich areas in the world. In the 1980s it produced 60% of the USSR's oil, half of its natural gas, 30% of its coal and 26% of its timber. Who controls its resources in the future will be a vital question for the newly independent states.

A number of towns in Siberia, like Surgut, have grown rapidly. Surgut is an oil town on the banks of the River Ob, about 800 kilometres north of Omsk. Its population more than doubled from 100 000 in 1977 to 250 000 in 1990. This growth was due to an increase in the number of mining jobs in the area. High wages and fairly good accommodation helped to attract people. The Surgut oil and gas company produces over one million barrels of oil a day, and the planners want to develop other activities. A hotel and international airport are planned. However, the problems of living and working in a hostile environment remain.

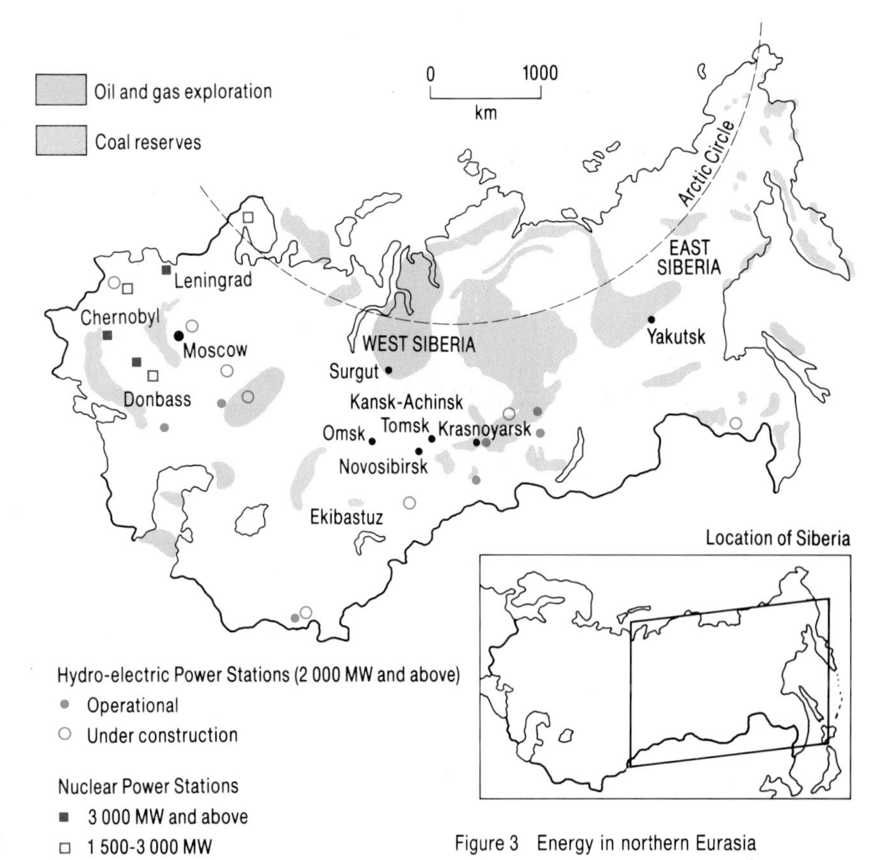

Figure 3 Energy in northern Eurasia

Activities

1 Study the climate figures in Figure 1 carefully.
   - *a* Copy the graph axes in Figure 1, then use the figures to complete the two climate graphs.
   - *b* Calculate the average temperatures for London and Verkhoyansk.
   - *c* What do you notice about the range of temperature (difference between highest and lowest temperature) in each place?
   - *d* Suggest two ways that precipitation is likely to vary between London and Verkhoyansk.

2 *a* From the photographs and other data on pages 52–53 describe what you think it would be like to live in Siberia. What advantages and disadvantages can you see?
   - *b* How might *i* farmers; and *ii* construction workers be affected?
   - *c* Would you like to live in Surgut or not? Explain your answer.

3 *a* Which types of energy are found in Siberia?
   - *b* Why do you think that hydro-electric power is not found there?

4 Which of the problems listed in Figure 4 do you think would be the most difficult one to overcome? Why? Discuss this in groups and see if you can reach any agreement about it.

Problems of living and working in Siberia

- lack of roads, manpower and amenities (schools, hospitals)
- intense cold means that the floors of houses have to be up to 30cms thick, and special construction methods have also been pioneered for the pipelines that are so important.
- it is difficult to operate drilling and welding equipment at very low temperatures
- Siberia is remote and even within the region distances are huge
- the environment at present is relatively unspoilt, so must be carefully protected. There are many dangers from power station emissions and dust, as well as the waste from processing other minerals like zinc and lead

Figure 4

5 Figure 5 shows some of the steps which must be taken to develop a region's resources. Put the five stages in the correct order and draw a flow diagram to show your answer.

Figure 5 Developing a resource

Dictionary

conservation reducing the wasteful uses of energy so that supplies are protected and therefore last longer

fossil fuels fuels like coal, oil and natural gas which are formed from the remains of plants or animals

geothermal energy power derived from the natural warmth of the earth's interior.

non-renewable energy types of energy which are limited in supply, and which will one day become exhausted

nuclear fission the process of splitting atoms of uranium or plutonium, which release huge amounts of heat

primary energy energy which comes directly from natural sources, usually either biomass fuels or fossil fuels

renewable energy sources of energy which will never become exhausted because their supply regenerates itself, e.g. solar, tidal or wind power

secondary energy energy produced by transforming primary energy, e.g. by changing coal into electricity

5 Places in the wider world

5.1 The superpowers compared

Nations vary enormously in their size and importance. A country's status may be due to its area, population, the size of its economy, the volume and variety of its natural resources or the value of its trade with other countries, or a combination of these factors.

Among the more industrialised nations of the world, perhaps three countries stand out as more 'important' than others in several key respects. These are the United States of America (USA), the area formerly known as the Soviet Union (USSR) and Japan (Figure 1), sometimes referred to as **superpowers**. Between them these three countries account for 12.5% of the world's population and 25% of the land area.

In physical terms these countries are very different. Japan is relatively small and mountains dominate about 80% of its land area. It has few natural resources and consequently relies heavily on imports, both of raw materials and energy. The USA and USSR on the other hand occupy massive land areas, and have rich mineral and energy resources. The USSR stretches into the Arctic Circle (as does Alaska in the USA) and forests cover huge areas.

Different reasons account for the importance of each country. Is the USA a superpower because of its large army, successful industries, huge wealth or its capacity to launch rockets and people into space? Why do you think the USSR and Japan may be regarded as a superpower? Figure 2 shows some of the comparisons between the three superpowers.

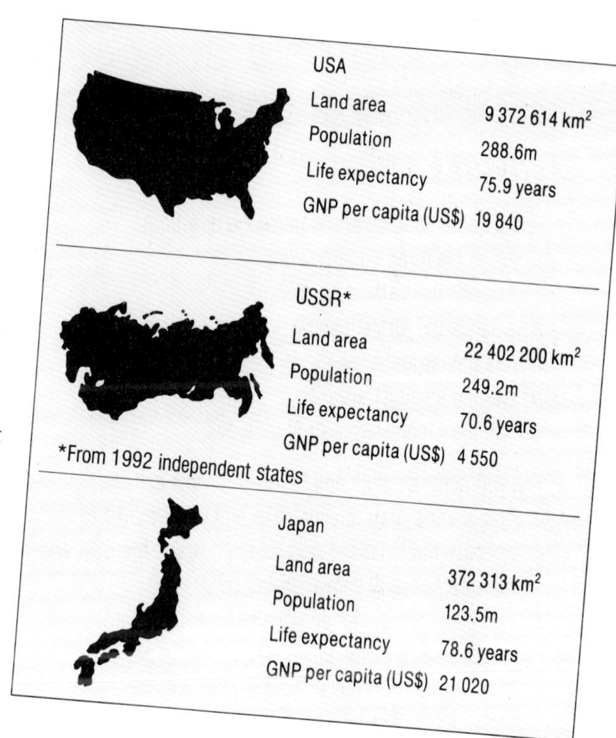

Figure 1 USA, USSR and Japan: some indicators

Figure 2 Table of comparisons

	Japan	USA	USSR until 1992
% of labour force in: .... agriculture .... industry .... services	8.0 23.6 68.4	3.0 19.0 78.0	20.0 39.0 41.0
Main imports	Crude petroleum, clothing, fish, methane gas, aluminium, logs, iron-ore, coal, chemicals	Foodstuffs, chemicals, oil, machinery and clothing.	Machinery (agricultural and industrial), foodstuffs
Main exports	Cars, scientific instruments, electronic goods, steel products, integrated circuits, cameras	Foodstuffs, coal, electrical machinery, chemicals	Oil & oil products, timber, iron-ore, machinery, gas and coal
Urban population (as % of total)	77	75	66
Total GDP (Gross Domestic Product) in US$ billion	2 844	4 847	399
Military spending (% of GNP)	1.0	6.7	11.5
Exports/imports ratio	144	69	95

The fortunes of countries change with the passage of time. Little more than a century ago, three different countries were global superpowers. Britain, France and Spain had huge empires around the world which they had exploited to become rich themselves. Now most of their colonies (in Africa, Latin America and the Pacific) have been returned to their rightful owners, and are independent countries. In the future, Japan and the USA might not always occupy the important positions which they do today. China is developing fast, and some of the **newly industrialising countries** (NICs) of Southeast Asia (see Chapter 10.4) are gaining ground.

Until 1992 the USSR was regarded as a superpower but with its breakup into independent states, or a loose federation, its superpower status has disappeared. It is difficult to know how powerful these states will be in the future, or if a new Eurasia superpower will emerge.

Activities

1 Use an atlas to answer the following questions:
Which of the three superpowers:
- *i* extends the furthest north
- *ii* extends the furthest south
- *iii* has the largest area
- *iv* has the smallest area
- *v* has the greatest spread of latitude?

2 You will need an atlas and Figure 1 for this activity.
- *a* Find a world map in your atlas and use Figure 1 to compare the locations and sizes of Japan, the USA and the area formerly known as the USSR.
- *b* Calculate the population density for each of the countries. Express your answer in people per km^2.
- *c* Choose *one* superpower, and explain why the population is distributed unevenly. You could refer to Chapter 7.1 to help you).

3 Work in groups of three for this activity. Each person should choose to represent one of the superpowers. Now study Figure 2. Why do you think the country that you represent is a superpower? Choose one single statistic or piece of information from Figure 2 that you believe makes your country very important. Discuss what you think with the others in your group.
- *a* Which piece of information did you each choose? Can you agree what makes a country a superpower?
- *b* Now do some library research on the country you chose. Find out some more about its economy. What natural resources does it have? What are its main industries? Does the country have a successful trade policy (more exports than imports)? Write your findings as short notes. Try to include some figures/statistics.
- *c* Compare the notes you made in *b* with those made by the other people in your group. Discuss the similarities and differences between the three superpowers. Refer also to the information in this Unit. Summarise your findings on one side of A4. You should include statistics and might want to make some comparisons using simple graphs, tables or by showing information on maps.

5.2 Industry, energy and environment in Japan

Manufacturing industry develops in most countries due to an abundance of raw materials which can be processed or cheap energy supplies. Japan has developed into a world superpower without either of these advantages. The massive expansion of manufacturing industry which began in the 1960s has turned Japan into one of the most effective manufacturing nations of the world. There has, however, been a cost to the environment.

Japanese products are known for their quality all over the world: Honda and Nissan cars; cameras from Canon and Minolta; TVs produced by Toshiba and Sony; and office equipment from Citizen and NEC. Japan's industries today are highly efficient and modern. Yet just 45 years ago the whole country lay in ruins at the end of the Second World War.

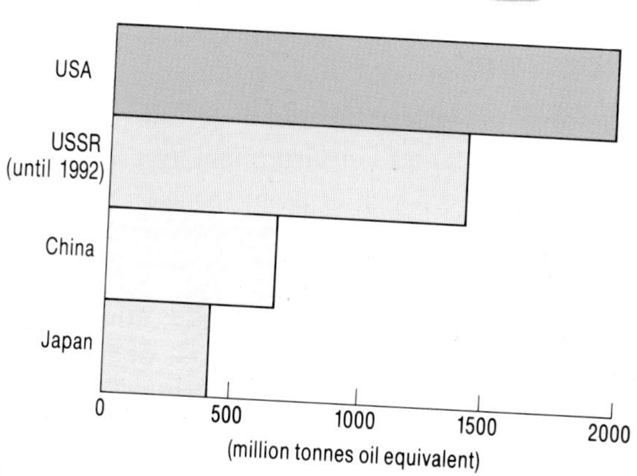

Figure 1 Energy consumption 1989

Energy

A rapid increase in energy consumption accompanied the expansion of Japanese industry throughout the 1950s and 1960s. However, Japan has little **indigenous** energy, so most has to be imported. Her consumption is today the fourth highest in the world after the USA, the Soviet Union and China (Figure 1). Oil is the largest single form of energy used, accounting for over 60% of Japan's total consumption.

In the early 1970s oil price rises caused shock waves around the world. Since then, Japan has reduced her **dependence** on oil by abandoning industries like aluminium smelting which used a lot of oil, and developing alternative energies, like geothermal power. Dependence on imported oil has, as a result, been reduced from 80% of total energy needs in 1972 to only 53% in 1988.

Location of industry

Heavy reliance on imported fuels helps us to understand the location pattern for Japan's factories. As the map shows, (Figure 2), manufacturing industry is unevenly distributed, with most factories concentrated around the coast. These are the locations with the lowest **production costs** for industry. Raw materials like iron-ore, copper, and other bulky goods arrive at modern ports in tankers and bulk carriers. Energy in the form of coal, oil and liquefied natural gas also comes ashore here. In addition, most people already inhabit the coast as inland areas are mountainous.

Manufacturing activity is concentrated in locations where people (both a labour supply and market) live, where materials and energy can be assembled cheaply, and where goods can easily be loaded onto ships for quick export overseas. Suitable flat sites for factories are so rare in Japan's crowded coastal areas (Figure 3), however, that many factories are actually built on land which has been **reclaimed** from the sea.

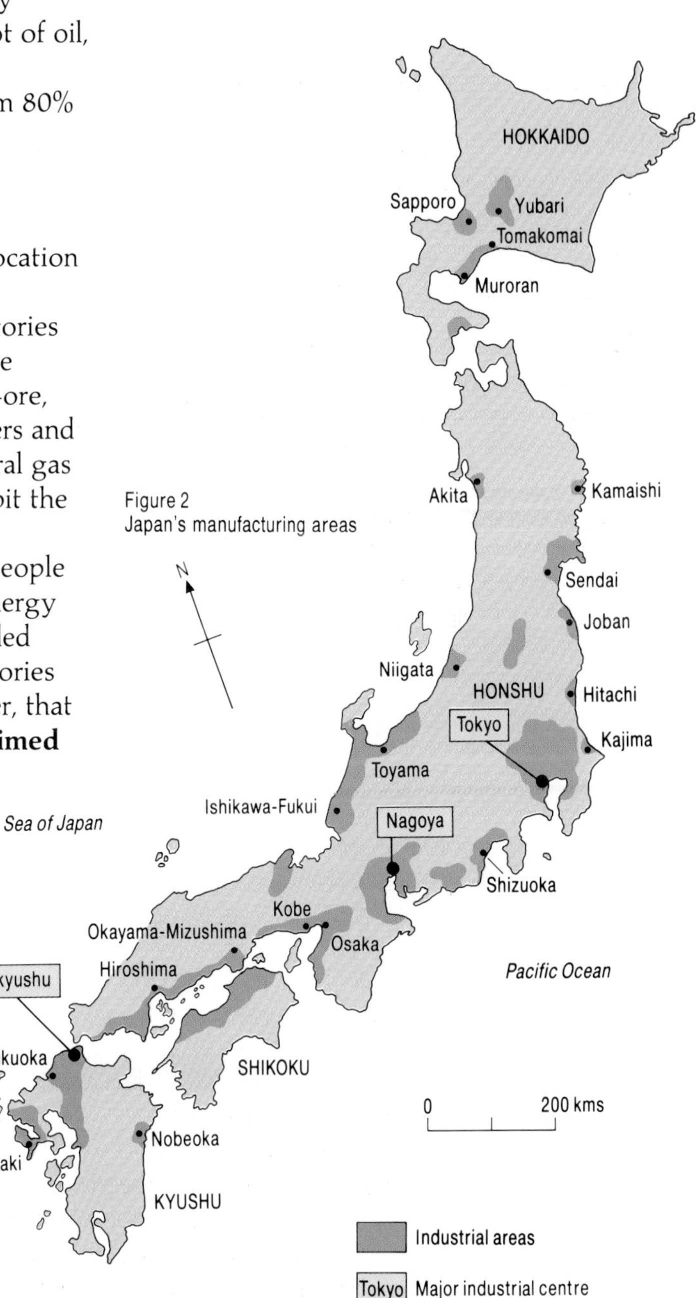

Figure 2
Japan's manufacturing areas

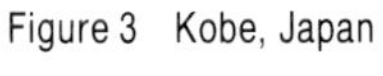
Figure 3 Kobe, Japan

Environment

Economic growth of around 4–5% each year in the 1980s caused problems for Japan's environment: overcrowded housing, traffic congestion and a lack of open space all resulted. However, it was the more rapid growth achieved from 1950–1974 – over 10% each year – which had more serious effects. Much of this growth was due to industries expanding. As factories and people were generally located quite close together because of the lack of space in Japan, when factories discharged their **effluents**, these often seriously affected the health of local residents. One tragic example concerns what happened to the people who lived around the shores of Minamata Bay in southern Japan (Figure 4).

The Minamata incident was not isolated. In the 1950s and 1960s, industrial growth caused Japan's environment to suffer in many ways. Water quality deteriorated, and city dwellers often had great difficulty breathing the badly polluted air (Figure 5). The police force even had to issue masks to officers on traffic duty in Tokyo. However, new laws in the late 1960s improved the situation. Levels of several major air pollutants have fallen (Figure 6). Water, too, is much cleaner, although there are still some problems. Lake Biwa which provides water for 13 million people in the Osaka area is polluted. Around 90% of the sewage pumped into it is untreated. Despite a cleaning-up programme and a ban on detergents containing phosphorous, the lake is still very dirty.

Location
Mimamata Bay on the island of Kyushu in Southern Japan.

Cause
The Chisso Chemical Corporation was pumping effluent containing mercury into Minamata Bay. The water in the bay became contaminated with the poisonous mercury, which entered the food chain through fish. Local people became ill after eating the fish.

Symptoms
Many people suffered the effects of mercury poisoning: including loss of hearing, vision and speech, and even partial paralysis. Some locals had fits, and babies were born with deformities.

Victims
By 1980 over 300 people were reported dead due to mercury poisoning in the area. Over 1000 people were seriously ill and 6000 people were claiming compensation from the company. Up to 50 000 more people were thought to be suffering some effects of mercury poisoning.

Figure 4 Minamata disease

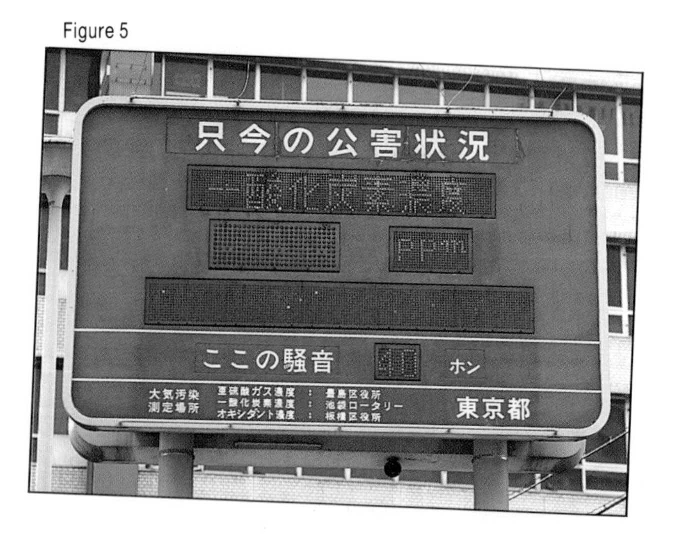

Figure 5

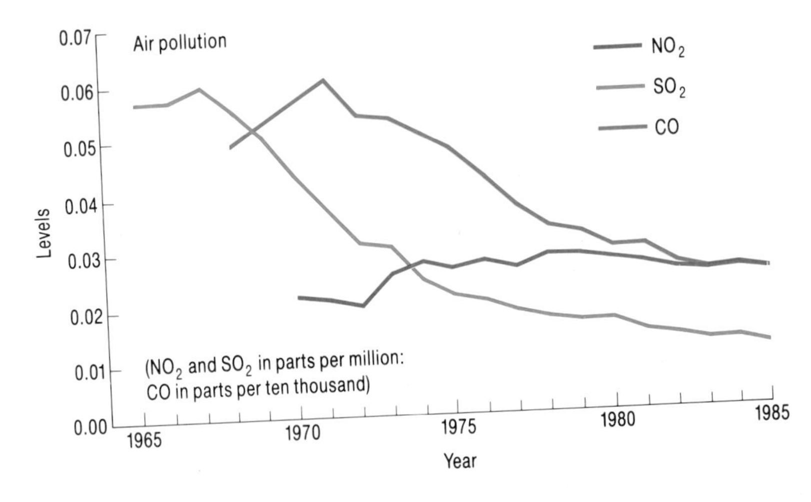

Figure 6

Activities

1 a In groups of three or four, brainstorm a list of Japanese products and companies.
  b Now look through some magazines and newspapers. Cut out some advertisements for products made by Japanese companies and include them in your notes.
  c What type of product does Japan mainly seem to manufacture and export?

2 Estimate the energy consumption in each of the four countries shown in Figure 1.

3 You will need an outline map of Japan for this activity. Study your atlas and the map in Figure 2 carefully.
   i Locate and label the cities of Fukuoka, Hiroshima, Kitakyushu, Kobe, Muroran, Nagasaki, Nagoya, Niigata, Okayama, Osaka, Sapporo, Sendai and Tokyo.
   ii Shade the industrial areas shown in Figure 2.
   iii Mark and label the Sea of Japan and the Pacific Ocean.

4 *a* What do you notice about the distribution of Japan's industry?
   b What has Japan's use of energy got to do with the location of industry? Suggest one other reason why industries are found in the locations shown.

5 The pollution in Minamata Bay affected many groups of people. Study Figure 4. Here are some of the things which local people said:

A
'My life has been ruined. I am no longer able to speak properly and have difficulty walking. My wife died last year after three serious convulsions. The doctors say this was due to mercury poisoning. The company must pay for the damage and distress they cause. We should even consider closing them down.'

B
'If the country is to be successful then our factories must be allowed to grow without any restriction. They must be left to produce as much as possible at the lowest possible cost. They know best what they are doing.'

C
'Some regulation is needed. If factories are left to do what they want, and fail to consider their neighbours and the environment, then both will suffer. The government must encourage factories to behave properly and to control the pollution they cause.'

a Which of the three views do you agree with and why?
b Read the third passage (C) again. How do you think that governments might 'encourage' factories to behave properly?
c Do factories in your local area behave properly? Look out for any evidence that local factories are helping or harming the environment. You could contact a local factory to ask what they are doing to improve or protect their environment. Watch for items in local newspapers concerning factories and the environment.

5.3 China – the giant of Asia

Our study of Japan proves that a country does not need a large area to become an economic superpower. It has a small area, yet is one of the world's most advanced economies. China, its nearest neighbour on the mainland of Asia, is very different. It has a larger area than Japan, as well as the world's largest population. However its economy is not as strong. China is one of the world's poorer or **'economically developing countries'**.

In this unit and the next we will take a detailed look at China. First, the general geography of the country will be explored. The effect of China's natural features on population distribution will be examined, as will some of the physical contrasts between one part of China and another. In the next unit we will look at some statistics which are used as **indicators of development** to see what they can tell us about life in China.

	Area ('000 km^2)	Population 1990 (million)
China	9 597	1 139.0
USSR (until 1992)	22 400	288.6
Canada	9 976	26.5
USA	9 363	249.2
Japan	372	123.5
UK	245	57.2

Figure 1

1 Landscapes and environments

With an area of 9.6 million km^2, China is the world's third largest country after the USSR and Canada (Figure 1). Its population of 1.14 billion represents 20% of the world total.

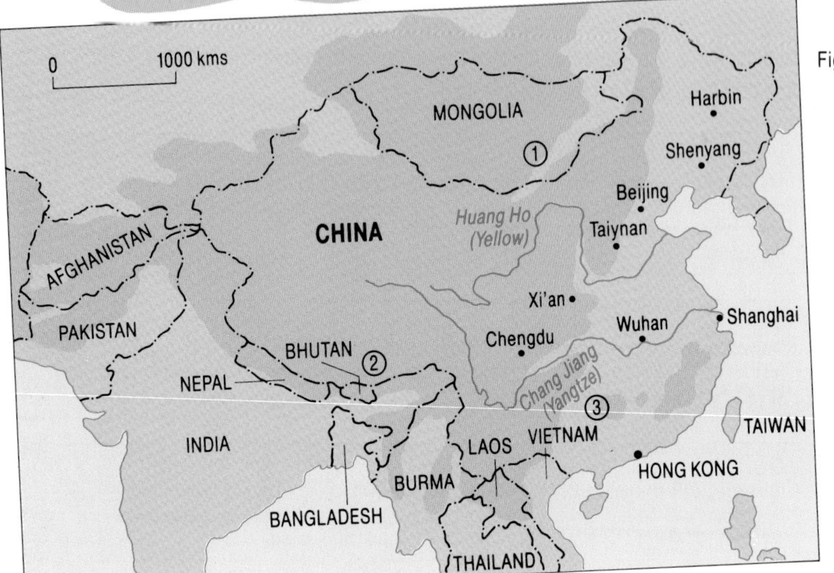

Figure 2 Landscapes and environments of China

Figure 3

China (Figure 2) has a huge area – 39 times larger than the UK. It extends from inside the tropics to the same latitude as southern Britain (from 18–53°N), stretching 4000 kms east to west, and over 3000 kms north to south. There are hot and cold deserts, high mountains, warm and fertile lowlands and areas of monsoon climate (Figure 3).

Huge variations in relief and climate help to explain the different landscapes (Figure 4). In southwest China, Tibet's landscape comprises high snow-capped peaks many over 7000 metres above sea-level (a.s.l.). They merge into the Himalayas in nearby Nepal. In northern China, the altitude of the land in Inner Mongolia is between 1000–2000 metres a.s.l. Along the east coast, in the provinces of Shandong and Jiangsu especially, the land is much lower (200 metres a.s.l.). This is the **North China Plain**.

China's climate is different from that of the UK. Inside China too, the climate varies greatly: South of Shanghai a monsoon climate brings hot and wet weather all year round. The North China Plain is warm and wet, while further north in Manchuria the climate is cooler, though the summers are still very wet. Inland, there are large temperature extremes typical of **continental climates**.

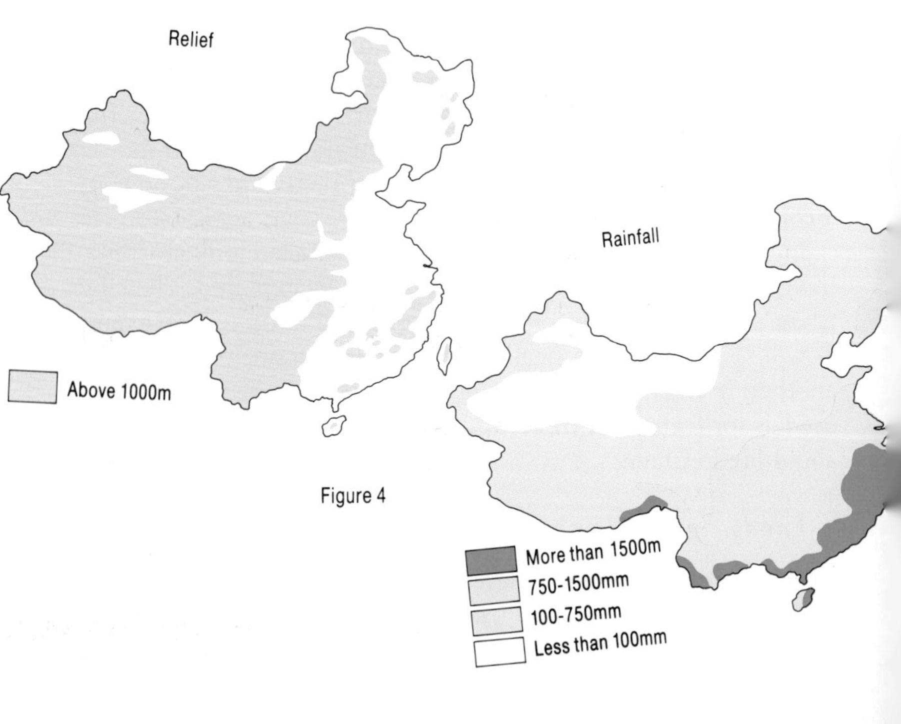

Figure 4

2 *Population distribution*

China is very large, and has a variety of different geographical environments. Its landscapes are very different as we saw in

POPULATION DENSITY 1985 (people per km^2)

1	Sichuan	180	11	Guangxi	168	21	Jilin	123
2	Shandong	503	12	Liaoning	253	22	Inner Mongolia	17
3	Henan	462	13	Yunnan	86	23	Xinjiang	9
4	Jiangsu	606	14	Jiangxi	208	24	Ningxia	62
5	Hebei	296	15	Shaanxi	146	25	Qinghai	6
6	Guangdong	295	16	Guizhou	168	26	Tibet	2
7	Hunan	268	17	Shanxi	168	**S**	Shanghai	1967
8	Anhui	370	18	Fujian	224	**B**	Beijing	571
9	Hubei	263	19	Gansu	45	**T**	Tianjin	714
10	Zhejiang	396	20	Heilongjiang	71			

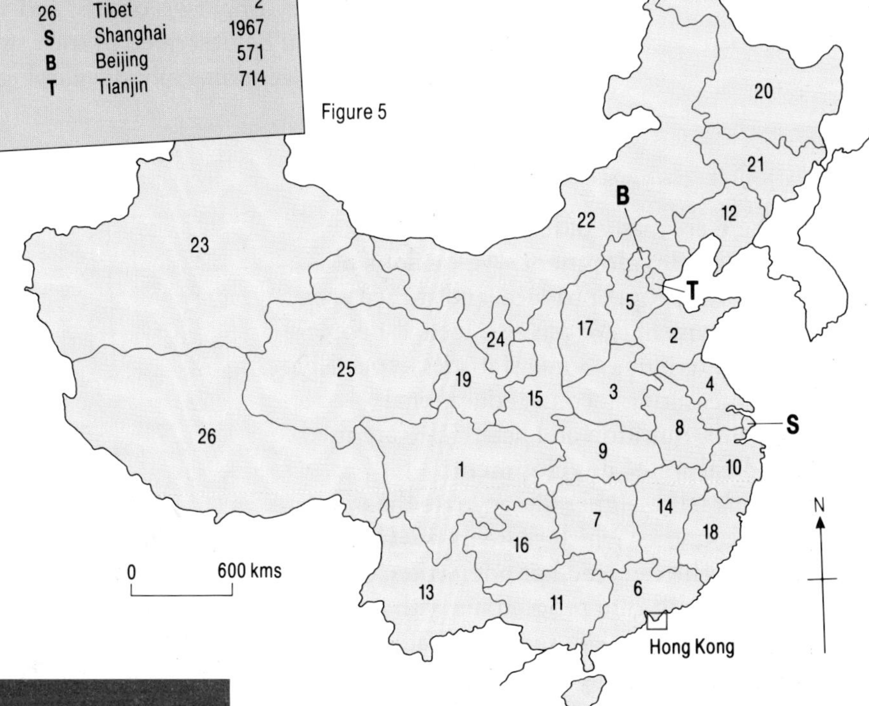

Figure 5

Figure 3, and the pattern of population distribution is very uneven. The density figures in Figure 5 confirm this. From the maps in this unit see if you can decide which parts of China are likely to be the most crowded.

China contains some of both the emptiest and the most crowded lands on earth. While Tibet has a density of just 2 people per square kilometre, Shanghai has over 1967 people per square kilometre!

Activities

1 China has the largest population in the world, but is it the most crowded country?
  a Using the data in Figure 1 calculate the population density (in people per square kilometre) for each of the six countries.
  b List the countries in rank order, placing the most crowded ones first.

2 Study Figure 2 carefully.
  a In which direction do China's two main rivers flow? Why do you think this is?
  b Estimate the lengths of the two rivers shown.
  c Suggest two reasons why land near rivers might be likely to have a high density of population.

3 With the help of an atlas, estimate the changes in average relief as you move from China's border with Nepal, northeastwards towards it capital city, Beijing.

4 *a* Just three of the many different landscapes of China are pictured in Figure 3. Match each photograph to one of the locations numbered 1, 2 or 3 on the map (Figure 2).
  b Explain your choice in each case.

5 Carefully examine all of the evidence in this unit.
  a Describe briefly where you might expect China's population to be mostly located.
  a Suggest reasons for the pattern of population distribution that you expect.

6 Study climate graphs in your atlas.
  a List three ways in which China's climate differs from that in the United Kingdom.
  b What factors other than climate help to influence the distribution of population in a locality?

7 You will need a blank outline map of China for this activity, with the provinces marked.
  a Plot a choropleth map of population density for China using the data in Figure 5. The number of each province corresponds with the number on the map outline.

For each category below choose a colour (or shading) and complete the map outline carefully.

Density:	*colour/shading*
i Under 20 people per sq. km	light
ii 21–100 people per sq. km.	↓
iii 101–300 people per sq. km.	
iv 301–500 people per sq. km.	
v Over 501 people per sq. km.	dark

  b Summarise briefly and in your own words the pattern which your map shows.

5.4 Is China an economically developing country?

China is often described as an 'economically developing country', and part of the 'Third World'. What does this mean? Can a country whose size is only exceeded by only two others, and which has the largest population in the world be described in such simple terms? And what does it mean to be an 'economically developing country' anyway?

There are many different ways of measuring **development**. We can look at how much people produce, and at the types of employment. We can also look at people's standard of living. Some statistics, especially those measuring income, educational standards, nutrition and health care are used as **indicators of development**.

China has a higher literacy rate than most of the countries which share its borders. In addition she can feed her population, and has a good health-care programme with relatively few child deaths (Figure 1). The rate of increase in China's population is one of the lowest in Asia, thanks partly to the government's one-child policy (see Unit 6.3). China's annual population growth rate between 1960–1990 was 1.8% compared with 3.0% in Pakistan and 2.7% in Bangladesh.

It is also possible to discover what life is like in China from looking at how people live. The Mai family (Figure 2) live in Changchun in Jilin province. The head of the household is Kim Mai. His wife, Sung, is a nurse and works at a local clinic. They live in an apartment on the outskirts of the city with their child. How typical are they though? This is something the photograph does not tell us. We would need much more information to help us decide how developed the country is.

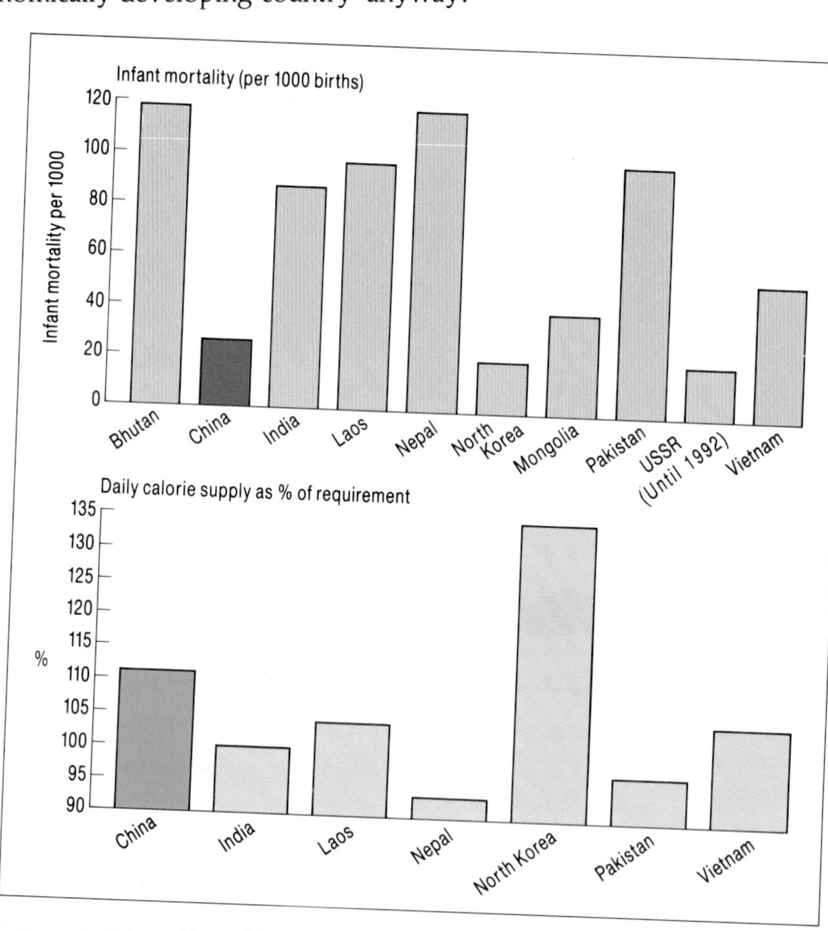

Figure 1 China and her neighbours

Are all parts of China equally developed?

It is important to remember that statistics can be just as difficult to interpret as photographs. They also often mean little for a large country like China. We saw in the last Unit the enormous physical differences between one region and another. There are also differences

Figure 2

Poster of the one-child family policy

in human geography between China's main regions.

To find out about these, we can examine statistics for each of China's provinces. Lets look at industrial output (Figure 3). Some provinces clearly have more industry than others. If we take China's average industrial output as an indicator of development, we might conclude that there is little worthwhile industry. However some coastal areas like the provinces of Jiangsu and Shanghai, have huge industries. Others like Yunnan, Mongolia and Tibet have almost no industrial output.

Some other indicators of development vary just as much. So contrasts in levels of development within a country may be as great as those between countries (Figure 5). However, levels of development do change over time. China's government is following policies designed to develop agriculture and industry (Figure 4), and to improve living standards for its population.

		billion yuan			billion yuan
1	Sichuan	40-60	16	Guizhou	0-10
2	Shandong	60-80	17	Shanxi	20-40
3	Henan	20-40	18	Fujian	10-20
4	Jiangsu	>80	19	Gansu	10-20
5	Hebei	40-60	20	Heilongjiang	20-40
6	Guangdong	40-60	21	Jilin	20-40
7	Hunan	20-40	22	Inner Mongolia	0-10
8	Anhui	20-40	23	Xinjiang	0-10
9	Hubei	40-60	24	Ningxia	10-20
10	Zhejiang	40-60	25	Qinghai	0-10
11	Guangxi	10-20	26	Tibet	0-10
12	Liaoning	60-80	S	Shanghai	>80
13	Yunnan	10-20	B	Beijing	20-40
14	Jiangxi	10-20	T	Tianjin	20-40
15	Shaanxi	10-20			

Figure 3 Gross output value of industry, 1985

Figure 4

Figure 5 Contrasts in development

	Life expectancy in years (1990)	Adult literacy rate (%) (1985)	Real GDP US$ per capita	Daily calorie supply (% of requirement)	Under 5 mortality rate (per 1000 live births)	Birth rate (per 1000)	Death rate (per 1000)	Population per Doctor
Bangladesh	51.8	32.2	720	83	184	40	13	6730
Brazil	65.6	78.5	4,620	111	85	26	7	1080
China	70.1	68.2	2,470	111	43	19	6	1000
Egypt	60.3	44.6	1,930	132	94	30	8	770
Ghana	55.0	52.8	970	76	143	42	11	14890
India	59.1	44.1	870	100	145	31	10	2520
Kenya	59.7	65.0	1,010	92	111	50	9	9970
Mexico	69.7	84.7	5,320	135	51	26	5	1240
Nigeria	51.5	42.7	1,030	90	170	48	14	7990
Pakistan	57.7	31.0	1,790	97	162	41	10	2910
Peru	63.0	82.0	3,080	93	119	31	7	1040
Venezuela	70.0	85.7	5,650	102	44	28	5	700
All developing countries	62.8	60	2,170	107	116	29	9	4590
Industrial countries	74.5	-	14,350	132	18	13	9	460
World average	65.5	-	4,340	113	108	26	9	3780

Activities

1 You will need to work in pairs for this activity. Try to agree answers to the following questions:

a What exactly does the word 'development' mean?

b Give some examples of 'development'

- in your own area;
- somewhere else in the United Kingdom;
- somewhere else in the world.

c Is all 'development' good for the people it affects? Give examples.

2 List five different methods you could use to find out or measure how developed a place is.

3 Two 'indicators of development' are shown in Figure 1. Does it suggest that China is more or less developed than its neighbours? Give as full an answer as you can.

4 a Imagine the Mai family (shown in Figure 2) were to move from Jilin province to Jiangsu province. How far (approximately) would this move be, and in what direction?

b What climate change might they experience?

5 You should work in groups of five for this activity. Each member of the group should work on one of the first five columns in Figure 5.

a Rank the 12 countries in your column – assign **low** rank numbers (1, 2 etc.) for data suggesting a **low** level of development; e.g. Nigeria, with a low life expectancy should have a low rank.

b Now calculate a combined 'Index of Development' by adding the ranks together for each country. Which country listed has the highest 'Index of Development'? Which has the lowest Index?

c Rewrite the list in rank order (most developed countries first).

d What does a low 'Index of Development' suggest about a country?

6 Write a paragraph describing what you have learnt about how developed China is compared with the other countries listed. Make some comparisons with the data included in Figure 5 for all developing countries, industrial countries and the world average.

Dictionary

dependence – relying heavily on one or a limited number of resources

effluents – waste products of human activity (industrial, agricultural or domestic)

indicators of development – the various statistical measurements e.g. literacy rates, income levels etc. which help to show the level of development reached by a place

indigenous – resources which are naturally occurring within a country rather than having to be imported into it

newly industrialising countries (NICs) – developing countries which are achieving high rates of manufacturing growth

production costs – the amount of money required by an economic enterprise (farm or factory) to produce a product in a given location

reclaimed – land which was once below sea-level and which has been drained so that it may be used for human activities e.g. industry

superpowers – countries which because of their size, population or resources have power and influence

6 People and quality of life

6.1 Worlds apart: the 'North-South' divide

You share this planet with over 5 billion other people. In many ways they are like you. We all share the same basic needs, including food and shelter, and hope to get a satisfying job and to live comfortably. However, our chances of achieving these hopes are influenced by where we are born. The gap between the rich industrialised countries (called the 'North') and the poorer developing countries (called the 'South') is probably wider today than ever before.

The causes of this gap are many and varied. They are historic and economic as well as environmental. The countries of the 'North' have hindered the development of those in the 'South'. In the nineteenth century, most of Africa, Asia and South America was colonised by European nations. Their people and resources were exploited. Today the 'South' owes huge sums of money to the 'North' and depends on it for food and other aid, especially in times of particular hardship such as famine, drought or flood.

The real difference between life in the 'North' and 'South' can best be seen by looking at three families – one in Peru, one in the USA, and one in Japan.

1 The Romero family in Peru

The Romero family live in a large squatter settlement outside Lima, the Peruvian capital. Maria sells fruit in the city while Tomas works in a small engineering factory. They have two children (see figure 1). The family is close, and all are hardworking. Most days Maria works 10 hours (Figure 2). Each day she makes about $2.

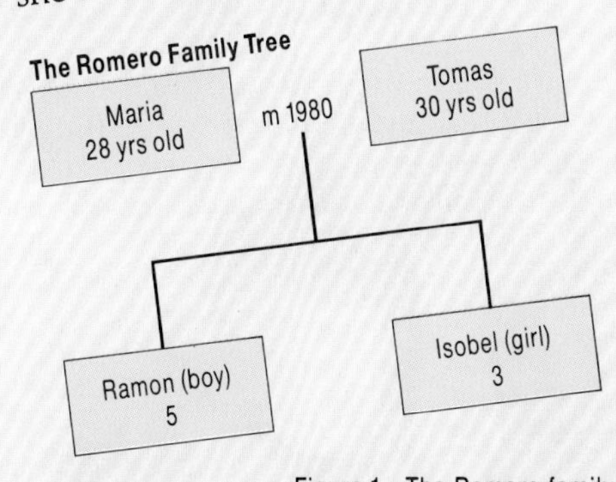

Figure 1 The Romero family

The Romeros will probably never be able to move from their present home, a small one-roomed hut, built on a steep hillside. The roof is made from corrugated iron and leaks when it rains, and the nearest clean water is a 10 minute walk away down the hill. Maria and Tomas hope they can give their children a better chance than they had. The children are learning to read and write, though they cannot afford to send them to school every day.

Figure 2 Maria's day

5.10 am: Maria is woken by Isobel's bad cough
She gets up then walks 1.5 kms to fetch the day's water

6.25 am: Maria leaves home for the 75 minute bus journey into town She visits the wholesale market to buy the day's stock

8.15 am: She looks for a good pitch in one of Lima's central squares
Here Maria stands for 8-10 hours each day

7 pm: Maria arrives home exhausted
She still has to cook a meal for Tomas and do some washing

2 *The Scott family in the USA*

In Sunnyvale in California, the Scott family (Figure 3) has a rather different way of life. Cheryl and Steve are a two-car family and have a luxurious home with a pool. Steve works for Apple Computers as a New Product Executive, while Cheryl runs the newsdesk at a local TV station. They are professional people with busy lives. Their children, Gary, John and Laura, each have their own bedroom. It was Gary's birthday last week, and his parents gave him a complete baseball kit. Next month the family is looking forward to a skiing holiday in Colorado. The children each expect to stay in school or college until they are 22 or 23 years old.

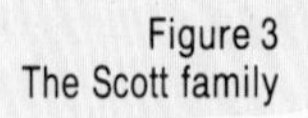

Figure 3
The Scott family

3 *The Ando family in Japan*

In Japan, on the other side of the world, is the Ando family. They live on the island of Kyushu in Southern Japan. Mr Ando is the Head of a small nursery school. His wife is looking for a part-time job, though he is not happy about this. They have four children, and live in a small old house on the outskirts of Oita City with Mr Ando's parents (Figure 4). Though he works very long hours, like most people in Japan, Mr Ando is well-paid, and was able to buy a second family car last year.

Figure 4 The Ando family

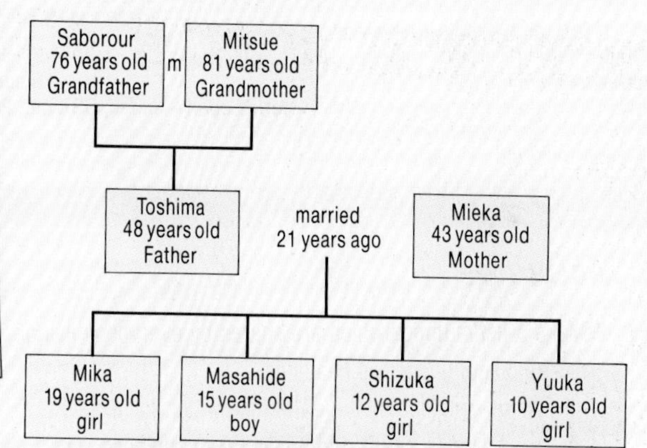

Mr Ando's working day

Mr Ando is the Head Teacher in a Nursery School four miles from home. There are 257 children at his school, mostly 3 or 4 years old.

6.15 am awoken by alarm
6.30 am leave home by car for work
7.20 am Mr Ando greets the teachers who have arrived early to plan the day ahead
8.15 am children begin arriving
8.30 am school starts with everybody together in the school yard doing exercises and singing the school song.
9.20 am Mr Ando has a routine visit from a local official of the Education Board
10.15 am some parents call to see mr Ando about moving their daughter to the school
11.00 am Mr Ando leave Oita Airport for the 1-hour flight to Tokyo to meet Education Officials over a working lunch
2.30 pm the meeting is over and Mr Ando heads back to the airport and his flight to Oita
4.10 pm back in school to take charge of the children cleaning their classrooms
4.30 pm school is over for the children, but the teachers meet with Mr Ando to plan a school trip to the local zoo
6.00 pm most of the teachers finish work and go home
6.45 pm Mr Ando checks the buildings are secure then heads home to his family

These three families live in very different countries (Figure 5). Not only are there differences between 'North' (Japan and the USA) and 'South' (Peru), but also inside the 'North' between Japan and the USA. They have contrasting lifestyles, and their children are likely to face very different futures. Why do you think this might be? Is it fair, when we all share the same planet, that some people have much better prospects for the future than others?

	PERU	USA	JAPAN
1990 Population (million)	21.6	249.2	123.5
1988 GNP per capita ($)	1300	19 840	21 020
Life expectancy (years)	63.0	75.9	78.6
Calories per day	2138	3643	2808
Under 5 mortality (deaths per '000 live births)	119	10	6
Literacy rate (%)	84	99	95
Secondary school enrolment (%)	64	99	96
Population with access to safe drinking water (%)	61	100	100

Figure 5
Worlds apart – Japan, USA and Peru

Activities

1 Make a list of things which are shared by everybody living on the planet under two headings:
- things provided by the earth (like water, for example);
- basic human needs and hopes (like happiness, for example).

2 What do you think is meant by the gap between 'North' and 'South'? Can you think of any examples of how this gap might affect people?

3 How are the lives of the children in the Scott and Romero families (Figures 1 and 3) likely to be different *i* now; *ii* in the future?

4 Read through the cartoon strip of Maria Romero's day (Figure 2).
a In small groups devise a similar cartoon strip illustrating a day in the life of Cheryl Scott (the American family's mother) or the mother of a family in Britain.
b Imagine that Maria and the mother in your cartoon could change places for a week. Choose one of the women. Write a description of her main impressions of the other's life, at the end of the week.

5 Study Figure 4 carefully.
a In what ways is the Ando family in Japan different from your own family?
b Keep a 'working diary' for a member of your family, like the one shown for Mr Ando. Are they similar or very different?

6 a List the things which all three families featured in this unit have in common.
b What difference do you notice between the Romero children and the Scott children?
c How do you think these differences might affect their prospects in life?
d Do you think they are really 'worlds apart'?

7 Look at Figure 5.
a How is life improved by being born in the USA or Japan, rather than in Peru?
b Choose what you think are the 3 most important measures of development from the table. Draw a graph or pictogram to represent each one.
c Can you think of any other indicators which should have been added to the table?
d Can you see a connection between any of these indicators?

6.2 Measuring development

The world we live in is constantly changing. For example, the amount of money spent on food in your home varies from week to week as prices change. Most of the time, prices are increasing. This doesn't matter if people's incomes rise as fast as the prices in the shops, but incomes change at different rates, and some families become richer while others may become poorer.

Figure 1

Figure 2 The North-South divide

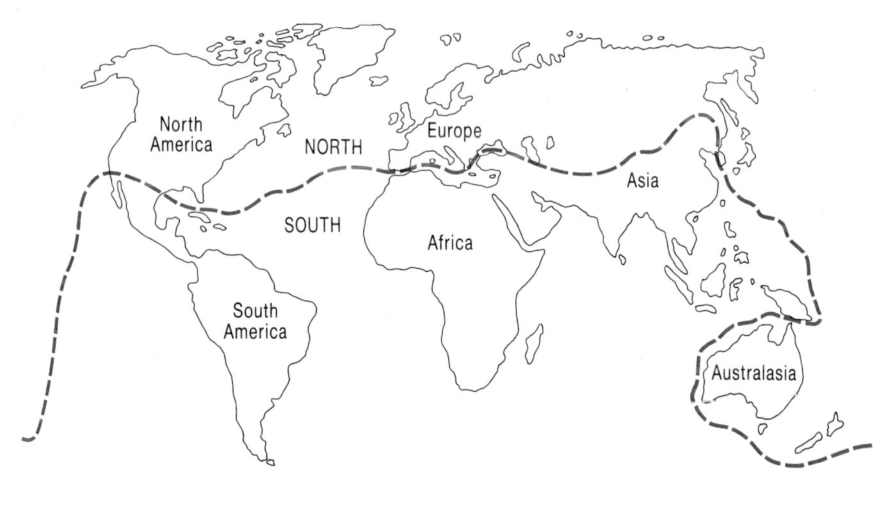

Similar changes are going on throughout the world. The prices which countries charge for what they grow, mine or manufacture alter for many reasons. When they increase, the country's income rises and its people may become richer. They may also fall, making the country and its people poorer. As a country's income changes so does its level of **development.**

Development is a very difficult idea to define. It is really about change for the better As countries develop they should be able to meet basic requirements for food, shelter, decent education, reasonable health and the opportunity to get a job. Figure 1 shows some photographs which indicate different levels of development. Which one do you think is the most developed and why? How do you think development can be measured?

The nations of the world are all at different levels of development. Some, generally those in North America, Australasia and Europe are mostly rich and industrialised (the 'North'), whereas those in Asia, South America and Africa (the 'South') are poor (Figures 2 and 3).

Figure 3 The North-South gap: Some indicators

	'SOUTH'	'NORTH'
Life expectancy at birth (years)	47	73
Infant mortality rate (per 1 000 of pop.)	132	18
Average daily calorie intake per head	2048	3361
Adult literacy rate (%)	32	99
% of population with access to safe water	34	99
Doctors per 100 000 of population	11	204
Telephones per 1 000 of population	3	603

The wealth gap between them has increased in the last 30 years (Figure 4).

One of the indicators most often used to measure development is **Gross National Product** (GNP). This is the total value of the wealth produced (goods and services) by a country each year. It is more useful to divide this figure by the country's population. This shows how much wealth is produced, on average, by each person (or GNP per capita). Some countries like Saudi Arabia have a high GNP, while many of the people who live there are actually quite poor, because the wealth is very poorly distributed.

There are actually many ways of measuring how developed a country is. Figure 5 shows some of these (including GNP per capita in column 2). It is useful to be able to compare different measures of development to see whether they are linked. We may find that as incomes rise, life expectancy increases.

The images we looked at in Figure 1 showed that in addition to contrasts in development between 'North' and 'South', there are also often major contrasts inside countries and cities. Measuring development is complicated!

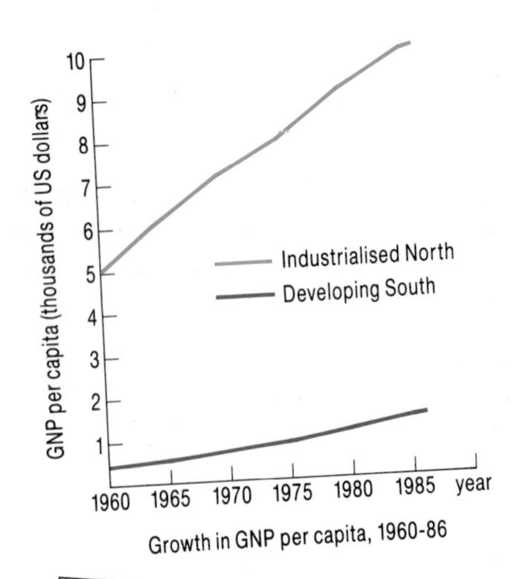

Growth in GNP per capita, 1960-86

The 'richest' GNP per capita ($US) 1987		
1.	Switzerland	21 330
2.	United States	18 530
3.	Norway	17 190
4.	U.Arab Emirates	15 830
5.	Japan	15 760

The 'poorest' GNP per capita ($US) 1987		
1.	Ethiopia	130
2.	Bhutan	150
2.	Chad	150
2.	Zaire	150
5.	Bangladesh	160
5.	Malawi	160
5.	Nepal	160

Figure 4 World wealth: the growing gap

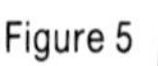
Figure 5

	Life (yrs) Expectancy	GNP per Capita $	People per Doctor	% employed in primary	Av. Annual popⁿ growth %	Energy consumption (kgs oil equiv.)
Australia	78	11 920	520	7	1.4	4710
Bangladesh	50	160	9 690	75	2.6	46
Brazil	65	1 810	1 300	31	2.2	830
Canada	76	14 120	550	5	1.1	8 945
Ethiopia	46	120	88 190	80	2.4	21
Japan	78	12 840	740	11	0.7	3 186
Norway	77	15 400	460	8	0.3	8 803
UK	75	8 870	680	3	0.1	3 802
USA	75	17480	500	4	1.0	7 193

Columns 1,2,6 = 1986 data Column 5 = 1980-86 average Column 3 = 1981 Column 4 = 1980

Activities

1 *a* Try to define in your own words what is meant by 'North' and 'South'.

b Sort out these 16 countries into two lists – one of countries in the 'North', and a second of countries in the 'South':

Austria; Australia; Brazil; Canada; Chad; Ethiopia; India; Italy; Japan; Kenya; New Zealand; Peru; Sweden; Thailand; USA; Zaire.

Use an atlas and Figure 2 to help you.

c Explain in your own words what is happening to the gap between 'North' and 'South'. Figure 4 might help.

d Are all the *richest* countries listed in Figure 4 in the 'North'? Check the map carefully, with the help of an atlas.

2 On a sheet of graph paper, use the different measures of development in Figure 5 to draw scattergraphs to compare:

a Energy consumption (x-axis) with life expectancy (y-axis);

b GNP per capita (x-axis) with % population in primary employment (y-axis).

c Compare Figure 5 with the table in 5.4 Figure 5.

6.3 Growing population

We live in an increasingly crowded world (Figure 1). The world population total exceeded 5 billion on July 11th 1987, was estimated at 5.3 billion in 1990, and looks set to reach 6 billion by the end of the century. Population is increasing in most countries and has been doing so for decades. About 95% of the increase over the next two decades is expected to occur in the less developed countries (LDCs), where rates of increase are generally higher.

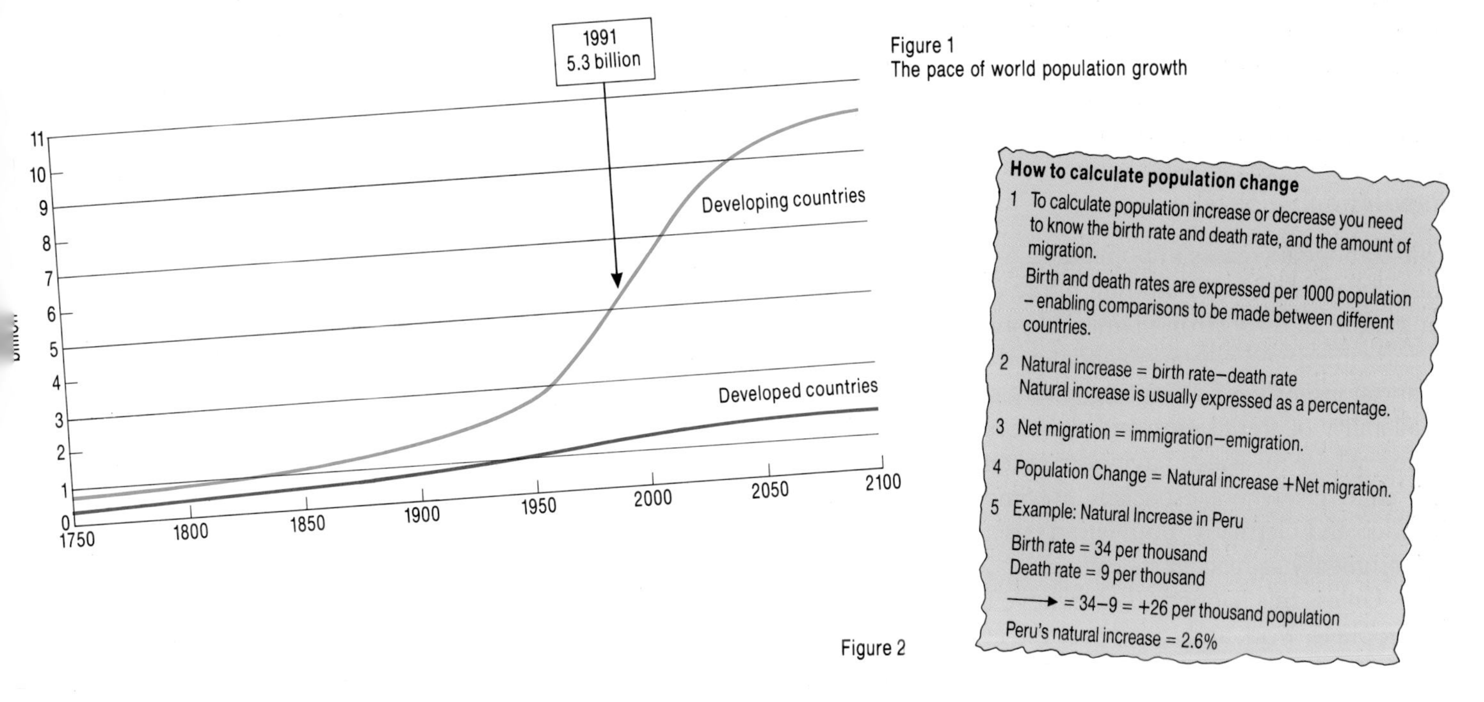

Figure 1
The pace of world population growth

How to calculate population change

1 To calculate population increase or decrease you need to know the birth rate and death rate, and the amount of migration.

Birth and death rates are expressed per 1000 population – enabling comparisons to be made between different countries.

2 Natural increase = birth rate–death rate
Natural increase is usually expressed as a percentage.

3 Net migration = immigration–emigration.

4 Population Change = Natural increase +Net migration.

5 Example: Natural Increase in Peru

Birth rate = 34 per thousand
Death rate = 9 per thousand
→ = 34–9 = +26 per thousand population
Peru's natural increase = 2.6%

Figure 2

How does population change?

The **birth rate** and **death rate** are the key to finding out what is happening to a country's population total. When the birth-rate exceeds the death-rate, population goes up. This is called **natural increase**. A country's population can also change by **migration**. People move in and out of countries more often today than in the past. Figure 2 shows you how to calculate population change.

Is there a population problem?

The population of many developing countries has risen faster than their agricultural output, so they have become less able to feed themselves (Figure 3). In about 70 countries, food production per head has decreased since the 1970s. This is especially true in Africa. The health of 340 million people is seriously at risk simply because they have too little to eat.

Figure 3 Food production and population growth

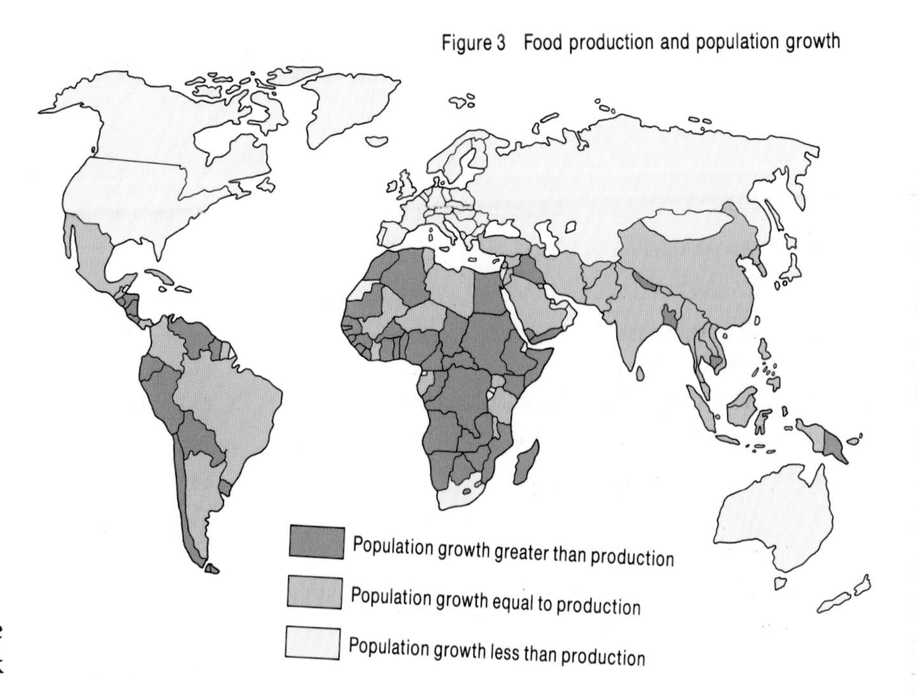

There are very good reasons why the birth-rates in developing countries are high. Most people work on the land and need large families to provide labour. Children often die young, so large families increase the chances of some surviving. Parents depend on their children to support them in old age.

The age and sex structure of a population can be shown using **population pyramids**. The shape of these pyramids differs between developed and developing countries (see Figure 4). The broad base of Pyramid A indicates a high birth rate – more mouths to be fed and jobs to be created!

The diagram representing developed countries (Pyramid B) actually looks less like a pyramid. There is a more even distribution of people in all age-groups. People living in developed countries like this have a high life-expectancy, and so more survive into old age.

Population policies

Due to huge increases in population, some governments have introduced policies for limiting future growth. China, Taiwan and Singapore all have strong family planning programmes. Measures include improved education about and access to contraception, financial incentives for limiting family size, later marriages, and wider availability of sterilisation and abortion. A strict policy is enforced in China, where measures have been taken to limit each family to only one child. Elsewhere, especially in some European countries like Sweden and Germany, population is actually falling. The German government has reacted by calling for 200 000 more babies each year. Unless this happens they believe there will be a serious lack of people to work and to support the ever-growing proportion of older people.

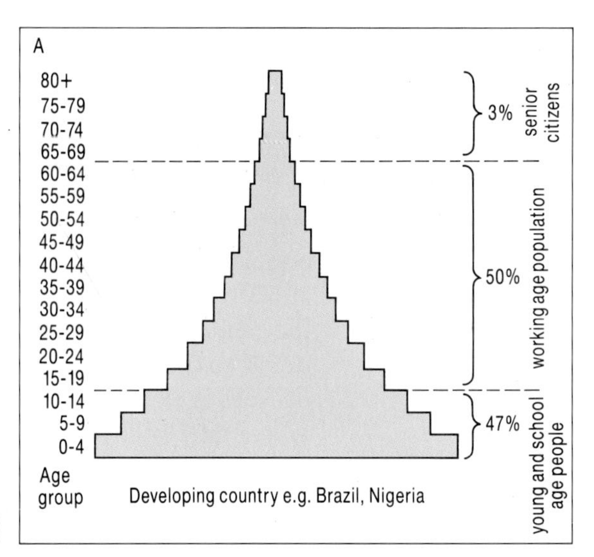

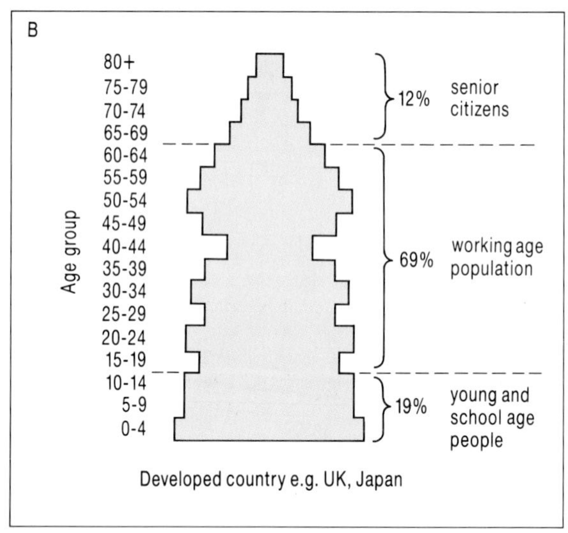

Figure 4
Model population pyramids for developed and developing countries

Activities

1 Read this unit carefully, then discuss the following question with a friend, and report your views to the rest of the class. Should the world's growing population be a cause for concern?

2 Calculate the birth rate for the following countries. Show your full working.

a 600 births in a country with a population of 70 000.

b 120 000 births in a country with a population of 6 000 000.

c 25 births in a country with a population of 4 200.

3 a The table below shows average birth-rates for 1985-89 for six countries. Copy and complete the table.

Country	Birth Rate	Death rate	Natural Increase (per 1000)	Natural Increase %
Australia	15.6	7.7	....	....
Bangladesh	41.7	15.6	....	....
Peru	34.3	6.8	....	....
Senegal	46.4	19.4	....	....
USA	15.7	9.0	....	....
Germany	10.6	12.4	....	....

b Which countries do you think are developed and which are developing? Why?

c Which country is the odd one out and why?

4 India is one of the world's most populated countries as you will see from Figure 5. It was also one of the first to devise a family planning policy. Imagine the government have asked you to **help spread the message about the importance of family planning** to the entire population. Working alone or in a group. Prepare **either**:

a a poster which will be distributed by the government;

or

b the script of a radio appeal for broadcast on All-India Radio.

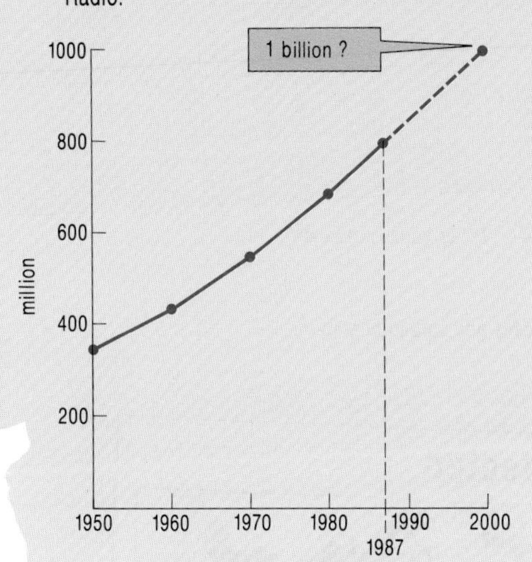

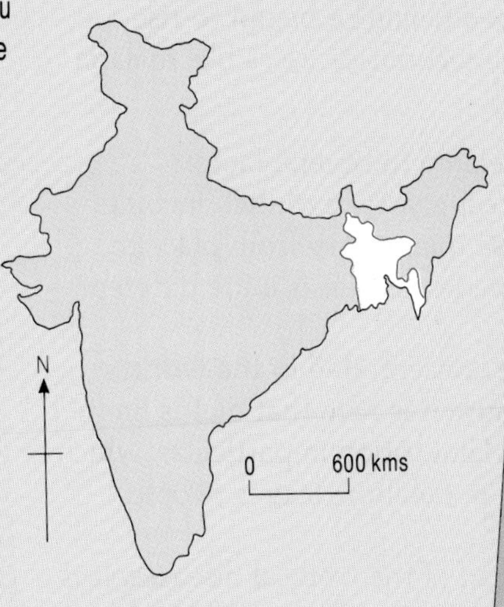

Figure 5
Population growth in India

- India has 15% of the world's population but only 2.4% land area
- About 16 million is added to the population total each year at the present rate
- In 1952 India was one of the first countries to introduce an official government family planning policy
- Birth rates have been reduced significantly but targets have not been met
- India's family planning programme (unlike that in China) is entirely voluntary

FACT FILE

Population	Growth rate	Safe water accessibility	Life expectancy	Income per head	Female literacy
810m (1989)	1.72% p.a.	57%	58 yrs	$300 per year	29%

6.4 Health for all?

We have already seen in Unit 6.1 how people's life chances are significantly affected by where they are born in the world. Place of birth also has a major effect on how many years you can expect to live, how healthy you are likely to be, and how you will die.

Over most of this century a number of encouraging trends have been observed:

- more and more young children are surviving into adulthood as infant mortality rates decrease
- people are generally living longer as health care improves and diseases become treatable
- many killer diseases have been wiped out over large parts of the earth's surface, or have at least become controllable.

However, the news is not all good. In the 1980s many developing countries had economic problems. Commodity prices fell, forcing them to borrow money when interest rates were rising. The result in many countries was a decline in per capita income of 10-25% between 1980-85. Less money was spent on health care in most of Africa and Latin America with disastrous consequences:

- **infant mortality** rates either stopped falling or began to rise
- **malnutrition** worsened and some infectious diseases like malaria and yellow-fever began to spread

The quality of a person's health is related to several factors including: the cleanliness of the water supply, type of diet, income level and access to health care. As these things vary from place to place, the pattern of disease in developed countries is quite different from that in developing countries.

Around 97% of all infant deaths are concentrated in the world's less developed nations (Figure 1), because it is here that diet is limited and clean water is difficult to obtain. Malnutrition in particular, which affects more than 1 in 5 of the world's population, leaves people weak and more susceptible to disease.

Malaria is one of the most widespread of the tropical diseases. It is a problem in over 60 countries (Figure 2) and each year kills more than one million children in Africa.

Disease or condition	Developed Countries	Less Developed Countries
Diseases of early infancy	2	8
Infectious and parasitic diseases	8	40
Heart and circulatory diseases	54	19
Cancers	19	5
Accidents	6	5
Other	11	23

Figure 1 Major causes of death

Figure 2 Causes and spread of Malaria

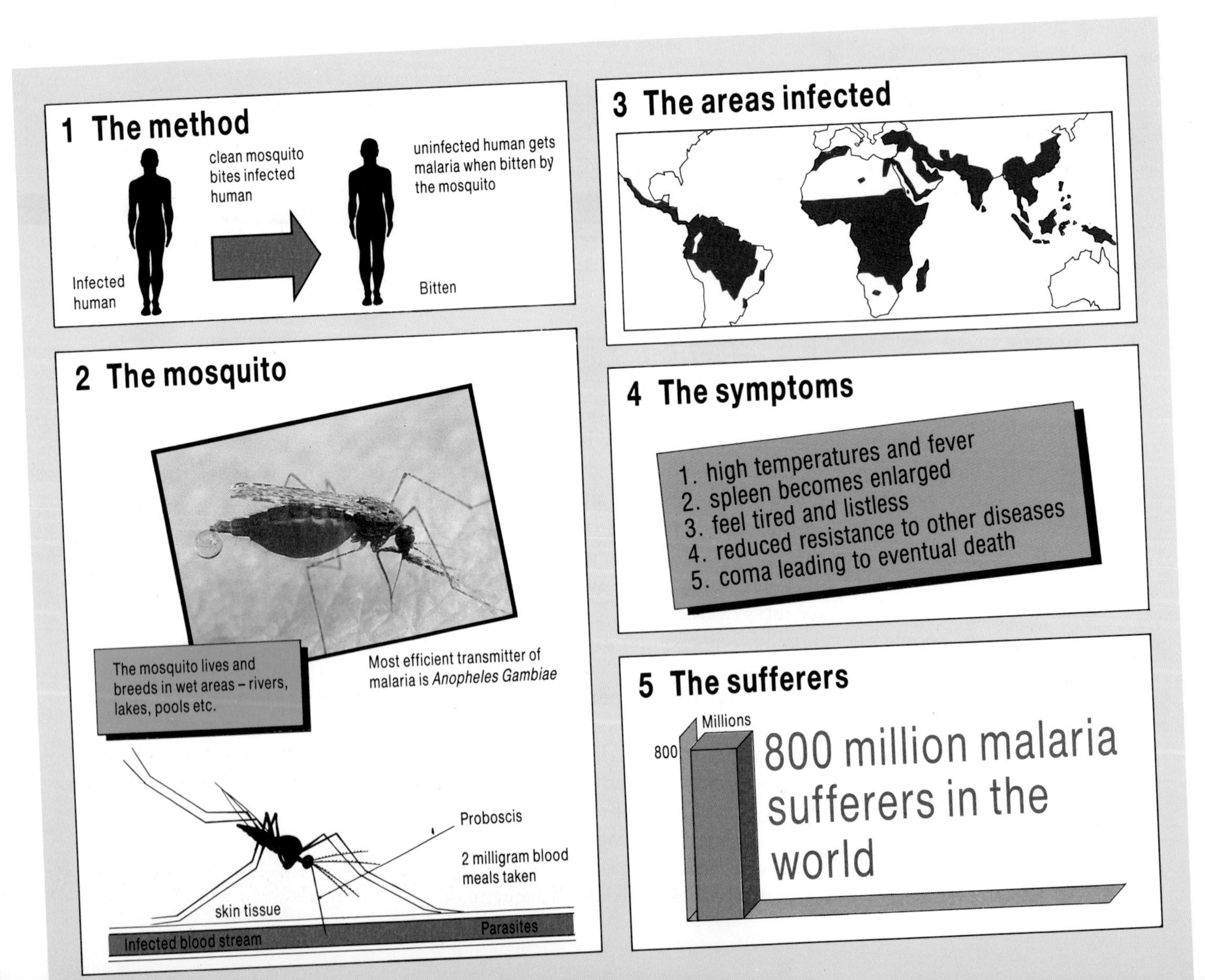

While some diseases may be eliminated or brought under control by thorough inoculation programmes or careful health education, new diseases are likely to replace them. The disease Aids, which was first diagnosed only in 1981, is already thought to affect 500 000 people, with a further 10 million carriers of the virus worldwide.

Many countries now spend most of their health budgets on hospital services which serve only a small number of people, while **primary health care** (education and prevention in local communities) is left underfunded (see Figure 3). For the same amount of money that it costs to train one doctor, about 30 community health workers could be trained in basic health protection. They would be able to help a far greater number of people than one overworked doctor.

Using money sensibly is critical. The challenge is to improve the health of people all over the world. By the year 2000, the World Health Organisation has set a minimum life expectancy in all countries of 60 years and an infant mortality rate of under 50 deaths per 1000 births. There is still a long way to go before these targets are achieved (Figure 4).

Figure 3
The health pyramid

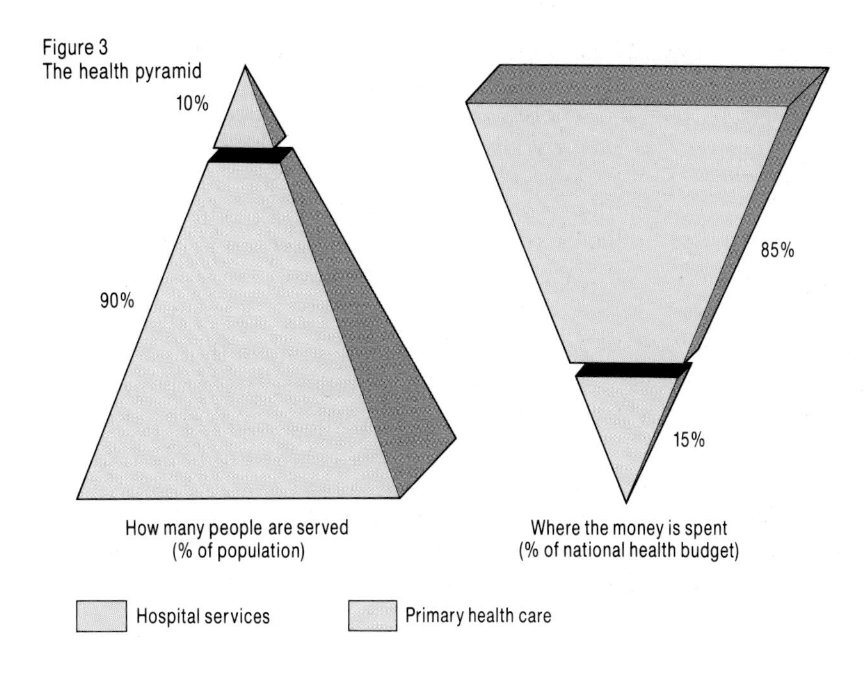

Figure 4 Progress towards World Health Organisation targets for the year 2000

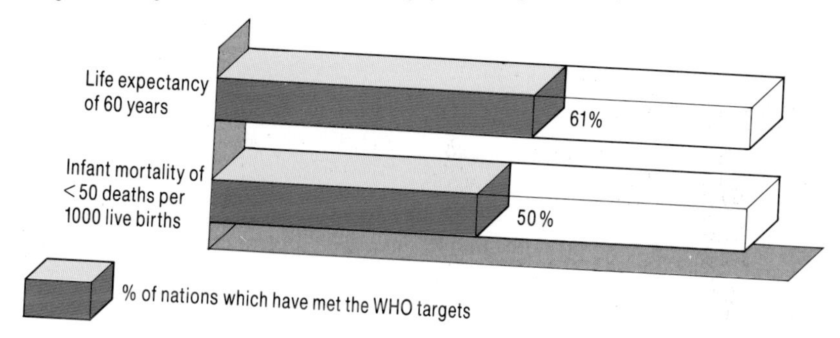

Activities

1 a Make two lists: *i* those foods which are nutritious and good for you; and *ii* those foods which you should avoid.

b Why do you think people in less developed countries have a different diet than you?

2 a Study Figure 2, then design your own poster to warn the people in the Amazon Basin about malaria. Try to make suggestions about how they can recognise the disease and more importantly how they can avoid catching it. Remember to make the poster as visual as possible, because illiteracy rates are high.

b Use the school and/or public library to find out about either *i* bilharzia; or *ii* cholera or *iii* sleeping sickness (trypanosomiasis). For your chosen disease, find out its symptoms, where it is most common (draw a map), how it is spread and what is being done to control it. Draw up a report summarising your findings.

3 The Health Pyramid is shown in Figure 3.

a What does it suggest that most money is spent on in most countries? How many people benefit?

b If you were a government adviser on health spending would you suggest any changes? Explain your answer.

6.5 Aid, debt and closing the gap.

We have seen how the gap between 'North' and 'South' has been growing. One real sign of this is the huge international debt crisis. By the end of 1989 the 109 countries in the 'South' owed a staggering $1.29 trillion ($1 290 000 000 000) to governments and banks in the 'North'. That's more than $240 for every single person alive on the planet today!

Between 1980-1989 the size of the debt more than doubled (Figure 1), and is now so huge that many countries cannot afford even the interest payments, and will probably never be able to pay off their debts completely. Zambia's debt is smaller than most (Figure 2). If Zambia's entire population gave every penny of their earnings to help pay the country's debt starting tomorrow morning, it would take about three and a half years before things were back to normal!

Figure 1 The growing problem

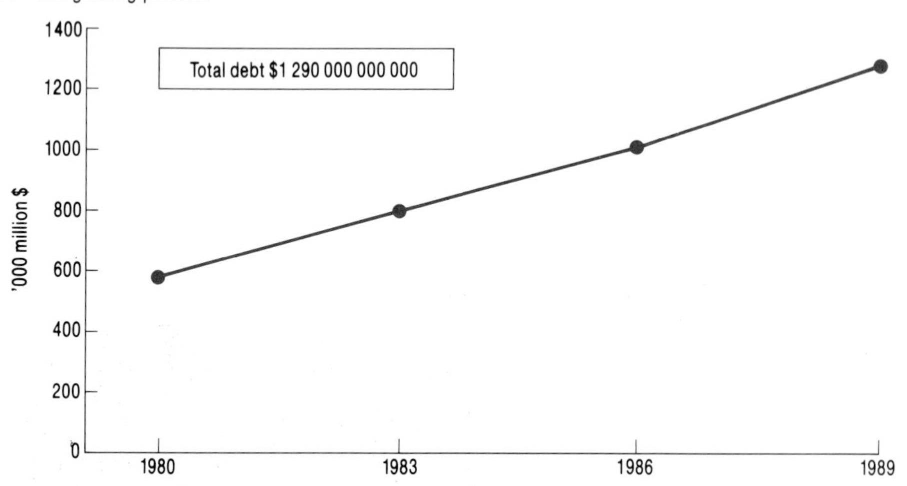

Country	Debt outstanding 1989 ($bn)
All developing countries	1 290
Argentina	61.9
Bolivia	5.8
Brazil	112.7
Chile	18.5
Colombia	11.4
Ecuador	11.5
India	41.1
Indonesia	42.1
Ivory Coast	14.0
Korea (Republic)	40.1
Mexico	102.6
Morocco	20.8
Nicaragua	8.6
Nigeria	18.6
Peru	19.9
Philippines	28.5
Sudan	6.7
Thailand	17.9
Venezuela	34.1
Zambia	5.3

Figure 2
The international debt crisis

You may have contributed money to the economically developing countries of the world by buying the Band Aid record, taking part in a 'fun-run' for Sport Aid, or organising a sponsored event for 'Comic Relief'. Huge sums are raised in this way. Each year too, the governments of the richer countries give large amounts of food, technical and financial aid. Despite these efforts, however, 1989 was the seventh year running when more money flowed out of the developing countries of the 'South' than flowed into them.

Activities

1 *a* How big was the international debt in *i* 1980 *ii* 1989?
b With interest rates at 10% a year, calculate how much interest the developing countries would have to pay on their 1989 debt. How much would this be each day?

2 *a* Figure 2 shows some of the biggest debtors in the world. What is their combined debt?
b Present the data in the form of a bar chart. Arrange the bars so that those representing the largest debts are on the right-hand side of the chart, and those representing the smallest debts are on the left.
c In which continent are the three biggest debtors located?

3 Using Figure 3 to help you, explain in your own words why many countries got into debt, and are finding it difficult to get out.

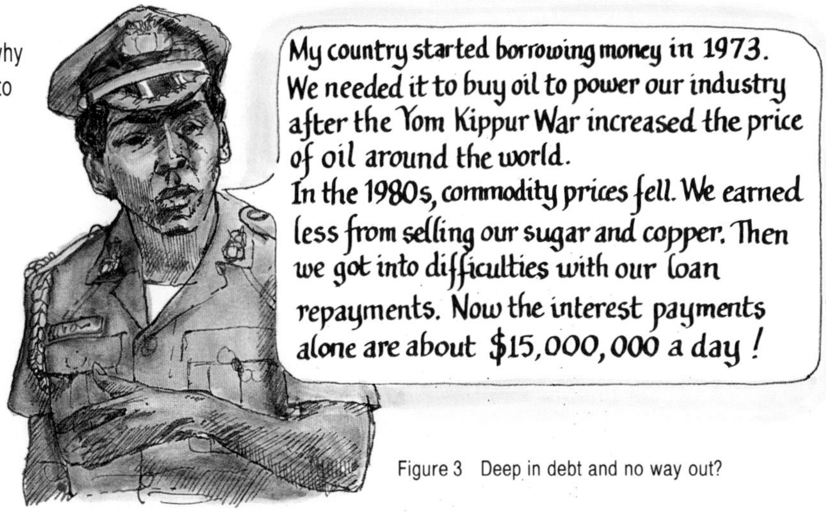

My country started borrowing money in 1973. We needed it to buy oil to power our industry after the Yom Kippur War increased the price of oil around the world.
In the 1980s, commodity prices fell. We earned less from selling our sugar and copper. Then we got into difficulties with our loan repayments. Now the interest payments alone are about $15,000,000 a day!

Figure 3 Deep in debt and no way out?

6.6 Refugees

Vietnam Refugees

Lee Chang is a hardworking businessman (Figure 1). He has a wife and three children. Until they were forced to leave Vietnam three years ago, the Chang family were quite successful, owning their own house and living comfortably. Mr Chang ran a small garage. He employed three people to help repair trucks, cars and bicycles.

During 1989, the Changs were forced to abandon their home in Vung Tau near Ho Chi Minh City (Saigon). They left because Mr Chang disagreed strongly with the policies of the government, who confiscated his business and moved the family out of their house. Like thousands of others, they decided to leave Vietnam. During the perilous boat journey across the South China Sea to Hong Kong (Figure 2) their young son died because of the poor conditions.

Figure 1

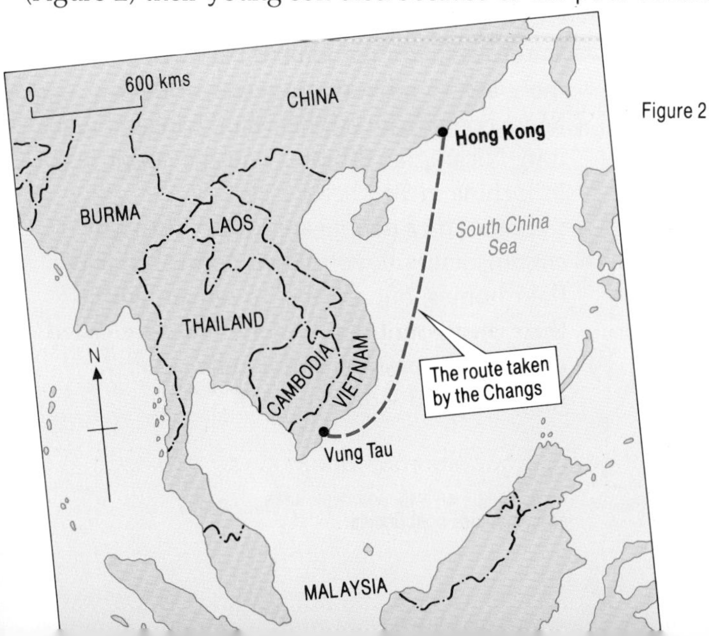

Figure 2

Today, the family are waiting along with thousands of others in a refugee camp (Figure 3), hoping that another country will give them a chance to rebuild their lives. They are regarded as **illegal migrants**. All they have left are the clothes they are wearing and a small amount of money Mr Chang managed to smuggle out of Vietnam.

The Changs are not the first or the last to leave Vietnam. Over one million people have fled the country since the war with the USA ended in 1975 and during the war with Kampuchea which followed. The peak year was 1979 when about 250 000 people left. This number had been declining, but in the summer sailing season in each of the last three years the number has crept up to around 70 000. Many of the 'boat people' end up in Hong Kong (Figure 4) before being moved on elsewhere or **repatriated**. Some estimates suggest that 200 000 'boat people' have drowned during the journey over the years. Despite their illegal status, Vietnamese 'boat people' have been allowed to settle in many countries (Figure 5).

Figure 3 Vietnamese refugees

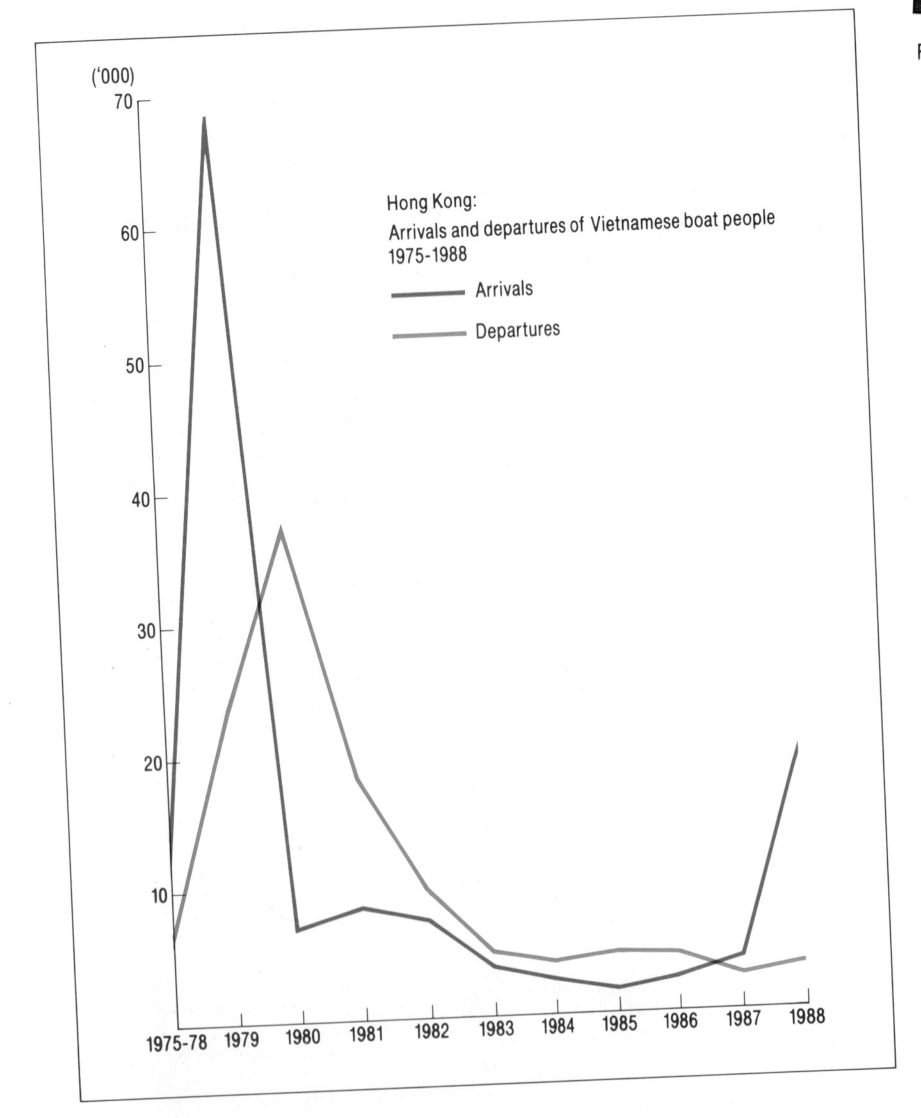

People who are forced to leave their homes and country because they fear persecution on account of their race, religion, nationality, social group or political opinions are classed as **refugees** by the United Nations. Today, there are 15 million refugees worldwide. Most come from Afghanistan, Mozambique, Iran, Nicaragua, Ethiopia and the countries of Indochina in Southeast Asia.

Sometimes people are forced, through circumstances beyond their control to leave their homes, but are able to remain within their own country's borders. They are called **displaced persons**, and number over 7 million worldwide (Figure 6).

Figure 4
Hong Kong – arrivals and departures of Vietnamese boat people

Destinations of refugees from Vietnam (up to 1990)		
Country	Number of refugees accepted	Number in camps awaiting interview and resettlement
Australia	70 000	
Canada	90 000	
China	260 000	
France	90 000	
Germany	22 000	
Great Britain	21 000	
Hong Kong	9000	56 000
Indonesia	5100	7000
Italy	3000	
Malaysia	5000	20 000
New Zealand	3000	
Norway	4000	
Phillipines	26 000	10 000
Thailand	16 900	14 000
USA	630 000	

Figure 5

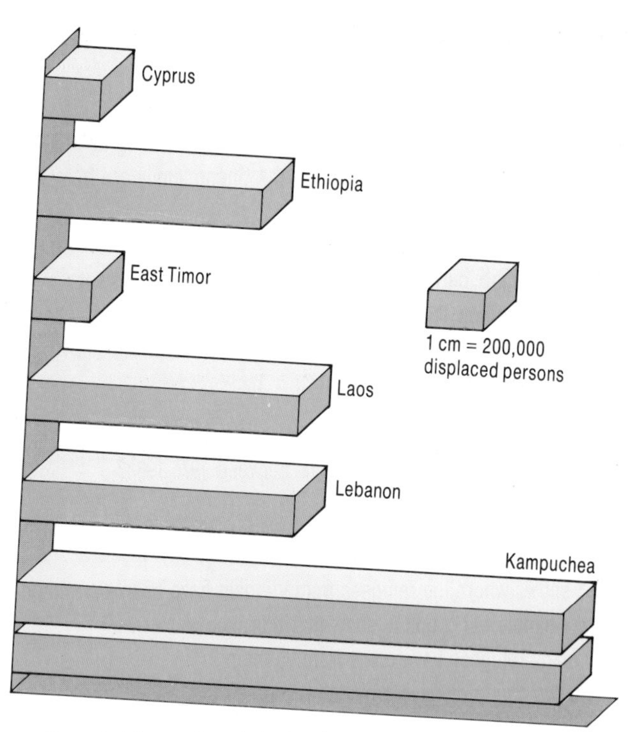

Figure 6 The number of displaced persons

Refugees from Eastern Europe

1989 saw dramatic changes in Eastern Europe – communist governments fell and the Berlin Wall was effectively dismantled. Many countries opened their borders, and lifted the restrictions which had prevented people from leaving them. Romania, Czechoslovakia and Bulgaria are now much freer than for many years and East Germany has joined with West Germany to form a united country. Despite the new freedoms, almost one million people have left the 'east' for a new life in the 'west'.

The Future

The world seems to be entering a fairly peaceful period. More elected governments and less persecution should result in fewer refugees. However, those who are forced from their homes due to natural disasters like floods and famines are also called refugees, though they do not fit the United Nations definition. Research into the greenhouse effect has led to concern that the number of refugees in the future (Figure 7) will be much greater than now. The world's refugee problem may just be beginning!

Figure 7

Climate change could cause world refugee crisis

The world is facing a massive increase in the number of refugees in the next century as the result of the "greenhouse effect" warned Sir Crispin Tickell, the UK permanent representative at the United Nations.

There were less than 5 million refugees in 1978 and almost 14 million in 1988 and this did not include undocumented people – probably well over 10 million.

"It requires a leap of the imagination to work out the numbers which would be on the move in the event of global warming on present estimates. Nearly a third of humanity lives within 60 kms of a coastline. A rise in mean sea level of just 0.25cm would have substantial effects," he said.

Many living in areas like the deltas of the Nile, Ganges and Yangtse would be forced out of their homes and livelihood. Some islands, such as the Maldives, Kiribati, Tuvalu and the Marshall Islands would become uninhabitable.

Countries like Bangladesh with more than 100 million people, and Egypt with 70 million people, would be particularly affected.

If just one per cent of a future world population of 6 billion were affected that would mean 60 million people on the move.

"60 million would represent a problem of an order of magnitude which no one has ever had to face.

Refugees create huge problems. There would be little prospect of return; shelter, food and medical care would be hard to find; they would be living in an alien environment with alien customs, religions, eating habits and agriculture.

In virtually all countries the growing numbers of refugees would cast a dark and lengthening shadow. Within a country they would represent a dangerous element in what would be growing difficulties of social and economic management," he said.

Secondary effects such as disorder, terrorism, civil war, economic breakdown or bankruptcy could become endemic. Willingness to help others may be limited.

Humankind was now "getting the bill" for a problem it had created itself. It was a bill that it may not be able to meet, but there was much that could be done if the world had a mind to.

He suggested new energy policies, reduced consumption of fossil fuels especially coal and oil, development of alternative sources from nuclear to solar, reducing the burning of fuel wood.

British Overseas Development, June 1989

Activities

1 a Look at the photograph of Lee Chang (Figure 1). Use an atlas to help you draw a sketch map of the location of the country that the Chang family are from, and of Hong Kong where they are now.
  b How long do you estimate the sea journey is?
  c Do you think the journey was hazardous? Explain your answer.
  d Try to imagine how the Chang family must feel about what they have been through. How must they have felt in the week just before they left for the sea voyage to Hong Kong?

2 Study Figure 4 carefully.
  a What was the peak year for arrivals in Hong Kong?
  b What was the total number of arrivals between 1975-1988?
  c Describe the recent trends briefly.
  d Why did the situation become worrying in 1988?

3 Figure 5 shows where the refugees from Vietnam have been accommodated.
  a Draw a simple bar graph to show this information.
  b How many refugees have come from Vietnam ?
  c Which two countries have provided homes for the largest number of refugees?
  d Why do you think these countries have helped Vietnam so much?

4 a Explain the difference between a refugee and a displaced person.
  b Calculate the number of displaced people in each of the countries listed in Figure 6.
  c For any one country see if you can discover why so many people have been displaced from their homes. A little bit of library research may be necessary.

5 Study the article about the effects of climate change (Figure 7).
  a How is climate change going to lead to more refugees?
  b Which countries may be particularly affected?
  c If just 1% of a future world population were affected, how many people could become refugees? How does this compare with the number of refugees in the world now?
  d List the sorts of problems that the author predicts.

6 As time goes on, the locations from which refugees come change. Keep a close eye on the newspapers as well as radio and TV news bulletins while you are studying this unit. Cut out or write down any information about refugees that you see or hear.

Dictionary

birth rate the number of births per 1 000 of the population

death rate the number of deaths per 1 000 of the population

displaced persons people who are forced, by circumstances beyond their control, to leave their homes, but are able to remain within the borders of their own country

Gross National Product (GNP) the total value of goods and services produced in a country, and a measure of its wealth

illegal migrants those people who move from one country to another, and try to settle without permission

primary health care a relatively cheap form of health care where the emphasis is on preventing disease and improving overall health. It is usually administered at local community level

refugees people who are forced to leave their homes and country because they fear persecution on account of their race, religion, nationality, social group or political opinions

repatriation the process of sending illegal migrants back to the country of their origin, often against their will

7 Settlement

7.1 People patterns

Have you ever noticed anything odd about the distribution of holidaymakers on a beach in the summer? Unless a beach is very full, the pattern is likely to be uneven (Figure 1). Many reasons influence where on a beach people choose to settle: some are near the amusements on the promenade or the ice-cream stall; others prefer to be in a quiet area; there are also people who like to sun-bathe near the pier, or to take advantage of the shelter provided by the cliffs. There may also be patches of pollution to be avoided!

If we examine larger areas of landscape like towns, countries or whole continents, we can also see uneven people patterns (Figure 2a). Some areas seem to be popular and crowded, while others have few people living in them and appear almost empty. **Population density** can be calculated by dividing the population of a country or area by its area. The result indicates how many people inhabit the area per km². Crowded areas have a high density of population, while empty areas have a low density.

Figure 1 People patterns on a beach

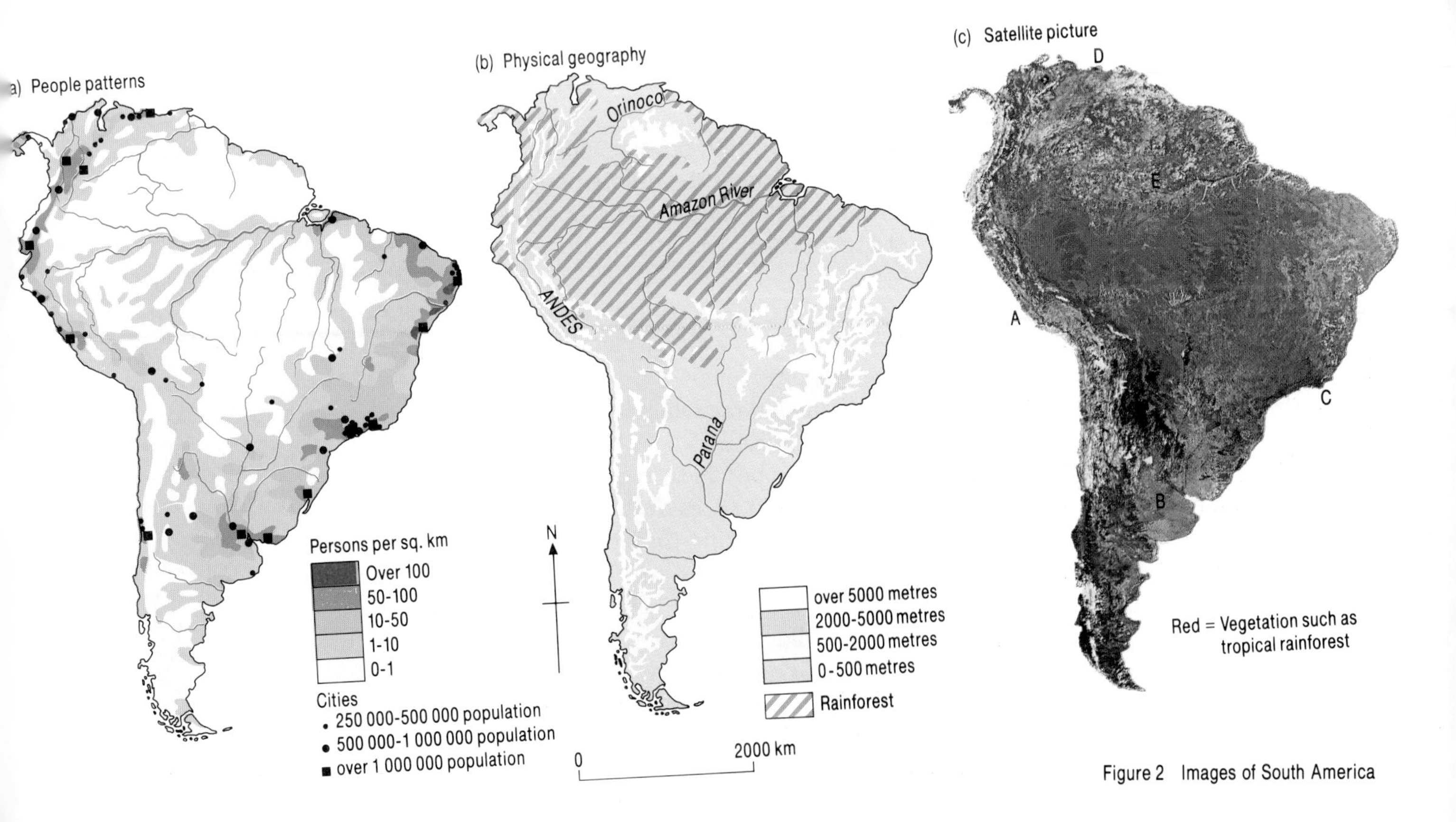

Figure 2 Images of South America

Densities vary considerably from place to place (Figure 3). Mountainous areas, for example, often have densities of under one person per km², while cities like New York, Mexico City and Tokyo have densities of over 5000 people per km²! There are districts within these cities which accommodate up to 50 000 people per km²!

Figure 3

World Population Distribution

The differences in population density around the world (Figure 5) are very marked.

1 Areas of high density, e.g. Western Europe and the northeastern USA, usually have one or more of the following characteristics:
- the landscape is flat and not too high above sea-level – this allows people to settle easily and live comfortably, e.g. the Netherlands
- the soils are deep and fertile – making the large-scale growing of food crops possible, e.g. the Great Plains of the United States and Soviet 'steppes'
- the climate is moderate and rainfall is sufficient for agriculture, e.g. areas in temperate latitudes
- they are near the coast or beside rivers – here land is often flat and construction easy. Also **accessibility** is good both inland and with other countries, making the site ideal for industries which need raw materials or those who need to trade, e.g. the St. Lawrence Valley in Canada, the Mississippi Valley in the USA and the Rhine Valley in Europe
- they have good mineral or energy resources – providing both employment for people and an attraction for industries, e.g. the gold and diamond mines in South Africa and the minerals of the Canadian Shield and Siberia

2 Areas of low density, e.g. Australia, usually have one or more of the following characteristics:
- the landscape is hilly and may be high above sea-level – this makes farming, construction and settlement difficult, e.g. the Great Dividing Range in eastern Australia and the mountains of Japan
- the soils are thin and poor – this makes them useless for cultivation, e.g. the Scottish Highlands and mountainous areas (the Rockies) of the western USA
- the climate is extreme – this limits agriculture and settlement. Special construction techniques may be required, and the costs of heating or air-conditioning may be high, e.g. in Alaska and the Yukon low temperatures and permafrost are a problem whereas in summer parts of the central USA experience temperatures of over 32°C (100°F)
- they cannot be reached very easily (inaccessible) and are often in inland locations – this remoteness makes places unattractive for most people and industries
- there are few economic resources – this limits the possibility of economic development and means few employment opportunities

Activities

1 Draw a simple plan of the distribution of holidaymakers on the beach in Figure 1. Label the factors which you think have influenced their location.

2 Try to produce very simple dot maps to show the distribution pattern of the people in your class at different times during the school day. You may need to do a survey at each of these times to find out where your classmates are located. You will need a map of the school's catchment area for *a* and a simple plan of the school buildings for *b–f*.
a 7.00 am; *b* 8.30 am; *c* 9.00 am;
d 11.20 am; *e* 12.30 pm; *f* 2.45 pm.

3 Study Figure 2a, b, and c carefully.
a With the help of an atlas name cities A, B, C and D shown on Figure 2c.
b Name River E and Mountain Range F.
c Write a short **description** of the pattern of population density in the continent.
d **Explain** the pattern you have described.

4 Study Figure 3. Each of the photographs shows a different part of the world.
a Write a sentence for each describing the number of people living in the area;
b Choose one phrase from the list below which best sums up the population density of each scene:

HIGH DENSITY **MEDIUM DENSITY** **LOW DENSITY**

5 Population Density can be calculated by doing this calculation:
Population Density = Population ÷ Area

a Copy and complete the table shown in Figure 4, by working out the remaining densities.
b Rank the countries in descending order (those with a high population density first).

Figure 4

Country	Population (million in 1990)	Area (million km²)	Population density (people per km²)
Australia	16.7	7.69	2.17
Bangladesh	115.6	0.14	
Brazil	150.3	8.51	17.66
France	56.1	0.55	
India	853.3	3.29	
Japan	123.4	0.37	
Kenya	25.1	0.58	43.27
Netherlands	14.7	0.04	367.50
Nigeria	113.0	0.92	122.82
Peru	22.3	1.28	
South Korea	66.5	0.09	738.80
United Kingdom	56.9	0.24	
USA	249.2	9.37	
USSR (Until 1992)	288.0	22.40	
West Germany	60.5	0.25	242.0

6 *a* What is the population density in each of the locations marked on the world map Figure 5 (A–F)?
b Use your atlas to suggest one reason to explain the high or low density in each case.
You could present your answers to (a) and (b) in the form of a table.

Figure 5 Population distribution

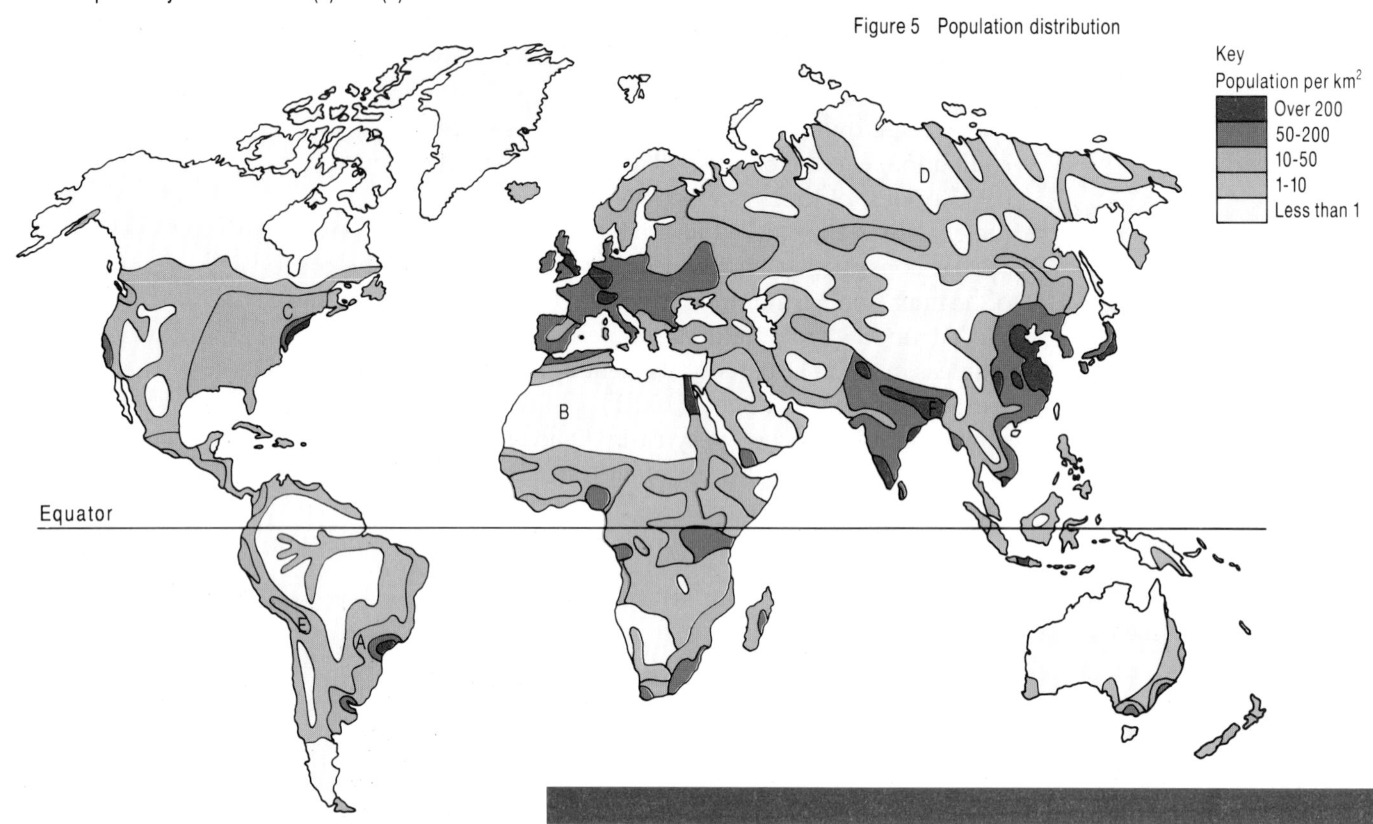

7.2 Expanding cities

A continuous drift of population towards the world's towns and cities has been the most important population trend over the last century. Since 1960, the number of people living in cities has doubled. It now stands at over 2.2 billion out of a world population total of 5.3 billion. This trend, called **urbanisation**, looks set to continue (Figure 1).

The balance of the world's urban population is also changing, because the cities in the developing world are growing more quickly than those elsewhere. In 1985 the world had 10 **megacities** (with populations of 10 million+). Seven were in the 'South'. The number of megacities in the 'South' will increase to 21 out of an estimated 25 by the year 2000 (Figure 2).

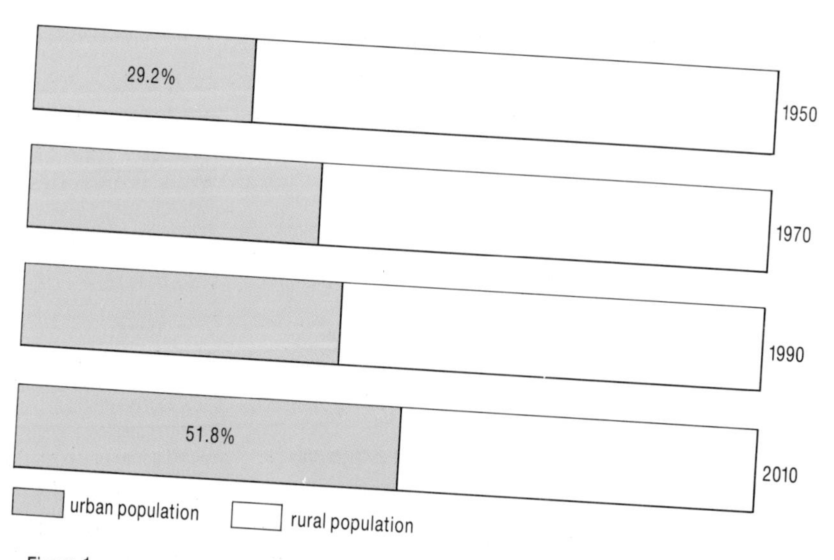

Figure 1
The world's growing urban population

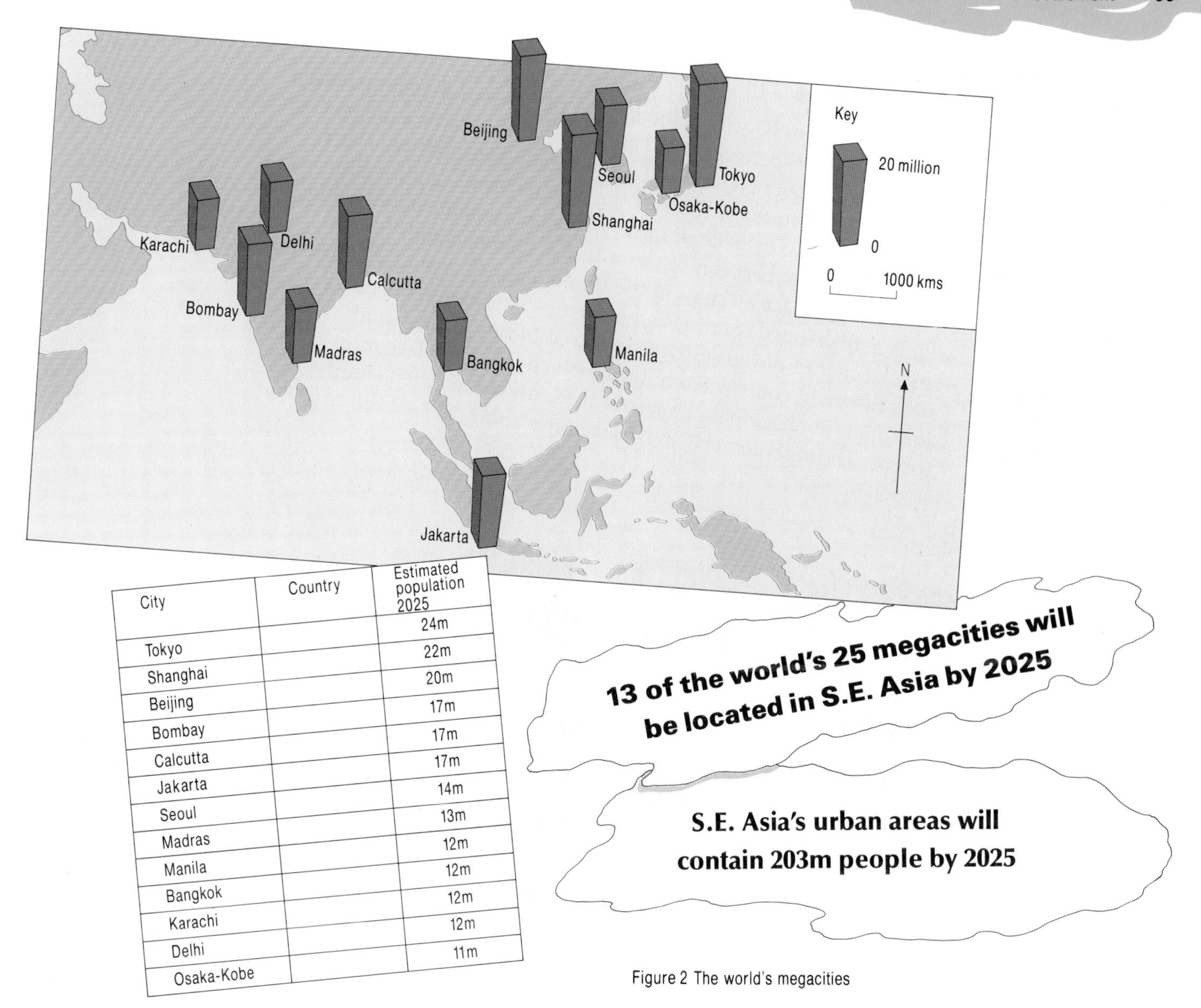

City	Country	Estimated population 2025
Tokyo		24m
Shanghai		22m
Beijing		20m
Bombay		17m
Calcutta		17m
Jakarta		17m
Seoul		14m
Madras		13m
Manila		12m
Bangkok		12m
Karachi		12m
Delhi		12m
Osaka-Kobe		11m

Figure 2 The world's megacities

Most of the world's cities are growing due to natural increase (see Unit 6.3) as well as massive migration. **Migration** is fed by a powerful combination of 'push' and 'pull' factors. **Push factors** force people to leave the countryside, while **pull factors** are the reasons they are attracted to cities. A combination of these factors has led to a massive influx of people into the cities of the 'South'. One recent estimate puts the overall figure at over 3000 people per hour! This amounts to an annual rate of over 3%. By 2025 it is estimated that these cities will contain four times as many people as those in more developed nations. By the same date there are likely to be three times as many 'millionaire' cities (with a population of 1 million +) in the 'South' than in the 'North'.

Growing cities need more housing, medical facilities and jobs to satisfy the demands of their new residents. These are difficult to provide in the wealthy cities of the 'North', and place a greater strain on the limited resources of cities in the economically developing countries.

Case-Study: Lagos in Nigeria

Lagos (Figure 3) in Nigeria is the largest city in Africa. Its population multiplied 8 times between 1960 and 1980 as it became a magnet for people from all over Nigeria and elsewhere in West Africa. There were jobs and homes for some of the new residents, but for the majority it was to be a life of misery, unemployment, and housing conditions that at best can be described as cramped and unsatisfactory. Like all cities in the world, Lagos has slums. Unlike the slums in developed countries which are old run-down buildings that have fallen into disrepair, those in the countries of the 'South' are areas of newly constructed housing which generally lack most amenities. In developing countries these areas are called **shanty towns**. These settlements in Lagos house about 75% of the city's population.

Population of Greater Lagos

Year	Number
1950	250 000
1960	400 000
1970	1 450 000
1980	2 900 000
1987	4 000 000

Figure 3 Problem cities, case-study: Lagos

In developing countries as a whole about half of all city dwellers live in single-room huts or shacks built from make-shift materials, and with few amenities such as running water or electricity. There are others who are far worse off and have nowhere at all to call home, and no roof over their heads. The numbers involved are large, so city authorities have a huge problem.

There are various ways of improving the situation. One solution is to try and stop the exodus from rural areas by improving conditions there. Another is to enable people in the cities to improve their own make-shift housing through **self-help schemes** (Figure 4). There are many difficulties however; building materials are often hard to obtain or are expensive. Money is short, and the problem in most developing world cities is huge and needs urgent attention.

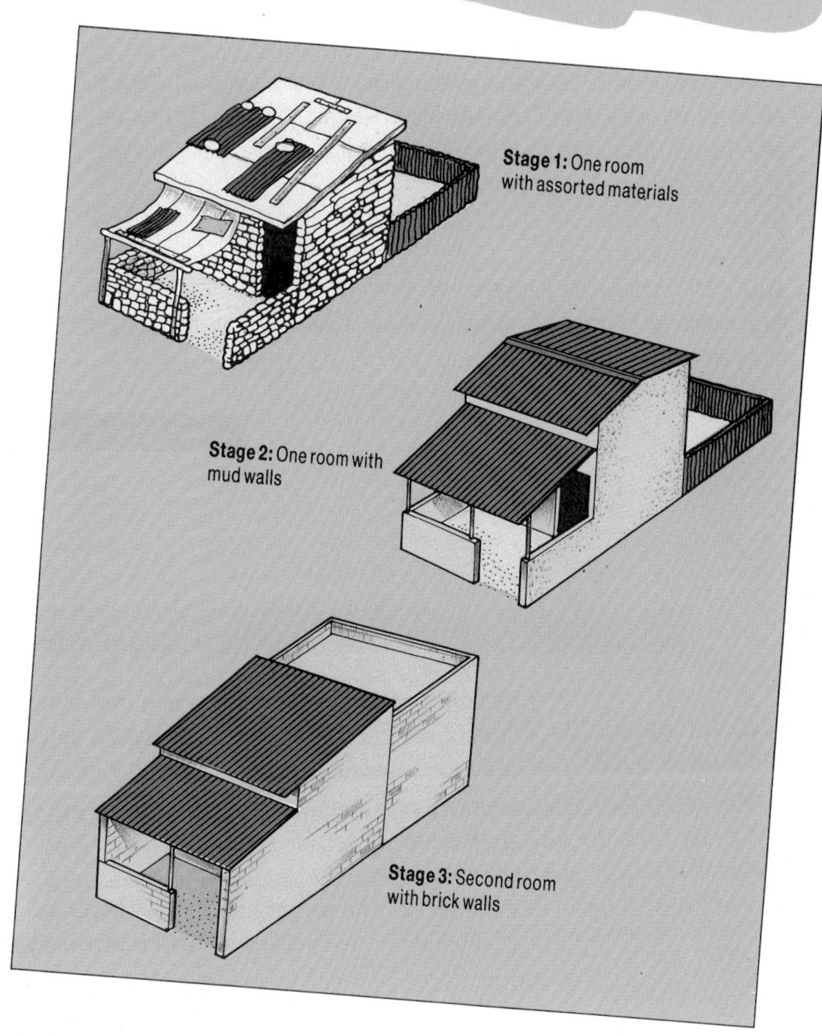

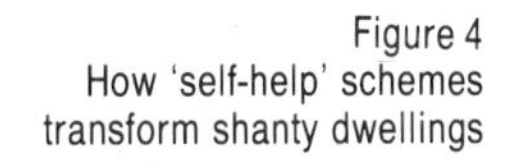
Figure 4
How 'self-help' schemes transform shanty dwellings

Activities

1 Use Figure 1 to calculate what percentage of the world's population lived in cities in: *i* 1970; *ii* 1990.

2 You will need an atlas for this activity.

a Copy and complete the table in Figure 2, by adding the country for each city.

b How many people will live in megacities in *i* Japan; *ii* India; and *iii* China in 2025?

c Use your atlas to find out where the world's largest cities are located now. Write a short description of their location.

3 a Complete the two definitions below:

i Urbanisation is ....

ii Migration is ....

b Study Figure 3. Imagine you have been left behind in a small village in the countryside in a developing country after your older brother and sister have left home to make a new life in a nearby city. **Either:** Working in a small group write a short play to show what you feel about this. Now act out the play for the rest of the class.

Or: Write an account describing what life is like in the countryside and what your feelings are about your brother and sister moving to the city.

4 Look at the photograph in Figure 3(b). It shows part of Lagos in Nigeria.

a Do you expect third world cities to look like this? Is there anything that surprises you about the photograph?

b Draw a line-graph to show how the population of Lagos has changed since 1950. Now use your graph to predict what the population will be by the year 2000.

c Make a list of 5 things that you think might attract people to cities like this.

5 *a* A young couple shown are shortly going to move to Lagos from their village some 240 kms away to the north. They were interviewed recently about the reasons for their decision. Seven quotations from the interview are shown. Make two lists – one of **push** factors the second of **pull** factors.

b Do you agree with their decision to leave? What do *you* think you might have done in the same position?

c Make a list of some of the problems they might experience on entering the city.

d What effects will the migration of many young couples have on the rural areas they leave behind?

6 Self-help schemes like the one shown in Figure 4 have been used in some countries to improve shanty dwellings.

a Describe what happens to the house as the scheme goes ahead.

b List two advantages of self-help schemes like this.

c What alternatives can you think of to deal with the problem of shanty towns?

7.3 World metropolis

Urbanisation is a worldwide process, and is not just confined to the less developed countries. It has produced settlements of varying sizes ranging from a small village at one end of the **urban hierarchy** to a huge sprawling super-city called a **megalopolis** at the other end. As you go further up the hierarchy, the size and importance of the settlement grows.

At the top of the urban hierarchy, there are a small number of cities which deserve the title 'world metropolis'. Cities like New York, London, Paris, Rome, Los Angeles and Tokyo have large populations living at quite high densities. They cover such large areas that they are clearly visible from satellites circling the earth. These cities have many **functions.** New York, for example, is a financial, entertainment, shopping, media and tourist centre (Figure 1). A combination of political, retail and commercial power gives the largest cities a special importance.

Figure 1

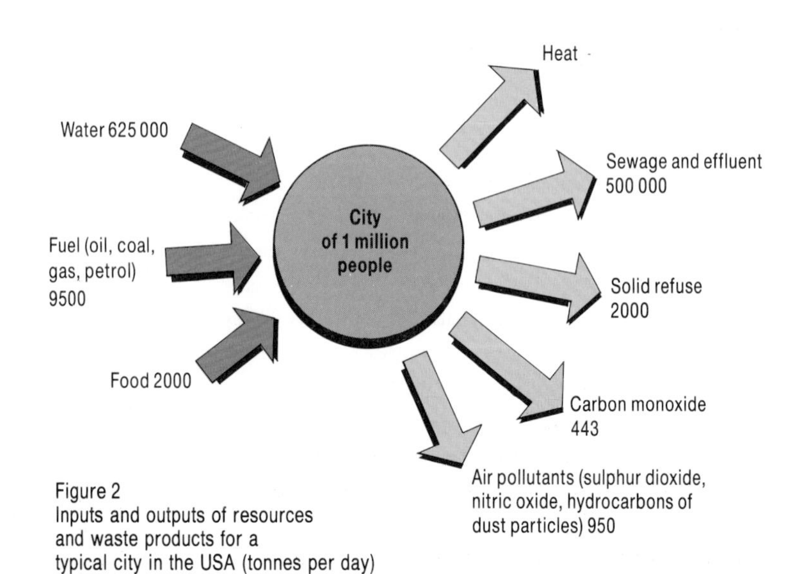

Figure 2
Inputs and outputs of resources and waste products for a typical city in the USA (tonnes per day)

We will look at three important aspects of cities in the developed world using London, New York and Tokyo as examples.

1 The City as a System

Cities are not just collections of buildings, but are more like living things. They are **systems** which require raw materials (inputs) to make them function, as well as waste products or outputs. Figure 2 shows the daily requirements of a typical American city with one million inhabitants, and the waste they produce, in the form of refuse, sewage and the gases which pollute the air. These outputs frequently travel far beyond the cities where they are produced – sewage is dumped at sea, refuse used for distant landfill, and air pollution may travel across entire continents.

2 Importance of the Central Business District

At the heart of all cities is a **central business district (CBD)** where commercial and retail enterprises are concentrated. This is the area with the best **accessibility**, so land prices are high. London's CBD includes the main shopping streets like Oxford Street and Regent Street, the entertainment areas around Leicester Square as well as the financial areas including the Stock Exchange and the Bank of England. Many buildings in the CBD are either several storeys high or are skyscrapers, because the cost of land makes it cheaper to build upwards than outwards.

3 Landuse patterns

Cities often seem chaotic places with little order or pattern. They contain many different land-uses. Shops, offices, transport, housing and open space have to compete for good sites. However, because some land-uses locate in the same areas, it is often possible to detect a pattern. Tokyo, the Japanese capital city, is a complex and crowded metropolis (Figure 3). Around the central area are several sub-centres like Shinjuku which are almost cities in themselves (Figure 4). Even here, the complex land-use pattern may be simplified.

> In the centre of Shinjuku, the largest and most bustling of Tokyo's new business centres, stands the Sumitomo Building, a forty-two-storey, triple-sided, hollow-cored edifice which houses several of Japan's most famous corporations.
>
> Directly to your right is Shinjuku Station used by three million people every day. Twenty railway lines meet here. Altogether they handle 3000 train departures daily.
>
> Looking to the west you have a panoramic view of the Kanto Plain, the industrial heartland of modern Japan, where thirty-five million people live and work. Here are their factories, homes, dormitories, offices and schools, all jam-packed together, competing for space and survival.
>
> Inside Japan, Peter Tasker

Figure 3

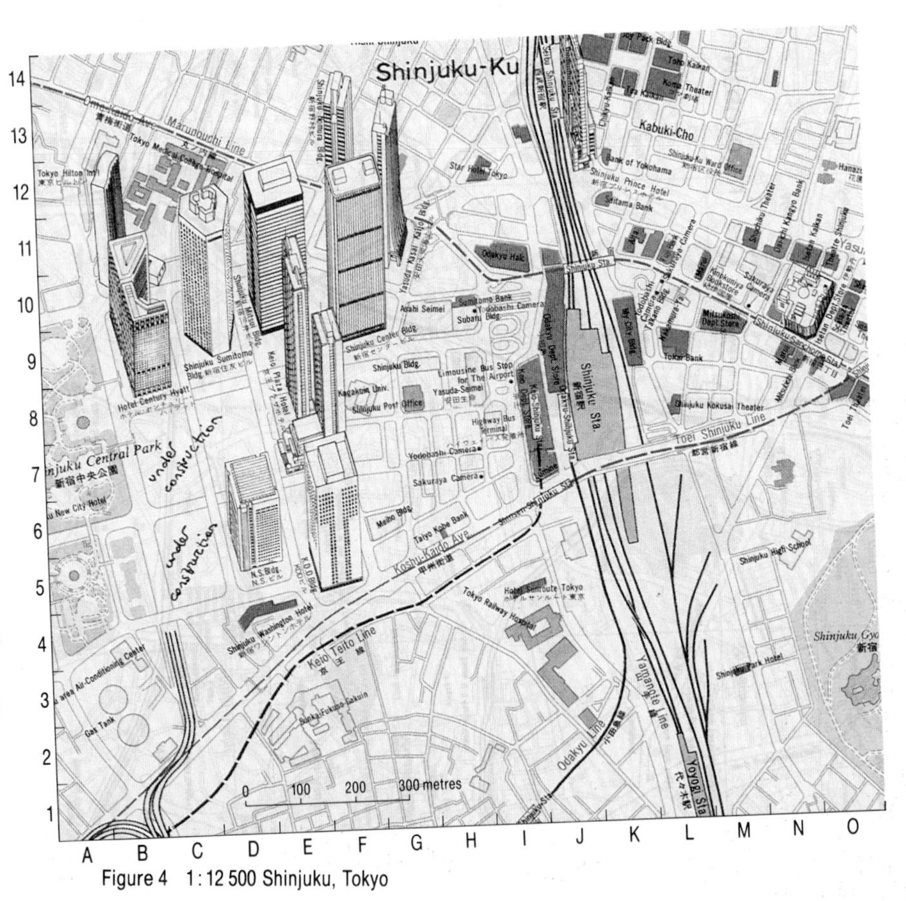

Figure 4 1:12 500 Shinjuku, Tokyo

Living in a world metropolis like New York, Tokyo or London has advantages as well as problems. The best things include large well-stocked shops, plenty of job opportunities, and a variety of cinemas, theatres and clubs. However, the picture is not all positive. Cities are often congested, dirty and unpleasant. They have become dangerous places as crime has increased. For all their problems many people live in cities, and will probably continue to do so for some time to come. However, the city of the future may well look very different to that of today as we will see later in this chapter.

Activities

1 a What is meant by the term 'function' when talking about settlements?

b Working in groups, list the functions of the nearest city to where you live. Give an example of each one, e.g. being a centre for shopping is an important function. An example of this would be a large department store or enclosed shopping complex.

2 Calculate the shortest walking distance between:

a Hotel Sunroute Tokyo (ref J5) and the pond in Shinjuku Central Park (ref B7).

b Bank of Yokohama (ref L12) to the Shinjuku Sumitomo Building (ref D10).

c Draw a simple route map from the station (ref K10) to the central park in Shinjuku.

3 a Make a tracing overlay of Shinjuku using the map in Figure 4.
Draw a full grid using the guidelines shown. For each square decide the most important single land-use shown, from the list below. Then colour each square according to its main land-use. Add a key to your map.

Land-uses:	Office buildings	Open space
	Commercial (shops and hotels)	Services (hospitals, theatres etc)
	Transport (railways and roads)	Residential areas

b Write a description of land-use in Shinjuku. Which are the most important land-uses? Where are they found? Is there any pattern (Does land-use change as you go away from the central area for example, or do land-uses relate to transport routes)?

4 Try the word puzzle (Figure 5). The answers are all places in New York. The name of a world metropolis is spelt out downwards.

Figure 5

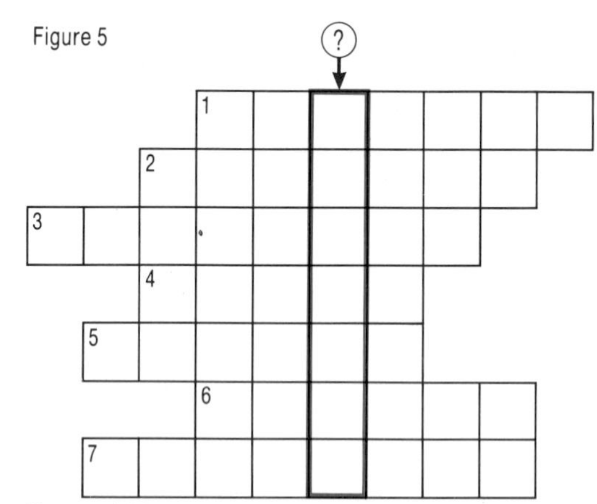

Clues All the answers are found somewhere in New York
1 Large Park
2 Famous statue
3 The home of the musical
4 Famous NY department store
5 A river west of Manhattan Island
6 Residential neighbourhood
7 One of the five boroughs

Project idea
Do some research on one of the cities named in this unit as a world metropolis. Write a report. In it try to provide answers to the following questions:

- Where is it located (site and situation)?
- How large is the city?
- How quickly is it growing (past, present and future)?
- What are its major functions?
- Does it have any problems at present?

7.4 City present .... City future

Many of the world's great urban areas are in a state of crisis. As the number and size of cities has increased in both developed and developing parts of the world, they have come under increasing strain.

As urban growth continues, the problems of cities affect more and more people. Remember, seven out of every ten people in the world live in urban areas. Overcrowding, traffic congestion and delays, high property prices and pollution are familiar to many of these people.

Urban problems do vary from place to place, but as Figures 1 and 2 show, some problems are common to most cities of the world. As a result, the cities of the future will have to be very different from the cities of today.

Figure 1 Crisis in the world's cities

Developed Cities:

- in the late-1970s New York City almost went bankrupt;
- the road system and public transport in London is full to capacity;
- water supply is a problem for cities in very dry areas like Los Angeles and Las Vegas;
- urban ghettos dominate many cities eg Harlem (New York); Watts (Los Angeles) and St Pauls (Bristol). Here as well as in other parts of large developed cities, drug-dealing and violence can be common;
- in 1960 over 40 million US citizens lived in cities which did not meet air safety standards for ozone and CO. Some European cities like Athens and Budapest are as bad.

Developing Cities:

- poverty, unemployment and poor housing can be expected by more than half the population of most developing world cities;
- traffic is so bad in Lagos that you can drive into the city on Mondays, Wednesdays and Fridays only if your car registration begins with an odd number;
- 1000 tons of pollutants falls each day on Greater Bombay;
- in Bogota, Colombia, some 60% of the population lives in slums and shanty towns; and only 200 of India's 3000+ cities have full or partial sewage systems;
- air pollution in Mexico City is six times the accepted limits for humans. Living there and breathing its air is said to be equivalent to smoking 40 cigarettes a day.

Figure 2 Urban problems

There are two main ways in which our cities might change:

1 Planned cities

Planners are now at work trying to solve the problems of the world's cities. They can make a real difference to the quality of the environment in many ways: by devising new road schemes, building new shopping areas, designing business parks and industrial areas, and improving housing. All face the problems of working with an environment that is already under great strain. One alternative is to allow planners to design and build cities, called **new towns**, on **greenfield sites** where little or no settlement exists.

In the last four decades many countries have developed new towns. Whole communities have been constructed in areas outside existing towns and cities. Because these are planned from the start, overcrowding and conflicts between land-uses, e.g. people and cars, people and industry, can be avoided. The United Kingdom has many new towns such as Milton Keynes, Crawley, Stevenage, Cumbernauld and Harlow.

Some countries have built new capital cities on greenfield sites. Canberra and Brasilia, the capitals of Australia and Brazil are the best-known examples. Others are being built in Tanzania and Nigeria.

The site of the new Brazilian capital was chosen in 1952. It was decided to build the city on the deserted central plateau, well away from existing population centres on the east coast. The city was to be a **growth pole** to help redistribute Brazil's population more evenly by attracting population towards the interior. Brasilia, which became the capital in 1960, now covers an area of 8800 km². Its population has increased to over 1.6 million. The unique design of the city (Figure 3) has led to it being designated as one of UNESCO's World Heritage Sites.

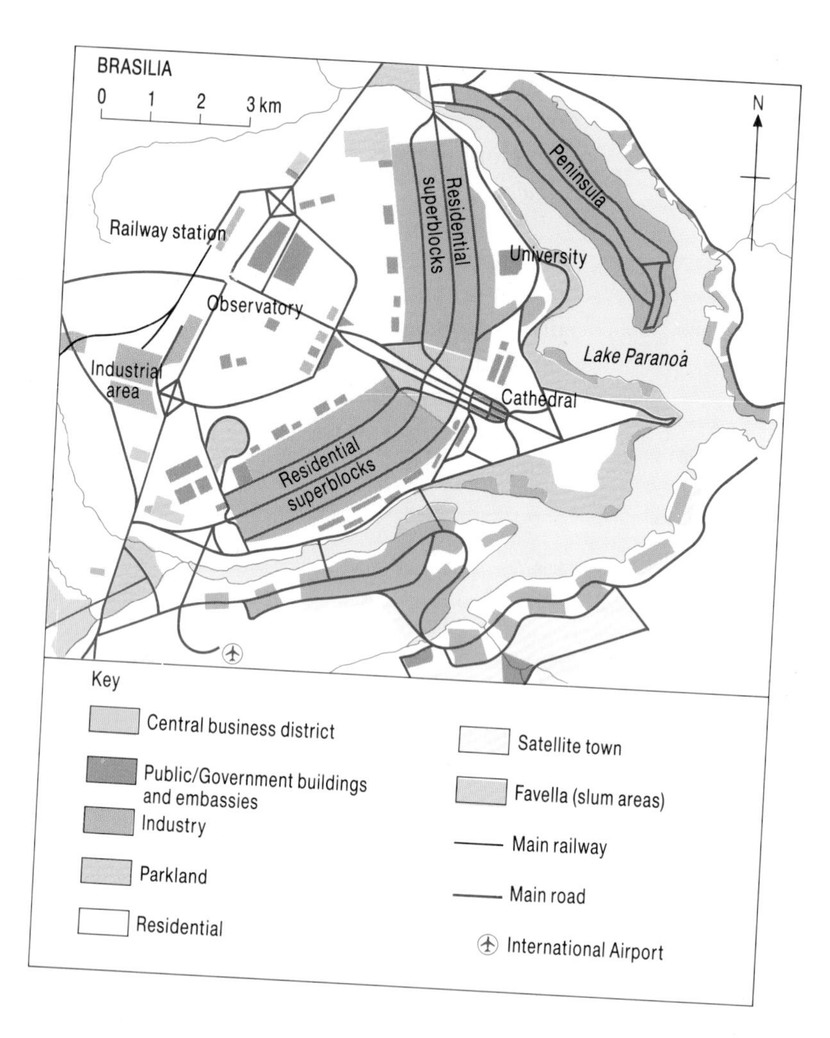

Figure 3 Brasilia

2 Dispersed cities

Changes in technology may mean that in future we no longer need the sort of cities that we have today. There are already some signs of this. In future cities could spread to cover much greater areas, but be made up of a series of small communities which are linked together (Figure 4). There will in these future **dispersed cities** be many different types of environment – ranging from rural landscapes and small villages to science parks, large out-of-town superstores and more conventional city centres.

Many people who are fed up with overcrowded, expensive and polluted cities are voting with their feet, and leaving them in favour of small villages in adjacent areas. In much of Western Europe and the United States of America, small rural communities have grown rapidly. This trend looks set to grow. Increasingly people will no longer need city centres and their amenities: home computers and fax machines are already enabling more people to work from home; shopping and banking can be done by computer or at out-of-town centres; and people's quality of life will be improved by more attractive and cleaner surroundings.

Changes in technology and lifestyles allow us to develop new environments in which to live and work so the city of tomorrow will probably be very different to the city of today.

Figure 4
The dispersed city

Activities

1 Study Figures 1 and 2.

a Make a list of the main problems of cities shown in Figure 1.

b Write a newspaper article (about 300 words) which features an interview with some of the residents of one of the cities named about its problems. The headline provided by your Editor is:

'Concern grows over city crisis ...'

c Identify the main urban problem in each of the photographs shown in Figure 2. Invent a suitable caption for each one.

d Draw a sketch of part of an urban area you are familiar with. The sketch should illustrate a different urban problem, e.g. litter and vandalism, from those shown in Figure 2. Provide a caption for the sketch.

2 Complete the following sentences by choosing the correct ending from those provided:

	Choose from
	....locations with little existing settlement
a Urban problems are	....purpose-built and planned communities
b Growth poles are	....areas which develop and expand rapidly
c New towns are	....found in almost all urban areas
d Greenfield sites are.............	....only found in developed countries
	....places where farming is planned

3 Imagine that an alien has just landed on earth from another planet. Its spacecraft circled the earth and saw vast empty spaces. It lands near one of the cities shown in Figure 2. What sort of reaction do you think the alien would have? Prepare a report to be sent back to the alien's home planet – it can be a serious piece of writing, or a sketch with notes or perhaps a poem or a cartoon strip. You could even script a scene to be acted out in class between the alien and the city's mayor.

4 Brasilia is the new capital of Brazil (Figure 3). Choose one other new capital city (either built or planned) and do some research to find out more about it. Choose from: Canberra (Australia), Abuja (Nigeria), or Dodoma (Tanzania). Try to:

- include a map to show its location compared with the old capital
- discover why a new capital was built or is planned
- find out something about the design and layout of the capital.

Figure 5 Planning Capitalia

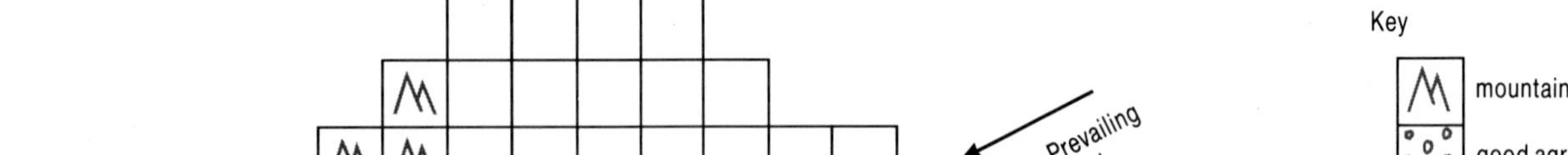

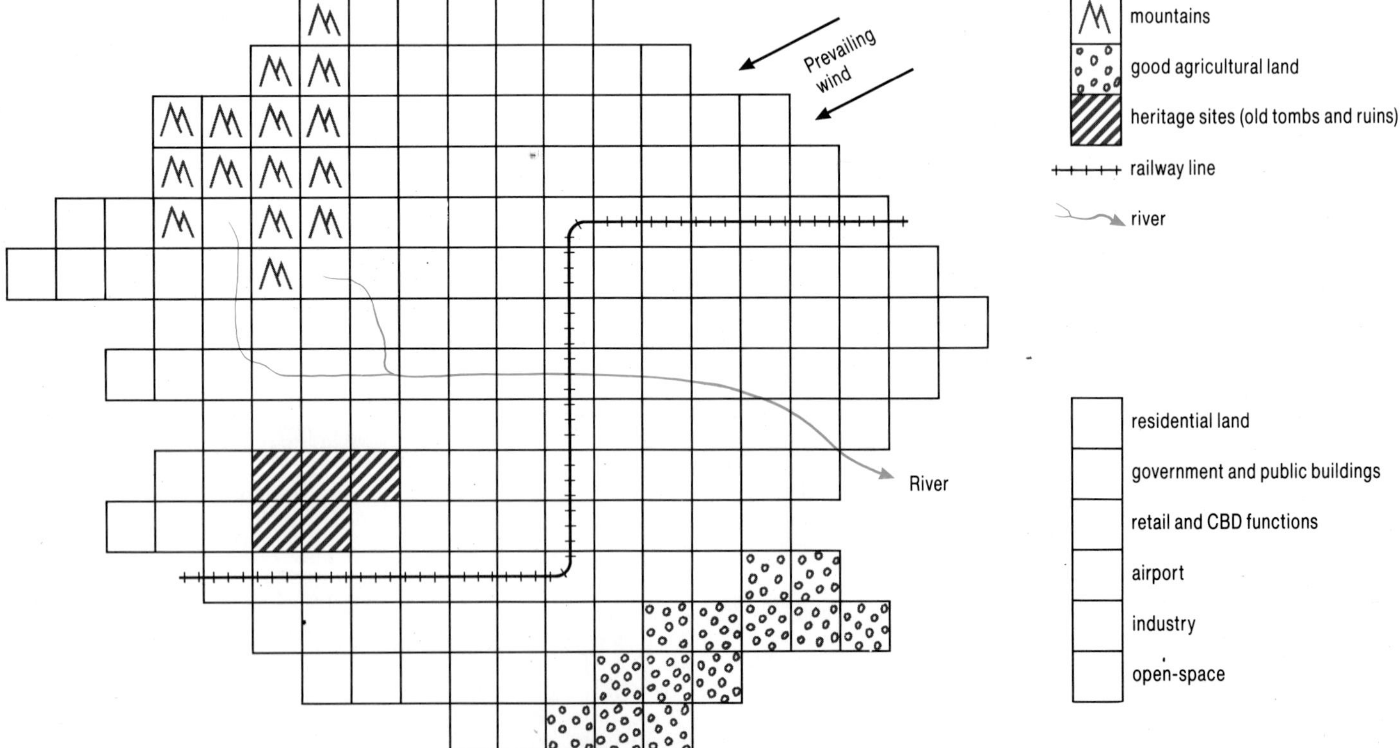

5 Organise a class debate to discuss what you think cities of the future will be like. Here are a few questions to discuss:

- Will they be like the dispersed city shown in Figure 4 or not?
- Would you like to live in such a city?
- What advantages and disadvantages do you think there would be?
- Will cities in the next century be like those of today?

Write an account of what you think the city of tomorrow will be like; you can include diagrams, sketches or plans.

6 You will need a copy of Figure 5 for this activity.
Try to design the land-use layout for **Capitalia**, the new capital city for a small island in the Mediterranean Sea. The area shown in Figure 5 is the site which has been selected by the government. You must design a suitable land-use pattern and layout for the new capital.

Each square represents one unit of area. The new capital must have:

- residential land (12 units)
- government and public buildings (5 units)
- retail and other central area functions (5 units)
- an airport (1 unit)
- industrial land (4 units)
- open-space (2 units)

You may build on any square apart from those designated as mountains. You might like to look at the plan of Brasilia (figure 3) for ideas before you start. Use a different colour for each land-use. Think carefully about each location you choose. For each square check the key to see if there is anything important to note. Complete the key.

Dictionary

accessibility whether a place is easy to get to or not
central business district (CBD) the part of a town or city containing the larger shops, offices and banks
dispersed city one possible form of future city which covers a large area and comprises many small communities linked together
greenfield site a development site with little or no existing settlement
growth pole location which grows and expands rapidly
megacities cities with more than 10 million inhabitants
megalopolis a very large urban area consisting of a network or chain of individual cities linked together, or 'super-city'
new town a purpose-built and planned community, usually constructed on a greenfield site
population density a measure of crowding which relates the population of a place to its area
self-help schemes schemes (usually house construction projects) which are low-cost and use local materials and labour, designed to improve lifestyles, e.g. housing projects
shanty towns settlements constructed from make-shift materials
urbanisation the process by which an increasing proportion of a country's population is coming to live in towns and cities

8 Transport, communications and trade

8.1 Growing networks

People and goods depend on **transport systems** for movement. We take them for granted, until they break down or inconvenience us. Over time, waterways, roads, railways and air routes have gradually developed into the intricate **networks** which exist today. Even in a small area transport networks can be complex (Figure 1).

But why do transport networks develop? This mainly happens for three reasons:

- to open up an area and allow the development of its resources, e.g. the Trans-Siberian railway (Figure 2a) and the highways which run through the northern parts of Canada and Alaska.
- for strategic reasons ... to demonstrate effective settlement, join with other networks and provide access for military personnel and facilities, e.g. the highway through Amazonia in Brazil (Figure 2b); an airport demonstrates a British presence in the Falkland Islands.
- to allow the movement of goods and services (trade) as well as of people between settlements, e.g. the M25 motorway around London (Figure 2c), and the Channel Tunnel etc.

Figure 1

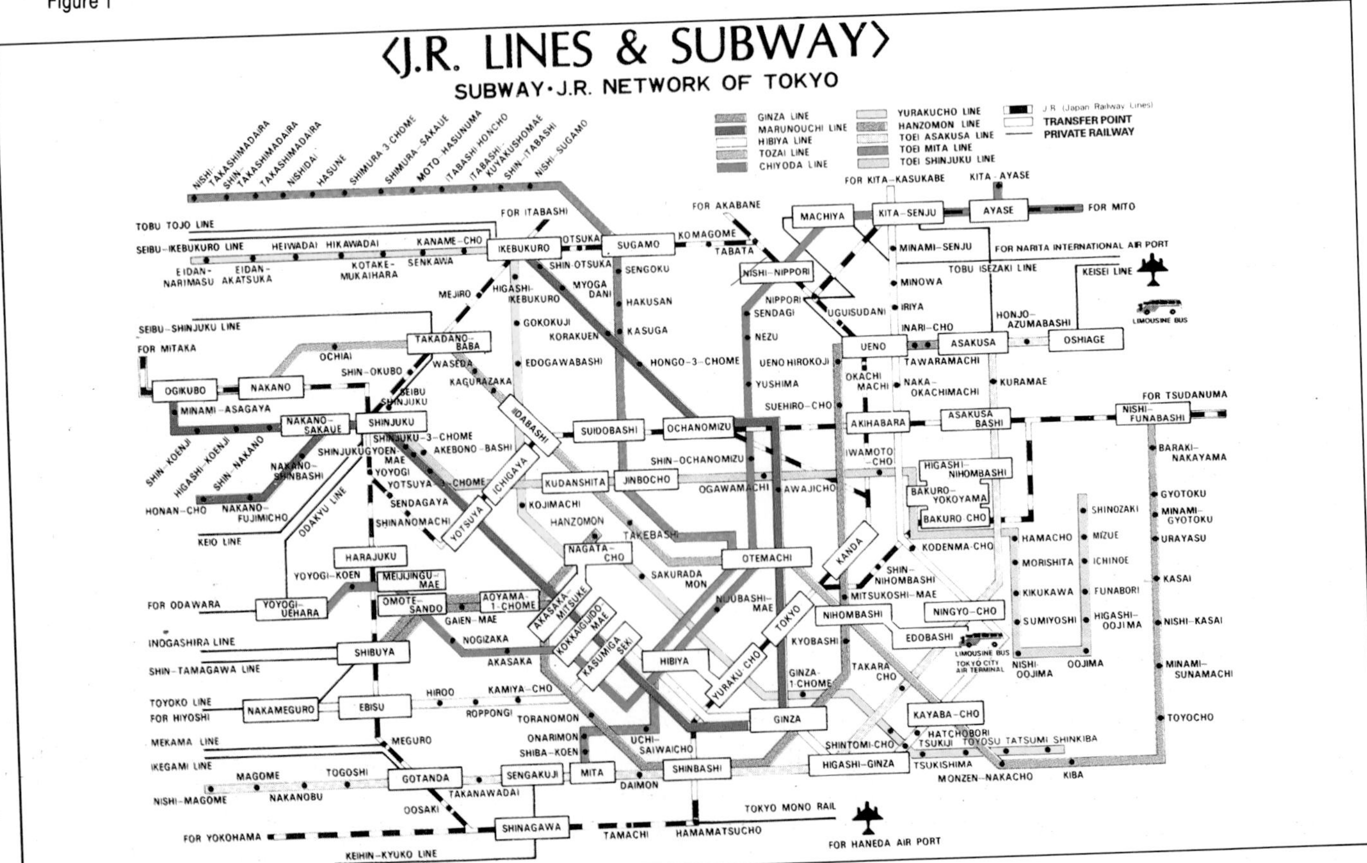

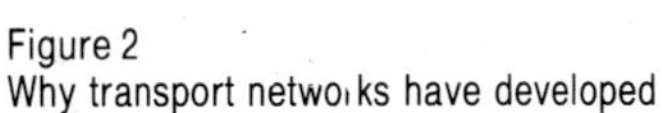

Figure 2
Why transport netwoıks have developed

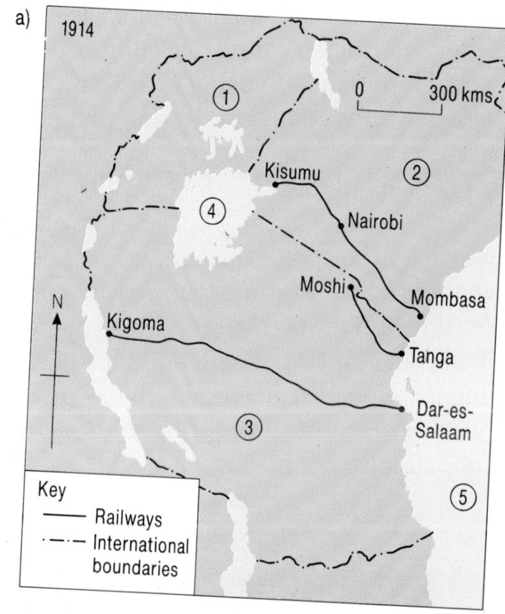

Figure 3 Changing rail network in East Africa

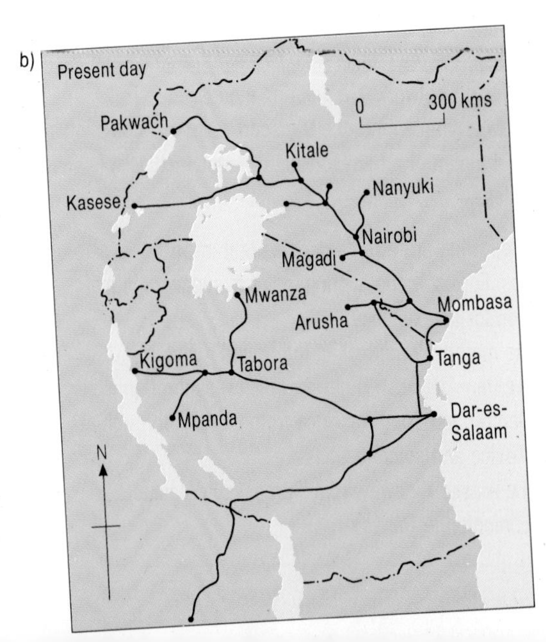

Examining and measuring networks

Today, there are more ways of moving from one place to another than ever before. A choice of **routes** often exists between places, which form a pattern on the landscape or a **network**. By examining maps of transport networks over time, we can see how many routes there are and how the transport network is changing (Figure 3). Keep a watch to see how the transport network changes near where you live: new roads might be built or a railway line closed; there may be plans for an airport to be constructed nearby, or for a river to be straightened and dredged so that it can be used by ships.

As well as comparing networks visually, they can be measured very simply. One of the best measures to show how well-developed the network is the Beta index (β):

$$\text{Beta index} = \frac{\text{Number of links}}{\text{Number of nodes}}$$

A **link** is a route or line which joins two places, and a **node** is a point where two or more links meet or the point at the end of a link. A simple network whose places are not well-connected might have a Beta Index of less than one. However, the higher the Beta Index, the better and more connected the network is (Figure 4). There may be a link between the general level of development in a country or region, and the Beta Index.

Case-Study: Linking the main islands of Japan

Having a well-developed and connected transport network is important for every country. This is especially the case when the country is made up of islands like Japan. Turn to a map of Japan in your atlas and look up the islands and cities mentioned below.

Only since 1988 have all four main islands of Hokkaido, Honshu, Shikoku and Kyushu been connected by road or rail, either in a tunnel or over a bridge (Figure 5). Until then the main link between Honshu and the northern island of Hokkaido was a ferry service and an air link. In 1988 however, the world's longest underwater passage, the 53.85 kilometre long Seikan Tunnel, was completed, carrying a new rail link.

In the same year the Seto Ohashi (or Great Bridge of Seto) was opened, to link Honshu with Shikoku across the Seto Inland Sea. This has reduced the crossing-time from over one hour to just 15 minutes, as well as making it more convenient. Farm produce and fish from Shikoku can now be sold in huge cities like Osaka, Kobe and Kyoto while they are still very fresh, injecting new life into the island's economy. Hotels are also being built to provide accommodation for the tourists who are expected to visit Shikoku now that the journey is easier.

The plan behind these improvements in Japan's transport system is to encourage economic and population growth away from the Tokyo area, which by the end of this century will be a massive urban sprawl. The Japanese hope to ensure that a major city can be reached by road in under three hours, no matter where you happen to live. As well as improvements in the road network, the rail and air transport systems are being developed. The world-famous 'shinkansen' or bullet train already connects most of the principal cities, and travels at an average speed of 220 kms. per hour.

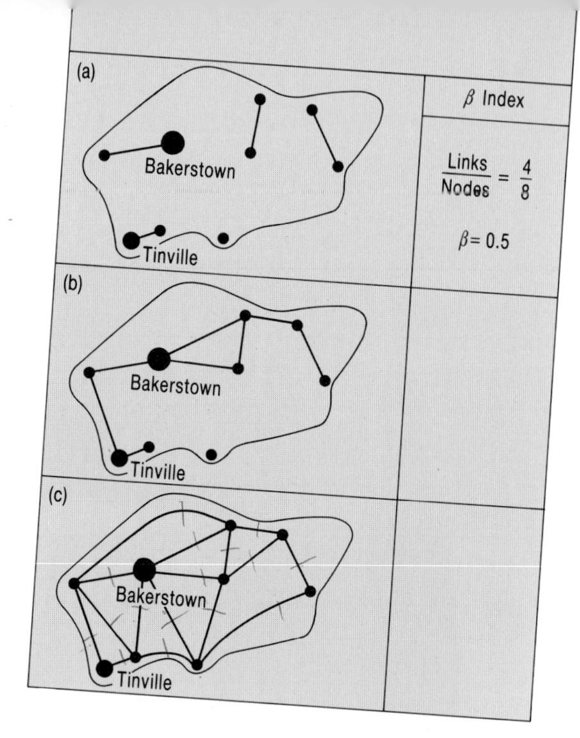

Figure 4 Transport network development on Loaf Island

Figure 5 Linking the islands of Japan

Activities

1 *a* Explain the main difference between: *i* a route and a transport network; *ii* a link and a node.
b Draw a simple map of a transport route you use often.
c Find a map of a transport network and include it in your notes.

2 The following are three examples of transport networks or routes. For each one, work in pairs to suggest the main reason for its existence:
a the motorway network in the United Kingdom
b the Pan-American Highway which runs through North, Central and South America from the USA through Mexico and south to Chile
c the Alaska Highway from Fairbanks in Alaska to Edmonton in Canada

3 Many cities have railway systems (overland as well as underground) which help to move people around. Figure 1 shows the network which operates in Tokyo.
a How many underground lines are there in Tokyo?
b Find a map of London's underground railway system. Describe any similarities between this system and Tokyo's network.
c The main stations on the network are shown in boxes indicating they are also transfer points. Which line would you take to reach the station at Ginza (Tokyo's main shopping area) from:
i Shinjuku; *ii* Ueno; and *iii* Nakameguro?
d How does the Hanzomon line differ from the others shown?
e the JR (Japan Railway) lines are shown on the map. Make a sketch of this network, marking only the principal stations
f Why is no scale shown on the map?

4 You will need an atlas for this activity. Study Figure 3 carefully.
 a Name the three countries marked 1, 2 and 3 on map A.
 b Name the lake (4) and the ocean (5).
 c Describe how the transport network changed between 1914 and the present day.
 d Which two countries shown on Map B are not connected to the railway network?
 e Why do you think that most routes run from east to west?

5 Figure 4 shows how Loaf Island's transport network has developed over time. The βindex for network (a) has been calculated.
 a Work out the Beta Index for (b) and (c).
 b Which network is the best connected and most developed?

6 You will need an atlas for this activity.
 a Why is transport within Japan difficult? (Use your atlas to help find the answer).
 b How is a farmer in Kyushu or Hokkaido going to benefit from the new links which have been built?
 c What type of transport might allow easy access between cities on the different islands?
 d Suggest some of the problems which may have been encountered when building the Seikan Tunnel between Honshu and Hokkaido.
 e Imagine you were a passenger in an an aeroplane, flying from south to north over Japan. *i* List the main links between islands in the order you would see them. *ii* Your plane would also overfly these cities: Osaka, Kumamoto, Tokyo, Sapporo, Hiroshima, Okayama, Sendai and Nagoya. List these in the order you would see them.

8.2 Types of transport

As transport systems grow and more people use them, they become congested. Roads, railways, sea routes and even the airways can only cope with a certain volume of traffic before conditions become dangerous (Figure 1). All transport needs some form of **traffic management** to ensure its efficient running and to help prevent accidents. On the railways for example traffic management is carried out by trackside signalling equipment; the airways are managed by more sophisticated radar apparatus (see Figure 2).

Figure 1

Figure 2

1 Competing modes of transport

There are several types or **modes of transport**, each with particular advantages and disadvantages. Road and rail are the most frequently used, but air transport, the waterways (canals, rivers and oceans) and pipelines all provide alternatives for some types of goods.

It is important to choose the best mode of transport for the particular items which need to be moved. Figure 3 shows some of the advantages and disadvantages of each of the main modes. Much depends on the distance they need to be moved. Speed, directness of route, and efficiency of journey are all key factors. So too is cost. Road transport is the cheapest over short distances but water is more economical for longer journeys.

Figure 3

Mode	Advantages	Disadvantages
Rail		Costs of construction, maintenance and operation are quite high
Road	Direct door-to-door journeys possible	
Air		May be disrupted by weather conditions
Sea		Generally a slow form of transport
Pipeline	Fast and efficient transport is possible on a continuous basis	

2 Environmental impacts of transport development

The different forms of transport have varying effects on the environment – we are all aware of the dangers of car exhausts, for example. All modes of transport require some change of land-use and many also cause pollution. Figure 4 shows how some impacts of a new road can be reduced.

Figure 4 How the impacts of the new roads can be reduced

Transport is provided to improve the flows of goods and people. As a result it may affect the growth of settlements – a new railway line might lead to a town's expansion, while an airport may cause people to desert their homes in a small village under the main flight-path.

The M25 motorway around London illustrates some of the impacts of a major transport scheme (Figure 5). Construction began in 1975, with the final section completed 12 years later. The 188-kilometre motorway was built to take 85 000 vehicles a day, but has become so busy that by 1991 some sections were being used by twice as many vehicles. The landscape near the motorway has changed in many ways – offices and shopping-centres have been constructed, and the demand for commercial land (and its price) have both increased, but so too have pollution levels. Some farms have been split in two, with motorway bridges providing the only link for some farmers to reach their distant fields. Are these impacts good or bad? Are the benefits of new transport schemes like the M25 worth the cost to the environment? And what about the earth's more fragile environments? The former Soviet government built a 3100-kilometre railway, the Baikal-Amur Mainline (BAM) Railway, through Siberia from Lake Baikal to the Pacific. Should this have been allowed? What might its effects be?

Some of the worst environmental effects of transport can be reduced by advances in technology, but despite this, we must consider the likely impacts of transport schemes very carefully in the future.

Figure 5 Impact of M25

Activities

1 a What group of people is responsible for traffic management of: *i* road traffic; *ii* sea traffic; *iii* air traffic?

b Why do you think traffic management is so important?

c Although the cartoon in Figure 1 is light-hearted, and is supposed to amuse, what serious message does it convey?

2 a Make a copy of the table in Figure 3, taking a full page in your notes. Add as much information as you can in each of the blank boxes.

b You may have experienced journeys using each of the first four modes of transport named in Figure 3 (it is unlikely that you have travelled far by pipeline!). List the most recent journey you have made by each mode and compare your list with a partner. Which modes were used for the longer distances? Which do you use most often?

3 The list below shows the origin and destination of items requiring transport. Suggest the most appropriate mode of transport in each case, and give a reason for your choice:

i Oil exported from Kuwait to the United States of America

ii Fresh-cut flowers to a wholesale market in London from Jersey

iii Swedish iron-ore is required by steelworks in Japan

iv This group of people must travel from London to Manchester;

v Soviet oil is to be exported to Hungary

4 Using price, speed, directness of route and any other indicators you consider to be useful:

a Compare cars and airplanes as a means of moving people;

b Compare trains and trucks as a means of moving cargo.

5 Carefully study the different views about the building of the M25 motorway shown in Figure 5.
  a First, make two lists: one of the statements in favour of the M25, and another of those against it. Add at least one statement of your own to each list, then make your mind up about the new road.
  b Next, get together with two or three classmates. Discuss what you think, and combine the best arguments from each of your lists.
  c You have been asked to write a short article for a London evening newspaper to mark the 10th anniversary of the M25's opening. Write and present your article like a real news story. Choose a suitable headline and include at least one illustration (perhaps a map or a cartoon?). The best articles could be displayed in the classroom.
  d Ask your teacher to organise a debate about the M25.

6 You will need to visit the library for this activity. Look in the *Encyclopaedia Britannica* or other reference books to find out about the following transport developments. The geography section might also be worth looking at. Choose **one** development to work on:
- the Trans-Amazonian Highway in Brazil
- the Baikal-Amur Mainline (BAM) Railway
- the Karakoram Highway in Northern Pakistan
- the Channel Tunnel between Britain and France

For your chosen development:
  a describe the transport route briefly (include a map)
  b suggest its likely effects on the environment

8.3 International trade

One key function of transport, in addition to enabling people to get from one place to another, is transporting goods and services. A quick look at the food on the shelves in the local supermarket next time you are shopping, or at the labels in the clothes you are wearing, should reveal just how many things actually come from overseas. We would find it difficult to survive without being able to buy goods from other countries. In order to earn the money to do this, we must sell some British goods and services abroad. This process is called **international trade**.

Trade is a two-way process. When products or services are sold to other countries they are called **exports**, but when they are bought from other countries they are called **imports**. It is important for countries to try and keep their import bill smaller than their export bill. If they can do this their **balance of payments** will be in surplus. It is rather like having to work hard to earn some money before you can go and spend it! Try to discover whether the current UK balance of payments is in surplus or in deficit.

There are three main reasons why there is trade between countries:
- some resources which we need, like iron-ore to make steel, are found in other countries
- many of the food items we like to eat, like oranges and bananas, will not grow in our climate, so must be brought from overseas
- the price and availability of land, labour and raw materials varies from country to country, so some products are easier and cheaper to buy from abroad than to make in the United Kingdom

Trading patterns

The volume (and value) of goods involved in international trade has grown steadily in the last two centuries. In 1988, total world trade amounted to over US$2 840 billion, and involved virtually every

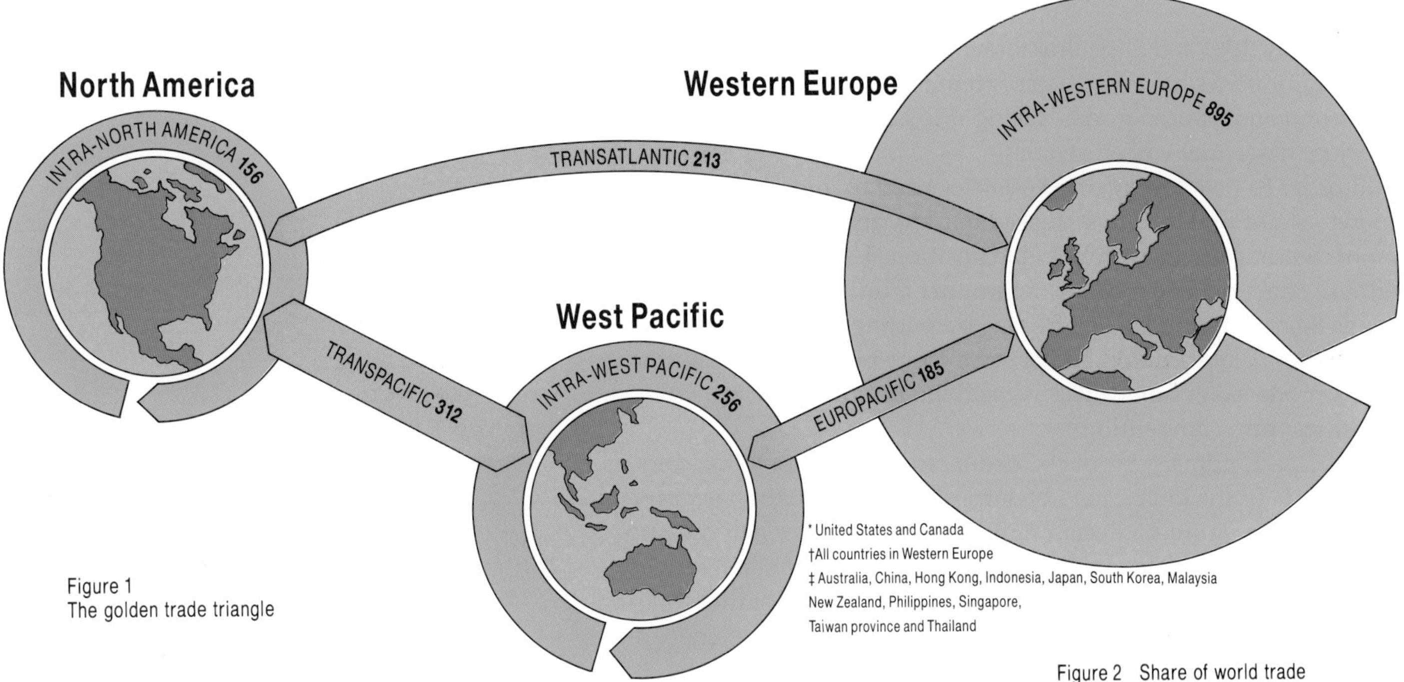

Figure 1
The golden trade triangle

Figure 2 Share of world trade
% breakdown of key merchandise trade flows, 1988

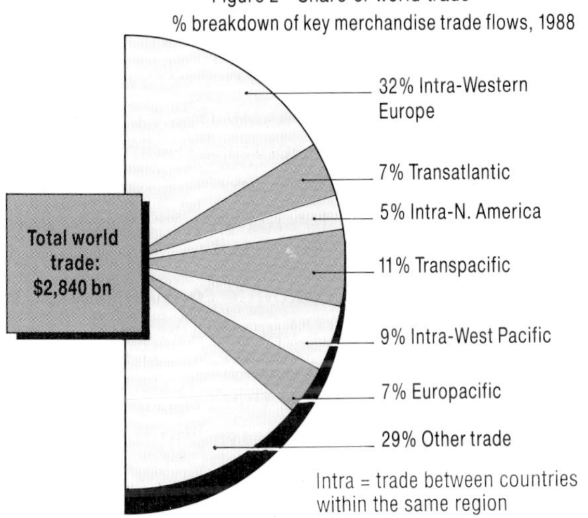

country in the world. It included all sorts of items from ships and shoes to cement and cars, from oil and oranges to stocks and shares. As most nations depend, to a greater or lesser extent, on trade, they are said to be **interdependent**. The pattern of exports and imports is uneven however. Trade in some regions is more significant than elsewhere (Figures 1 and 2). In money terms, Western Europe, Japan and the USA dominate world trade, but many smaller countries depend heavily on buying and selling in the world markets.

The type of trade also varies from place to place. Traded items fall into one of three categories:

- **primary products**: including food and natural resources produced from the sea, land or mined from beneath the ground. Cereals, fruit, fish and iron-ore are all primary products
- **manufactured goods**: items which have been made in factories
- **services**: many nations concentrate on the export of a single type of product. They may have very rich soil and a good climate and so are good for farming. Perhaps they have cheap labour and low-cost **raw materials** and are an ideal location for manufacturing, or there may be special expertise in providing services.

The trade trap

Despite hundreds of years of trade, a huge **wealth-gap** still remains between the rich countries of the 'North' and the poorer countries of the 'South' (as you saw in Chapter 6 Units 1 and 2). This is largely because the present system of international trade operates unfairly.

Many poor countries depend heavily on exporting primary products like bauxite or sugar, copper or tin (see Figure 3). The prices of such **commodities** vary a great deal. During the 1980s many commodity prices fell: between 1980-87 the price of minerals fell by

Figure 3
Developing country economies dependent on primary products

Map of country	Commodity	% export earnings	Country
La Paz	Tin	30%	**Bolivia**
Lima	Copper Lead Zinc	35%	**Peru**
Santiago	Copper	40%	**Chile**
Kingston	Bauxite	50%	**Jamaica**
Kinshasa	Copper Cobalt	50%	**Zaire**
Lusaka	Copper	85%	**Zambia**

6%, food by 10% and agricultural raw materials by 4%. While commodity prices have fluctuated, an index which measures the prices of manufactured goods, taking into account the effects of inflation, has actually risen steadily.

In order to develop, poorer countries need to import manufactured goods, whose prices have increased quickly, and which they cannot afford. So they are in an impossible position. This is made worse because some richer countries use **import controls** to prevent certain goods being imported. They do this by putting taxes or **tariffs** on imports to make them more expensive for people to buy than the goods produced at home. This helps them to protect their own industries from competition.

In the past, primary products amounted to up to three-quarters of the exports of the developing countries. Today's situation is different however (see Figure 4). Recent figures show that over half the non-fuel exports of the developing countries are now manufactured goods. Even if the newly industrialising countries of Southeast Asia (Singapore, Taiwan, Hong Kong and South Korea) are excluded, primary products still only amount to 35% of non-fuel exports.

	1955	1986
Primary products (food, agriculture, raw materials, minerals and ores etc.)	90%	35%
Manufactured goods	10%	65%

only non-fuel exports are represented in these figures

Figure 4 The changing composition of exports from developing countries

Trading blocs

A key feature of trade today is the existence of a number of large **trading blocs**. One important trading bloc is the European Community, others include:

- **Andean pact** – an area with common tariffs which includes Bolivia, Ecuador, Peru and Venezuela
- **West African economic community** – includes Ivory Coast, Mali, Mauritania, Niger and Senegal

These are groups of countries who co-operate on trade matters. The general idea behind these trading blocs is to create a free market between group members. Trading is simplified and sometimes tariffs are abolished.

Much world trade is controlled by large **transnational companies** (TNCs). Examples include Unilever, Rio Tinto Zinc, British American Tobacco (BAT) and Lonrho. Such companies are usually based in rich industrialised countries, but invest their money wherever it will make the greatest profit. We will look at TNCs in Chapter 10. They trade primary products (from their plantations and mines), manufactured goods (from their factories and workshops), and services (from their hotel operations and transport companies).

Black gold: Case-study of oil

Oil is perhaps the most important single commodity traded in the world today. It has a great variety of different uses (see Figure 5). The main oil producing region is the Middle East, while the main consumers are the industrialised nations of Western Europe, North America and Japan. The result is that massive transfers of oil by sea are required (see Figure 6) from the producing areas to the consuming nations. These occur in large, purpose-built vessels known as **VLCCs (very large crude carriers)**.

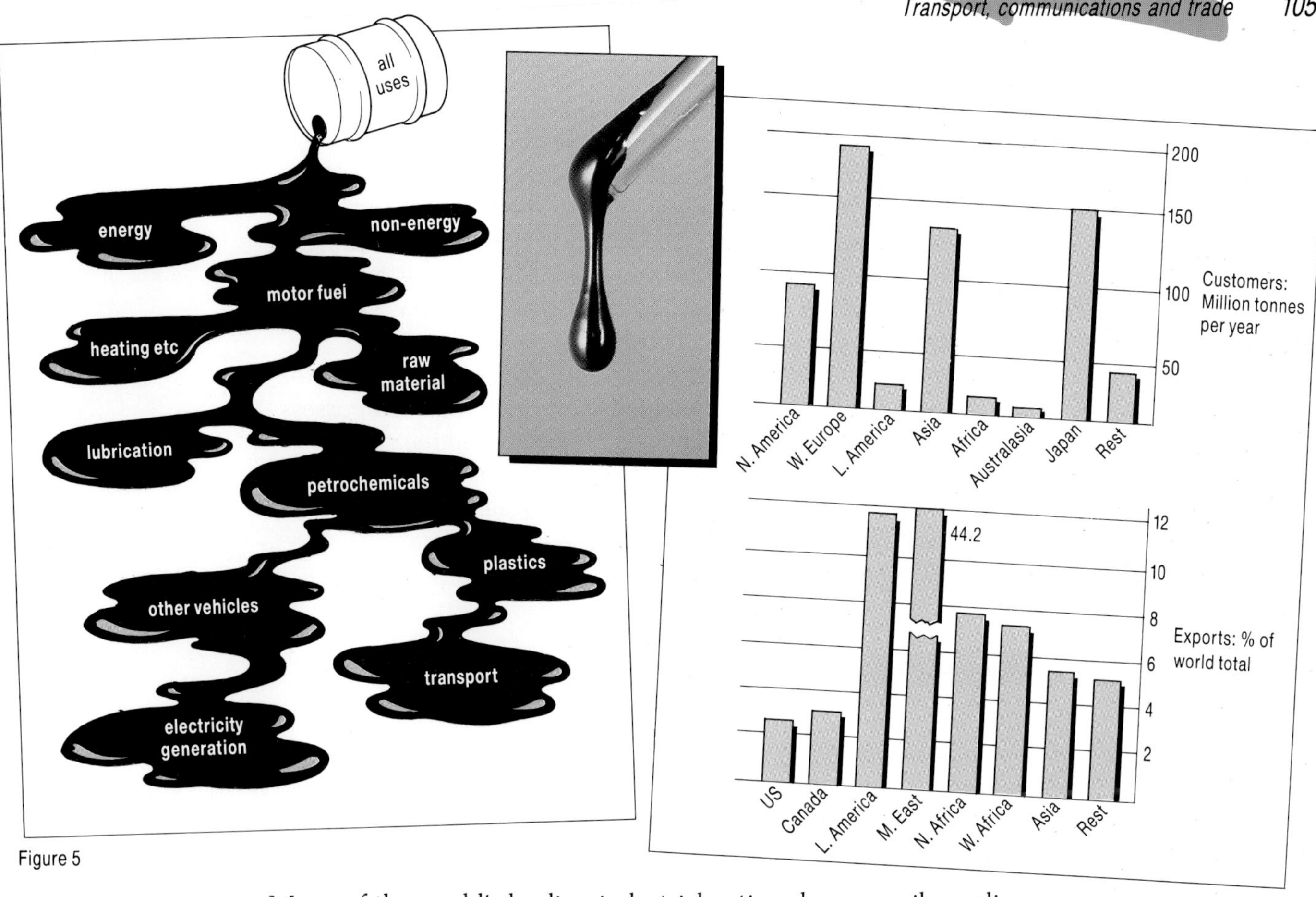

Figure 5

Many of the world's leading industrial nations have no oil supplies of their own, and so are dependent on imports and international trade. Japan, for example, uses 5 million barrels of oil each day to keep her industries operating, and all of this has to be imported! West Germany has to import 97% of the 2.3 million barrels of oil she requires each day.

Figure 6

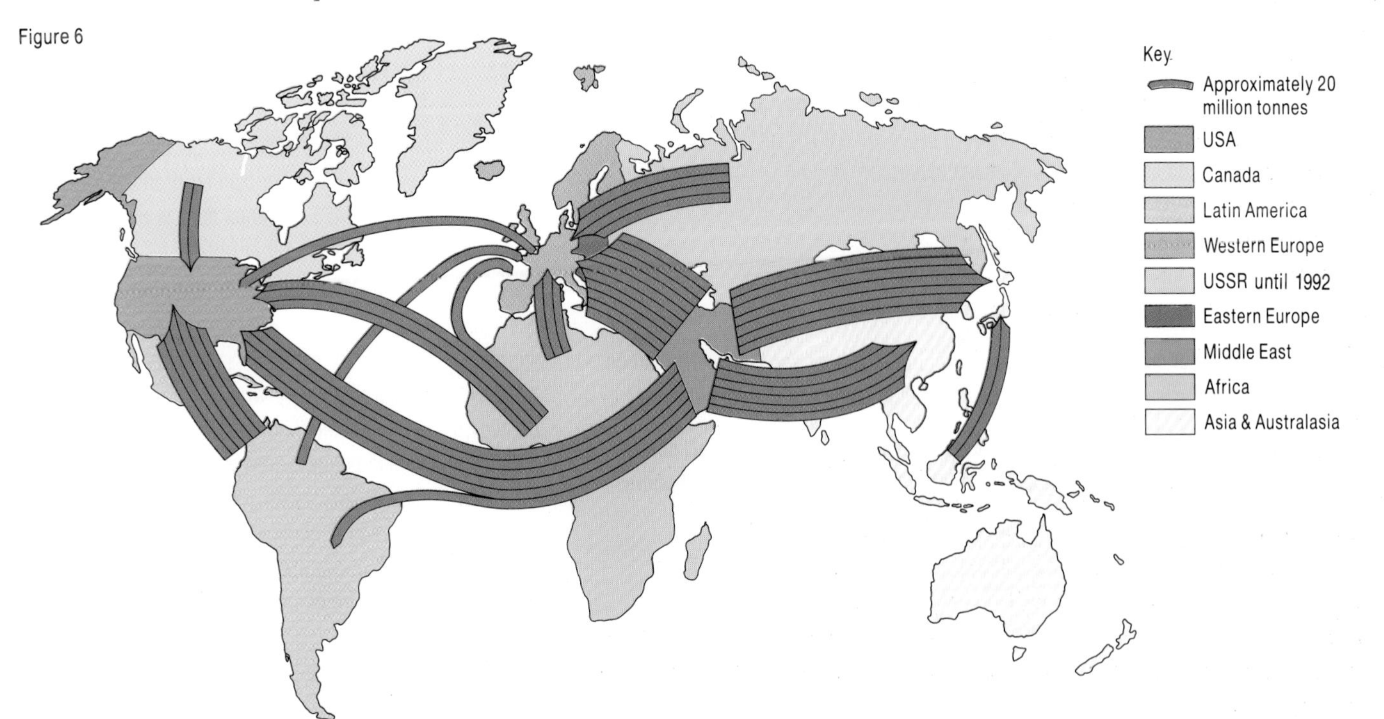

Oil continues to be one of the most important sources of energy in the world. Proven reserves increased from 541 billion barrels in 1969 to 1012 billion barrels in 1989. Most of these reserves (66%) are in the Middle East. This overwhelming concentration of such an important resource in a small part of the world poses certain dangers. The Middle East is a politically unstable area as Iraq's invasion of Kuwait in 1990 and the war which followed clearly demonstrated, so uninterrupted supplies cannot be guaranteed.

The international trading of oil is crucial to the development of the world. Because it is such a key commodity, the countries that possess oil reserves also have great power. Many have formed the Organisation of Oil Producing and Exporting Countries (**OPEC**). There are, however, risks attached to the large-scale movements of oil by sea. Spillages and accidents occur from time to time, threatening the environment (see Chapter 12.4).

Activities

1 *a* Explain the following in your own words:
i Why does international trade take place?
ii What is the difference between imports and exports?
b Find out the main exports of these countries: Brazil; United Kingdom; Zambia; China, Japan; India; and the USA. (Hint: many atlases contain this information).

2 *a* Examine 10 items of food from the kitchen at home. Choose a mixture of tins, packets, fruit and vegetables, and meat and dairy products. Find out which of the 10 items were imported, and where they came from. List this information, then draw a map showing the countries of origin.
b Compare your list and map with others in the class. What did you learn about where our food comes from?

3 Figure 1 shows some of the world's most important trade flows. Study the diagram carefully.
a Which of the six trade flows shown is the most important? Why do you think that this might be so?
b Calculate the total value of the six flows shown.
c What percentage of total world trade (US $2840 billion) does your answer in *b* represent?

4 The following is a list of primary products, manufactured goods or services which can be traded. Draw up a table with three columns placing each item in the correct column:

ships; banking fees; timber; shoes; overseas hotel bill; salmon; holiday hire car; coal; fish fingers; wheat; sightseeing tour of Venice; computer printer; zinc ore; stocks and shares; steel girders

5 Figure 4 shows the composition of exports from developing countries between 1955 and 1986.
a Draw two divided bars (each 10 cms long) to show this information.
b Describe the main changes.
c How do you think these changes might be related to the way that the prices of commodities and manufactured goods have changed?

6 The items which were exported from Cuba and Denmark are shown below:

Cuba	%	Denmark	%
Sugar	77	Industrial goods	72
Mining	6	Agricultural products	16
Tobacco	2	Canned meat & milk	3
Seafoods	2	Other goods	9
Agricultural goods	4		
Other goods	9		

a Show these figures as pie-charts.
b Study these figures carefully, then decide whether each of the statements below is *true* or *false*:
i Cuba's exports are mainly primary products;
ii Denmark's trade is dominated by a single item;
iii Manufactured goods are important exports for Cuba;
iv Both countries are over-dependent on one category of export;
v The Commodity Price Index will affect Denmark more than Cuba.

7 You will need a blank world outline map and an atlas for this activity. Read the section on trading blocs again. On your map plot the three trading blocs mentioned. Use a different colour for each. Remember to include a key.

8 Figure 6 contains a map showing the world's main oil producers.

a Draw a pie chart to show the relative importance of Africa; North America; Latin America; Eurasia (the former USSR and Eastern Europe); the Middle East; Western Europe; Asia and Australasia.

b Why do you think that Japan and Western Europe are larger oil consumers than Latin America and Africa?

9 Oil movements are very significant in world trade. Figure 6 shows 14 of the major flows. For example some 140 million tonnes of oil are exported from the Middle East to Japan. Copy and complete the table below, listing all the flows in decreasing order of size:

	From	To	Size (million tonnes)
1.			
2.			
3.			
4.			
5.			
6.			

8.4 Information flows

Methods of communication are changing. We have seen how improvements in transport technology have allowed goods to be moved further and more quickly. However, **information** also needs to be moved around.

For the last century, the postal service has served this function. The first postal system in the United Kingdom (1840) allowed letters posted in one location to be delivered in another. Sometimes, the delivery would take many days. Today, information can be 'transported' between locations virtually instantaneously. The postal system has been replaced by a new generation of communications equipment: the telephone, television, satellite and facsimile or 'fax' machine (see Figure 1).

Figure 1 Modern communications

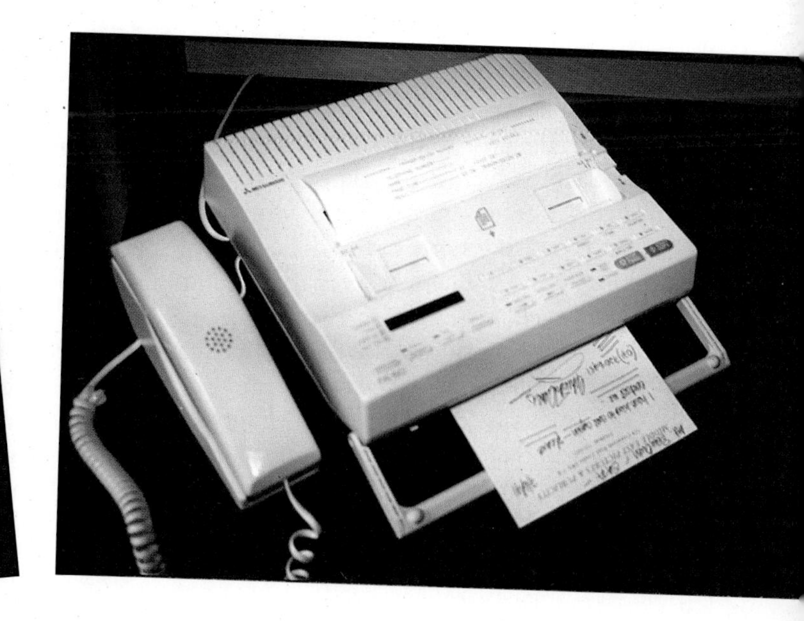

Communicating information is so much a part of our lives today that we take it for granted. Information flows are important for business people as well as in our leisure activities. Most households have a telephone, and depend on it quite heavily. Televisions too have rapidly become established features in most households. In addition we rely on satellites to provide data for our daily weather forecasts and to quickly relay information about events that are occurring on the other side of the world.

The growth in the use of the telephone is a good example of how information flows have developed. The telephone was developed just over a century ago in 1876. Most households in the developed world now have at least one telephone, as do an increasing number of cars (Figure 2). Telephone traffic is growing at around 20% each year.

Figure 2

Telephones are not just used over short distances (see Figure 3). The volume of international telephone traffic increased from 5 billion minutes to over 30 billion minutes between 1980 and 1990. It is predicted that by the year 2000, the total number of minutes involved in international calls will exceed 150 billion.

While much of the international traffic is accounted for by people talking to one another, a growing proportion is due to the growth in the use of facsimile or 'fax' machines. These allow documents to be transmitted via the telephone line. The 'fax' machine codes the document into electronic pulses which pass down the telephone line. At the other end another fax machine decodes the pulses and the document appears from the machine in its original form.

Transmission by 'fax' is quick and almost instantaneous. Text and pictures and plans can all be transmitted. Once the 'fax' machine has been bought, the cost to the sender is just the cost of the phone call. There are many advantages: communication is quick and relatively cheap; 'faxes' can be sent across the globe even when the office there is shut; and there are none of the difficulties of speaking to someone on a poor telephone line who perhaps does not understand spoken English very well.

All around the world the use of the 'fax' machine is growing. Over 50% of all the telephone traffic across the Pacific Ocean is accounted for by 'fax' transmissions. Here in the United Kingdom a recent survey showed that 600 000 firms are using 'fax' machines, and that a massive 38 million pages are transmitted by 'fax' and are whizzing their way around the country every day!

International telephone traffic in millions of minutes – 1988	Outgoing	Incoming
Australia	415	331
Canada	358	250
France	1570	1690
Italy	785	1075
Japan	529	553
Mexico	211	504
Netherlands	706	577
Singapore	152	126
S.Korea	131	230
Switzerland	1014	851
UK	1729	1814
USA	5325	3155
W.Germany	2479	2080

Canada figures do not include traffic to and from the USA and Mexico   Financial Times 8.6.90

Figure 3

Satellites too have become increasingly useful. They collect and transmit data on the weather; help scan the earth's surface for resources; monitor military movements; transmit radio and television signals and perform a variety of other useful tasks.

One of the most useful satellites is Meteosat (Figure 4), which, as its name suggests, is used to collect and transmit data on the weather from land stations, ocean buoys, ships, aircraft and weather balloons.

Meteosat is positioned in **geostationary** orbit 36 000 kilometres above the equator over Ghana. This gives it an excellent view over the whole of Europe and Africa. Every 30 minutes it sends a picture to earth, to be decoded. Data is provided about cloud cover, height and type; sea and cloud temperatures; wind direction and speed; and the distribution of water vapour in the upper atmosphere. Meteosat has also been used to map vegetation and soil as well as climatic hazards such as hurricanes.

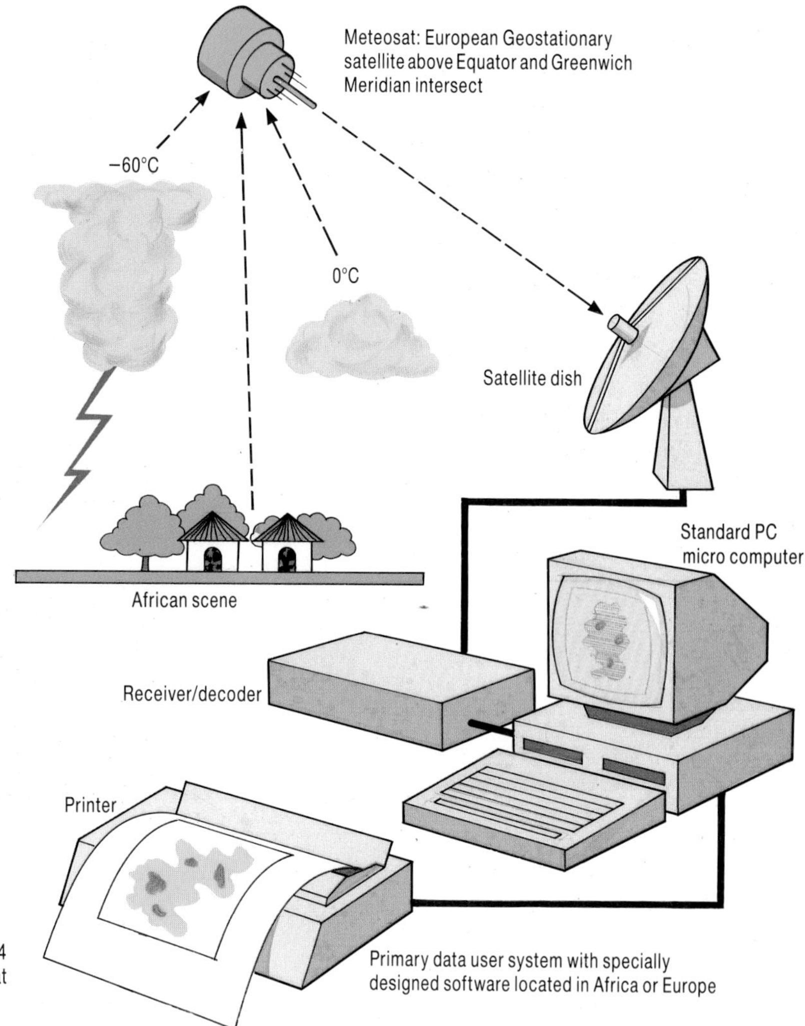

Figure 4
How data is processed from Meteosat

Activities

1 Rewrite the following sentences matching the 'heads' and 'tails':

Head	Tail
a Fax machines ...	... allow people to talk to one another;
b Satellites are used to ...	... carries moving pictures as well as data;
c Telephones ...	... transmit documents around the world;
d Television ...	... record and relay weather data;

2 *a* Keep a log to see how many times your telephone is used at home during a one-week period. You will need your family's co-operation for this. You might also try to measure the length of time you spend on each call. In the log record which calls are local. At the end of the week work out the percentage of local calls.

b Do a survey in your class to see what use is made of the 'fax' by parents at work. Try to find out how often faxes are sent and how many are received on average per week. What benefits has the fax brought to their work, and what costs are involved?

3 Use the data shown in Figure 3 to answer these questions.

a *i* Which country of those shown has the greatest volume of outgoing telephone traffic?

ii Which country had the highest overall volume of telephone traffic?

b Can you suggest any reasons why this is the case?

c Is all this traffic made up of people talking to one another?

4 You will need a blank world outline map for this activity. For each of the 13 countries in Figure 3, calculate the total amount of international telephone traffic by adding together the figures for outgoing and incoming calls. Now plot this information on your blank world map by using proportional bars. Use a suitable scale: 1 cm = 1 000 million minutes. Divide each bar into two to show the proportion of outgoing and incoming calls.

5 Figure 5 shows the last posting dates for airmail post being sent abroad before Christmas for 15 countries.

a Copy the table. Using an atlas complete Column 3 by calculating the distance between the UK and each of the countries named (if the country is large use the capital city to measure from).

b Plot a scattergraph to see if there is a correlation between the distance items have to travel (x-axis) and the number of days before Christmas items have to be posted (y-axis).

c Look at your scattergraph. Is it always true that items of mail travelling furthest have to be posted earliest? Explain.

Country	① Last posting date (for airmail)	② Number of days before Christmas	③ Distance from the UK
Australia	7 December	18	
Bhutan	1 December	24	
Canada	7 December	18	
Egypt	7 December	18	
France	14 December	11	
Gambia	7 December	18	
Greece	7 December	18	
Hungary	14 December	11	
Italy	10 December	15	
Japan	7 December	18	
Nicaragua	14 December	11	
Norway	14 December	11	
Saudi Arabia	10 December	15	
Solomon Islands	1 December	24	
USA	7 December	18	

Figure 5

Dictionary

balance of payments an account which shows the total of a country's imports and its exports

barrel (of oil) the standard unit which measures oil production. One barrel of oil is equivalent to 35 imperial gallons (42 US gallons)

commodities primary products traded on world markets

exports goods or services which are sold and sent out to another country

geostationary a satellite positioned above a point on the earth's surface and rotating at the same speed as the earth is said to be geostationary as it appears to be motionless in the sky above that point

import controls restrictions on imports of goods. These can take the form of taxes (or tariffs) to make imports more expensive, or outright bans

imports goods or services which are bought from overseas

interdependent nations of the world rely heavily on each other because trade flows are so complex

international trade the buying and selling of goods and services between nations

networks patterns made in the landscape by a number of routes which are joined together

node the point at the end of a link, or where two or more links meet

primary products food produced from the land or sea, or natural resources mined from beneath the ground

tariffs duties or taxes which are commonly applied to imports

transport systems networks of routes and the vehicles which operate them

VLCCs an abbreviation for Very Large Crude Carriers. These are large purpose-built ships for transporting huge quantities of oil

wealth-gap the difference in wealth between rich and poor countries

9 Farming

9.1 Feeding the world

Many people on this planet share one major problem – they have not got enough to eat (Figure 1). Yet more people are involved in food production than in any other activity. The four people featured in Figure 2 are all farmers. Apart from that one fact, there are few similarities between them. They have different homes, grow different crops, and have different opportunities, problems and pests to cope with. However, in their own way, each of these four people is a key part of the world food production process that keeps most of the planet's five billion people alive.

Figure 1

Figure 2

In recent decades, the world's farmers have generally maintained a steady increase in food production (Figure 3). Each year, an extra 90 million people must be fed, and this target has usually been achieved. The figures show that the increase in food production (2.7% per annum) has kept ahead of the increase in population (1.7% per annum). This should mean that there is enough food for everybody in the world. As we have already seen though, in Chapter 6, some people in the world do not have enough to eat and are starving. The map in Figure 4 shows every country's food supply in terms of calories. There are important differences from continent to continent.

	1965	1975	1985
cereals	1 005 926	1 372 727	1 847 436
root crops	489 283	553 230	587 336
meat, milk, fish	501 748	606 277	748 013
oil crops, pulses, fruit, vegetables	514 161	653 611	821 659

Figure 3 World production ('000 metric tonnes) of selected food crops

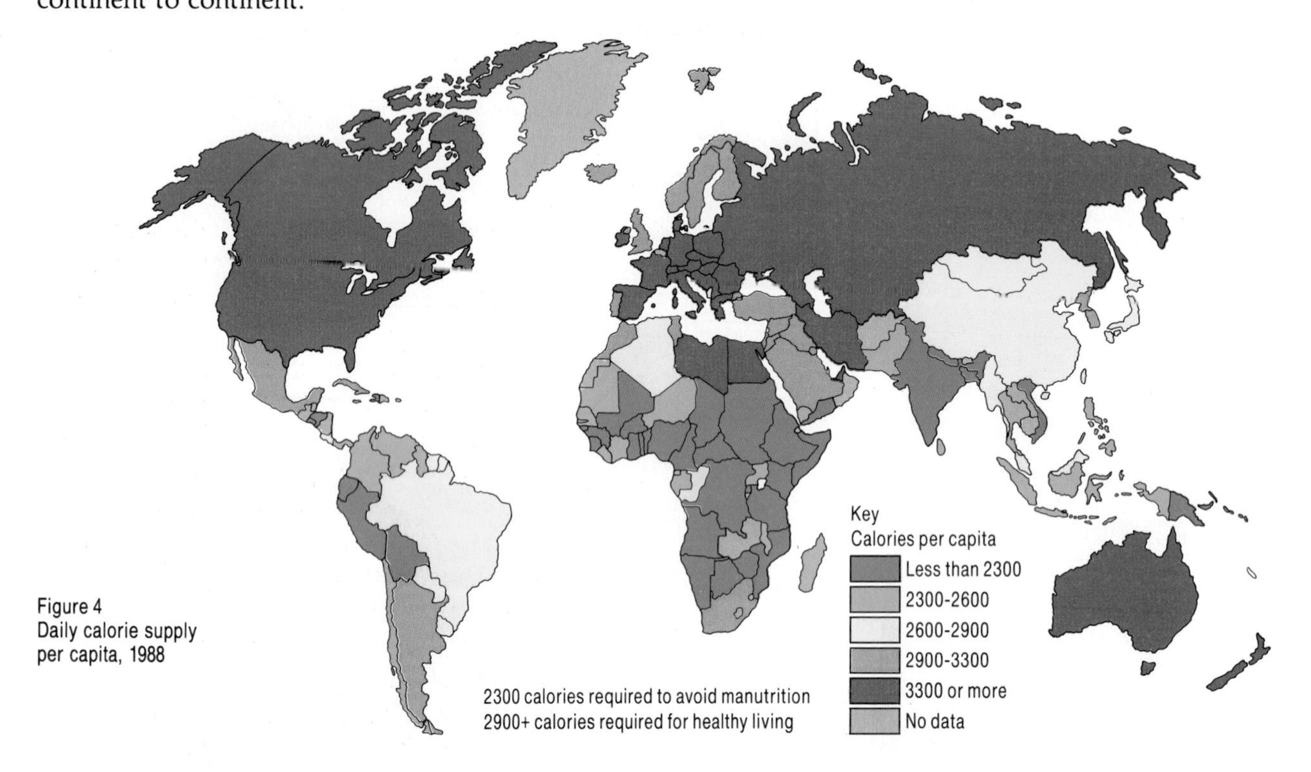

Figure 4
Daily calorie supply per capita, 1988

The outlook for the future is not hopeful. In some countries, food production has fallen behind population growth. Between 1979-87 there was a decline in cereal production per person in 51 of the 95 developing countries. To get over this problem, more food must be bought from other countries: food imports by developing countries more than trebled from 20 to 70 million tonnes between 1970-1984. They could exceed 110 million tonnes by the year 2000. Much of these imports will come from the grain surpluses usually produced by the farmers of North America. Continued increases in grain output, however, are not guaranteed. In 1988, world cereal output per person was the lowest since 1977 due to a serious drought. They may in the future suffer further as a result of the greenhouse effect (Chapter 3.4).

The growth in world food production since 1945 has been achieved by increased **productivity** rather than by increasing the amount of land used for agriculture. This was the result of:

- increasing the use of chemical **fertilisers** (up by nine times in the last 35 years)
- developing and using new varieties of seed which produce **higher yielding varieties** (HYV) and are more **disease-resistant**
- extending the use of **irrigation** which allows farming in places which were previously too dry. There are today almost 271 million hectares of irrigated land around the world
- using more chemical **pesticides**, to control the damage done to crops by insects and other forms of pests and disease.

The map in Figure 4 shows that only a limited amount of food is available in some countries. It is estimated that by the year 2000, some 36 countries, with a combined population of 486 million, will be unable to feed themselves from their own lands. As developing countries' debts increase they are less able to afford food imports, so the situation is worsening.

	% of world population	% share of world food supplies
Europe	25	48
USA and Canada	8	20
Far East	40	14
South America	10	8
Africa	10	4

Figure 6

Figure 5
Exotic fruits and their countries of origin

Fruit	Countries of origin
Carambola (star fruit)	Brazil Israel
Papaya (paw paw)	Brazil West Indies South America
Limes	Brazil West Indies
Lychees	South Africa Madagascar Far East
Guavas	Brazil West Indies
Mangoes	Israel Brazil Mexico South Africa Kenya West Indies
Pineapples	Ivory Coast Kenya South Africa

Although only a small proportion of the earth's land area is suitable for agriculture, much of that which is being used could be used more effectively to produce more food. Developing countries alone could produce enough to feed 33 billion people – more than six times the current world total! To do this though, every square metre of usable land would have to be farmed, huge amounts of fertiliser and pesticides would be required, and meat production (requiring a lot of land) would need to be eliminated.

One reason why so many people in the world today lack a basic supply of food is that instead of growing food for themselves and their families, they produce **cash crops** such as tea, coffee, rubber and exotic fruits, which are exported for people overseas to buy. Although not all of us eat exotic fruits like guavas or pineapples, many varieties can now be found on the shelves of our supermarkets (Figure 5). Producing crops for export instead of basic food crops for consumption is one reason why many people are starving. They are locked into a kind of 'global food machine', the output of which is highly **specialised**, and which is mainly controlled by the rich industrialised countries of the 'North'.

Activities

1 a World food production is something most of us do not know enough about. Carefully read the statements below. The answers are not in the text. Which statements **do you think** are true ?

i enough food is produced to feed the world's entire population;

ii more than half the world's population live in countries where agriculture provides more than one-third of the national income;

iii about half the world's cereal crops are fed to animals;

iv two-thirds of the world's population live in countries where they on average have under 3 000 calories a day to sustain them;

v farmland in southeast Asia is capable of producing higher grain yields than in most developing countries;

vi millions of pounds are paid by governments to produce food that cannot be sold and which ends up being stored or destroyed.

b Now get into groups of 3 or 4, and compare your answers to *a* with others in your group. Discuss your answers and try to agree on a list of true statements between you. When you have an agreed list your teacher will tell you which statements are true.

c Now imagine that a visitor from another planet were to be given the list of statements in *a* above, and to see some of the people who are dying of starvation (like those in Figure 1). What message might be sent home describing food production on earth?

2 You should work in small groups for this activity.

a Study the photographs in Figure 2. Suggest a location where each photograph could have been taken.

b Do you think the farmer in each photograph is producing food for sale or for consumption by his/her family?

3 *a* Copy the axes below, and draw line graphs to show the trend in the production of selected food crops between 1965 and 1985. Use the data in Figure 3 for this exercise.

b In your own words briefly describe the trends shown.

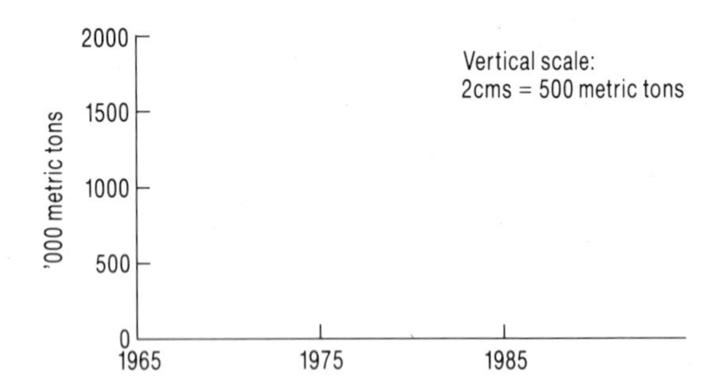

4 The map (Figure 4) shows the daily calorie supply per head in most countries of the world.

a Use an atlas to name:

- 3 countries where calorie levels are totally inadequate (<2300);
- 3 countries where calorie levels are inadequate (2300-2600);
- 3 countries where calorie levels are less than desirable (2600-2900);
- 3 countries where calorie levels are adequate (2900-3300);
- 3 countries where calorie levels are too high (>3300).

b In which continent is the supply of calories likely to cause most concern to the world community?

c Study the map. Which countries have calorie levels which surprise you, either because you thought they would be higher or lower?

d Use a science text to find out more about calories. Why are people trying to lose weight often concerned about their calorie intake?

5 You will need two blank world outline maps for this activity, and an atlas.

a The exotic fruits shown in Figure 5 are becoming common on our supermarket shelves. Mark the countries of origin on one of the outline world maps.

b Make a rough estimate for each fruit of the distance it has had to be brought to reach your supermarket.

c Organise a survey of imported fruit and vegetables in your local supermarket. Choose 10 different imported vegetables and 10 fruits. Check the information on the shelves or the packaging to find the country of origin for each. Mark these locations on the second world map. Use small sketches or a key to indicate which items come from which locations.

d What have you learnt about the production of food as a result of the activities in this question?

6 Many modern techniques are being used by farmers in different parts of the world.

a What are chemical fertilisers being used for?

b How can the land be fertilised without them?

c What do you personally feel about farmers using chemicals to help them produce the food we eat? What dangers does it raise?

7 *a* In your own words explain what Figure 6 shows about the way in which the world's food resources and population are distributed.

b Suggest two ways in which this situation could be improved.

9.2 World farming systems

With over two billion people involved in agricultural production (almost 40% of the global population), it is not surprising that there are many different types of farming (see the map and photographs in Figure 1).

Figure 1
World farming types

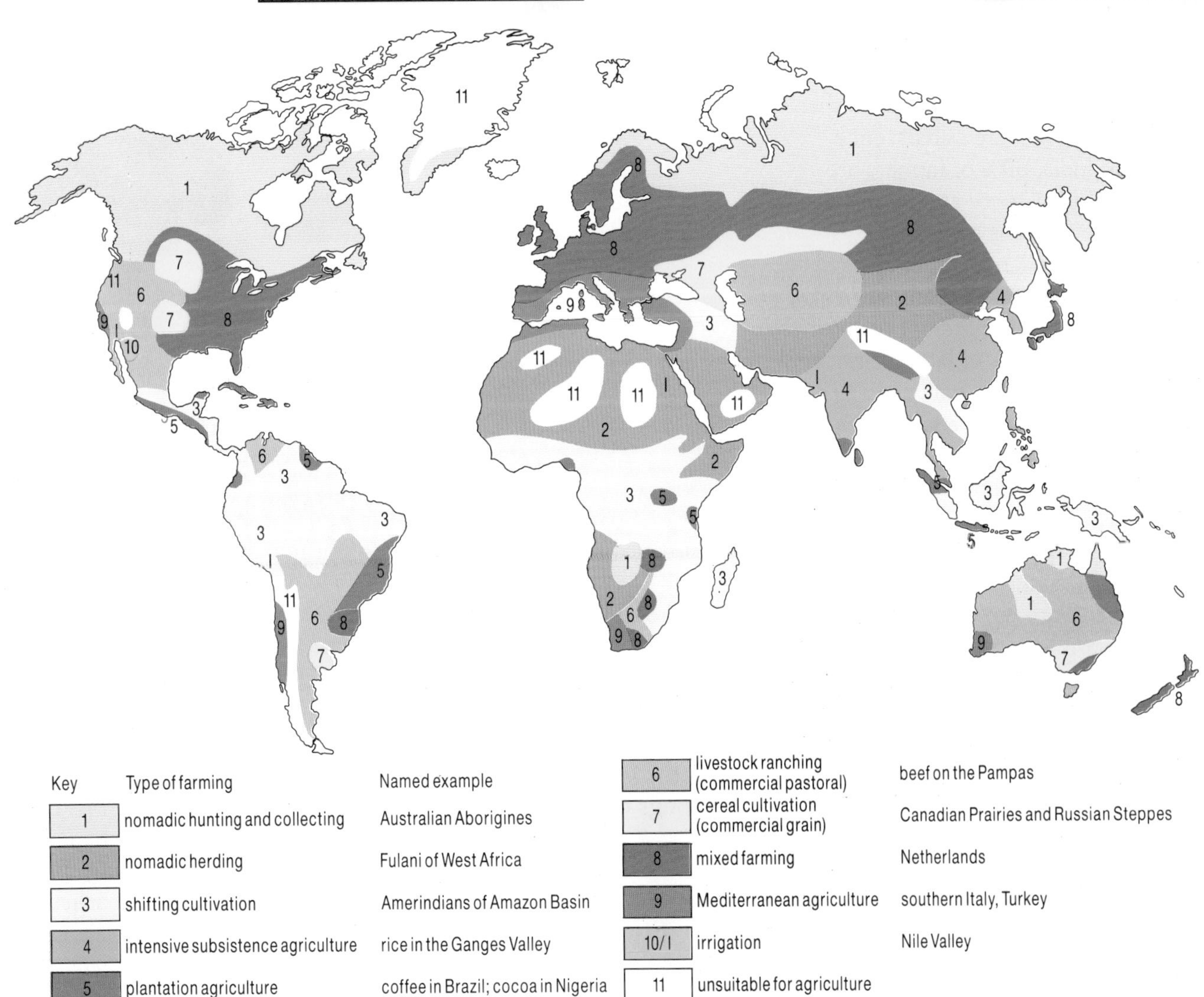

Types of farming

Farms can be classified in various ways

- *by their products:* farms are usually defined as **arable** or **pastoral**. Arable farms produce crops while pastoral farms concentrate on rearing livestock. Farms with both types of activity are called **mixed farms**.
- *the mobility of farm activities:* most farmers remain in one location without moving about, they are **sedentary**. Some farmers need to move from pasture to pasture with their animals, or shift from one patch of forest to another in order to achieve a satisfactory output. These are known as **nomadic** farmers.
- *the purpose of farming:* the growing of crops and rearing of animals is usually done so that the products can be sold at market (see Figure 2). This is **commercial** farming. In some parts of the world however, farmers grow food for their own (and their family's) consumption rather than for sale. They are **subsistence** farmers. In India, 80% of farmers are engaged in subsistence agriculture, while in Africa the figure is some 60%.
- *their organisation:* land, labour and capital, are basic requirements on any farm, and they may be used in different proportions. When large amounts of labour or capital are used on relatively small areas of land, farming is **intensive**. If a large area of land is used, in relation to the amount of capital or labour, then farming is **extensive**.

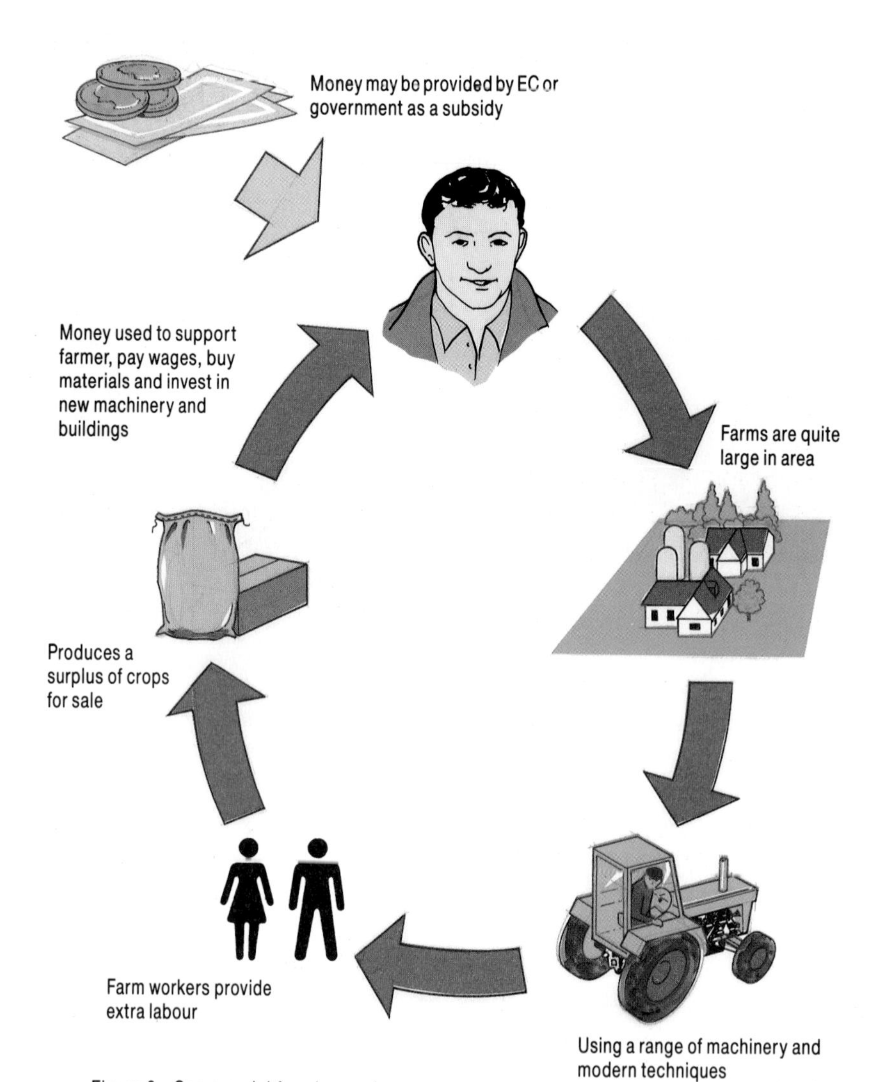

Figure 2 Commercial farming cycle

These four characteristics each describe one aspect of a particular farming type. They can be combined to build a picture of the sort of farming which is occurring in a given location.

Though they vary considerably in organisation and output, there are some similarities between farms of different types. As you saw in *Exploring Geography 1*, farms can be regarded as systems. There are several **inputs** and these are converted into products (or **outputs**) by a variety of farm **processes**. In a commercial farm these are taken to market and sold. Some of the money obtained is returned to the farm (as **feedback**), where it can be used to improve buildings or machinery and buy new inputs the next year.

Changes in farming

Farms do not remain the same year after year. They are dynamic systems. Changes might include the type of crop being grown or the level of technology being used. Farms respond to changes in the wider world. If demand increases for a new crop, as has been the case for soya in recent years, farmers will adjust their land-use patterns. The prices which farmers receive for their crops on world markets also bring about changes. Soil conditions may deteriorate causing the farmer to rotate the crop growing in a particular field. In the longer term, climate change may bring about more major changes.

Activities

1 a Use the map in Figure 1 (and an atlas if you need one) to identify the **main** farming type/s found in the following countries:

a India *b* United Kingdom *c* Italy *d* Egypt
e Peru *f* Japan *g* Nigeria *h* Brazil
i USA *j* China

b Look at the photographs in Figure 1 and suggest which farming type each one shows.

2 a Copy and complete these sentences:

- Arable farming involves growing ....
- Farmers who move around are called .... farmers.
- Most farmers in the developed countries produce their crops for sale at market and are known as .... farmers.
- Farms with livestock and crops are called .... farms.

b Study Figure 2. Now try to sketch a similar diagram which illustrates and explains subsistence farming.

- First decide the best order for the labels listed on the right.
- Now add illustrations to make your diagram look interesting and to help explain the labels.

Subsistence Farming

1 A variety of crops is grown to give the family a balanced diet

2 Subsistence farms are usually small family-operated plots using simple tools

3 Seeds are planted and the farmer tends the crop and weeds the plot

4 Pests, disease, and climatic hazards mean that usually everything that is produced is consumed by the family

5 Sometimes a small surplus is produced which can be traded in the village for another crop or perhaps sold for cash

3 a Work in groups of 3 or 4 to classify the different types of farming listed in the table. For each type listed, there is a photograph around the map in Figure 1, to help you make the right decisions. After discussing each photograph, try to agree an accurate description. One example has been done for you.

b Now copy and complete the table entering your agreed answers.

	Wheat production on prairies in Canada	Cattle herding in Mali	Rice farming in S.E Asia	Market Gardening in the UK	Sheep rearing in Australia	Banana plantations in C.America	Shifting cultivation in Indonesia	Goat herding in the Sahara	Hunters and rubber tappers in Amazonia
Arable	✓								
Pastoral									
Nomadic									
Sedentary	✓								
Commercial	✓								
Subsistence									
Intensive									
Extensive	✓								

4 Look carefully at the words below. Each word is the name of an agricultural product, but the letters have been jumbled up. Try to work out the correct name of each product and say whether or not you think it could be grown under normal conditions in this country.

THEWA, LARBEY, CUTEEL, RAGESP, MALB, RUGAS, ETA, EFFOCE, BERRUB, NAGSOME, IWIK, CIER, EFEB, ESAP, NORC, NABSANA, NOTTOC, CONBA

9.3 Farming in the developing world

Agricultural produce from farms in the developing world is as good and varied as from farms elsewhere (see Figure 1). Basic **staple foodstuffs** like rice, maize and cassava are grown as well as more colourful and exotic fruits and vegetables. Among the animals reared are sheep, goats, cattle and pigs. Millions of people in these countries do for themselves something that many of us are unable to do, namely, they grow sufficient food to feed themselves and their families, without having to visit the supermarket!

One of the major problems facing farmers in the developing world is the unfair distribution of land. Often the majority of the land is owned by a few wealthy landowners (see Figure 2a). As a result, the majority of farms are too small to be able to provide a reasonable living for their owners. Almost half the holdings in the developing world are under 1 hectare (the size of a football pitch), and another 20% are smaller than 2 hectares. When a farmer dies, the land is traditionally divided between the male children. With large families persisting, many plots have become too small to be successful. As a result, almost half the rural population of the less developed world are landless, and their numbers are growing (see Figure 2b).

The large numbers of people with either smallholdings or no land at all engage in **subsistence** farming. Often they are also nomadic, wandering from place to place. The remainder tend to work on the large estates and **plantations** which are owned by large overseas companies. These are the two examples we will look at in this unit.

Figure 1

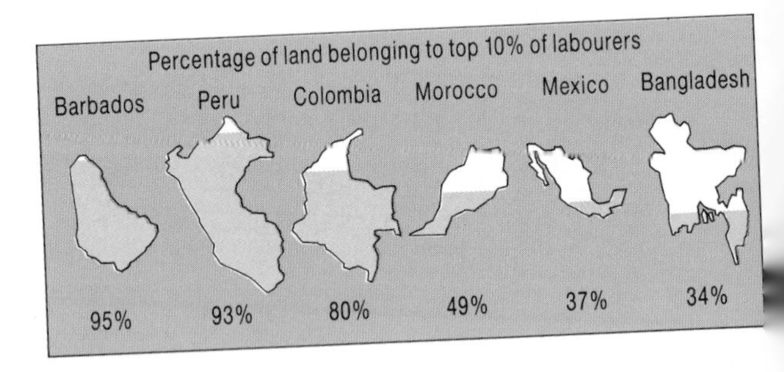

Figure 2a

1 Subsistence farming

There are many types of subsistence farming. One common type is found in the world's tropical forests, where large numbers of peasants who own no land themselves try to provide food for themselves and their families. Their particular type of farming is known as **slash and burn**, because it involves clearing and burning the rainforest.

In slash and burn farming, the people first have to find a suitable area of forest on which to settle and farm. Then they clear the trees and other vegetation with large knives called **machetes**. The cleared vegetation is piled up and burnt. The ashes are scattered over the plot and act as a fertiliser for the soil, making it ready for seeds to be planted. For a few years this soil will produce reasonably good crops but after a time the heavy tropical rains begin to wash the soil away and erode it. Gradually crop yields fall. The peasants are forced to move to a new plot where the whole process is repeated.

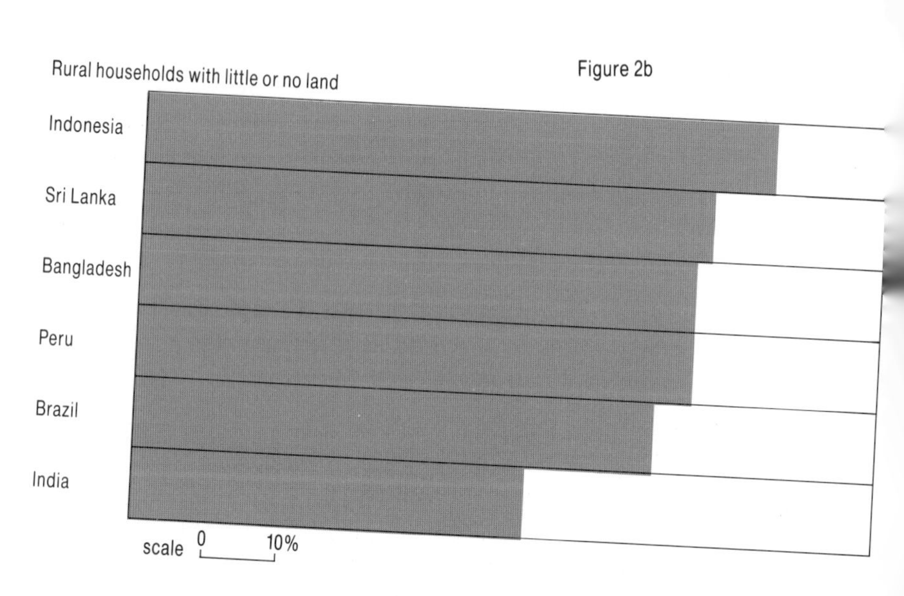

Figure 2b

Subsistence plots are usually planted with a variety of crops growing to different heights. They are sometimes called 'kitchen gardens'. Although they look jumbled, everything is actually carefully planned, and can be managed by a small labour force. A small plot can usually support a family for several years, before they must move on. However, the forest and its soils are gradually being destroyed by this process.

2 *Plantation farming*

Plantations are huge farms employing large labour forces, usually to produce a single product for export. This **monoculture** is damaging to the soil because, although chemical fertilisers are sometimes used, the same nutrients are repeatedly removed. A good example of plantation farming is the production of sugar in Mauritius.

Plantations are economical to run, because large areas of the same crop are easy to look after. Seeds and other materials can be bought cheaply in bulk. However, plantations are often criticised because the workers may live in poor conditions and be badly paid. The **cash crops** produced are usually exported, so plantations do not help to feed local people.

Many plantations in developing countries are owned by companies operating from overseas. The multinational Unilever, for example, operates three rubber plantations and an oil palm estate in Nigeria (Figure 3) through a local company called Pamol Nigeria Limited (PNL). On these estates, which cover over 6000 hectares, the conditions are better than on some plantations. All the workers live in rent-free accommodation on the estates, and the company provides them with free medical treatment and recreational facilities.

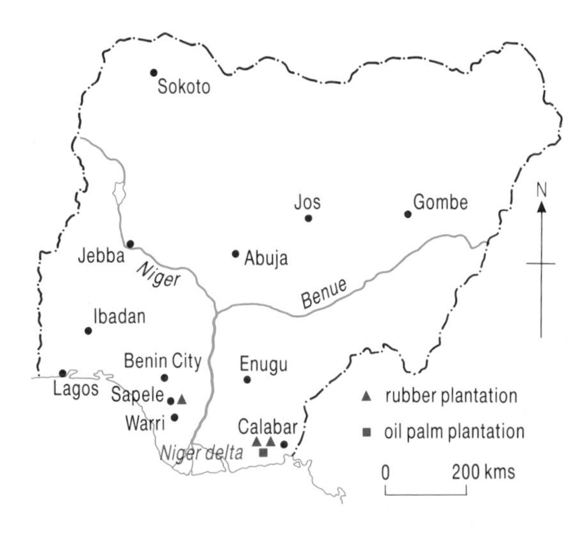

Figure 3 Unilever plantations, Nigeria

Activities

1 Study Figure 2 carefully before answering this question.
   a Calculate how much land is owned by the bottom 90% of landowners in each of the 6 countries shown in Figure 2a.
   b Look at Figure 2b, and use the scale to find out the percentage of rural households with little or no land in the six countries shown.
   c Imagine you are a trainee newspaper reporter, with the job of investigating the distribution of land in developing countries. You have found these statistics. They are so surprising that the Editor gives you the opportunity to write the lead story for tomorrow's front page. Write an article of about 300 words summarising what you have discovered. Suggest what effects the distribution of land might have on farming. You could include an imaginary interview with a government official or a small landless farmer.

2 a Explain what subsistence farming is. (You may need to look back to Unit 9.2).
   b What name is given to the sort of subsistence farming which involves clearing the forest with a machete? How might this activity harm the soil?
   c List five major differences between a subsistence farm and a farm in a developed country like the UK or the USA.
   d Try to explain how the slash and burn method of farming works:
   Either: draw a series of four or five simple labelled sketches or cartoons;
   Or: devise a flow diagram to show the sequence of operations.

3 a List three important differences between subsistence farming and plantation farming.
   b What sort of products are grown on plantations?
   c What advantages are there of growing crops on plantations?

4 Find out about one plantation crop chosen from – tea; rubber; coffee; tobacco. For the crop you have chosen, use an atlas, encyclopaedia and other reference books to describe:

- where the product is grown (include a map);
- the climatic conditions required; and
- the method of cultivation.

5 The following words are all contained somewhere in the grid, Figure 4. How many of them can you find? (They are hidden vertically, horizontally, forwards and backwards.)

ARABLE COMMERCIAL INTENSIVE ORGANIC STAPLE
CASH CROP FIELD NOMADIC PASTORAL SUBSISTENCE

N	Z	P	C	A	S	H	C	R	O	P	M
O	A	R	N	S	U	L	W	R	T	U	L
M	B	P	E	L	B	A	R	A	G	Z	U
A	M	A	S	A	S	T	R	U	M	L	O
D	R	S	I	R	I	P	W	L	D	K	R
I	N	T	E	N	S	I	V	E	L	I	G
C	N	O	P	S	T	A	P	L	E	R	A
L	X	R	O	L	E	D	F	I	I	Q	N
N	U	A	L	P	N	T	P	A	F	H	I
O	N	L	A	I	C	R	E	M	M	O	C
G	N	I	U	L	E	F	W	G	O	N	J

Figure 4

9.4 Developed world farming

Western Europe, North America and Japan contain some of the most productive farmland in the world. Most farming in these areas is intensive and uses large amounts of capital and/or labour so **yields** are high. Huge amounts of **capital** have enabled farmers to buy the latest machinery and to use chemical pesticides and fertilisers. Japan, for example, uses more than 20 times as much fertiliser as Africa (Figure 1).

In addition to having good equipment, chemical fertilisers and higher-yielding seed varieties (HYVs), farmers in the developing countries receive money from their governments. Farmers in many countries are given subsidies to produce particular products, and benefit from a system of **guaranteed prices**. European farmers are so successful with some crops that they can feed themselves, and are still able to export products, as do North American farmers. Canadian and American wheat and other grains play an important role in maintaining food supplies around the world.

Farmers have been so successful that huge **crop surpluses** have been produced, especially in the European Community (EC). Governments are asking farmers to **set-aside** part of their farmland for non-agricultural uses, like tourism and small industries, in the hope that this will reduce overall food production. Farmers are given financial incentives to do this. Even with a successful set-aside policy, it is likely that many farms will have to close in the next few years.

Country	Fertiliser Use (kgs/hectare)	GNP Per Capita $US in 1988
Australia	25	12 390
Brazil	35	2 280
China	176	330
Egypt	357	650
France	308	16 080
India	43	330
Japan	435	21 040
Mauritius	256	1 810
Netherlands	789	14 530
Nigeria	9	290
Peru	22	1 440
Tanzania	5	160
UK	368	12 800
USA	101	19 780
W.Germany	423	18 530

Figure 1

A comparison of farming in Japan and the United States

The range of farm products in North America is enormous. This is because the continent covers several climatic belts from **temperate** latitudes in the north where wheat is grown, to the **sub-tropics** in the south where citrus fruits, grapes, rice, tobacco and other products are cultivated. Japan is much smaller, so the range of products is smaller than in the USA. The nation is self-sufficient only in rice, despite high productivity in many products. Other foods like wheat, maize, fruit, and some meats have to be imported.

There are many important contrasts between farming in the USA and Japan (Figure 2). Farm size, methods, and cropping patterns all vary. At the same time however, similar trends are occurring in both countries – the number of farmers is decreasing and the cultivated area is declining, while average farm size is increasing. One other key difference between the two countries, is that agricultural land is very scarce in Japan as much of the land is mountainous.

	USA	JAPAN
Agricultural land	431 million hectares	5.4 million hectares
Agricultural land per capita	118.5 hectares	1.1. hectares
Agricultural population	3.6 million	4.9 million
Main product	wheat and other cereals	rice

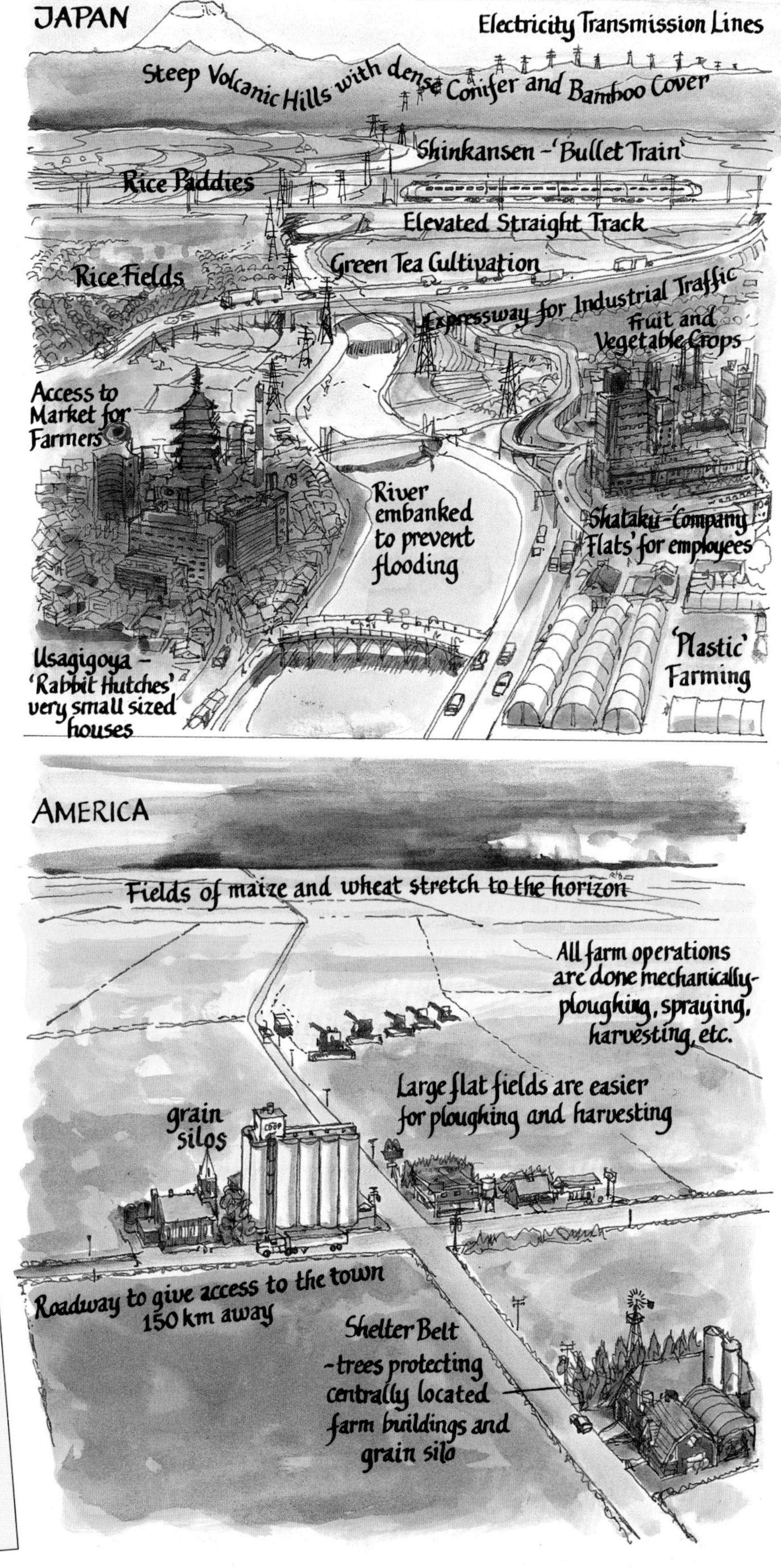

Figure 2 Farming comparison – USA and Japan

Activities

1 Why are the farmlands of North America, Japan and Western Europe able to be very productive?

2 The statistics in Figure 1 show the amount of fertiliser used by each of 15 nations along with each country's Gross National Product (GNP).

a Name the four countries which use the most fertiliser per hectare, and the four countries using the least fertiliser per hectare.

b Use an atlas to compare the size (area) of the two groups of countries you identified in *a*. What do you notice?

3 In small groups imagine that you jointly own and run a farm in the south of France. You have heard a rumour that the French government thinks that you have been too successful, because your farm's output has contributed to the wine lake and the grain mountain.

a What is your reaction to this? Try to agree what you are going to say to the government official who is to visit tomorrow to tell you officially to reduce your farm's output.

b You learn that at least 30% of your farm must be taken out of agricultural production for the next ten years. What do you propose to do with this land? Look at the farm's location in an atlas. It is near Toulon, about 40 kilometres southeast of Marseille.

4 a Compare and contrast farming in the United States with that in Japan. Figure 2 is a good starting point, but use your atlas and visit the library as well to use their reference books and encyclopaedia. In one paragraph describe some of the similarities you discover, and in another paragraph mention the differences. Suggest reasons why there are some differences.

b Farming varies considerably from one area to another in a large country like the USA. Choose one region (either Florida, California or the Great Plains) and investigate the sort of farming practised. Write a short account. Try to include some details of the region's climate as well as details of the types of farms and farm products.

5 a Study the statistics in Figure 3 carefully.

- For each country calculate how much agricultural land there is per farmer. Divide the number of farmers (column b) into the total agricultural area (column a).
- Show the results as a bar chart. Write a few sentences describing what you found.
- Using an atlas to help you, try to suggest some reasons for the variation in agricultural area per farmer which exists.

b Look at the figures for wheat production.

- What percentage of world output comes from the seven nations shown?
- Use an atlas to name at least two other countries where a substantial amount of wheat is produced.
- Use the figures to draw a pie-chart showing world wheat production. The difference between the total production from the seven countries shown, and the world total can be shown as OTHERS.

c Decide whether these sentences are true or false after studying the table of statistics in Figure 3:

- China and Japan have less agricultural land per capita than the UK and France.
- The USA has more agricultural land per capita than Canada.
- Almost half the world's agricultural labour force lives in China.
- Canada has more agricultural land than anywhere else.
- The UK has more farm workers than Japan.
- The USA is the largest producer of maize and soybeans listed.
- China produces more than one-third of the world's rice.
- The USA is the largest wheat producer in the world.
- France produces twice as much milk as the UK.

Figure 3 Selected agricultural statistics

	(a) Total Agriculture Area ('000 ha)	(b) Number of farmers ('000)	Main farm products (thousand metric tonnes)						
			Wheat	Rice	Maize (corn)	Soy beans	Vegetables and melons	fruit	cow's milk
USSR*	605 415	25 022	83 000	2 600	15 000	550	31 785	18 200	97 765
USA	431 382	3 640	65 992	6 171	225 180	57 114	28 098	22 460	64 954
China	386 582	444 956	85 286	171 479	62 250	10 519	99 705	12 040	2 568
Canada	70 380	550	23 900	-	7 393	1 063	2 060	770	8 200
France	31 197	1 679	29 030	61	11 839	58	7 391	13 788	33 000
UK	18 641	697	11 700	-	1	-	3 920	510	16 250
Japan	5 358	4 935	874	14 578	-	238	15 407	5 862	7 377
World	4 628 098	1 059 013	510 029	465 970	490 155	100 833	402 445	312 353	458 023

*From 1992 independent states

9.5 Important issues in farming today

Farming today is in a state of crisis. In some areas millions of people are starving, while huge crop surpluses are being produced elsewhere; the environment is being damaged with rivers polluted, hedgerows uprooted and many species of wildlife under threat; and huge volumes of topsoil are being lost each year through soil erosion.

The importance of agriculture to the survival of the human race is widely recognised. The industry provides the basic food supplies which keep us alive, and is also the largest employer in the world. However, not all farmland is equally productive (see Figure 1). The problems are most serious for the economically developing countries, where there are more mouths to feed, and large areas of land are devoted to producing cash crops for export.

Many problems concern farmers today. These vary in size and scale, and also differ from one location to another. We will look at just a few of the questions raised by these problems in this unit:

1 Do new ideas and machines benefit farmers and the environment?
2 Why are huge quantities of soil being eroded each year?
3 Can irrigation help farmers increase their output?
4 What can be done about the locust problem?

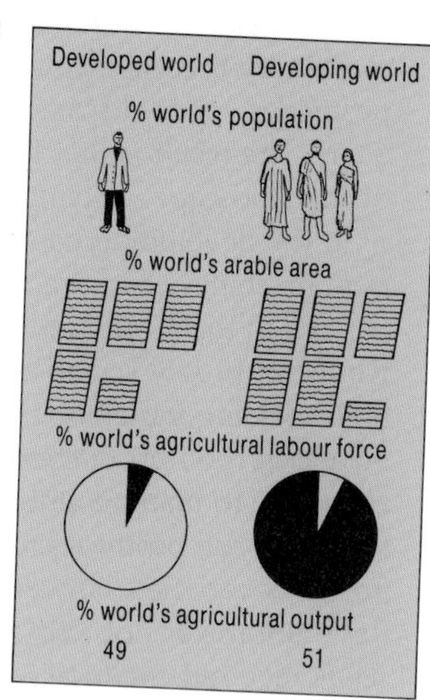

Figure 1

1 Do new ideas and machines benefit farmers and the environment?

Many farmers in developed countries have invested huge sums of money in new machinery, seeds and other means of keeping food production high at a time when people are deserting farming in large numbers. Each year in Britain, about 4000 farmworkers leave the land, and the number of farms falls by over 5000. This **depopulation** has had a major effect on the rural areas (Figure 2). Similar effects are being seen in the United States, Japan and elsewhere.

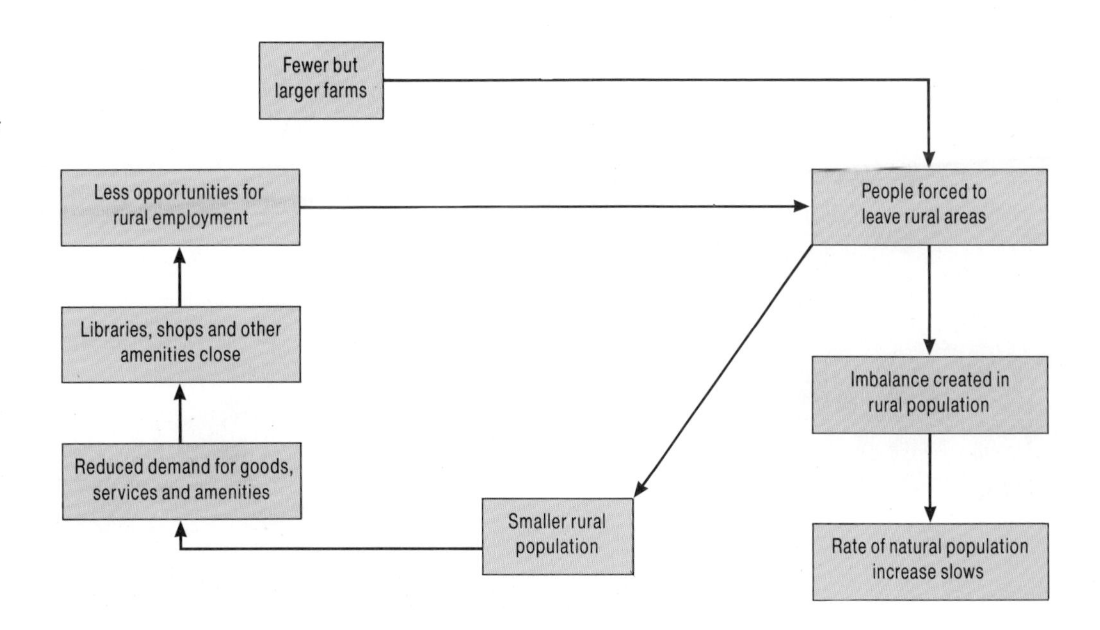

Figure 2
Effects of change in farm size and number

Modern technology (methods and machinery) means that farming today can damage the environment. Hedgerows are being torn up creating large fields; heavy machinery is compacting the soil; and pesticides sprayed from airplanes affect large areas. The result is that the entire appearance of the landscape is being changed (Figure 3).

In the developing countries too, modern farm machinery and practices are having an impact. In the 1960s and 1970s, the **Green Revolution** saw scientists producing new high yielding varieties (HYVs). These increased food production and so proved attractive to many countries. Some new strains of rice produced four times as much as previous varieties. However, the Green Revolution was not a total success. The new seeds required chemical fertilisers and pesticides which are expensive. More irrigation was needed and new machinery required, which many farmers could not afford to maintain, or even provide the fuel to run.

Figure 3 Countryside under threat

Figure 4 Which technology is best?

Another problem has been trying to choose the most appropriate technologies (Figure 4) to help farmers in developing countries improve their output. Large new tractors and combine harvesters have in the past been used by these farmers, but they are not very energy efficient, may not withstand the difficult conditions, and spare parts may be hard to obtain. However, at the other extreme, the simple tools used by many peasant farmers mean that work is hard and slow. The best way forward is by using **intermediate technology**. This equipment is usually low in cost, made from local materials, and is easy to use and maintain. In many ways it is more appropriate to the needs of the people – this is why it is sometimes called **appropriate technology**.

2 Why are huge quantities of soil being eroded each year?

Each year, as a result of **soil erosion**, the world's farmers lose an estimated 24 billion tons of topsoil from their croplands. This reduces crop yields as well as the potential growing area. The loss of soil around the world during the 1980s was equivalent to half of all the soil used to grow crops in the USA. Soil erosion is caused by a lack of care of the land surface, and can be reduced if more attention is given to looking after it (Figure 5).

Figure 5 Causes of soil erosion

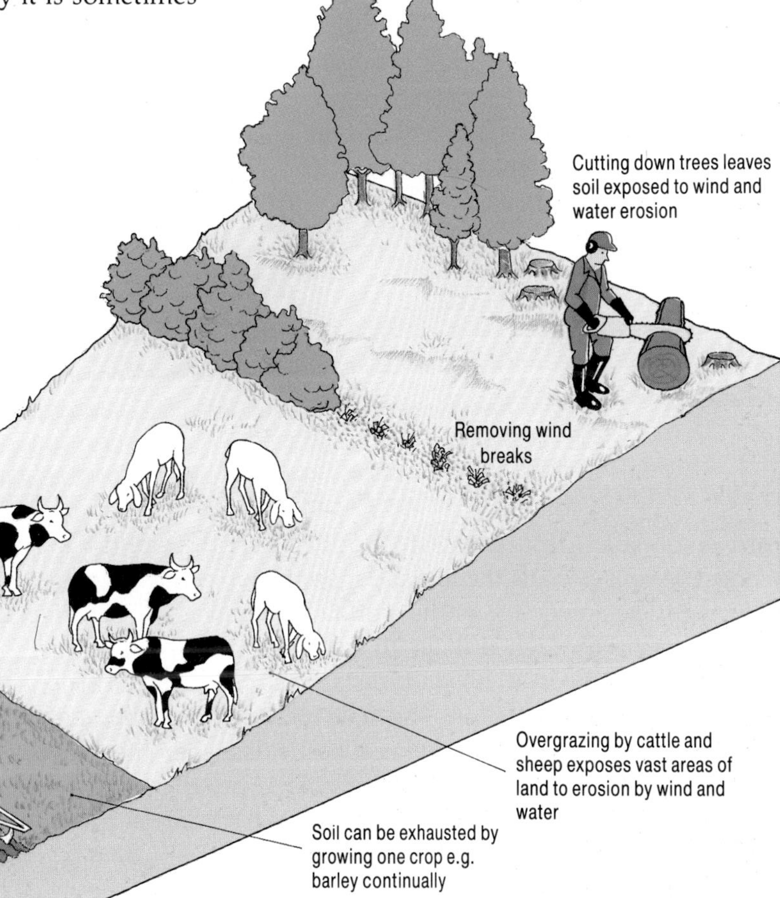

3 Can irrigation help farmers increase their output?

Every year, millions of hectares of cropland are lost as cities and highways spread across the countryside, or soil becomes eroded. However, the irrigated area has gradually grown. It doubled between 1900-1950, and has increased even faster since then (Figure 6). As a result of **irrigation**, areas which were once too dry to farm can be artificially watered, making crop cultivation possible. In 1990, about one-third of the global harvest came from irrigated areas. Countries like China, India, Egypt and Japan rely on irrigated land for over 50% of their domestic food production.

Figure 6

Irrigated area in the world 1950-2000

Year	Area of irrigated cropland (ha)
1950	94
1960	136
1970	188
1980	236
1990	259
2000	279*

*estimate

Irrigation schemes often involve constructing huge dams, like the Aswan Dam in Egypt. But it is also possible to irrigate land with a simple system of canals, channels and sprinklers. All these different methods can befound in the dry southwestern corner of Cyprus (Figure 7) where the Paphos Irrigation Project has brought 36 million cubic metres of water to an area whose annual rainfall is under 300mm. The huge Asprokremmos dam can store 51 million cubic metres of water, which is led to the fields via a specially constructed canal, and delivered to the crops by pipelines, drip irrigation and sprinklers. The result is that avocados, grapes, lemons, groundnuts, melons and oranges are all able to grow here.

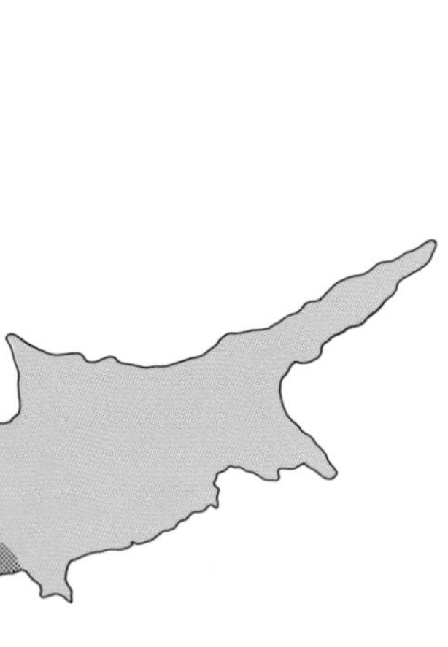

Figure 7 Paphos irrigation project, Cyprus

4 What can be done about the locust problem?

Insect pests cause great damage to crops all over the world. One of the most serious pests is the locust (Figure 8), which has its main home in Africa. Some 10% of the world's land area is subject to locust attack. The insect, which is about 10 cms long, travels in swarms containing as many as 40 billion locusts. These swarms can strip a huge area of all its vegetation. The main method for dealing with locusts is to spray them with chemical pesticides when they are at their weakest, before they are able to fly. They are then said to be in their 'hopper' stage. Even at this stage they are capable of great destruction. When fully active, a locust can consume its own body weight in vegetation every 24 hours!

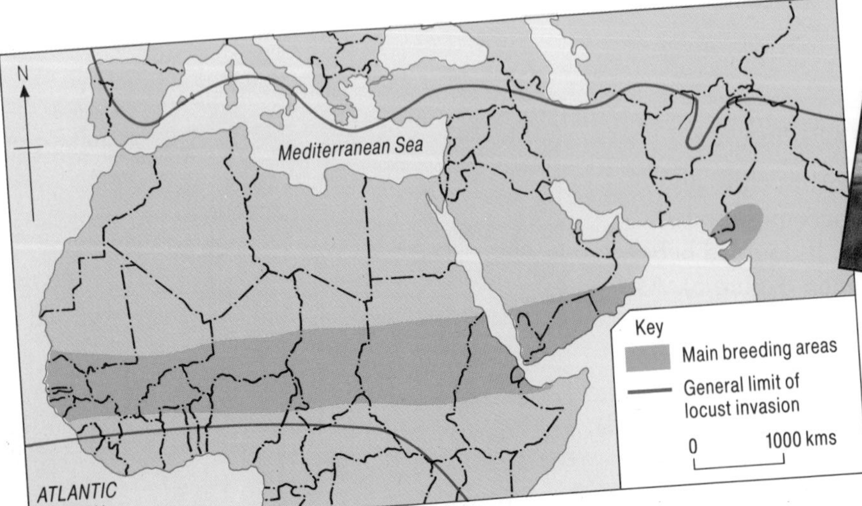

Figure 8 Locust breeding and invasion

Activities

1 Copy and complete the paragraph below, using the following word-list. You will need to have read this unit carefully.

Word-list.

● Irrigation ● Surpluses ● Desertification ● Slash and Burn
● Famine ● Rainforests ● Greenhouse effect ● Subsidies

Many aspects of world farming are causing concern today. In Europe, government ---------- cause large ---------- of grain and butter to build up, while elsewhere in the world, -------- is a problem and people are dying. In the ----------- of Brazil and Indonesia, trees are being cut down by peasant farmers practising a type of farming called --------------

Sands are advancing in a process called ----------- in one-third of the earth's land area. At the same time, some desert areas are being cultivated as a result of ---------- . In the future, climate may change as a result of the ---------------. This could have a very dramatic effect on agriculture.

2 The distribution of population, arable land and farm labour-force between developed and developing countries is shown in Figure 1.

a Estimate the percentage from the diagram for each of these.

b Outline two main differences between developed and developing countries.

3 *a* You will need to work in pairs for this activity. Discuss each of the four statements below with your partner. Which do you agree with and why?

BUTTERFLIES ARE NICE TO LOOK AT BUT ARE NOT USEFUL CREATURES. THEY ARE NOT WORTH PRESERVING

MODERN FARMING IS DANGEROUS BUT IT DOES HELP TO PROVIDE US WITH CHEAP FOOD.

IT IS A DISASTER THAT ALMOST ALL OUR CHALK DOWNLAND HAS BEEN DESTROYED. SUCH HABITATS ARE AN IMPORTANT NATIONAL ASSET AND SHOULD BE PROTECTED FOR OUR CHILDREN.

FARMERS SHOULD NOT BE ALLOWED TO PRODUCE SURPLUS FOOD. NO MORE MONEY SHOULD BE PAID TO THEM IN SUBSIDIES.

b Choose one of the statements which you have strong views about. Draw a small sketch or cartoon, or write a poem about it to illustrate your feelings.

4 *a* Choose two advantages and two disadvantages (from the list below) for farmers in developing countries of:

● advanced technology ● basic technology.

Advantages	Disadvantages
Simple to use	Costly to buy and to run
Requires few people	Work is laborious and slow
Provides work for many people	Methods are inefficient
Produces large amounts of food	Uses energy and creates unemployment

b Write a paragraph explaining why intermediate technology is often the most appropriate way of increasing productivity in developing countries.

5 *a* Make a list of the causes of soil erosion from the diagram in Figure 5.

b For each cause try to find an appropriate solution from the list below.

- contour ploughing (ploughing along the contour lines)
- planting areas with trees (afforestation)
- planting windbreaks
- converting ploughland back into pasture
- rotating crops from one year to the next
- greater control of grazing

c Design a poster for distribution to farmers which explains visually how they can change their methods to reduce the risk of soil erosion. You might choose to concentrate on one or two suggestions rather than trying to include them all. Remember the message must be clear, and interesting!

6 *a* Use the data in Figure 6 to draw a line graph to show how the world's irrigated area has increased since 1950.

b Do you notice anything about the amount of new land being irrigated now, compared to between 1950-60, or 1960-70?

7 Study Figure 8 which gives you some information about the locust, and the areas in which it breeds and is a pest. You will also need your atlas for this activity.

a In which continent is the locust problem most severe?

b Name six countries where locusts breed.

c Draw a sketch-map to show the areas where locust swarms are a problem.

d What sort of natural vegetation is mostly found in these locust breeding areas?

e If locusts can fly for about 130 kilometres each day, how long would it take a swarm to reach the Indian coastline from the Sudan coast?

f Find out about the locust's life cycle.

Dictionary

appropriate technology machinery, usually low in cost, which is suited to the conditions of the people who use it
capital money used on or invested in the farm
cash crops crops grown for sale and not for the direct use of the grower
commercial farms farms whose products are sold for profit at markets
depopulation the loss of population in an area
disease-resistant varieties of crop not affected by particular diseases. These special varieties can be produced by special breeding
extensive when large areas of land are farmed. May either involve animals being grazed or crops being grown
fertilisers nutrients which can be added to the soil in order to increase the output of crops. They can either be natural or chemical
guaranteed price a price which farmers are assured in advance they will receive for their products
high-yielding varieties (HYVs) new types of seed which have been specially bred to produce high yields
intensive using large amounts of capital or labour to produce a large amount of agricultural produce from a relatively small area
machete a long and heavy knife
mixed farm a farm where both animals and livestock products and crops are produced
monoculture a system of farming in which one crop is cultivated year after year, to the exclusion of others
organically grown produce which is grown without the addition of chemical fertilisers or pesticides
outputs the products of a system
pastoral farm a farm which concentrates on the production of livestock and their products
per capita an amount per head of the population
pesticides chemicals which are applied to the land or to crops in order to eliminate insects or other pests
plantations large estates which concentrate on the production of cash crops, usually under a system of monoculture
productivity the rate of output per unit of farmed area
sedentary farmers farmers who remain in one fixed location
set-aside amounts of land taken out of agricultural production in order to reduce surpluses
slash and burn method of subsistence agriculture involving the removal of forest cover followed by an exploitative method of farming
staple foodstuffs foods like rice, cassava or wheat which provide a substantial part of the diet in a particular region
subsistence farming farming which concentrates on the production of food for consumption rather than directly for sale
sub-tropics the region lying between the Tropic of Cancer and the Tropic of Capricorn
temperate the region lying between the tropics and the cold zone (between 23.5° and 66.5° in both hemispheres)
yields the amount of output per unit of farmed area

10 Industry

10.1 Patterns of work

The world of work today is very different from that which our parents and grandparents knew. The type of work being done and the tools and machinery which are used have changed, as have general working conditions and wage levels. However, major differences still exist in the working patterns and conditions between different countries.

In the last chapter, we looked at farming, one of the world's largest employers, but there are three categories of employment – **primary** (farming, fishing, forestry and mining), **secondary** (manufacturing) and **tertiary** (services). Every type of work fits into one of these categories. The resulting pattern, known as the **employment structure**, varies from one country to another (Figure 1).

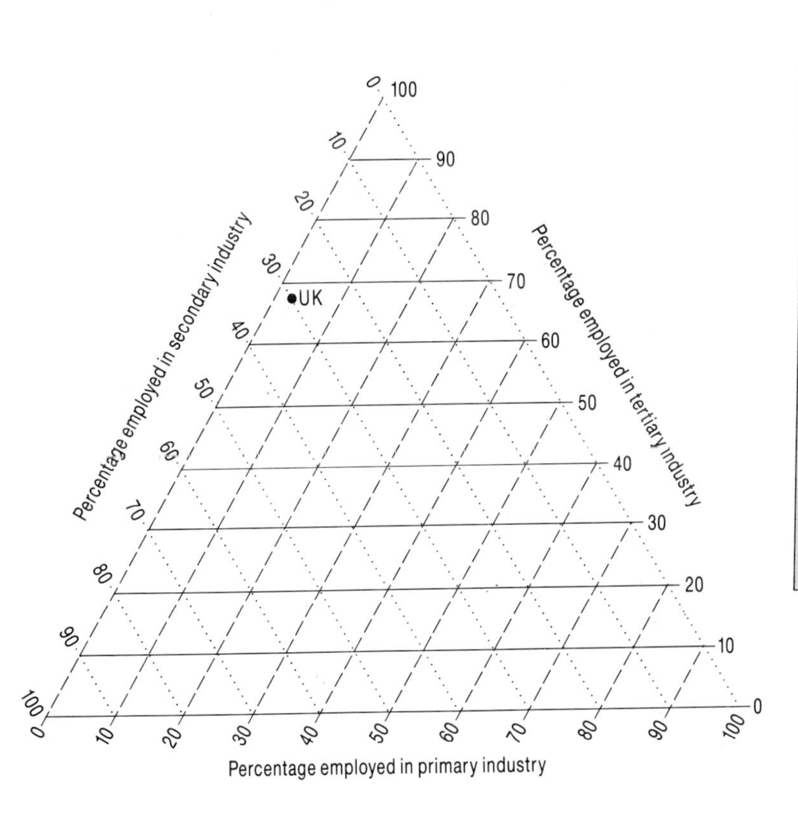

	% of workforce in		
	Primary	Secondary	Tertiary
China	72	–	–
India	72	11	17
Nigeria	54	19	27
South Africa	10	29	41
Peru	38	20	42
Brazil	30	24	46
Egypt	40	30	20
USA	3	27	70
USSR *	20	38	42
Japan	8	34	58
France	7	30	63
W.Germany	4	40	56
Spain	15	33	51
UK	2	30	68
Bangladesh	74	11	15
Burkina Faso	82	13	5

* From 1992 independent states

Figure 1
Employment structure – selected countries

The last 50 years have seen many changes in working patterns (Figure 2). The distribution of economic activity around the world has also changed. Traditionally, developed countries produced and exported manufactured goods, whereas agricultural products and raw materials came from economically developing countries. However, massive growth in manufacturing in some developing countries has altered this pattern. Companies must secure large profits for their shareholders, so manufacturing today takes place wherever **costs of production** can be minimised. Industries like iron and steelmaking, textiles, shipbuilding as well as food processing and the chemical industry, have been attracted to developing countries by large and cheap labour forces.

One reason why manufacturing industry today is easily able to move about is that its choice of location is not restricted by having to be sited near to its raw materials or to a power supply. Such industries are described as **footloose**, because both their raw materials and power supplies can be easily and relatively cheaply transported. In the eighteenth and nineteenth centuries, however, the situation was different. It was important for factories then to be near coalfields or deposits of raw materials. Transport was slow and difficult, and because industry was less efficient, larger quantities of the raw materials were required.

* Working conditions have substantially improved, with shorter hours and longer holidays than 50 years ago
* Location patterns have changed and industrial estates and science parks have developed
* The level of technology used in workplaces has increased e.g. computers, automation and even robots are found in the workplace!
* Service and financial (tertiary) industries have become major employers
* The scale of operation has increased as the world has become more interdependent. Much manufacturing is now global in scale, with capital locating where labour or raw materials costs are lowest
* Transnational companies e.g. Shell, ICI, Unilever, have spread their influence

Figure 2 Changes in the world of work 1940–1990

Robots welding truck cab at the Iveco-Ford Langley factory, Buckinghamshire

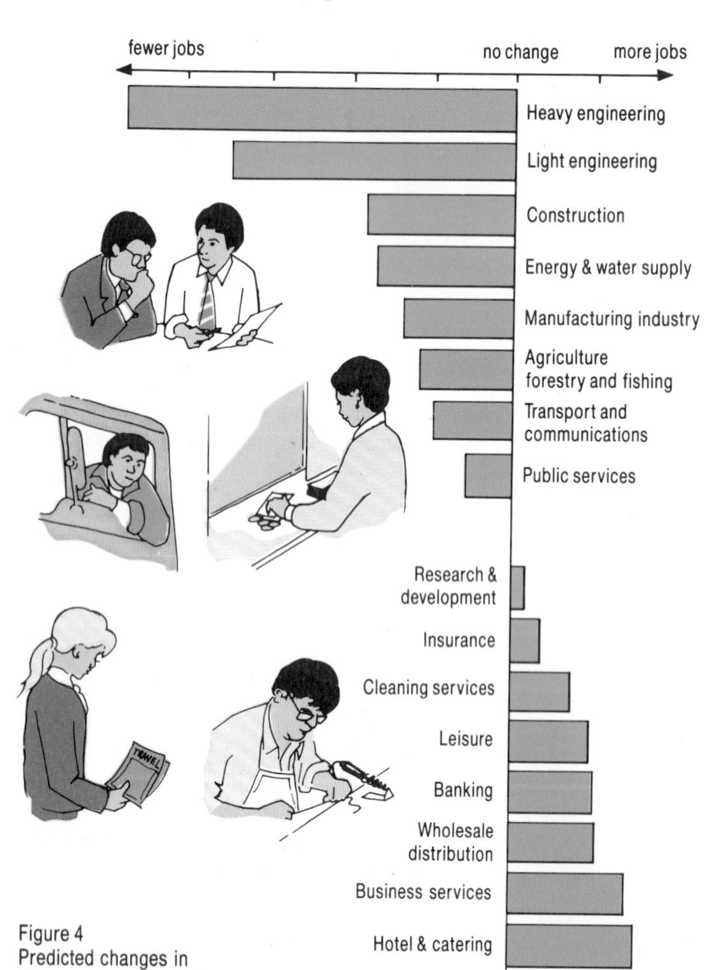

Figure 4 Predicted changes in UK employment in 1990s

Another factor contributing to changes in the global pattern of work, is that manufacturing industry has gradually become more **automated**. Machines and robots are being used to perform routine operations in many factories (Figure 3). This is causing job losses, as the automated factories require a labour force which is smaller in total, but more highly skilled.

In many countries, manufacturing is turning to new types of locations. Light industries, such as the manufacture of domestic appliances and light engineering are often located close to one another on **industrial estates**. New high-technology industries, like electronics and computer manufacturers, prefer to locate close to universities and in locations which have easy access to good transport systems. They also tend to locate near one another, often in purpose-built premises on estates called **science parks**.

Manufacturing is growing in many economically developing countries. Local industries are present along with those operated by large **transnational companies** (TNCs). However, industry is still concentrated in the rich industrialised 'North'. Just three nations: Japan, the United States of America and Germany account for over 50% of all production. Despite global manufacturing output growing by about seven times between 1950 and 1990, it has become a relatively less important employer than previously. To compensate for this process of **de-industrialisation** in many developed countries, employment in service industries, especially in retailing, financial services and tourism (Figure 4) has grown.

Activities

1 *a* What differences can you think of which exist between workplaces of today and those of a century ago?

b See if you can find out what sort of work your grandparents did for a living. Where did they work? What were the conditions like ?

2 To make sure you have learnt the differences between primary, secondary and tertiary work, draw up a table with three columns. Put each of the following types of work in the correct column:

- shoe-mender
- airline pilot
- cereal farmer
- bread maker
- potter
- secretary
- accountant
- assembly-line worker in car factory
- TV repair person
- coal-miner
- machinist in curtain factory

3 Carefully study the triangular graph in Figure 1(a). You will need a copy of Figure 1(a) for this activity.

a The employment structure of the UK is shown. Use the diagram to calculate the percentage of the workforce in each type of employment.

b Now on your copy of Figure 1(a) mark the positions of all the other countries listed in Figure 1(b).

c Are the countries evenly spread on your completed graph, or in clusters? Can the countries be divided into groups in any way?

4 You should work in small groups for this activity. In Activity 1 you thought about how workplaces changed up to the present day. Now look at the list of changes in Figure 2.

a In groups, discuss why you think these changes have come about. Try to think of an example of each change stated.

b Now add any other changes which have been missed from the list.

c Discuss how workplaces might have changed by the year 2010.
Either: write a summary of the changes your group thinks will happen;
Or: Draw sketches showing what you think the workplace of 2010 will look like.

5 Do you think it is a good idea for robots to do all the jobs in factories? Try to explain what you feel about this.

6 a Look at Figure 4 carefully. Which of the sentences below are accurate? Copy only those you think are correct:

- It is predicted that in the future there will be fewer jobs in transport and communications and construction.
- The heaviest UK job losses will probably occur in the hotel and catering sector.
- Insurance and banking are likely to employ more people in the future.
- Most of the new jobs to be created will be in service industries.

b With a partner, see if you can think of some of the reasons why:

- engineering is likely to decline so much;
- hotel and catering jobs are set to increase.

7 The table in Figure 5 shows the employment structure of a typical developed country and a typical developing country. Use this, and the other information you have learnt in this Unit, to summarise the main differences in employment structure between developing and developed countries.

Figure 5

Type of employment	% workforce in each type	
	Developed country	Developing country
Primary	5	70
Secondary	35	10
Tertiary	60	20

10.2 Large or small – which is best?

The word industry has many different meanings (Figure 1). It most often conjures up a picture of a factory or a steelworks. However, industries operate at a variety of scales (Figure 2), from small **cottage industries** to giant **transnational companies (TNCs)**.

Cottage industries do not need a special building. They may take place in a spare room, shed or garage. Other industries require purpose-built factory accommodation. Industries operating at the largest scale may consist of a number of factories or **branch plants**, all linked together, but located in more than one continent.

Different types of work, primary, secondary and tertiary, may also be linked. A factory making Weetabix, for example, has links with its suppliers, the wheat farmers, as well as those who sell the finished products, the shops and supermarkets (Figure 3). In this way, most jobs can be seen as part of a **system**, with one job being dependent on another.

Figure 1 Types of industry

The next three units will look at manufacturing. Primary activities are dealt with in Chapter 4 (Energy) and Chapter 9 (Farming). The last Unit in this Chapter (10.5) will look at tertiary industry.

1 Locations matter

Whatever their size and scale, all manufacturing industries have important decisions to make. One problem which must be resolved before production occurs is – '*Where is the best place for the factory to be located?*'

Each industry has its own particular set of requirements. When examining locations, several questions must be asked:

- Where are our **raw materials** coming from? Which location will enable them to be obtained most easily and cheaply?
- How **accessible** is this location (for our workers, raw materials, and to our **market**) compared with the other locations?
- What is the **labour force** like? Will it be large enough, and have the skills and training needed? Do people work hard? Are strikes likely to be a problem?
- What sort of **social environment** is this for our workforce to live in (houses, schools, shops and other amenities)?
- Is the **site** suitable for our requirements (size? flat? close to water? strong enough to support large buildings?)
- Are there any special financial **incentives** from government (enterprise zones? freeports? special local authority advantages?)

The site shown in the photograph in Figure 4 near Derby, was chosen in 1989 by Toyota as the location of their new car factory. Toyota officials examined several sites in Britain before this one was chosen. They were looking for a large (> 100 hectares) flat site with strong enough bedrock to support a huge factory. The labour force needed to have engineering skills, and the site required excellent communications so that raw materials and components could easily be assembled and the finished cars transported to locations all over the UK and Europe.

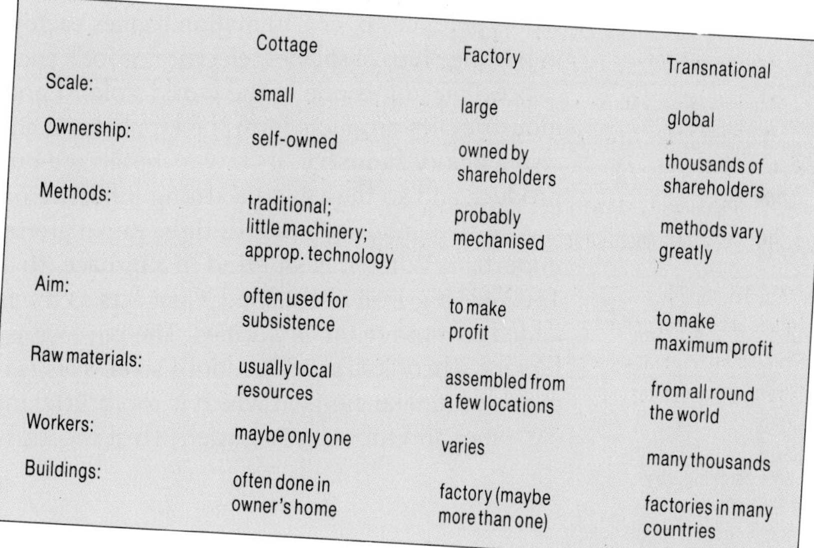

	Cottage	Factory	Transnational
Scale:	small	large	global
Ownership:	self-owned	owned by shareholders	thousands of shareholders
Methods:	traditional; little machinery; approp. technology	probably mechanised	methods vary greatly
Aim:	often used for subsistence	to make profit	to make maximum profit
Raw materials:	usually local resources	assembled from a few locations	from all round the world
Workers:	maybe only one	varies	many thousands
Buildings:	often done in owner's home	factory (maybe more than one)	factories in many countries

Figure 2

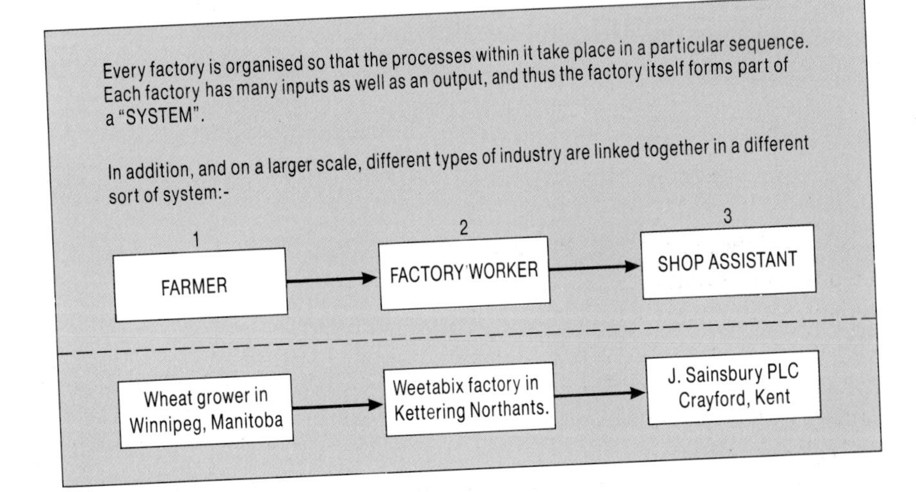

Figure 3 Links between types of work

Figure 4 Burnaston

2 The steel industry – a case-study

One important raw material required by the car industry is steel. The world produces over 750 million tonnes each year. Steel is also used in making ships, airplanes, electrical goods and machinery.

Steel-making is one of the world's oldest and most important industries. Its products form the inputs for many other industries. It is also a **heavy industry**. Its raw materials are bulky in relation to its product, and so they exert a strong influence on location.

The steel industry requires three raw materials. Iron-ore is the most important. When it is **smelted** in a furnace (to a temperature of over 1300°C.) pig-iron is obtained. Coal acts as the fuel, and limestone is added to remove the impurities. The pig-iron is taken to a steel furnace where it is processed into steel. This is cooled and can be moulded (unlike pig-iron which is too brittle) into different products, e.g. pipes and tubes, rails, girders, steel sheets, wire etc.

Figure 5
Japan's steel industry and its products

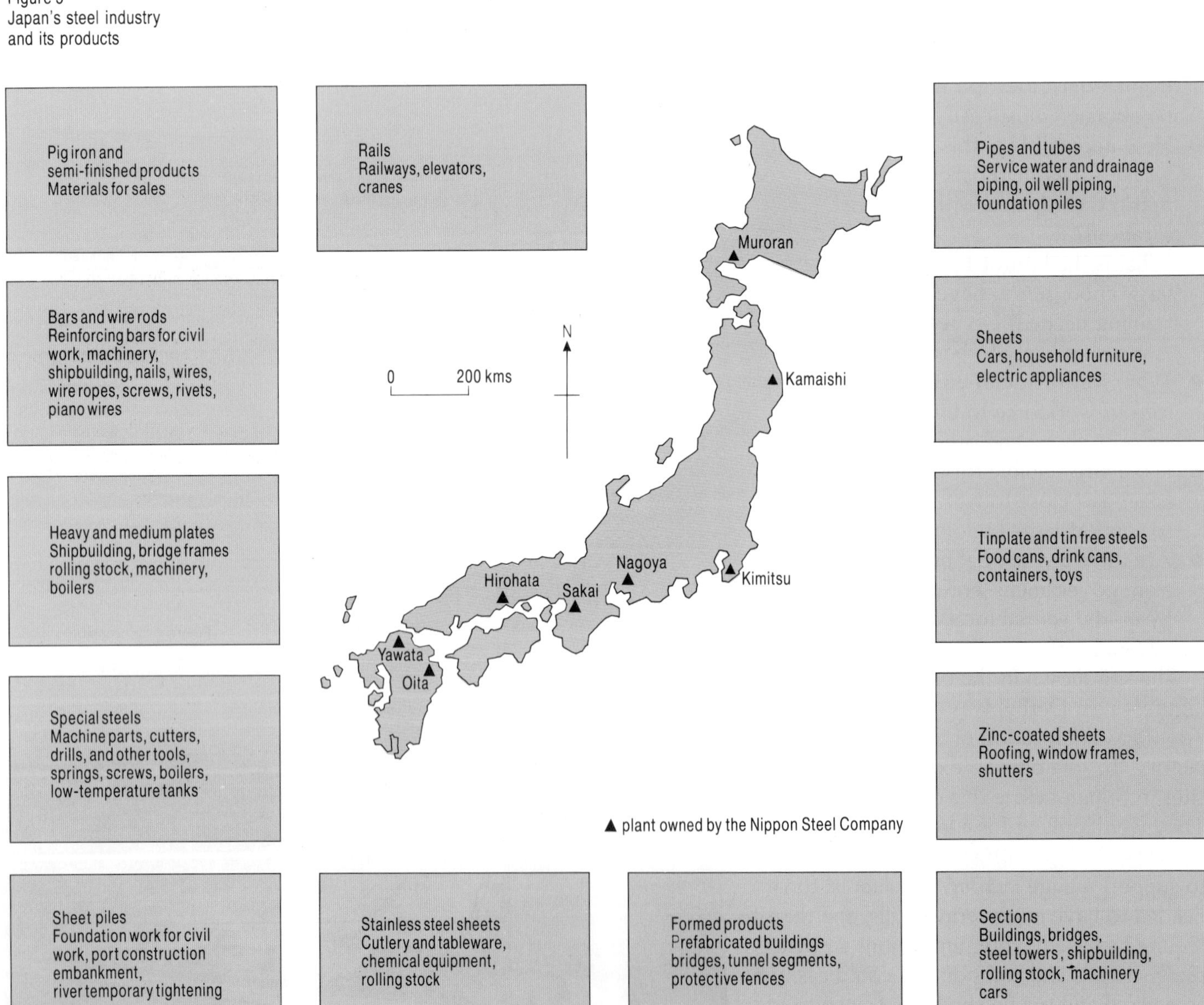

After the USSR, Japan is the largest maker of steel in the world, producing about 14% of the total output. Figure 5 shows the location of the plants belonging to Nippon Steel, the largest steel company in Japan. The range of products from its eight plants is impressive – especially because Japan has none of the raw materials needed for steel production. The Oita works is the newest steel plant owned by Nippon Steel. It was built entirely on reclaimed land. Like Nippon Steel's other plants almost all its raw materials are imported. The iron-ore comes mostly from Brazil and Australia and the coal from Australia, Canada and the USA (Figure 6). The importance of imported raw materials accounts for the coastal location of plants like this one. The Oita steelworks produces 8 million tonnes of steel each year.

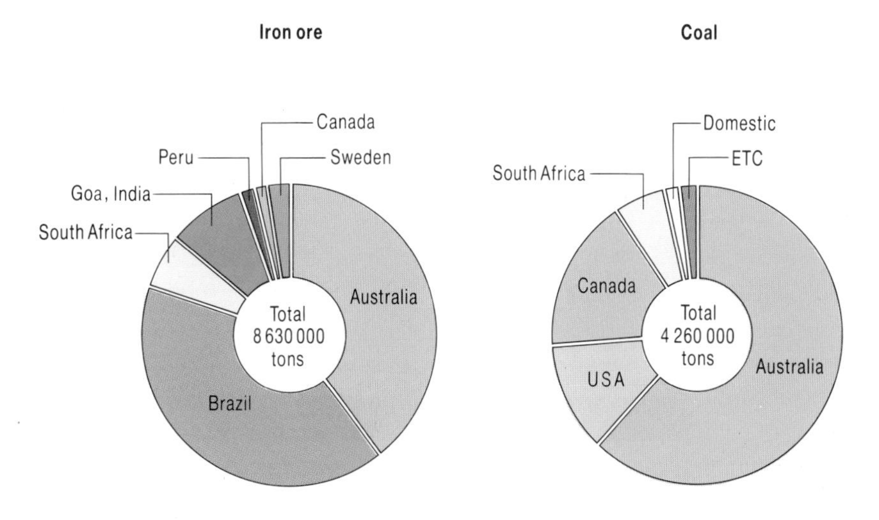

Figure 6 Sources of raw materials – Oita Works 1986

Activities

1 *a* Identify the products being made in each of the photographs in Figure 1.
b Choose one of these products and try to list some of the raw materials that would be necessary in its manufacture.

2 Do a survey of industry in your area to find out what types of work are available near your school. You will need to work in groups of four for this activity. Each person will need a local newspaper.
a Turn to the pages with general job vacancies. Each person should write down the first 25 job vacancies that they see. Now classify them into primary, secondary and tertiary types of job.
b Now add all your group's results together, to get a grand total for each job type. This should be a percentage because, between you, you have looked at 100 jobs.
c Draw a pie chart or a bar graph to show this data, then write a few sentences to describe your findings.

3 Study Figure 3 closely. It shows how making Weetabix is one link in a chain of jobs that stretches from Canada to your local supermarket.
a Identify which job is primary, secondary and tertiary (there is one in each category).
b Choose another manufactured product. Draw a similar diagram for this product, showing the jobs on which it depends. Follow the example shown to indicate what information you need. Think about where its raw materials come from and where it is sold.

4 Figure 4 shows the site chosen near Derby for the new Toyota car factory.
a If you were in the third year at a school near the new factory, and wanted to leave school after your GCSEs, would you welcome the new factory or not? Explain your answer.
b What benefits do you think it might bring to the local area?
c Is everybody going to be pleased to see this new development?
d Working in a small group, imagine that you had an opportunity to meet the officials from Toyota, to persuade them to locate their new factory in the nearest town to *your* school. How would you convince them that this was a good location?
You might choose to draw posters, make a short cassette tape, design an advertisement with a catchy slogan, or write a report.

5 You will need an atlas for this activity.
a Name the four islands which make up Japan.
b Name the steelworks shown in Figure 5 on each island.
c Which island has no steelworks?

6 You will need two blank world outline maps and an atlas for this activity.

a Study Figure 6 which shows the sources from which the Oita works obtains its supplies of coal and iron-ore. Locate the sources of coal on one map and iron-ore on the other. Do this by shading and naming the countries concerned.

b Add an arrow linking each country to Japan (by a sea-route) to show the probable path taken by the raw material on its journey. The width of the arrow should be proportional to the amount of raw materials being transported. Choose your own scale and show it clearly.

10.3 Changing industry

Patterns of work around the world are not the same, as we saw in Unit 10.1. They are in addition constantly changing. The balance between primary, secondary and tertiary jobs alters over time, as countries become more developed. For most countries, this change has been gradual, and has led to a greater proportion of the population working in the service (tertiary) sector, and fewer in manufacturing and primary production (see Figure 1).

Manufacturing industry itself is also in an almost constant state of change (Figure 2). Improvements in technology together with demand for new types of products are partly responsible for the changes that have occurred. In this Unit we will look at:

- one way of classifying manufacturing industries;
- a new type of product (electronics) and the growth it has brought to an area of California;
- the changes which are currently going on in the Soviet Union, which seem likely to transform its manufacturing industry.

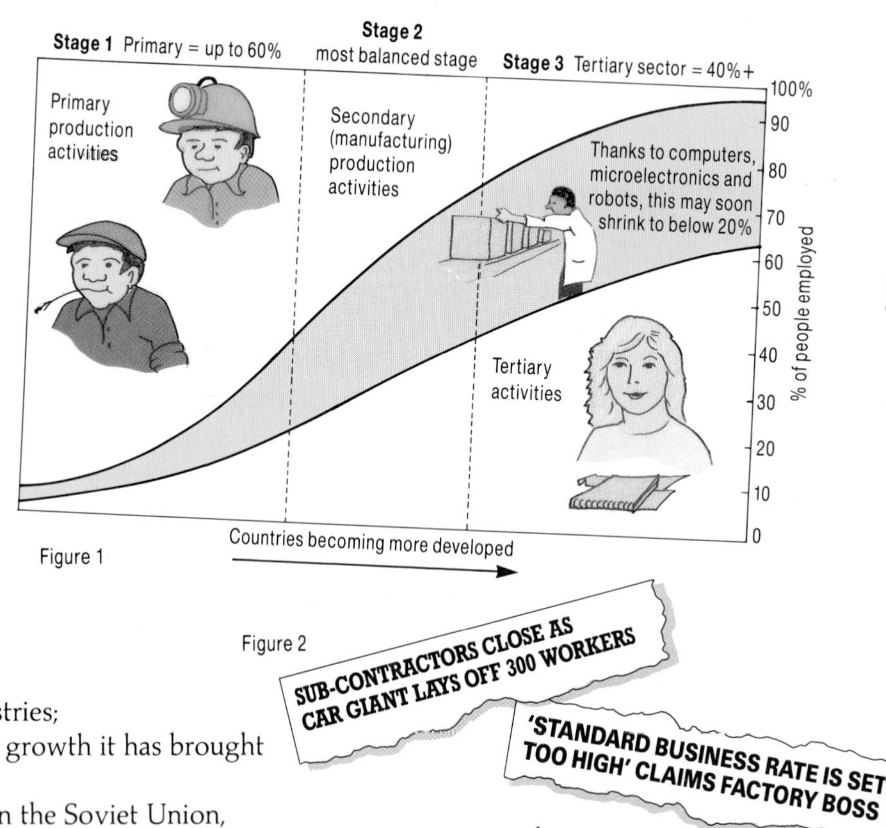

Figure 1

Figure 2

1 *Old and new industry in the UK*

A distinction can be made between the sort of industry found in Britain a century or more ago, and that found today. The **old industries** used heavy raw materials and employed a lot of people. They relied on rail, river and canals for transport. The products of these heavy industries were bulky. As they were often polluting they were sometimes also called 'smokestack' industries. Examples include iron and steel, metal smelting and shipbuilding.

Today, however, most manufacturing is done by industries with smaller labour forces and some **automation** in their manufacturing operations. Road transport is often used. These **new industries** are much cleaner than their older counterparts. They are also known as **light industries** as their products are easily transported. Examples include electronics, food processing and light engineering.

Figure 3
Pattern of manufacturing in the USA

2 Electronics in the USA – Silicon Valley, California

The main industrial area, or 'manufacturing belt' of the USA has for a long time been located in the northeastern part of the country. It extended from New York on the east coast inland to the Great Lakes (as Figure 3 shows). The iron and steel industry and car manufacturers have been major employers here for over a century. In the last 40 years, however, local industry has declined. Most new industrial jobs have developed in the south and west of the USA. One of the most important of these is the electronics industry.

California has become a key location for the electronics industry. Since it was first settled, a series of industries have dominated California's economy (Figure 4a). Most of the growth since the 1960s, however, has been in electronics and related industries (Figure 4b). As a result, California is now the USA's leading producer of high-technology goods. The centre of the development is Santa Clara county just south of San Francisco, where a 32 kilometre long strip of land has become known as '**Silicon Valley**' because it has such a high proportion of high-technology firms (Figure 5).

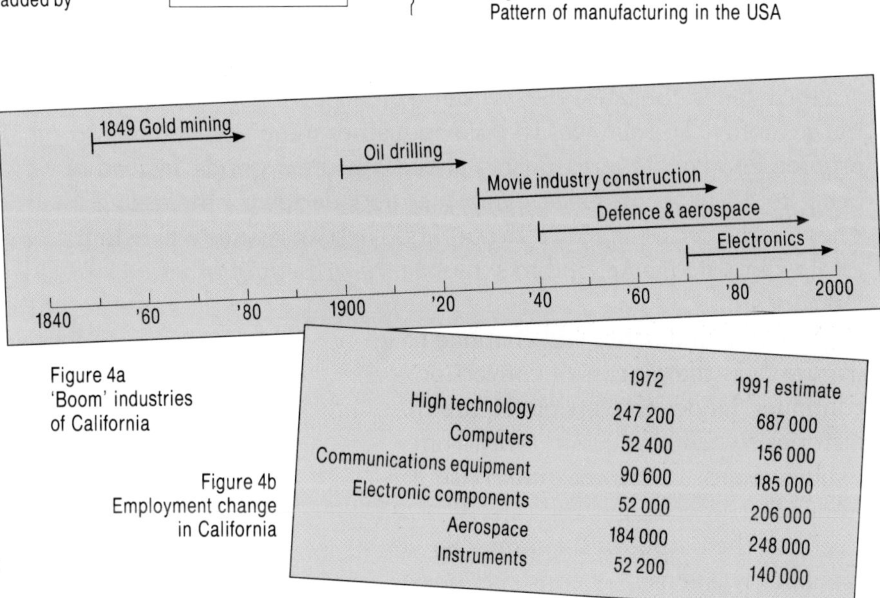

Figure 4a
'Boom' industries of California

Figure 4b
Employment change in California

	1972	1991 estimate
High technology	247 200	687 000
Computers	52 400	156 000
Communications equipment	90 600	185 000
Electronic components	52 000	206 000
Aerospace	184 000	248 000
Instruments	52 200	140 000

Figure 5 Silicon Valley

3 *Russia and the former Soviet Republics — sleeping giants?*

The 1990s have seen great changes in the former Soviet Union:

- the Union has dissolved and a commonwealth of independent states has been formed;
- the Baltic states have broken away completely;
- in 1992 the state abandoned its control of all prices. This left the market free to fix price levels.

These recent developments have brought great changes to the individual states.

The former Soviet economic and political system meant that industries had to employ many people, making the types of products ordered by the government. Most investment was devoted to producing military products rather than consumer goods. As the machinery was old and inefficient, two or three times more raw materials and energy were used to produce fewer products than elsewhere in Europe. The products were of low quality and the industries heavily polluted the environment (Figure 6).

Figure 6

However, in the late 1980s Mikail Gorbachev began restructuring the economy. The aim was to make industries more efficient, and to provide good quality, reasonably priced consumer goods. Instead of being told what to produce, companies now decide for themselves. They fix the prices and keep the profits. These measures will help to create a private market and to stimulate the growth of other industries.

Output of selected consumer goods in Soviet Union (1980-88)	1980	1985	1988
Cars (m.)	1.3	1.3	1.3
TV sets (m.)	7.5	9.4	9.6
Fridges and freezers (m.)	5.9	5.9	6.2
Footwear (m. pairs)	743	788	820
Washing machines (m.)	3.8	5.1	6.1

Figure 7

Consumer industries will continue to grow (Figure 7) as the process of conversion continues. Under conversion (Figure 8), factories switch production away from military goods to manufacture consumer goods like TVs, fridges and cars. By 1995, over half the output of the former Soviet republics will consist of consumer goods. Even the factory which makes the space stations is undergoing conversion. Now each year they also produce 220 000 bicycles, 130 000 pressure-cookers and 30 000 tents!

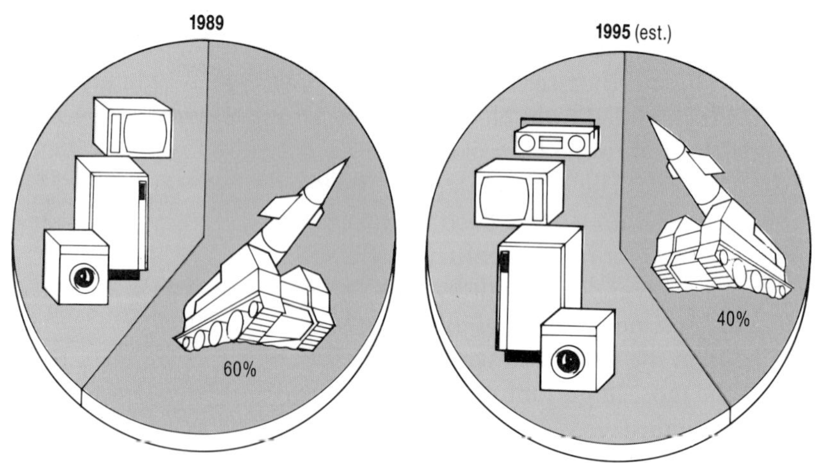

Figure 8 Conversion of Soviet factories from military to civilian output

Activities

1 *a* Turn back to Unit 10.1, and list the countries in Figure 1b. Now look at Figure 1 in this Unit. For each country on your list, decide whether it is in Stage 1, 2 or 3. Note this on your list.

b Suggest two ways that countries with only a small number of people employed in primary industry, are able to provide enough food to feed themselves.

2 You will need to work in pairs for this activity. Try to collect ten pictures or photographs of different types of manufacturing industry from magazines or newspapers. Make a display of the pictures for your classroom. For each one, note down whether it is a light or heavy industry. Examine each picture carefully to see whether you can see any evidence from 50 years ago in the machinery used or the products being made. Note any changes clearly.

3 *a* Using an atlas to help you, identify all those American cities in Figure 3, which are located inside one of the major manufacturing areas, and which have a very high value added by manufacturing.
b Describe how the locational pattern of manufacturing industry in the USA is changing.
c Draw your own map to show the USA's main manufacturing areas. Make sure you include the six main manufacturing areas shown on Figure 3. Label the following features:
- steelmaking areas near Chicago and Cleveland;
- the car industry of Detroit;
- the electronics industry in California;
- the petrochemical industries of New Jersey and the Gulf Coast.

Add any other major industries you have found.

4 Work in groups of three or four for this activity. Read the section about Silicon Valley again, then study Figures 4 and 5. You have been asked to design some material to be used in a presentation to a group of European visitors in San Francisco.

The purpose of the presentation is to explain to the visitors what Silicon Valley is, where it is, and how it has developed. The presentation is to be mostly visual, and will use an overhead projector. You have two A4 sheets of overhead transparency. Decide what information the visitors need to know, and how to present it to them. You will need some design skills here! Prepare your work on paper first. Your teacher may let the best ideas be put onto overhead transparencies and shown to the rest of the class.

5 *a* Draw a simple line graph showing how the production of cars, TV sets and washing machines in the USSR changed between 1980-1988.
b What is conversion?
c Why is the message shown by the pie charts in Figure 8 important?

10.4 Transnational companies and newly industrialising countries

1 Transnational companies (TNCs)

Much of the world's manufactured output comes from a relatively small number of huge companies, each of which has interests in more than one country. These firms, called **transnational companies** (TNCs) have their headquarters in the developed countries of the 'North', but frequently have mining, agricultural or manufacturing holdings in the 'South'.

Transnational companies have four main characteristics:

- **Size:** they are large and powerful organisations. Their annual turnovers are frequently larger than the Gross National Products of many countries, e.g. General Motors has a turnover larger than Switzerland and Shell has a turnover larger than South Africa.
- **International scale:** they have branch plants in many countries of the world – often in every continent.
- **Varied interests:** their activities are usually spread over a range of products and services.
- **Specialisation:** different activities occur in each country according to its characteristics, e.g. labour-intensive work is done where wages are low; research and development takes place where labour is skilled and information is plentiful.

Among the transnational companies are many whose names are well-known in this country. These include Shell, Grand Metropolitan, BP, Allied Lyons, American Express, ICI, Philips, and Unilever. The top 250 transnational companies employ 40 million people worldwide, while the top 100 TNCs account for over one-third of world trade.

Case-study of a transnational company – Lonrho plc

Over 134 000 people are employed by Lonrho. This group consists of over 1000 different companies operating in 100 countries in every continent (Figure 1). The group's turnover in 1989 was £5 billion. Its interests include primary (mining and agriculture), secondary (making textiles, steel and brewing) and tertiary (retailing, hotels and casinos, car showrooms) activities. Lonrho employees are involved in everything from goldmining in Zimbabwe to ranching in the USA (Figure 1).

Transnational companies are a major force in the world. There are good and bad things that can be said about them (see Figure 1). They have been criticised particularly for the way they operate in economically developing countries. Transnational companies do employ large numbers of people, and also contribute greatly to world trade. However, it is also believed that they have abused their power. For example, the low wages paid by some transnationals.

Figure 1
Lonrho operations worldwide

Ashanti gold mine – Ghana

Boran cattle – Kenya, part of Lonrho's 120 000 head of cattle world wide

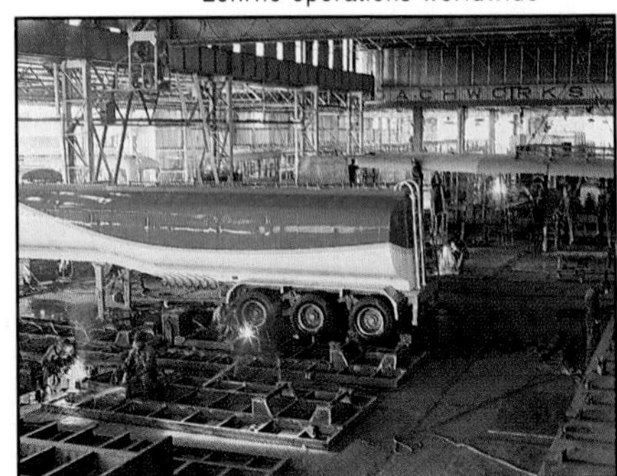

Petroleum tanker from Zambesi Coachworks, Zimbabwe

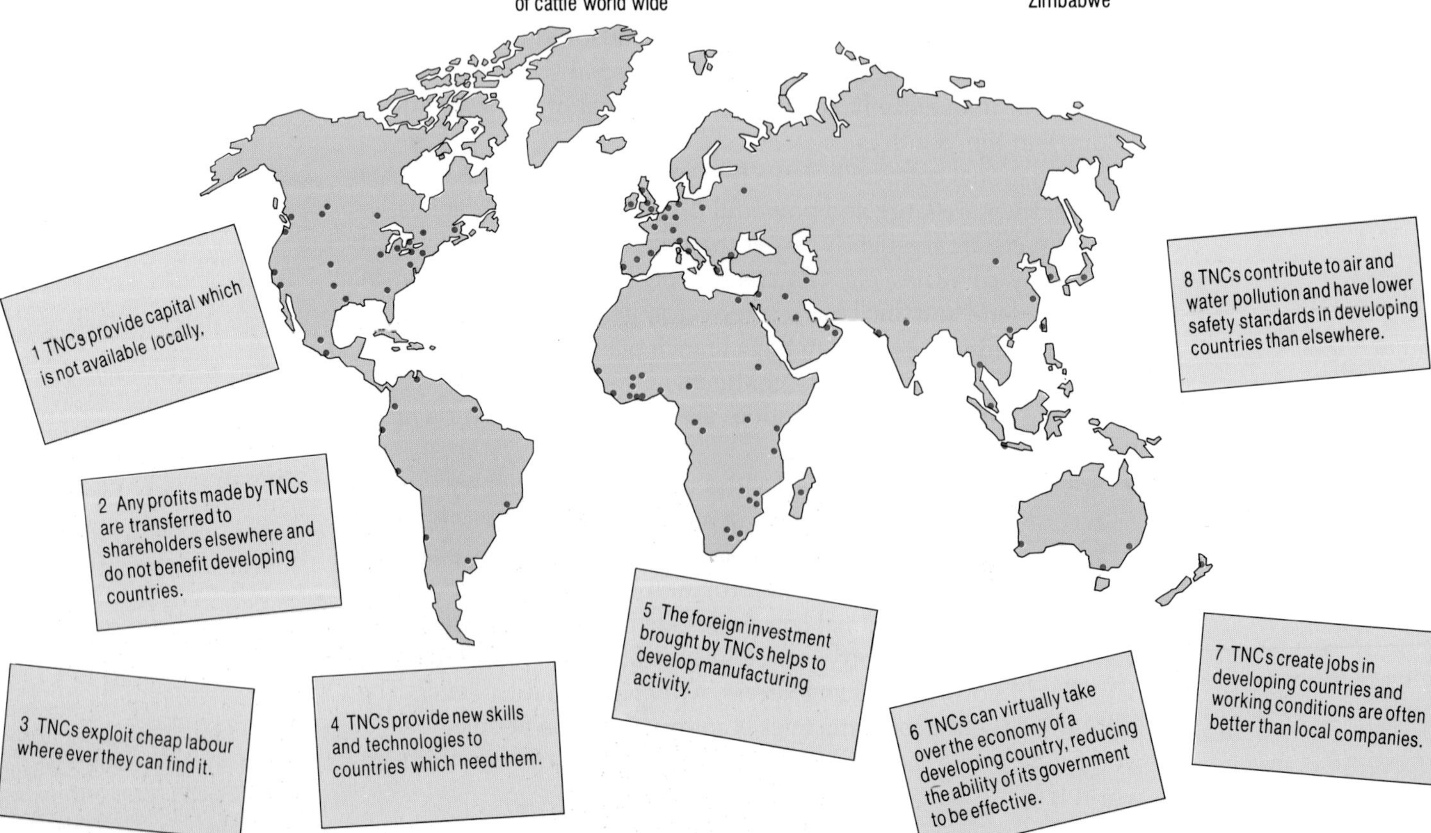

2 Newly industrialising countries (NICs)

In most developing countries, manufacturing industry faces problems in becoming established. Raw materials are often costly, the technology is limited, and workforces have had limited skills-training. For many years most primary products (agricultural or mineral) have been exported for processing elsewhere, so there is no tradition of manufacturing. In addition, average wages are so low that there is little demand for many manufactured goods. As a result, manufacturing industry contributes little more than 10% of national wealth in most developing countries.

The exception to this situation is found in a small group of countries known as **newly industrialised countries** or NICs. Here, manufacturing industry has grown rapidly, as have exports of manufactured goods. The best-known NICs are Hong Kong, Singapore, Taiwan and South Korea, which are together called the 'four little tigers' of southeast Asia. Economic growth here has been occurring at 3-5 times the rate of that in the older industrialised countries of Europe, North America and Japan (Figure 2).

Manufacturing industry has been attracted to the NICs because they have large labour forces which are adaptable and hard-working. In addition, wage levels are relatively low and the unions are weak. The countries are politically stable and keen to export their products overseas. Textiles, televisions, computer chips and even cars are being produced in huge quantities. South Korea has been so successful making cars, that output is planned to increase substantially by 1994 (Figure 3). Most of South Korea's cars are made by the Hyundai company which is known all over the world (Figure 4). Over 90% of the components they use are made in South Korea. Exports to the USA have grown to around 350 000 cars and in 1988 the company opened a factory in Canada designed to produce 100 000 cars a year for the North American market.

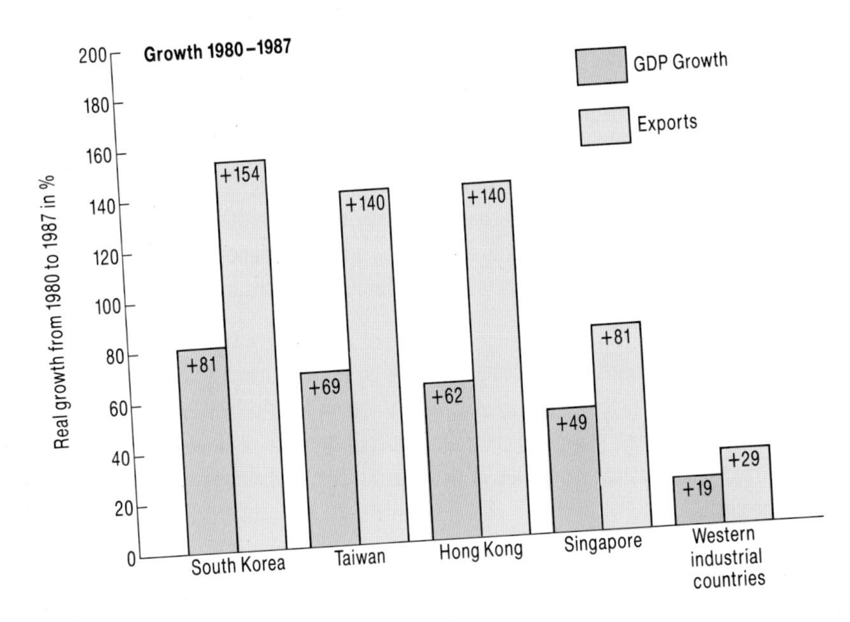

Figure 2

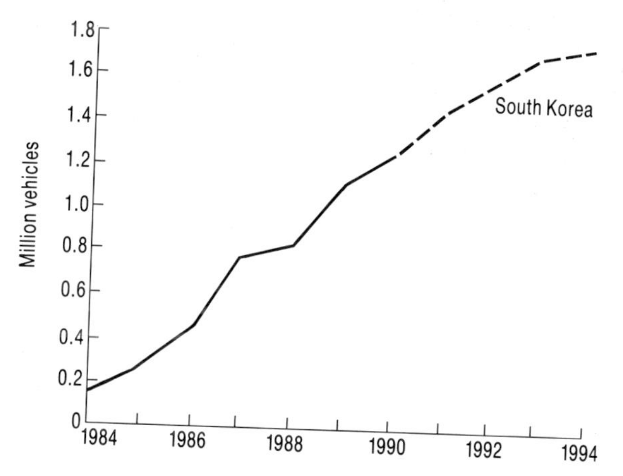

Figure 3 South Korea: growth of car production

Figure 4 Hyundai car factory

Activities

1 Decide which of the following statements about transnational companies (TNCs) are true:
- TNCs operate only in one country;
- TNCs often have interests in several products and services;
- TNCs are very large organisations with operations in more than one country;
- when you fly from one country to another you are a transnational;
- TNCs locate their activities wherever in the world conditions are best for them and costs are lowest.

2 Choose one of the transnational companies, and do some research on it in your local reference library. Try to find a copy of its Annual Report and Accounts. Note down: the number of employees; how many countries it operates in; size of turnover; and the range of products and services it provides. Write a short report on the company containing this information.

3 Look carefully at the map in Figure 1 which shows where Lonrho is located.
a How many continents does Lonrho operate in?
b In which continent does Lonrho have the largest presence?
c The photographs in Figure 1 show some of the activities which are undertaken by companies which are owned by Lonrho. Describe what sort of economic activity is occurring in each photograph. Is the activity primary, secondary or tertiary?

4 The statements in Figure 1 were made by people taking part in a debate on the role of transnational companies in economically developing countries.
a Some of the statements suggest that TNCs do a good job, while others are critical of them. Sort the eight statements out into two lists.
b Which set of statements do you most agree with and why?

5 You will need an atlas for this activity.
a Draw a sketch-map of Southeast Asia, which clearly locates and identifies the four newly industrialising countries (NICs) named in Figure 2. Mark the capital city of each one, and the main oceans in the area.
b Show the increase in the exports of these four NICs between 1980-87 (from Figure 2) on the map, as proportional bars.
c In which of the four countries did exports grow the most between1980 and 1987?
d Why do you think these countries have been able to develop their manufacturing industry and their exports so rapidly?
e Choose one of these four NICs. Design a poster to attract transnational companies to locate a large manufacturing operation there. State the advantages very clearly.

6 Study the graph of car production in South Korea (Figure 3).
a How many cars did South Korea produce in: *i* 1985; *ii* 1988; *iii* 1990?
b What is likely to happen to car production in South Korea up to 1994?
c Name South Korea's largest car producer.

10.5 Expanding services

As we have already seen in this chapter, patterns of work around the world are changing. Increasingly, people are being employed in jobs which are not concerned with extraction of natural resources (farming and mining) or with making things (manufacturing), but with providing services. These jobs are called tertiary jobs, and they are the main source of employment in many countries. In the United Kingdom for example, more than 15 million people out of a working population of 22 million are engaged in tertiary work.

Tertiary activities are varied, and many help to keep primary and secondary industries functioning properly. The main categories are:
- selling goods: wholesale and retail distribution;
- leisure, recreation, hotel and catering;
- financial services: banking and insurance;
- transport and communications;
- administration: government;
- professional services: teachers, doctors, dentists and lawyers.

Each type of tertiary work makes a contribution to our daily lives. We all need services. These are provided in offices as well as in a variety of specialist locations such as schools, hospitals, hotels, banks, shops, coach stations and health centres etc.

Offices have traditionally been located in the central areas of large towns and cities. These locations are easy for workers to reach and they provide good access to national and international transport networks. Central city locations are also likely to be able to provide the specialist services which may be required such as advertising agencies, financial services and lawyers. They are also **decision-making centres**, where governments operate.

London, Tokyo and New York all have large areas of offices. They specialise in banking, insurance and other financial services. The services offered by the City of London, and New York's Wall Street are known all over the world. However, even here, offices do not have a guaranteed future. The noise, pollution and congestion associated with city locations, together with their cost, is forcing many companies to look elsewhere.

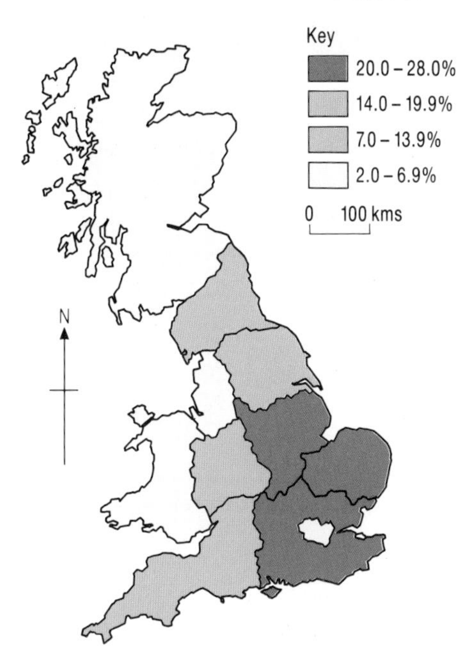

Figure 1 Service employment growth

In the United Kingdom, **greenfield sites** away from London are being chosen for new tertiary development. Parts of East Anglia, the East Midlands and South-East England are experiencing a more rapid growth in tertiary jobs than London (see Figure 1). Service sector employment grew in Reading and Croydon in the 1960s and 1970s. Cambridge grew in the 1980s and Ashford and Maidstone look set to expand in the mid-1990s once the Channel Tunnel opens.

London, which already has empty office space, is fighting back however. A massive new office development is underway at Canary Wharf in London's Docklands (Figure 2). This will give London another 10.4 million square feet of office space . Another huge redevelopment set to contain many offices is planned for the King's Cross area.

Figure 2 Canary Wharf

Elsewhere in the world, the search for new locations continues. It is being quickened by improvements in transport, and advances in technology such as the 'fax' machine (see Unit 8.4). Singapore and Hong Kong (Figure 3) are among the places which are beginning to attract large numbers of tertiary jobs. In the latter, almost one-fifth of national wealth is provided by financial and business services – about the same as manufacturing. More and more service sector jobs seem likely to be created in the countries of the South as their economies grow and their people become more wealthy.

Figure 3 Hong Kong, harbour view

Activities

1 From a local newspaper find advertisements for at least five different types of tertiary job. For each one, make a note of the job type, and decide what sort of building it will be located in.

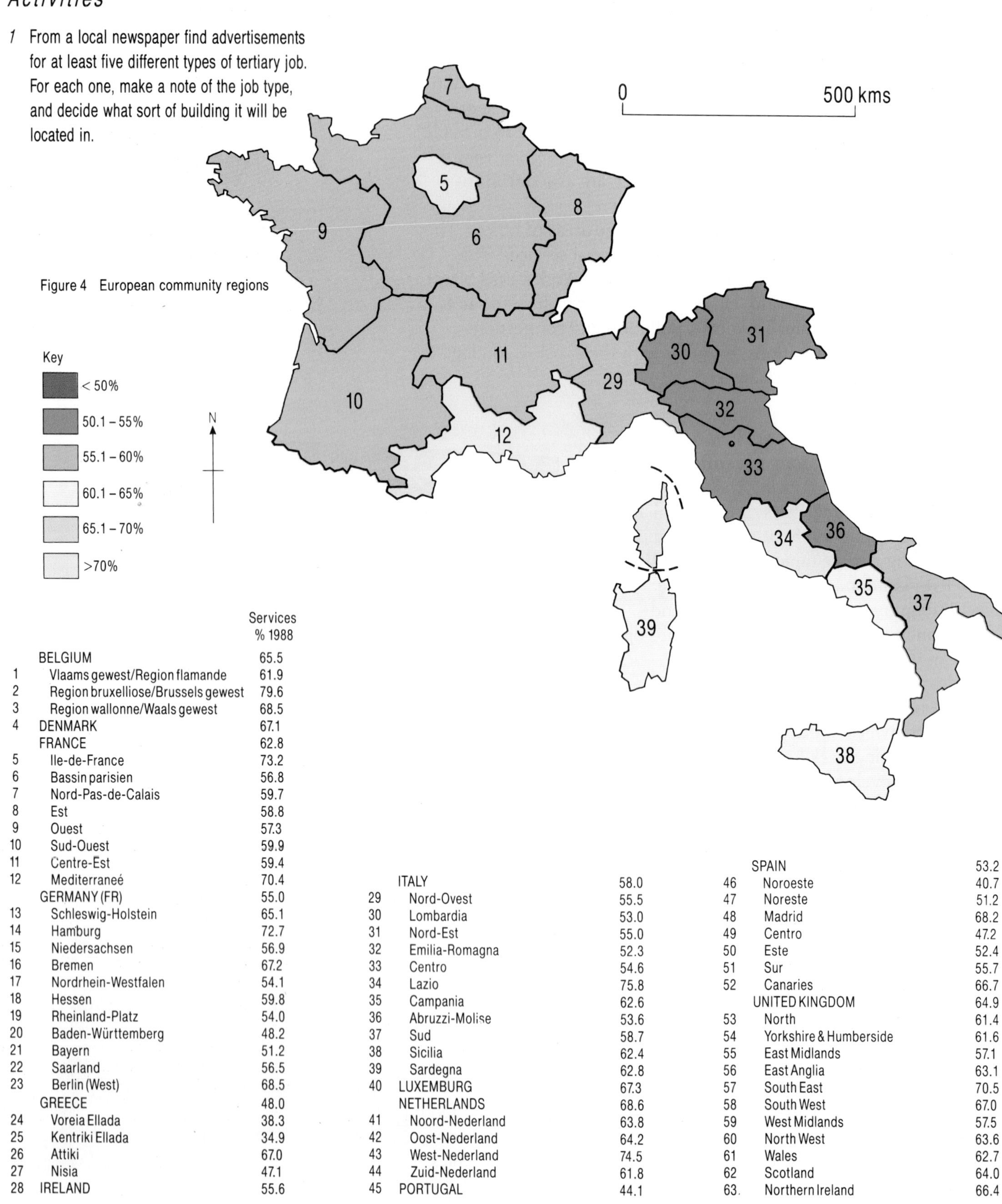

Figure 4 European community regions

		Services % 1988
	BELGIUM	65.5
1	Vlaams gewest/Region flamande	61.9
2	Region bruxelliose/Brussels gewest	79.6
3	Region wallonne/Waals gewest	68.5
4	DENMARK	67.1
	FRANCE	62.8
5	Ile-de-France	73.2
6	Bassin parisien	56.8
7	Nord-Pas-de-Calais	59.7
8	Est	58.8
9	Ouest	57.3
10	Sud-Ouest	59.9
11	Centre-Est	59.4
12	Mediterraneé	70.4
	GERMANY (FR)	55.0
13	Schleswig-Holstein	65.1
14	Hamburg	72.7
15	Niedersachsen	56.9
16	Bremen	67.2
17	Nordrhein-Westfalen	54.1
18	Hessen	59.8
19	Rheinland-Platz	54.0
20	Baden-Württemberg	48.2
21	Bayern	51.2
22	Saarland	56.5
23	Berlin (West)	68.5
	GREECE	48.0
24	Voreia Ellada	38.3
25	Kentriki Ellada	34.9
26	Attiki	67.0
27	Nisia	47.1
28	IRELAND	55.6
	ITALY	58.0
29	Nord-Ovest	55.5
30	Lombardia	53.0
31	Nord-Est	55.0
32	Emilia-Romagna	52.3
33	Centro	54.6
34	Lazio	75.8
35	Campania	62.6
36	Abruzzi-Molise	53.6
37	Sud	58.7
38	Sicilia	62.4
39	Sardegna	62.8
40	LUXEMBURG	67.3
	NETHERLANDS	68.6
41	Noord-Nederland	63.8
42	Oost-Nederland	64.2
43	West-Nederland	74.5
44	Zuid-Nederland	61.8
45	PORTUGAL	44.1
	SPAIN	53.2
46	Noroeste	40.7
47	Noreste	51.2
48	Madrid	68.2
49	Centro	47.2
50	Este	52.4
51	Sur	55.7
52	Canaries	66.7
	UNITED KINGDOM	64.9
53	North	61.4
54	Yorkshire & Humberside	61.6
55	East Midlands	57.1
56	East Anglia	63.1
57	South East	70.5
58	South West	67.0
59	West Midlands	57.5
60	North West	63.6
61	Wales	62.7
62	Scotland	64.0
63.	Northern Ireland	66.4

2 Decide whether each of the following sentences is true or false after examining the map in Figure 1.
- The greatest increase in service employment was in Southeastern England.
- Scotland had increases of between 7% and 13.9%.
- Increases in service employment were greater in the Northwest of England than in the Northeast.
- Service jobs grew in London and Wales at the same rate.

3 *a* Copy and complete the word-puzzle below. Clues have been provided for all the across words.

Clues Across.
1 A location in the Far East where tertiary jobs are important.
2 A machine that has made long distance communication much easier.
3 A site outside a town where some new tertiary development is taking place.
4 Another name for 'service' jobs.
5 The name of the Wharf in London's Docklands which will contain a huge 'office city'.
6 An important service job found in a school!

b Find out what word connected to tertiary employment runs down the puzzle.

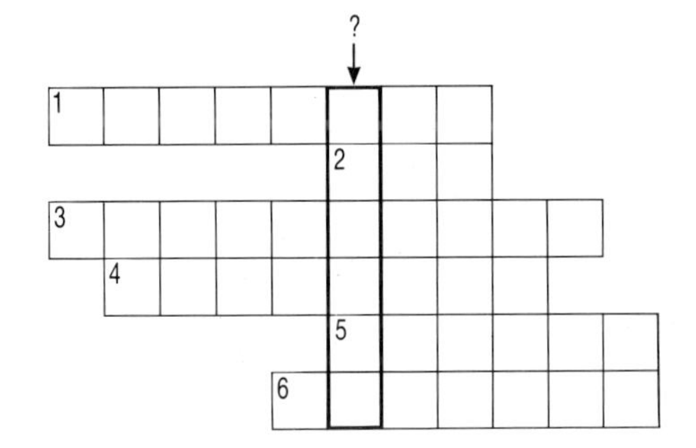

4 The distribution of tertiary employment is uneven. The statistics in Figure 4 show the situation in Europe.

a The map shows the distribution in France and Italy. What pattern can you see? What differences do you notice between Italy and France?

b On a map showing the regions of each country plot a *choropleth map* showing the pattern of tertiary jobs in the European Community. Choose six colours and complete the key (use light colours for the low percentages). Now shade in each area on the map using your key.

c Write a short description of the pattern you can see. Mention any areas with very high or low percentages of service employment.

d Try to suggest some reasons for the pattern you have observed.

Dictionary

automated using machinery to do the work once done by people

costs of production the total amount of money needed to produce a manufactured item, including raw materials and wage costs

cottage industries small-scale 'craft' industries which are usually carried out in homes rather than specialist factory buildings

decision-making centres centres of regional or national government

de-industrialisation the process by which manufacturing industry is becoming relatively less important as an employer

employment structure the division of jobs in any location between primary, secondary and tertiary sectors

footloose modern 'light' industries whose locations are not tied to sources of raw materials

greenfield sites undeveloped locations outside large population centres where many new secondary and tertiary industries prefer to locate

incentives sums of money or other inducements to encourage industries to locate in an area

11 Leisure and recreation

11.1 Time on our hands

Leisure, recreation and tourism have become increasingly popular in recent years. This is because today people have more time, money and opportunity than ever before (see Figure 1) to take part in a whole range of non-work activities.

Working hours in the 1990s are much shorter than in the 1960s, and most jobs have four or more weeks of paid holidays. This has given people more time to spend on leisure activity. Incomes have also risen, giving many people extra money to spend on hobbies, sport, travel and holidays (see Figure 2). There have also been improvements in transport which have allowed people to travel further and faster. In the United Kingdom, a motorway network gives fast access between towns, while international travel is available to millions due to cheaper air fares.

	1960s	1990s
Paid holiday (average)	1 week	4 weeks +
car ownership	40% households	65%+ households
likely holiday destinations	UK seaside, Southend/Scarborough	Greek Islands/ Florida, USA
travel by	Old car... Hillman Imp, Austin 35	Boeing 747
Sports/leisure facilities	Swimming baths	Leisure centre, ice-rink etc.

Figure 1 Changes in tourism

Figure 2

1 The growth in tourism

Thanks to cheap air transport, many people each year enjoy package holidays in the sun in Southern Spain and other parts of the Mediterranean. Some tourists travel even further. The United States of America became a popular destination in the 1980s when transatlantic air fares became cheaper. Now it is as easy to buy a **package holiday** to Florida or New York as it is to buy one to Spain!

The number of tourists worldwide has increased greatly (Figure 3) from just 25 million international tourists in 1950 to over 400 million by 1990. This looks likely to increase to 600 million by the end of the century. Every day in 1990, there were over 1.1 million people travelling outside their own country. The tourist industry employs over 100 million people, and accounts for 12% of the world's GNP.

People go on holiday and become tourists for different reasons (see Units 3 and 4 in this chapter). Some just want a break from work or are eager to enjoy the sun, while others are keen to experience a different culture. The Americans spend more on personal travel than any other nationality (Figure 4), while UK residents are the fourth highest spenders.

Years	International tourism arrivals (thousands)	Percentage rate of change
1950	25 282	
1960	69 296	174.09
1961	75 281	8.64
1962	81 329	8.03
1963	89 999	10.66
1964	104 506	16.12
1965	112 729	7.87
1966	119 797	6.27
1967	129 529	8.12
1968	130 899	1.06
1969	143 140	9.35
1970	159 690	11.56
1971	172 239	7.86
1972	181 851	5.58
1973	190 622	4.82
1974	197 117	3.41
1975	214 357	8.75
1976	220 719	2.97
1977	239 122	8.34
1978	257 366	7.63
1979	273 999	6.46
1980	284 841	3.96
1981	288 848	1.41
1982	286 780	−0.72
1983	284 173	−0.91
1984	312 434	9.94
1985	326 501	4.50
1986	334 543	2.46
1987	361 165	7.96
1988	393 160	8.86
1989	405 306	3.09

Figure 3

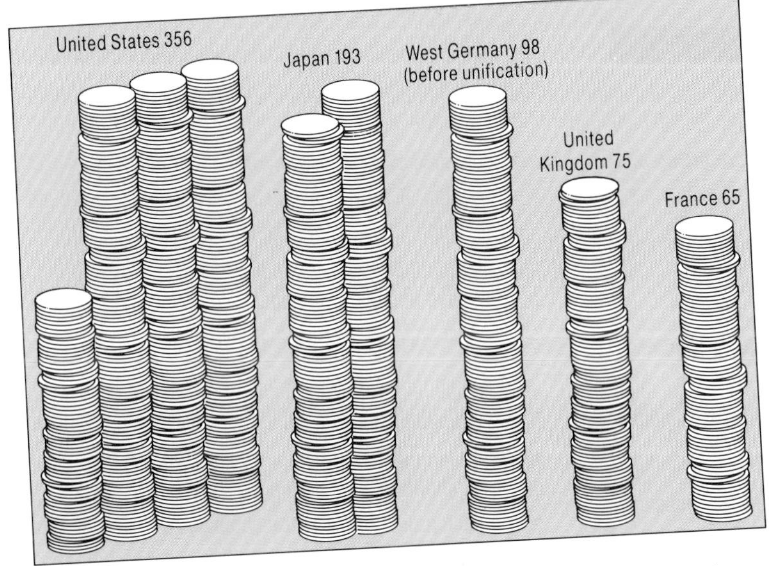

Figure 4 The big spenders

2 Sport, leisure and recreation

Some people prefer to spend their leisure time in other ways than going on holidays abroad. In this country for example, many people enjoy visiting the countryside. They may go on walks, play sport or visit the coast. Parts of the countryside have so many visitors, that they are being damaged (Figures 5) in various ways. **National Parks** have been created to protect particularly beautiful areas. Even here, footpaths are being worn away, wildlife is being disturbed and litter is spoiling the landscape.

Impact of leisure

Activity/cause	Impact
Walkers and climbers enjoy the open air	Disturbance to wildlife e.g. nesting and breeding birds
People walk on grass and footpaths	Grass and paths are worn away leading to soil erosion, gulleying and footpath erosion
Cars are used by many people to get to the countryside	Congestion and pollution are caused on narrow roads People leave litter
Access to many beaches is over sand-dunes – cars are parked on them	Sand-dunes, their vegetation and wildlife are damaged

Figure 5a

The Country Code

1 Guard against all risk of fire
2 Fasten all gates
3 Keep dogs under proper control
4 Keep to the paths across farmland
5 Avoid damaging fences, hedges and walls
6 Leave no litter
7 Safeguard water supplies
8 Protect wildlife, wild plants and trees
9 Go carefully on country roads
10 Respect the life of the countryside.

Figure 5b

Sport is another important leisure activity. Many sports should have special appeal for geographers (see Figure 6), as they use the earth's surface in various ways. Skiers and climbers are able to look at some spectacular mountain and glacial scenery; sailers and surfers need to know about coasts; walkers and cyclists are able to appreciate all sorts of landscapes; and **orienteering** might have been invented for geographers as it involves finding your way around a course by solving clues and using map reading skills!

Figure 6
'Geographical' sports

Activities

1 Study Figure 1, then explain in your own words why leisure and tourism have grown and changed in the last 30 years.

2
- Organise a survey to find out which hobbies and sports you and your classmates take part in regularly.
- Present this data in the form of bar charts or pie charts.
- Organise a survey to find out which places people in your class have visited on holiday in the last three years.
- Plot these places on a map of the UK, Europe or the world. Use an atlas to help you locate them.

3 a Ten different leisure activities are shown in Figure 2. Identify each of the activities.
b Which of these activities, if any, would not have been common thirty years ago? Ask an adult to help you with this activity. Suggest reasons for your answer.

4 a The statistics in Figure 3 show the number of international tourists each year since 1960. Draw a bar graph to show this information. Use the horizontal axis for the years (1960-2000) and the vertical axis for the number of tourists.
b On a tracing overlay draw a trend line, by marking the middle of the top of each bar, and then joining these points together. Try to predict how many tourists there will be in the year 2000.

5 Some of the impacts of visitors on the countryside are listed in Figure 5(a). A Country Code also exists to help people avoid damaging the countryside, Figure 5(b). Working in small groups, design a poster to show people how they should behave in the countryside. You might like to choose one or two points of the Code to concentrate on.

6 a Choose one of the sports in Figure 6 or another 'geographical sport' that you would like to try. Using an atlas, pick a location for your chosen sport. Explain your choice.
b What have you learnt in geography so far that might help you enjoy your chosen sport?

7 Ten luggage labels bearing the names of the airlines shown in Figure 7 were found in Manchester Airport at the end of a busy Tuesday in June. Flights from the ten countries shown arrived during the day. See if you can match each airline to the correct country. Work in pairs for this activity.

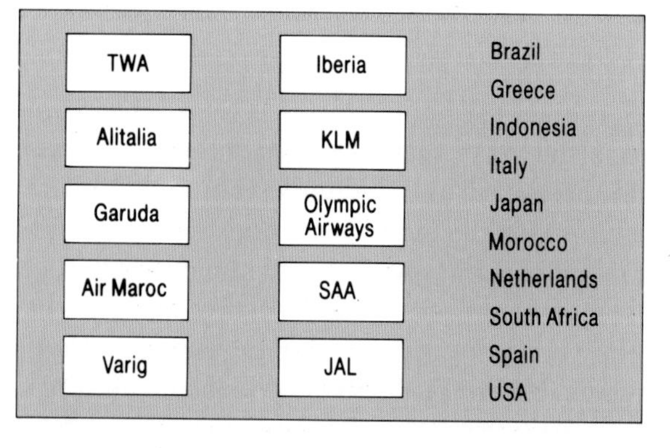

Figure 7

11.2 Visiting the great outdoors

Much of our leisure time is spent out of doors. A survey carried out in the UK in 1985 showed that people liked to take part in a wide variety of outdoor activities. Some like to drive or have picnics, while others enjoy sport or go for walks. Of course, the reasons why people like to visit 'the great outdoors' vary from one part of the world to another. The photographs in Figure 1 show different kinds of outdoor attractions. Each of these locations attracts visitors with special interests.

Figure 1
Attractions of the great outdoors

National Parks

People sometimes visit the countryside in such large numbers that they damage the very things (scenery, wildlife, ancient monuments etc.) they come to see. For this reason, some parts of the countryside have been designated as **National Parks** or **Game Parks**.

The UK has ten National Parks. Land in National Parks is protected from unwanted development, so that people may enjoy the natural landscape. However, in the UK land in National Parks is often owned by many people and organisations. There are often **conflicts** (Figure 2) between them and the general public who wish to see land left undeveloped. For example, large tracts of the Pembrokeshire Coast National Park are owned by the Ministry of Defence. Public access onto this land is often restricted, especially for military excercises.

Figure 2

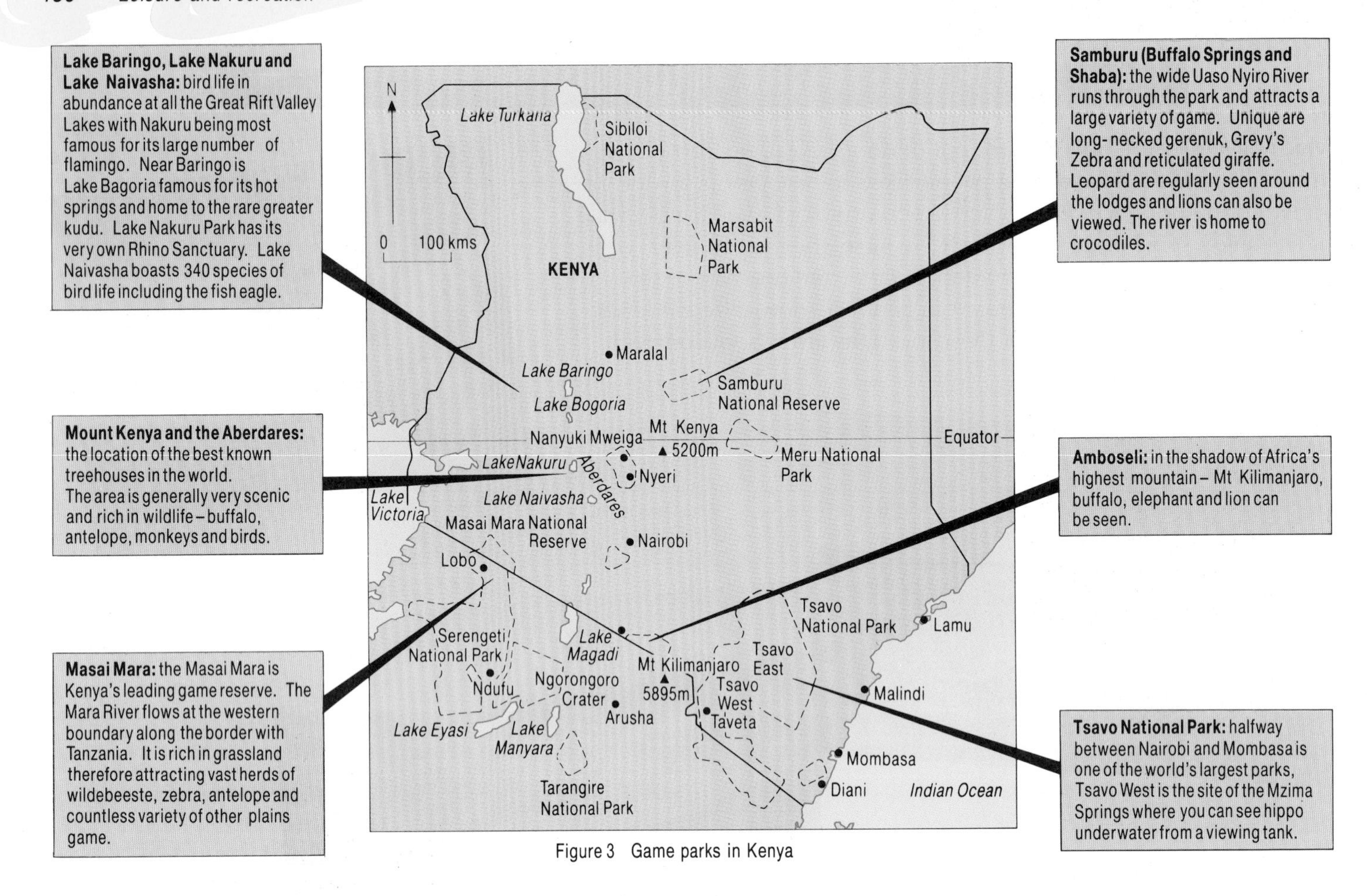

Figure 3 Game parks in Kenya

Other parts of the world have National Parks too. In the United States two of the most well-known are Yellowstone and Yosemite. In Africa the protected lands are known as Game Reserves or Game Parks. Kenya in particular has a number of these (Figure 3).

African Game Parks

The main priority in Game Parks is to protect the wildlife from extinction. However, this is not always as straightforward as it sounds. In the Amboseli Game Park near Mount Kilimanjaro, elephants are one of the species being protected. They are quite difficult animals to protect. A single elephant feeds for about 18 hours each day (Figure 4), consuming up to 150 kilograms of vegetation – including grass, leaves, roots and even the bark of trees. They often flatten bushes and small trees while feeding.The elephant does not use the food it eats very efficiently. Over 82 kilograms of waste is produced each day (55% of the food intake). When elephants are protected as they are in game parks, their numbers can increase rapidly leaving little vegetation for them to eat.

The Game reserves of Kenya and Tanzania have in recent years become popular destinations for safari holidays. Many people, especially those with an interest in wildlife, as well as photographers, like to see the animals close up, and many holidays now cater for these groups (Figure 5).

Figure 4

Figure 5 The booming business of safari holidays

Unprotected areas

Not all of the 'great outdoors' is protected land. There are huge areas of great beauty in many parts of the world, in which a variety of leisure activities occur. One such location is the island of Barbados in the Caribbean. Its location resulted in sugar cane being grown for centuries, but now tourism is one of its fastest expanding industries. Unspoilt beaches and high temperatures are the main attractions. But there are many other activities for visitors. Places like this will attract so many people that they may be spoilt.

In some places, **wilderness areas** exist, which are untouched by human activities. These have no roads, buildings, airports, power lines, mines or reservoirs. Even the discovery of tyre tracks means that an area is not a wilderness. The largest wilderness areas are in Antarctica, Greenland and Canada. There are large areas also in the USSR (34% of national area), Brazil (32%), Australia (30%) and Saudi Arabia (28%).

Activities

1 Write a few sentences saying what National Parks are for. Name some of the UK's 10 National Parks.

2 *a* Look at the photographs of the 'great outdoors' in Figure 1. What do you think might attract people to visit each place?

b Which of these landscapes would you like to visit and why?

c Write a short poem or a piece of descriptive writing about one of the scenes. Try to imagine what it would feel like to visit the landscape you have chosen.

3 There are quite often conflicts between the users of land in National Parks, as Figure 2 shows.

a List those features you can see which have been provided for tourists. Explain how you think that visitors might spoil this area.

b What other land uses can you see which might spoil the natural beauty of the land in the Park?

c Do you agree with the idea of National Parks – or should people be able to use land in any way they wish?

d Imagine you were in charge of a National Park. Choose two land uses to be removed from the Park. Which would you choose? Why?

e Two words are often used to describe the purpose of National Parks – preserve and conserve. Look these up in a dictionary and explain the difference. Which do you think should be the main purpose of National Parks?

4 You have been asked to provide a map to help visitors to Kenya decide which Game Reserves to visit.

i Start by drawing a fairly large sketch map of Kenya using Figure 3 and an atlas.

ii Mark the locations of the six Game Parks shown, and the Equator.

iii Read the description of the wildlife which can be seen in each park. List the key animals in each park.

iv Now design a symbol for each animal – it does not necessarily have to look like the animal!

v Mark **up to two** appropriate symbols on your map for each park.

You may do no writing on the map other than to name the parks. Do not forget to include a key, and to give your map a title.

5 Safari Holidays to East Africa (Kenya and Tanzania) are now big business. Find out what such a holiday would be like. Collect a brochure from the travel agents. Choose **one** of the **Safari holidays** in the brochure – it might be to visit one of the parks shown in Figure 3.

i Write a full account of what you would expect to see and do on your holiday – you could use some of the pictures in the brochure to illustrate your account. Use your atlas to add some details about the **climate**, **vegetation** and **wildlife**.

ii In addition explain how you would travel to start your holiday – the brochure will explain where the flights are from. Draw a map to show the route. Decide when you want to take the holiday (you cannot go during term-time!). Now work out its cost.

11.3 Cyprus: An island of tourists

If you visit Cyprus in the summer, you are more likely to meet people from other European countries than you are to encounter a Cypriot who lives on the island all year round! Like dozens of locations around the Mediterranean, the summer months are busy ones in Cyprus. There were almost 1.4 million visitors in 1989. Tourism has led to massive building programmes and brings income to the island. However, it also poses various problems. We will look at some of the most important ones in this Unit.

1 The growth of tourism

The location of Cyprus is a clue to its popularity with tourists (Figure 1). Its climate is hot and dry, especially in summer, when long and bright days with almost guaranteed sun attract the most visitors. The average temperature from June to September is over 30°C (Figure 2).

As well as its climate, Cyprus offers the visitor unspoilt beaches, and many interesting places to visit. The island has a history that goes back beyond Roman times, and there are many churches, mosaics, amphitheatres and monasteries to see as well as vineyards and beaches. Most hotels and other tourist facilities are modern. Most Cypriots speak English, and welcome visitors. There is a long association with the UK. Even today there is a large British military presence. Troops are stationed at Akrotiri and Dhakelia on the south coast.

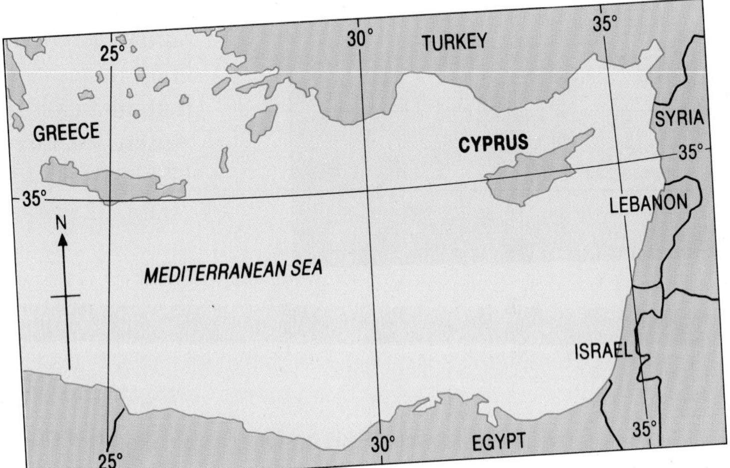

Figure 1 Location of Cyprus

2 Too many visitors? Which way forward?

Tourism has expanded so rapidly in Cyprus, that several problems have emerged (Figure 3).

- **Effect on turtle nesting grounds:** The arrival of tourists has had serious **ecological** consequences. The beaches have traditionally been the breeding grounds for the loggerhead and green turtles (Figure 3). Now, the beaches are needed for commercial development. Many tourists have invaded them, and so the turtles can no longer lay their eggs in safety. This has threatened their survival.

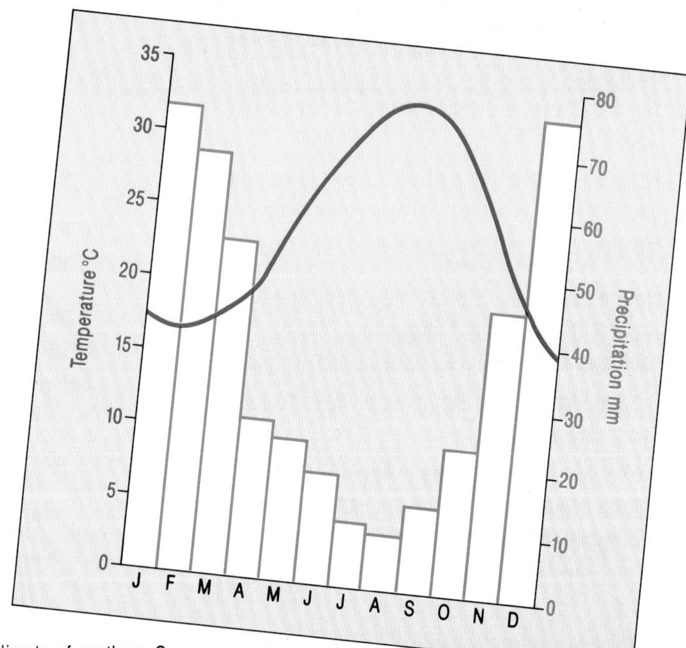

Figure 2 Climate of southern Cyprus

	J	F	M	A	M	J	J	A	S	O	N	D
Hrs. of sun per day	5	6	7	9	10	12	12	12	11	9	6	6
Days of rainfall	9	7	5	3	3	1	1	1	1	3	4	8

Figure 3 Principal resorts in Cyprus

The situation is so serious that hatcheries have been set up like the one at Lara (Figure 4). Government officials and wildlife groups watch over these beaches to ensure that the turtles can lay and hatch their eggs in safety. The Lara Beach Turtle Project releases over 4000 turtles into the sea each year. This is three or four times greater than when the beach was unprotected. If the turtles are to continue to survive, many beaches may have to be put off limits to tourists.

- **Destruction of wilderness areas:** Inland from the beaches of western Cyprus, is a remote area of unspoilt natural beauty called the Akamas peninsula (see Figure 3). Developers want to build a motorway through the area and encourage tourists by building hotels. The mountain scenery in this arid part of Cyprus is delicate, and an influx of visitors could seriously damage the area. Conservationists are trying to halt all development, and want the area designated as a National Park.
- **Political conflict:** The first difficulty came in 1974, when the Turkish government claimed that northern Cyprus belonged to Turkey rather than to Greece, and sent its troops in to claim the territory. The island is now split into two. Tourism is developing on both sides, but most progress has been made on the southern 'Greek' side of the 'green line' separating the two communities.

Figure 4 Turtle hatchery

- **Destruction of traditional lifestyles:** Massive development has changed the coastline. Small fishing villages like Ayia Napa, in the southeast of the island, have been transformed into bright, modern resorts. Here, there are discos and restaurants, traffic congestion, brash new hotels and crowds of visitors. The old atmosphere and traditions are fast disappearing. Even the local people are being forced from their homes near the sea, so that developers can build more hotels and apartments for visitors.
- **Damage to ancient monuments:** Cyprus has a large number of historic monuments and sites like the spectacular remains of an ancient city at Kourion, west of Limassol, which date back to Roman times. As the number of tourists increases, sites like this will be under greater pressure. Car parks and other facilities will have to be provided, and there is a great risk that the ancient remains will be damaged by so many visitors.

The authorities must decide how they want tourism to develop in Cyprus. Should they encourage as many visitors as possible, by building cheap hotels, or aim to attract a smaller number of wealthier visitors by trying to provide facilities that will be attractive to them only. Already some voices are calling for a halt to new development (Figure 5), so that important decisions can be made.

Government moves to limit development

ENOUGH!

By Alex Efthyvoulos

THE government announced long overdue measures yesterday to check uncontrolled tourist development along the island's coastline. The move coincided with an appeal by Dr Theodore Panayiotou of Harvard University, a Cypriot who is an international authority on the effect of economics and development on the environment, for the treatment of the environment as a "scarce resource in need of protection".

The government measures withdraw tax incentives for the tourist industry, impose stricter financing controls on new buildings, and freeze the issuing of all permits for the construction of new hotels and other tourist accommodation along the coastline for 10 months, beginning today.

The government action followed years of protest by environmental groups about the mindless destruction of the environment and the threat this posed for the survival of the tourist industry, a mainstay of the economy.

Cyprus Weekly 28 June 1989

Figure 5

Activities

1 You will need an atlas for this activity.

a Describe the location of Cyprus using Figure 1 and an atlas.

b
- Estimate the distance between the UK and Cyprus.
- Which direction is Cyprus from the UK?
- Describe the quickest sea-route to Cyprus from the UK, and mark it on a simple sketch map.

2 *a* Study the climate graph and figures for Cyprus (Figure 2). Use your atlas to list the differences between it and the climate of the UK.

b Look at the table below which shows the monthly pattern of visitors to Cyprus.

Tourist arrivals by month (%).

J	F	M	A	M	J	J	A	S	O	N	D
2.3	3.0	6.0	8.3	11.0	10.4	13.7	13.8	11.6	10.6	5.3	4.0

Draw an appropriate graph to show these figures.

c Explain in your own words why some months are more popular than others.

3 You should work in groups of three or four for this activity. Use Figure 3 and the text to decide how local people might feel about the growth of tourism in Cyprus. Discuss *a* and *b* before writing your answers:

a Summarise the problems that tourism can bring.

b List some of the ways that local people might benefit from the continued development of tourism.

c The newspaper article in Figure 5 describes the views of some people in Cyprus about the tourist industry. Write a letter to the newspaper saying whether you agree with the government blocking all new tourist development for 10 months.

4 Study some holiday brochures describing holidays in Cyprus.
- Draw a map to show where the main resorts are located. Your map should include: Ayia Napa, Paphos, Larnaca, Protaras, Limassol and Paralimni.
- Add the three locations shown in Figure 3 as being potential sources of conflict.
- Devise symbols to show what is available at each site e.g. beach, historical monument etc.
- Finally, add the capital city (Nicosia) and the location of the two main airports at Larnaca and Paphos.

5 Study Figure 4.

a Explain how people are interfering with the development of the turtles on the beaches of Cyprus.

b What do you think about this problem? Does it matter that the breeding grounds of the turtle are threatened – or should tourism be allowed to develop without restriction?

6 Imagine that you own a development site near the coast at Paphos in the southwest of Cyprus. You have three proposals for development

Proposal 1: involves building a small high-class hotel with 120 beds. It will provide five-star luxury accommodation, and will have its own golf course and casino. The aim is to attract only wealthy tourists. It will be built in the Cypriot style by local craftspeople. There will be extensive gardens and they will be landscaped. The hotel will only be three storeys high.

Proposal 2: involves building a massive hotel and apartment complex with accommodation for 870 people. It will have several restaurants serving English food, and two discos. The hotel will be British owned and managed. It will fill most of the site, and will be six storeys high.

Proposal 3: involves building a small holiday village complex. It will comprise small holiday chalets surrounding a central pool area and restaurant complex. They will be low-rise – a maximum of two storeys high.

All three proposals will cost about the same amount of money – but they are not equally popular with local people. Which one do you think that they would favour and why?

11.4 Tourism in the developing world

Statistics show that more of us are travelling overseas for our holidays. In 1950 only 25 million travellers crossed international borders. Today, this figure exceeds 400 million, and is still increasing. People who travel abroad on holiday are mostly fairly wealthy, live in developed countries, and usually choose to visit other developed countries. However, some of the world's economically developing countries like the Gambia, Kenya, India, Mexico, and the Caribbean islands, have been attracting more and more visitors (see Figure 1). Their share of world tourism is also increasing.

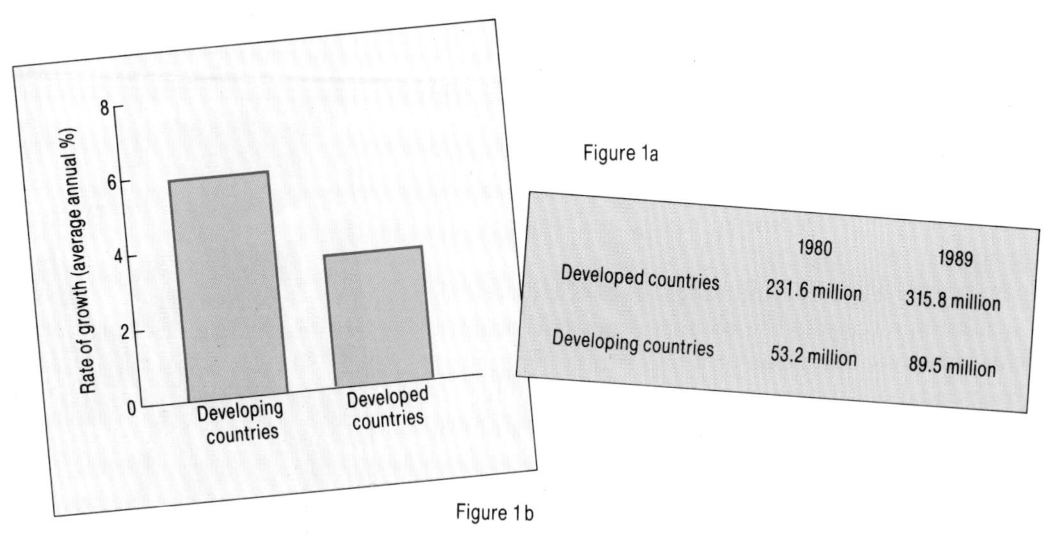

Figure 1a

	1980	1989
Developed countries	231.6 million	315.8 million
Developing countries	53.2 million	89.5 million

Figure 1b

Tourism is growing in the developing countries because many of them see it as a good way of getting foreign currency to pay for the manufactured goods and services that they need. It can also provide employment. Many developing countries already earn vast amounts from the industry. Kenya for example, earns more from tourism than from its traditional exports of coffee and tea. Mexico (Figure 2) earns 4% of its GNP from tourism, and aims to double the number of visitors in the next four years. All these are examples of countries who see tourism as a way of helping them become more developed.

Encouraging tourism can bring problems and difficulties as well as benefits (Figure 3). Tourists from developed countries sometimes feel superior to the people who live in the countries they are visiting. They can also fail to understand local customs. The local people who do get jobs often have little status – they are hotel clerks, chambermaids and waiters. The better-paid jobs usually go to foreigners.

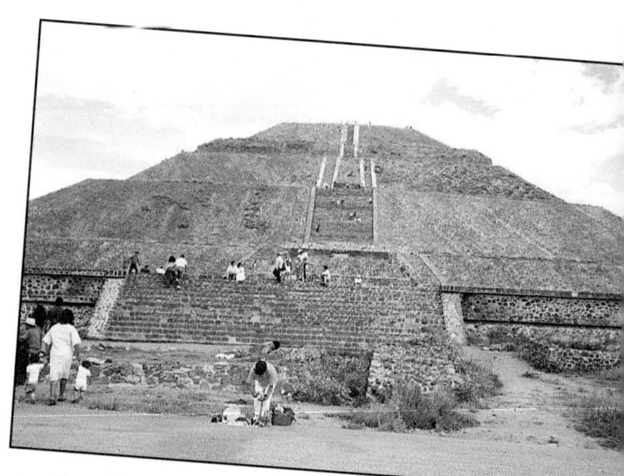

Figure 2

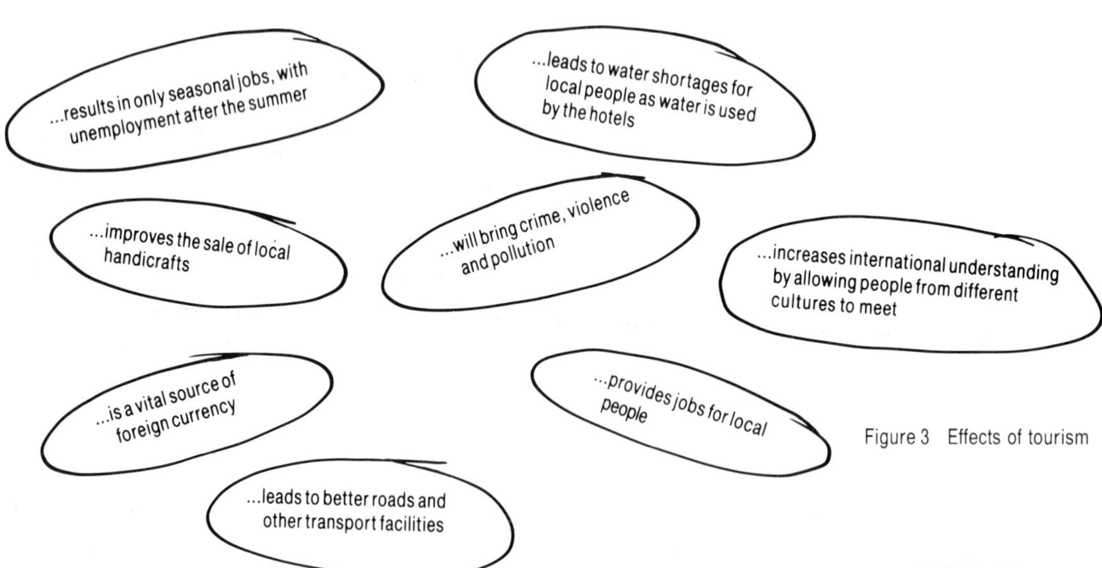

Figure 3 Effects of tourism

Figure 4

Local people, especially youngsters, may try to copy the dress and habits of the tourists they see – so destroying local traditions and culture. Youngsters have abandoned their traditional dress in favour of western-style jeans (Figure 4). Pop music has replaced the local slow-chanting songs, smoking has become common, and young people are rebelling against their parents.

The travel companies who want to build hotels in exotic locations claim that tourists will bring money to the country, and that local industries will benefit. However, things are not this simple. Tourists may bring money to spend, but often they spend it on items which have been imported. As a result, the money goes straight back out of the country again. Food, drink and even souvenirs have to be imported to satisfy the demand from the tourists. In Tahiti, the colourful sarongs worn by the dancing girls are actually imported.

A recent book about tourism claims that the developing countries have been turned into giant theme parks for the entertainment of rich people. Tourism is already important in Asia and parts of Africa (Figure 5), and the growth in the number of visitors to these areas will probably continue. If we are to stop spoiling our planet, then we must learn to be more responsible tourists (Figure 6).

	Africa	Asia/Pacific
1980	7.1 m	28.0 m
1985	9.9 m	39.9 m
1989	13.3 m	55.2 m
1995 (est.)	26.0 m	125.0 m
2000 (est.)	40.0 m	232.0 m

Figure 5 The growth of tourism (number of international arrivals)

1 Not all cultures share the same concept of time. Being aware of this can prevent upsets. Isn't the rat race one of the things you wanted to get away from?

2 Cameras invade privacy and can be offensive. Should you ask before snapping? How would you feel?

3 Why travel abroad only to eat the same old food? Could you prepare an authentic Ristafel?

4 Litter is offensive – where is the nearest bin?

5 We all love bargains but where was your souvenir made? How much was the person who made it paid?

6 Water is a scarce commodity in many countries. Should we take it for granted?

7 Try to use local transport. Which is more appropriate – car or camel?

8 Temples, shrines and sacred buildings ought to be respected. Should you remove your shoes or cover your arms, head or legs?

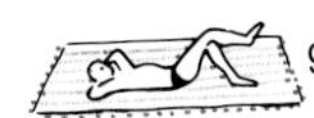

9 Concepts of modesty vary world wide. Is your acquisition of an "all over tan" offending anyone?

10 Respect the local countryside. Paths get worn out. Would a local guide help?

11 People are very similar world wide. We all want respect, courtesy and consideration. Be interested, learn how to greet people. Should you shake hands, place your palms together, bow?

12 Are you a responsible tourist? Will you be welcome back?

Figure 6 Responsible tourist quiz

Activities

1 You will need an atlas and some holiday brochures for this activity.

a Why do you think people wish to go on holiday to countries which are developing, like the Gambia, Kenya, India, Mexico and the Caribbean islands?

b In what ways are these places likely to be different from the more usual holiday destinations around the Mediterranean?

2 a Use the statistics in Figure 1(a) to calculate the percentage of tourists visiting developing countries in *i* 1980 and *ii* 1989.

b Draw a bar chart showing the percentage of visitors to developing countries.

c Use the annual rate of increase shown in Figure 1(b) to predict the number of tourists likely to visit developing countries by the year 2000.

3 Figure 2 shows one of the popular tourist destinations in Mexico. In groups of three or four, undertake a study of a tourist destination in a developing country. You may choose the Caribbean, the Gambia, Kenya, India or somewhere else. With the help of a travel brochure and the travel books in the library, explain in your own words why the place you have chosen is popular with tourists. Prepare a wall display. Include a location map; climate details; and some of the main things that tourists can see or do while on holiday in the destination you have chosen.

4 Tourism in developing countries can have some good and bad effects. A selection of these are listed in Figure 3.

a Draw up a table with two columns. Include the positive effects of tourism in one column and the negative effects in the other. Use the statements contained in Figure 3 for this. Try to think of at least one extra effect yourself to add to each column.

b Compare your table with a classmate. Do your lists agree? If not, talk about any difficulties, and see if you can produce a list you are both agreed on.

c In pairs again, look closely at the positive effects of tourism listed in your table. Which of the statements listed in this column do you think tourism to developing countries will really achieve?

5 Draw two line graphs to represent the data in Figure 5. This shows the growth in tourism to Africa and the Asia-Pacific regions.

11.5 People, leisure and the environment

As we saw earlier, increased prosperity, more leisure time and a stronger awareness of the environment, are causing many people to go into the countryside to enjoy their leisure time as well as for their holidays. This movement is putting many unspoilt parts of the world, like some of the great national parks, under threat. Even more remote 'wilderness' areas, like Antarctica, are beginning to be exploited for their tourist potential.

Another real danger lies much closer to our homes. The countryside surrounding our towns and cities is increasingly under threat from a whole variety of sources. Let's take a look at south-east England, which, with the opening of the Channel Tunnel in 1993 is set to become even more popular as a destination for many visitors.

Case-Study – South-east England

The population of south-east England has been growing for many years as people who work in London have sought more pleasant 'greener' locations in which to live and spend their leisure time and weekends.

This, together with several additional factors, is putting the environment of the region at risk:

- industrial development around some of the region's towns is causing many people to abandon working in London in preference for working nearer to home;
- developments in the transport infrastructure of the region, like the new Queen Elizabeth II bridge over the River Thames at Dartford and the completion of the M20 motorway linking London with the Kent Coast, increase the amount of traffic;
- the opening of the Channel Tunnel in 1993 will lead to more traffic on the roads and probably a greater influx of visitors and tourists to the towns of the South East, like Canterbury, Ashford and Maidstone.
- the continuing provision of extra shopping and leisure facilities, some of which are being built on greenfield sites, will be a further attraction, encouraging more visitors into the countryside. The massive new regional Lakeside Shopping Centre at Thurrock north of the bridge at Dartford and the Fantaseas Leisure Complex are two examples.

Is the countryside near you under threat from visitors? What sort of new facilities or changes are taking place in transport where you live? Will these increase your area's attractiveness? What effect will this have in the long term?

Maidstone: People, leisure and environment

Right at the heart of the county of Kent, in the midst of a now thriving region, lies the County Town of Maidstone. Its population has grown steadily from just 8 000 in 1801 to over 130 000 today. Despite its growth it is still surrounded by beautiful countryside – part of the 'Garden of England'. However, recent growth and the development of the town centre are placing increasing pressures on both the town and the countryside. The road system cannot cope, parking in the town centre is almost impossible, and there are further threats from out-of-town leisure complexes. Many of the small surrounding villages have lost their character as extra housing has been built to accommodate the overspill population from Maidstone.

Figure 1 Leeds Castle

Activities

The following activities are all based on the Ordnance Survey map extract (Figure 2). Study it carefully before attempting any of them.

1 a Identify *three* different types of leisure activity for which there is evidence on the map. Explain the evidence for each one.

b Suggest, with reasons, some leisure activities which might take place on the land to the north of the railway line which runs through the map extract.

c Name one way in which residents of Maidstone town centre have had their leisure activities provided for.

2 a What evidence is there of farming activity in this area?

b In what ways can farms be used in leisure activities? Think carefully – there is more than one answer!

Figure 2 1:50 000 Maidstone ©Crown Copyright

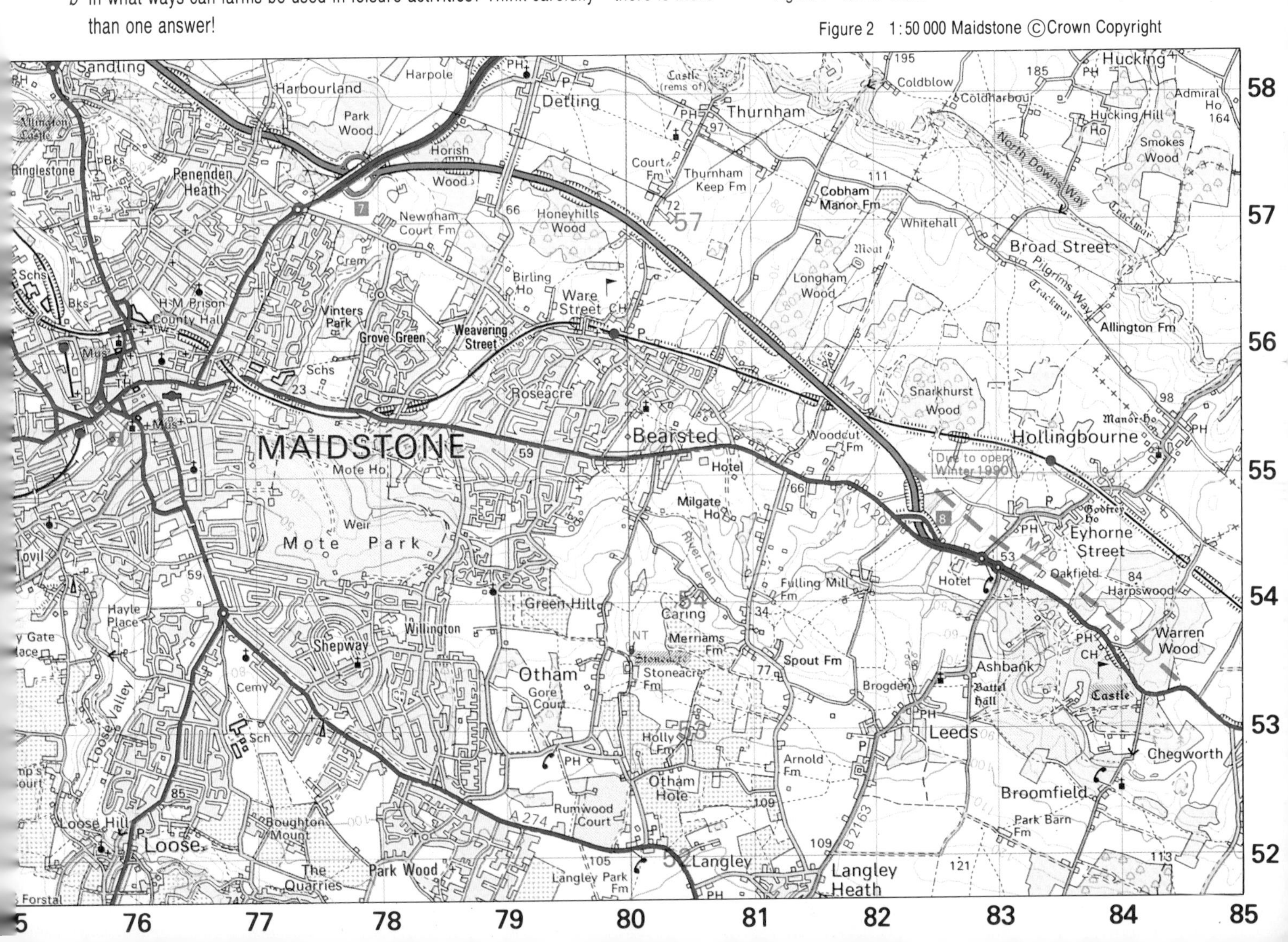

3 Give the 6-figure grid reference for the following:

- Tourist Information centre
- Maidstone Coach station
- County Hall
- Allington Castle

4 You should work in groups for this next activity. Woodcut Farm near Hollingbourne (817552) has been suggested as a possible site for a new all-seater stadium for Maidstone United Football Club. Examine its location carefully and list some of the advantages and disadvantages of this site. On balance does your group support the plan or not? Gives reasons to explain your decision.

5 Examine the photograph (Figure 1) carefully. It shows Leeds Castle, which is one of the area's most popular visitor attractions.

a Locate the castle on the map extract and give its 6-figure grid reference

b In which direction was the camera pointing when the photograph was taken?

6 a The photograph was taken from a hot air balloon. Using the photograph itself and evidence from the map, write a description of what you would see if you were in the balloon, as it drifted north from Leeds Castle to the edge of the extract at 837580. Take note of the relief and land use as well as any human activity.

b Now draw a sketch map of the physical and human features you have described.

7 How far is it (as the crow flies) from:

i Leeds Castle to the church at Thurnham?

ii Newnham Court farm (781570) to Hollingbourne railway station (834551)?

8 A hiker travelling along the North Downs Way in grid square 8357 decides to visit Leeds Castle, and asks you to describe the quickest route. Look carefully at the map then write out as full as you can the direction which the hiker must follow.

Dictionary

ecological relating to the environment and the systems of flora and fauna that live on the earth's surface

Game Park a carefully managed area of land (often in Africa) where animals like elephants, leopards, giraffe etc. are looked after and protected. The animals are allowed to roam about freely

National Park an area of special scenic beauty, which it is thought worth saving for people to enjoy. Development inside National Parks is restricted

orienteering a sport which involves navigating around an unfamiliar course, out-of-doors, by solving clues and using an Ordnance Survey map.

package holiday a holiday, all the different components of which (hotel, travel, tours etc.) can be bought together for one inclusive price

wilderness areas these are areas which are totally untouched by human activities

12 Ecosystems and environment

12.1 Ecosystems, environments and people

How does an ecosystem work?

As countries continue to develop economically, their environment is put under increasing pressure (Figure 1). An important part of any environment are the living things (plants and animals) which inhabit it, as well as its non-living elements (rock, climate, soil, air and water). All these elements together form an **ecosystem.**

Figure 1

Ecosystems vary in scale from a pond to an ocean, from a single tree to a global forest environment. One way of trying to understand ecosystems is to look at how they work. Within the living elements of an ecosystem, **nutrients** are stored and then moved from one part of the system to another. There are three main nutrient stores in ecosystems, as Figure 2 shows:

- **biomass** – all the plants and organisms;
- the **litter** – dead organisms matter on the land surface;
- the **soil** – broken down rock material together with rotted vegetation and animals.

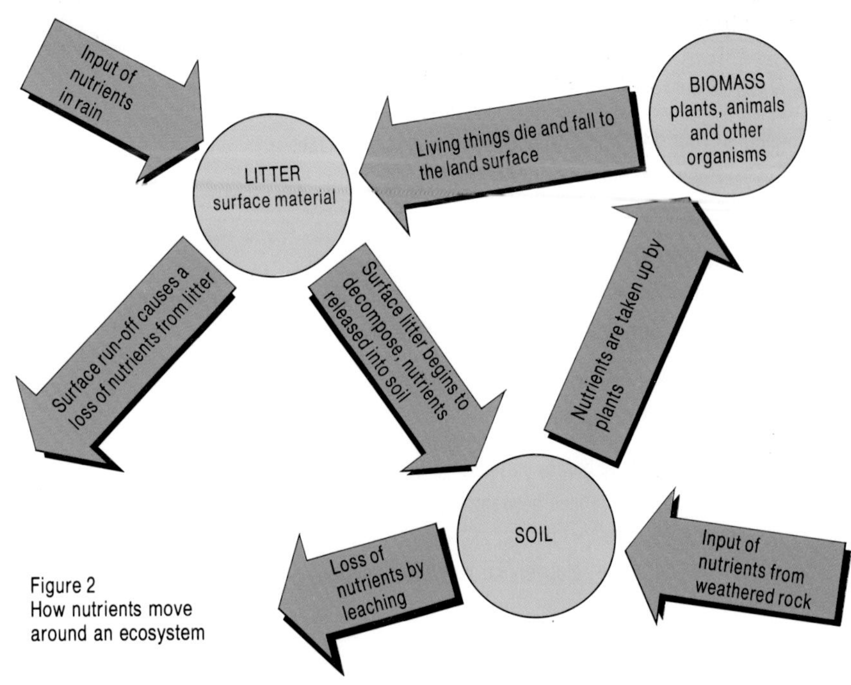

Figure 2
How nutrients move around an ecosystem

The relative size and importance of these three stores varies from one ecosystem to another (Figure 3). Coniferous forests have large litter stores but only small soil stores. This is because leaves which fall to the ground to form litter, decompose slowly due to low temperatures. The prairie grassland ecosystem has fewer nutrients stored in its vegetation and wildlife than coniferous forests, so has a smaller biomass. However, the soil store is quite large.

Human activity and ecosystems

All over the world today, ecosystems and environments are being threatened. The continued growth of the world's population (Unit 6.1) and an ever-increasing demand for natural resources means that human activities are having a severe impact on vast areas of the earth's surface. Modern industrial and farming practices and power-generation are also exerting great pressure on many natural environments.

The results of such human activity include:

- the destruction of the tropical rainforests (Unit 12.2)
- the contamination of land and sea (Units 12.3 and 12.4)
- the Greenhouse Effect (Unit 3.4)
- mining in remote areas (Unit 4.5).

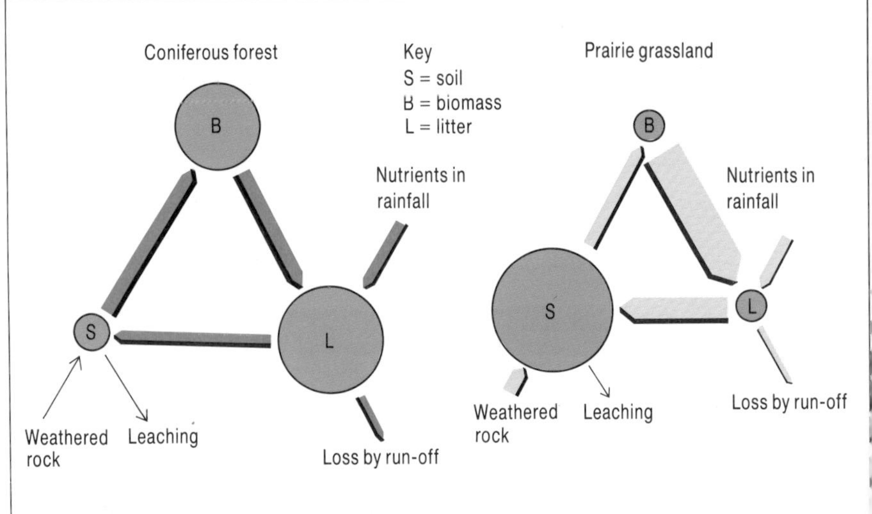

Figure 3

Activities

1 Explain in your own words what the following terms mean:
- ecosystem;
- biomass;
- nutrients.

2 Study the photographs in Figure 1.
  a Describe what is happening in each photograph.
  b Imagine that the photographs are to be used in a leaflet describing how ecosystems are under threat. Devise a caption for each photograph.

3 Study Figure 2. The working of an ecosystem is sometimes described as a cycle. Do you think that this term is appropriate?

4 Study Figure 3 carefully before you attempt this activity.
  a Summarise the differences between the coniferous forest ecosystem and the prairie grassland ecosystem.
  b Why is the litter store relatively large in the coniferous grasslands?
  c How does rainfall play a part in the cycling of nutrients in ecosystems?

5 For this activity you should work in groups of three or four.
  a Use this Unit and others in the book to make a list of damage done to ecosystems by human activity.
  b Now, in the same groups, think of an example of an ecosystem near your school that is being changed by human activity. Remember that ecosystems vary in scale. Write a short account describing what is happening to the ecosystem and why. It may be useful to look through some local newspapers.

12.2 Tropical rainforests – a fragile ecosystem

One of the earth's most fragile ecosystems on the planet is the tropical rainforest (Figure 1). At present, massive destruction or **deforestation** is taking place on a scale not seen before. The forests are being felled for a variety of reasons: for small-scale peasant farming; mining operations; extensive ranching; as well as to allow **logging** and highway construction (Figure 2).

Figure 1

The rate of destruction

About 7% of the earth's land surface is covered by tropical forests. The vegetation that makes up a rainforest only grows in the moist and hot conditions found near the equator. The area of rainforest, is being steadily reduced by human activities. The fastest destruction is in Amazonia in South America and on New Guinea and Borneo in the East Indies (as Figure 3 shows). The latest figures suggest that about 3% of the world's rainforests are being destroyed each year. By the year 2000, almost one-third of the existing rainforest could have disappeared.

Figure 2

Demands on land in Amazonia	%
Land already cleared	10
Area to be flooded for HEP	4.4
Oil deposits (Uriri Basin only)	0.3
Forest reserves maintained for timber production	15
Serra dos Carajas Project (iron ore extraction)	16
Softwood plantations	4.5
Colonisation up to 1989	13
Total officially earmarked for development	63
Land protected in national parks and reserves at end of 1987	3.4

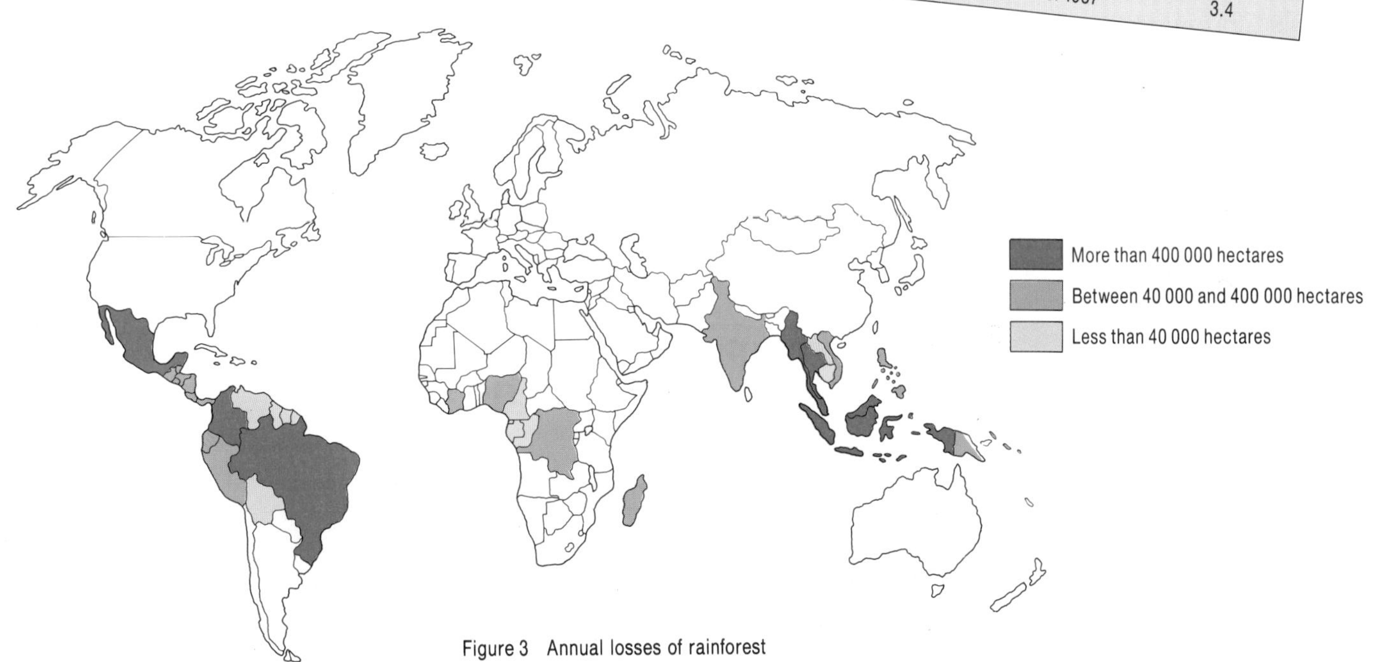

Figure 3 Annual losses of rainforest

A fragile ecosystem

Rainforest vegetation always looks lush and fertile. The trees are dense, and some grow up to 60 metres suggesting that the soil is fertile. This is far from true. In fact, most of the nutrients in the rainforest ecosystem are in the biomass rather than in the soil or litter (Figure 4). Once the trees are felled, the nutrients are lost and the ecosystem begins to collapse. This is why when rainforests are cleared they turn into barren and deserted places, often with the already thin soils being washed away by **soil erosion**.

A new season in the rainforest – the 'burning' season.

Much of the forest is being cleared by the vegetation being felled and then burnt (Figure 5). The problem has become so severe that satellites have recorded the smoke from the fires, especially in Amazonia. The period between July and October is when much of the felling takes place and has become known as **queimadas** (the burnings). More than 8000 fires were recorded in 1990.

The impacts of removing rainforest

Several serious problems result from deforestation:

- the **habitat** of large numbers of plants and animals is being destroyed. This has led to some species becoming extinct.
- with no trees to protect the soil, its nutrients are removed or **leached** by the heavy rain, leaving it infertile. With no tree roots to bind the soil, it may be washed away (soil erosion) and into rivers which silt up and flood.
- the burning process has added to the amount of carbon-dioxide (CO_2) in the atmosphere. This is a 'greenhouse' gas, and is one of the factors leading to global warming (see Unit 3.4).
- many Indian groups have been driven from their lands by those clearing the forest for road construction, mining or ranching. Some of these groups, like the Penan tribe in Indonesia (Figure 6) are under threat of extinction.

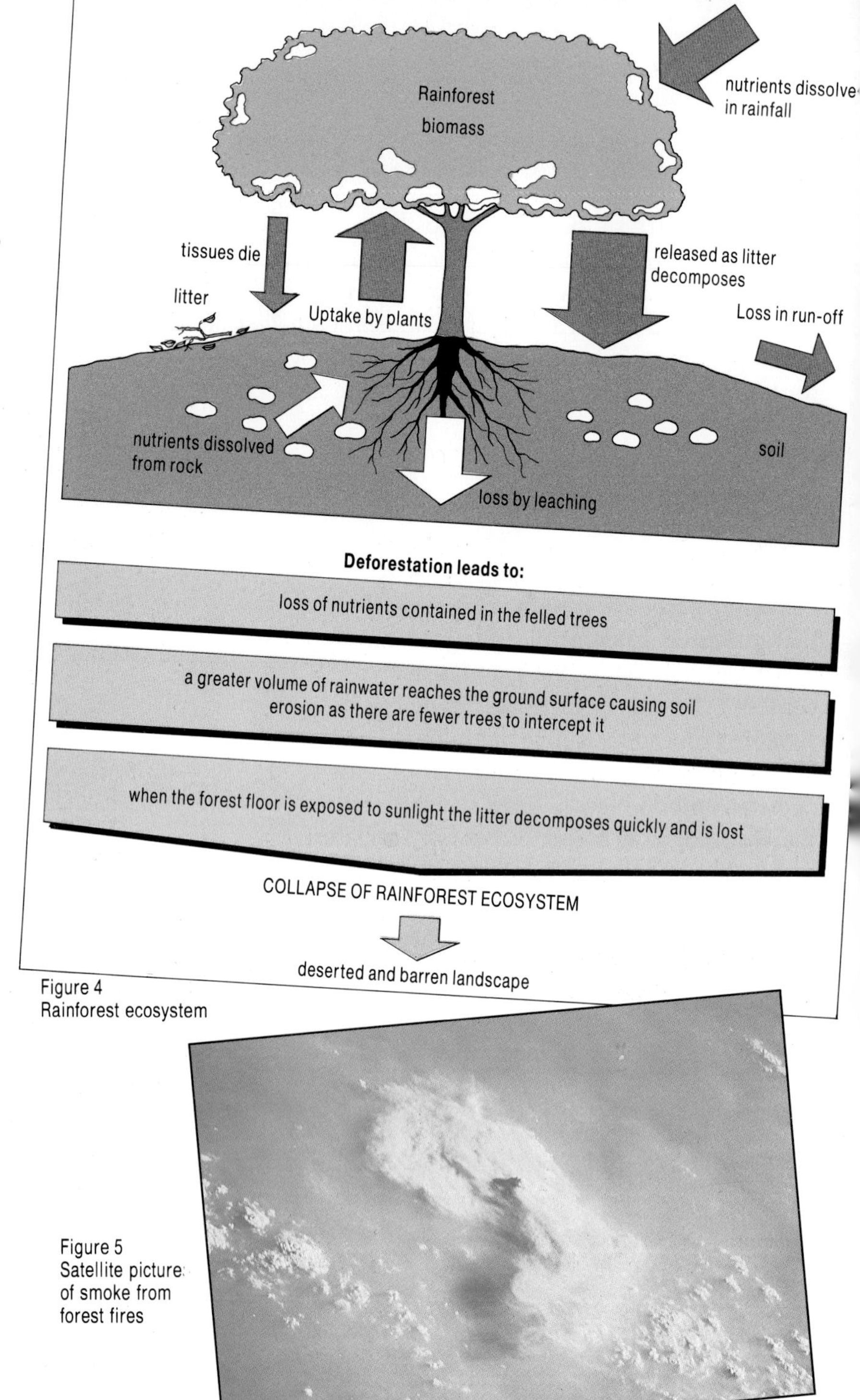

Figure 4
Rainforest ecosystem

Figure 5
Satellite picture of smoke from forest fires

Figure 6

'For years we resisted, but there is no reaction'

Logging is driving Malaysia's tribal people to extinction. Unga Paran an elder of the Penan Tribe in Sarawak, tells his story

Other Voices

BEFORE the logging our life was good. We got food and medicine from the jungle. The water was clear and the air was clean. Because of the logging, we now have hunger. There is no meat for my family, and there are many diseases. The situation is desperate. There is no end to the logging in Sarawak.

All our forests, mountains and rivers are being destroyed. In our jungle the air is full of dust and pollution. In four years the forest will be gone, the land will have died.

The forest has been our way of life for thousands of years. The Government say they give us development. This is a lie. If logging were not destroying our forest, there would be no development. Development is tied to destruction. What development they give is in exchange for our forest. I once heard an elder say: "However good you build a house for us, the house may last my lifetime, but will give no benefit to my grandchildren, like the forest."

Unga Paran is in London as a guest of Survival International.

Guardian 2.11.90

Halting the destruction

There are many ways that the destruction of the world's rainforests can be slowed down or stopped:

- governments could declare the rainforests to be protected land
- buying and selling tropical woods like mahogany could be made illegal
- cleared areas could be replanted with trees
- loans to tropical countries could be made dependent on them making sure that their rainforests were protected
- small-scale farmers who burn much of the rainforests because they have no land of their own could be given land to farm.

International pressure and action is needed if the destruction of the rainforest is to be halted before it is too late.

Activities

1 The photograph in Figure 1 shows what the rainforests actually look like.
  - *a* List as many words as you can to describe the scene.
  - *b* Do you think rainforests should be protected? Explain your answer.

2 Are the soils in the rainforests fertile or not? Explain your answer as simply as you can.

3 The chart in Figure 2 shows the different demands on land in Amazonia in South America which contains one of the world's largest rainforests.
  - *a* Draw up a simple table listing the demands in rank order according to how much land they involve (the high values should be at the top of the list).
  - *b* Where on your list is the 'Land protected in National Parks and reserves at the end of 1987'? What do you think about this?

4 You will need an atlas and a blank world outline map for this activity. Study the map in Figure 3 which shows the rate of rainforest destruction.
  - *a* First complete your outline map by shading the areas with tropical rainforests. On your map carefully mark and label the Equator and the Tropics of Cancer and Capricorn.
  - *b* With the help of your atlas, name three countries in each of the following categories:
    - where annual rainforest loss is over 400 000 hectares;
    - where annual rainforest loss is 40 000 – 400 000 hectares;
    - where annual rainforest loss is less than 40 000 hectares;
  - *c* Use your atlas to find out something about the climate of the areas where tropical rainforests grow. Either draw a climate graph or write a few sentences describing it.

5 You will need to work in groups of four or five for this activity. When you have read the evidence about the causes and effects of rainforest destruction, and calculated how long the rainforests will survive if we keep destroying them at current rates, have a discussion about the situation. See if you can provide answers to these questions:
  - Why are rainforests important to each and every one of us?
  - Are there alternatives to destroying rainforests?
  - What are the consequences of rainforest destruction?
  - How can governments and others be persuaded to protect and preserve the forests rather than destroy them?

  Share some of your conclusions and suggestions with the rest of the class when you have finished your group discussion.

6 Read the appeal in Figure 6 by Unga Paran from the Penan tribe which lives in Sarawak. What response do you have to his story? What can you do? Imagine you could send him a postcard. On one side write your answer to his message. On the other side, try to summarise in pictures, images or words (or both) what your personal feelings are about rainforests and the way they are being treated.

12.3 Fouling the nest – a dirty planet

All over the world, human activity is polluting the land, the oceans and the atmosphere (Figure 1). Continued industrial expansion, the burning of fossil fuels, extravagant use of chemicals in farming, the burning of the rainforests and the dumping of sewage and other wastes are taking their toll. The world's environment – land, sea and air – is slowly being ruined (Figure 2). All countries are responsible to some extent for this pollution, although the rich, industrialised countries of the 'North' are doing most damage at present.

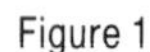

Figure 1

Fouling the nest – Soil Destruction

- There are hundreds of soil types in Britain alone. Soil types take thousands of years to form but can be destroyed in a fraction of the time. Throughout the world much valuable soil is under threat from human actions.
- At the current rate of soil loss it is probable that by the year 2000 there will be ⅓ less topsoil per person in the world.
- Soil is destroyed by a number of factors: intensive animal farming; soil erosion; hedge and forest clearance; use of chemicals; wind loss; water erosion; pollution.
- All of these factors reduce the fertility of the soil. Erosion reduces the thickness of the topsoil (see diagram) destroying the soil's ability to support vegetation.
- Soil is a vital part of the earth's natural resources and must be protected for the future.

- TOPSOIL: mixture of organic and mineral matter
- SUBSOIL: little organic matter; water-seeking tap roots
- PARENT MATERIAL: mineral material from which the upper soils are derived (may be rock, alluvium, glacial till etc)
- SOLID ROCK beneath, say, alluvium or glacial till; plays no role in providing soil materials

Figure 2

1 Pollution in Europe

There have been several major environmental problems in Europe recently:

- **acid rain** started killing the forests of Scandinavia and Germany;
- major pollution swept down the River Rhine;
- green **algae** started growing in the Adriatic sea around Rimini;
- a nuclear accident at Chernobyl sent a radioactive cloud over Europe
- pollution in the North Sea led to the death of 16 000 seals;
- bathers on beaches all over Europe began complaining about the quality of the water;
- cyclists in London began wearing gauze masks to protect themselves from the fumes pumped out by cars.

Many of these problems, e.g. acid rain, river pollution, nuclear accidents and water quality at sea, occur in one location, but their effects are spread over large areas. This has made international action on cleaning up the environment essential. The European Community (EC) is helping to draw up laws which will protect people all over Europe. They are prepared to take action against countries who break any of their rules about the environment (Figure 3).

The EC environment 'crime' scorecard *

COUNTRY	WATER	AIR	WASTE	CHEMICAL	NOISE	NATURE	TOTAL
Belgium	11	3	18	5	2	7	
Denmark	2	–	–	–	1	2	
France	15	3	2	1	–	20	
Greece	10	4	6	2	3	20	
Ireland	7	2	3	2	–	7	
Italy	9	4	10	2	3	12	
Luxembourg	5	2	2	–	1	2	
Netherlands	6	2	2	3	3	8	
Portugal	2	1	4	–	–	7	
Spain	12	2	10	4	–	29	
UK	16	5	3	3	–	4	
Germany	9	4	2	3	–	11	
TOTAL							

* each number represents the number of legal proceedings being taken on environmental grounds by the European Community against member states.

Figure 3

2 Dumping toxic waste

Problems created by industrialised countries in Europe and the USA are not confined to these areas. Many modern industries create poisonous (toxic) waste products. Increasingly these toxic wastes have been sent to third world countries and dumped there. The environmental organisation Greenpeace records 115 shipments of toxic waste to Latin American and African countries from 1986-88. The reason for dumping is clear: toxic waste can be dumped cheaply in third world countries. This is already happening in parts of West Africa (Figure 4).

Figure 4 West African trade in hazardous waste

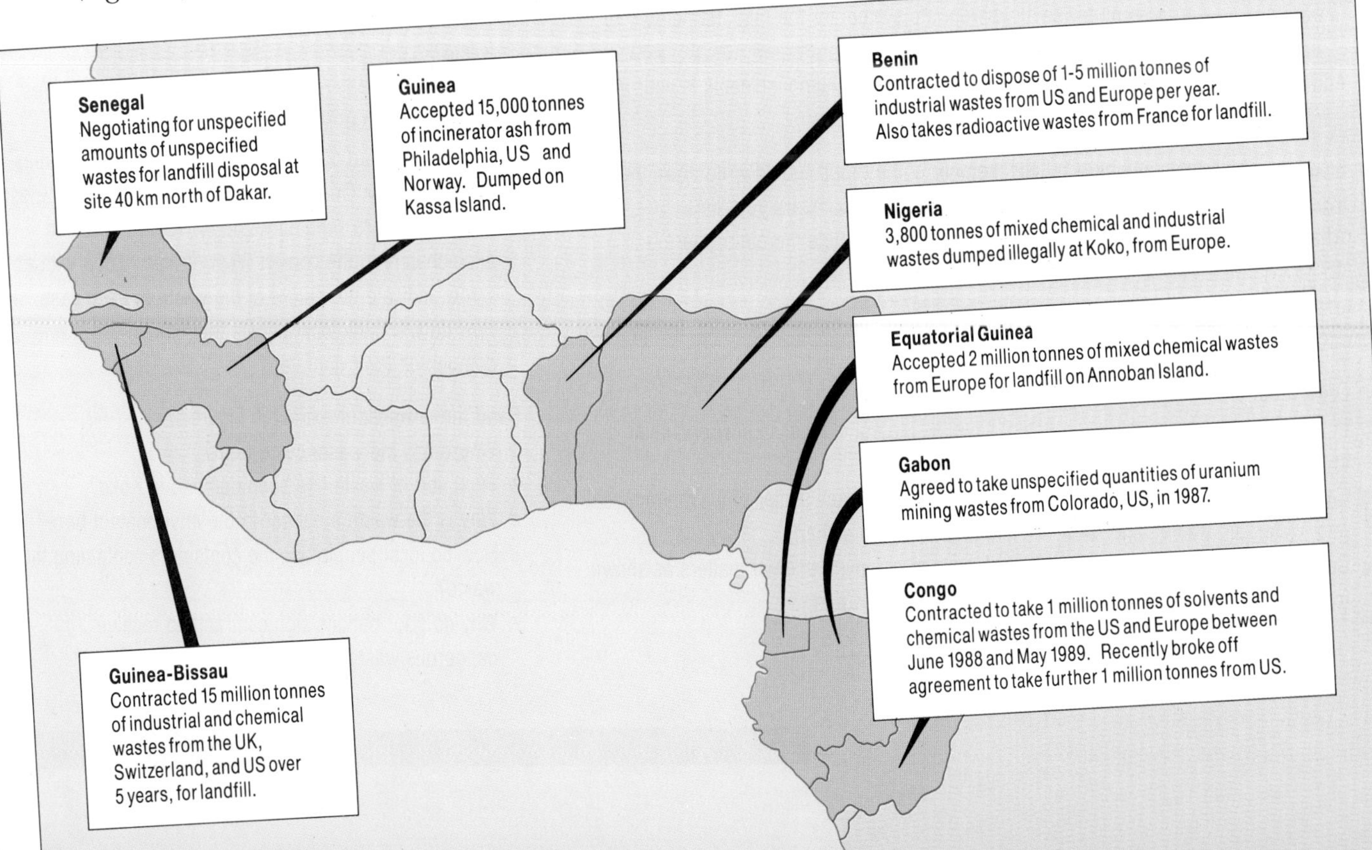

One example of the damage that can be caused concerns 15 000 tonnes of toxic incinerator ash from Philadelphia in the United States which was dumped on the Guinean island of Kassa in West Africa in 1988. It killed a large part of the island's vegetation. The importers were paid $40 per tonne. The same waste would have cost $1000 per tonne to dispose of in the United States, where there are strict laws to comply with. You can read about another example in Figure 5.

There is a growing amount of nuclear waste from nuclear power stations in Europe, the USA and Japan. This will have to be disposed of somewhere.

Deadly offer poor countries find hard to refuse

Charles Secrett

THE toxic waste dump at the backwater port of Koko on the banks of the river Niger in southern Nigeria is just that – a dump. Some 10,000 drums, holding 3,800 tonnes of industrial poisons shipped over from Italy, lie rotting in a small, L-shaped compound, surrounded by a 10 foot high, rickety wire fence. The site is unguarded and unmanaged. It is also illegal and extremely dangerous. At least half the drums are in a terrible state – crushed, burst, rusty and old. Many are leaking. Drums containing liquid chemicals are swelling under pressure as the fluids vaporise in the tropical heat. Large numbers hold volatile solvents with a low flash point. Some "smoke" on exposure to air. There is a very real risk of a spontaneous fire or explosion engulfing the sites.

Koko village is some 200 yards away. The closest building is the school. Despite their international toxic hazard warning labels, with skull and crossbone symbols, several drums have been emptied and carried away as useful storage containers by local people.

The owner of the compound, Mr. Sunday Nana, and his family live in a house less than 5 metres from the nearest stack of drums. From their porch you can hear the drums "popping" in the heat and smell acrid vapours wafting over.

The Koko wastes arrived in five shipments from Pisa between August 1987 and May 1988. They were smuggled into Nigeria by an Italian director, Gianfranco Rafaelli, of the Iruekpen Construction Company, using forged Italian cargo clearance papers and Nigerian import permits. Koko port officials were reportedly bribed to turn a blind eye.

To the fury of the Nigerian Government, which has been instrumental in persuading African nations to unite against toxic waste dumping, the unauthorised tip in their own backyard is embarrassing evidence of the difficulties of controlling the toxic trade between the North and South.

For desperately poor nations, the lucrative contracts offered by the waste merchants are hard to refuse. Earlier this year, Guinea-Bissau was offered a contract for 15 million tonnes of chemical residues from Europe and the US at $40 a tonne. The arrangement would have been worth $600 million over five years, or three times the country's GNP.

Guardian 15.7.88

Figure 5

Activities

1 You will need an outline map of Europe for this activity.

a *i* Read Section 1 of this Unit again, and mark the locations of the incidents mentioned on an outline map of Europe.

ii For each type of incident devise an appropriate symbol for the map. Remember to include these in your key.

b Add the locations of any other recent environmental or pollution incidents to your map.

2 Work in small groups of three or four for this activity.

a Study the photograph in Figure 1. Each member of the group should write down the first five words they think of when looking at the photograph. Compare your lists.

b What reasons can you think of to explain why factories pollute the atmosphere?

3 Study Figure 3.

a Calculate the total score for each EC country. Rewrite the list in rank order, listing those with the highest crime scores first.

b Draw a bar chart to show the 'score' of each country.

c In which two sectors of the environment have the largest number of environmental crimes been committed?

d Calculate the percentage of total crimes represented by each sector of the environment (e.g. water, air, waste), and show this information as a pie chart.

e Describe in your own words the UK's performance on environmental matters as shown in the table. Make some comparisons with other EC countries.

4 The map in Figure 4 shows the main countries of origin of some of the hazardous waste dumped in West Africa recently.

a Which countries seem to be the main providers of waste?

b Why is it that they choose to dump their waste in West Africa rather than at home?

c You will need an outline map of the world and an atlas for this activity. On the map outline shade the countries/areas which are sending waste to West Africa. Join each country to the correct West African nation with an arrow. Indicate the nature of the waste in each case.

d How do you think local people feel having this waste dumped on their doorstep?

5 Read the newspaper extract in Figure 5.

a Where has the waste come from?

b What sort of waste has been dumped in Koko?

c Why is the waste a danger to the environment here?

d How do local people use the containers containing the waste?

e Why do poor nations sign contracts to receive dangerous waste products?

12.4 Polluting the seas

Most human activities take place on land. This is where industrial waste, sewage sludge, and agricultural effluent are produced. But hese waste products are not confined to the land. Some pass into the mosphere and are dispersed as air pollution. Most pollutants oduced by people however, end up in the oceans, either by natural -off from the land, by deliberate dumping or by accidental age.

he oceans form a major part of the planet's life support system. y cover two-thirds of the earth's surface, and contain a wealth of , other animal and plant life (Figure 1). Oceans comprise many nponents which together form an **ecosystem.** They contain undant food both for the living organisms within them, and for mans.

Today, the world's oceans must absorb the **by-products** of ople's domestic, agricultural and industrial activities. Each year, lions of tonnes of pollutants find their way out to sea via rivers gure 2). Here, they result in water which is dirty and even ngerous, and do damage to the natural ocean ecosystems.

Figure 1

Figure 2

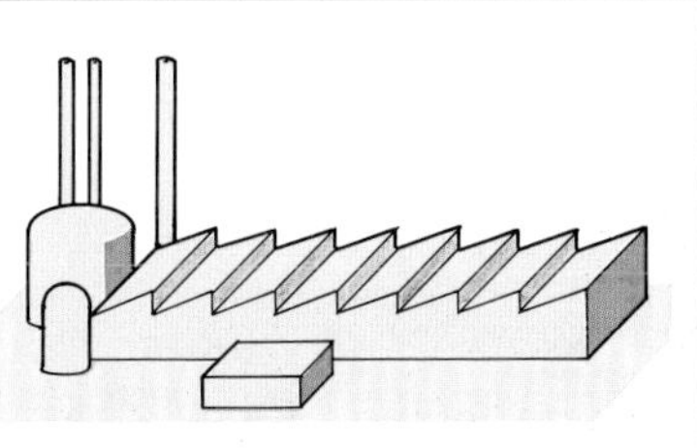

Industry
Much of the complex mix that goes into industrial waste ends up in the sea. Included in this are partially biodegradable food wastes, heavy metals, and persistent pesticides. It often takes a human casualty to alert us to the source of pollution.

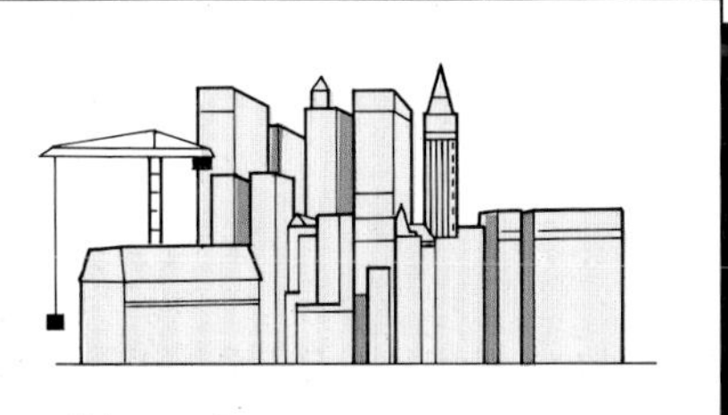

Urban centres
Municipal drainage systems pour out domestic and industrial sewage, contaminated with toxic chemicals, heavy metals, oil, and organic nutrients. Construction sites release enormous amounts of sediment into rivers.

Agricultural run-off
Pesticides and herbicides, not readily bio-degradable, are persistent pollutants. As they pass through marine food chains, their effect is concentrated. Nitrates from fertilizers over-enrich water, causing algal growth and eventual deoxygenation.

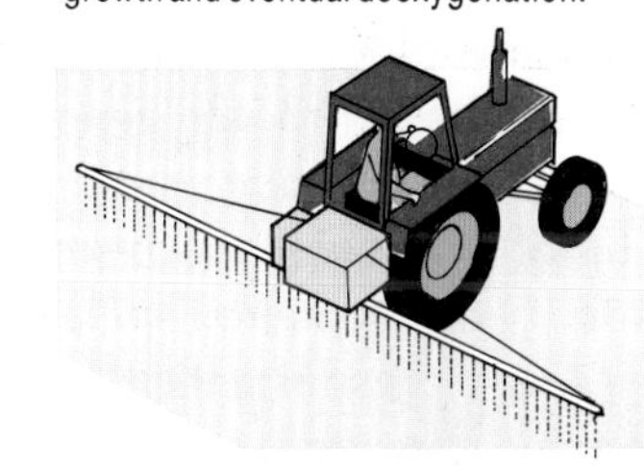

Oil spillages 20 billion tonnes of suspended matter and dissolved salts each year.
6 million tonnes of oil enter the sea each year by many different routes.

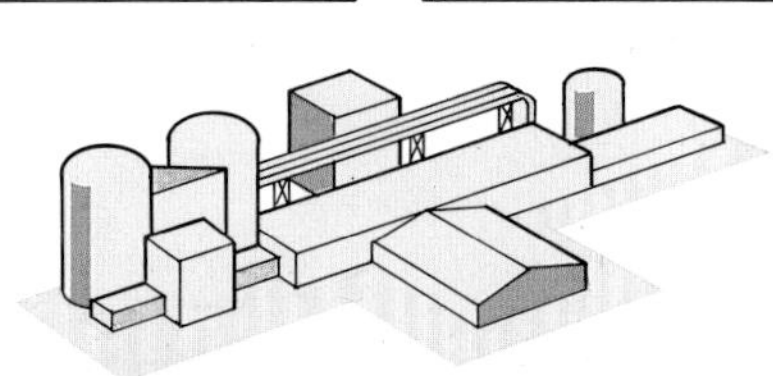

Nuclear reactors
Radioactive waste is discharged into coastal waters from nuclear reprocessing plants such as those at Sellafield (UK) and La Hague (France). Both plants have been implicated in sickness and deaths of local people.

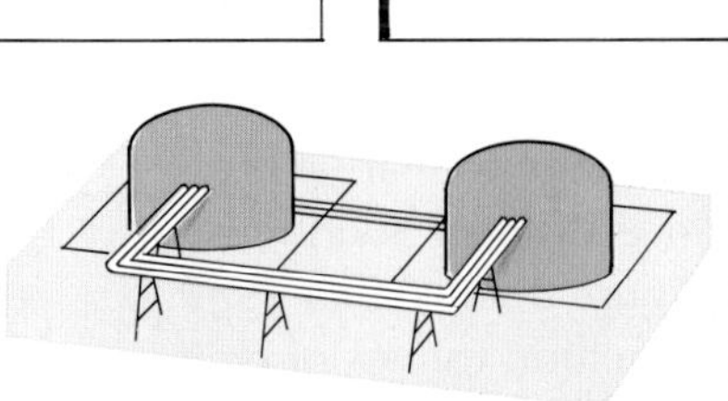

Oil refineries
Oil terminals tend to be sited along coasts, often built on valuable saltmarsh or near productive estuaries. Accidental oil loss and seepage from refineries contribute some 200,000 tonnes of oil annually to ocean pollution.

Sewage dumping
Nuclear dumping
Washing out of oil from tanks

The dumping of sewage sludge and industrial wastes is a major problem. Some countries have also dumped radioactive waste. A smaller problem, but one which received a lot of attention, is that of oil spills from supertankers.

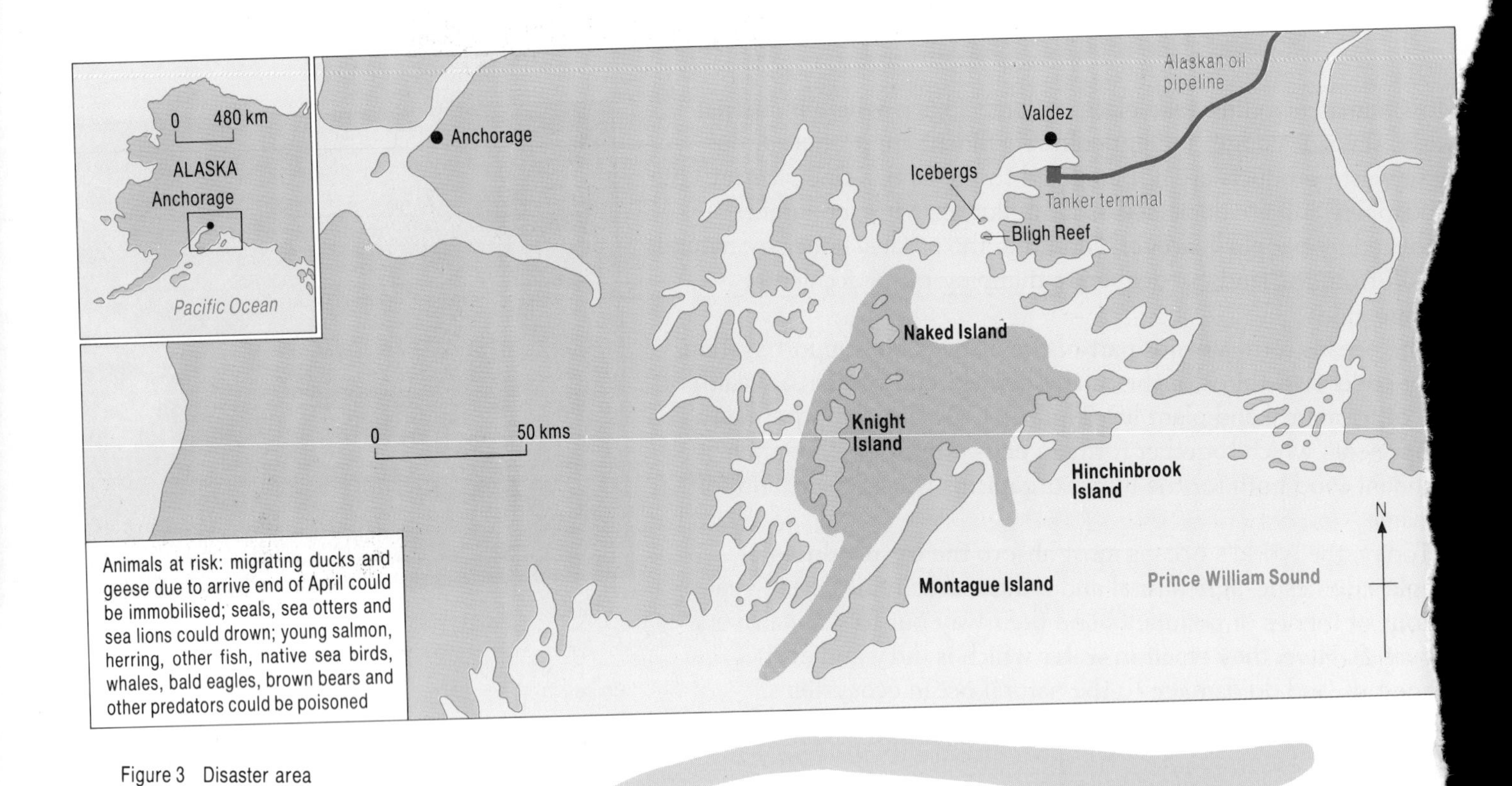

Figure 3 Disaster area

Figure 4 Alaskan wildlife at risk from oil

Salmon In late spring, salmon move upriver to spawn. The oil slick threatens three prime salmon hatcheries, now ringed by booms, that would have contributed to the $90 million catch expected this year.	**Grizzly Bear** Alaska is one of the last last refuges for large numbers of grizzlies. Although primarily vegetarians, they gorge in the spring on the millions of salmon migrating upstream.
Tufted Puffin These abundant birds breed in the cliffs of fjords and dive for fish and mollusks. When drifting oil coats the puffins, they may freeze because their feathers do not insulate them against the cold.	**Caribou** Every April 170,000 caribou migrate from the Yukon Territory to calving grounds in the Arctic National Wildlife Refuge. Proposed oil exploration on the coastal plain could threaten the herd.
Dall Sheep A type of bighorn, these surefooted white sheep inhabit mountains from the Kenai Peninsula to the Brooks Range	**Gray Wolf** This predator is endangered in all states except Alaska and Minnesota. About 8,000 gray wolves roam the tundra in search of caribou and other food.

Most sea and ocean pollution is the result of land-based activities like farming, transport, the generation of electricity and industrial processes. The remainder is caused by activities at sea, like the dumping of sewage. A much smaller contribution is made to sea pollution by accidental oil spillages – though these receive a lot of television and press attention when they happen, and can cause considerable damage.

Case-study: The Alaskan oil spill of 1989

Accidents involving oil tankers occur from time to time, causing large oil spillages. In 1967 the Torrey Canyon ran aground off Cornwall. Eleven years later the same thing happened to the Amoco Cadiz off the coastline of Brittany. In both accidents spilt oil polluted the sea and the adjacent coastline, and caused major damage to marine life.

The most recent accident took place in Prince William Sound just south of the Alaskan oil terminal at Valdez (Figure 3) in March 1989. A tanker called Exxon Valdez, loaded with 50 million tonnes of crude oil hit a **submerged** reef. Eight of the ship's thirteen oil tanks were punctured, and some 11 million tonnes (50 million litres) of heavy black crude oil leaked into the sea.

Alaska contains some of the most remarkable unspoilt scenery in the United States. Its mountains, forests, rivers and coastal waters contain a unique collection of wildlife. They are at risk from oil spills and the further development of oil-related activity (Figure 4).

The consequences of the Exxon Valdez oil pill just offshore were very serious. The oil loated ashore and coated some 3800 ilometres of Alaska's coastline. Three million irds lost their lives along with many other ypes of wildlife (Figure 5). The clean-up eration lasted 6 months and cost around 50 million. 85 planes and over a thousand s and other vessels were involved. In l 11,000 people were employed by Exxon help. Birds needed cleaning and sticky oil ches had to be treated on long stretches of st line.

After six months the clean-up, which had volved a variety of methods (Figure 6), was lted. Exxon claimed that about 50% of the ntaminated coastline had been 'treated'. wever, experts from the state of Alaska d that only 10% of this was actually fit for imal and plant life. So the effects of the oil ill will last for many years.

One positive result of the disaster is that it vill probably keep new oil-drilling operations way from the coastlines of California, Florida nd New England. This is because residents here will not want to risk their environments eing threatened by a similar accident to that in Alaska.

Figure 5
Wildlife killed by
Exxon Valdez oil spill. 1989

Figure 6 Methods of cleaning up oil spills

Accidents are rare, but when oil spills occur the oil industry has emergency procedures to minimise any damage.

1 **Dispersants:** Strong detergents can be sprayed on to the oil. These cause it to break up more quickly. However, dispersants cannot be used close to the shore or near fisheries as the chemicals are poisonous to marine life.

2 **Sinking:** Oil floats on the surface, but powdered chalk spread on the surface absorbs the oil and makes it sink. Although the surface is cleared quickly, the oil ends up on the sea bed where it can continue to damage the plants and animals living there.

3 **Absorption:** Materials such as straw, peat and polystyrene can be put on the water to absorb the oil. They continue to float and can be collected and disposed of. This method can only be used in calm conditions.

4 **Booms:** Floating barriers can be placed in the water to prevent the oil from spreading on to nearby beaches and wildlife areas. Small slicks can be surrounded by booms and the oil sucked from the surface into a tanker. Calm water is needed.

5 **Leave it:** If the oil spill is far out to sea it is often best to leave it and let natural processes break it up.

6 **Burning:** If the oil is at least 2mm thick it can be burnt off.

Activities

1 a List three different types of pollution found in the seas and oceans.

b Where does most marine pollution come from?

2 Copy and complete the following passage. Use the words in the word-list, but watch out for three 'red herrings'!

The oceans of the world cover - - - - - - - - - of the earth's surface. They contain a variety of animal and plant life. Fish and plants live together in a marine ecosystem, which provides - - - - - - for people.

The oceans contain many pollutants which are the - - - - - - - - - - of human activities such as - - - - - - - - and - - - - - - - - - -. About 83% of the sea's pollutants come from - - - - - - - - - - activities, while the remainder come from deliberate dumping of sewage or other wastes or from - - - - - - - - - - spills.

Word-list: accidental; by-products; deliberate; domestic; farming; food; industry; land-based; one-third; two-thirds.

3 a Study Figure 2. Explain the role of rivers in bringing pollution to the seas and oceans.

b How much ● material enters the world's oceans in suspension and solution; ● oil enters the world's oceans each year?

4 *a* Study the maps (Figure 3) which give an account of the events of the evening of March 24 1989. Write an account of these events in the style of a newspaper front page, making use of diagrams and maps.
Your account should be about 200 words long, and should include a suitable headline.

b The newspaper's Environment Correspondent is attending a Conference. Your Editor asks you to stand in for her, and write a supplement to your main article. In it you should outline the possible effects of the accident on the wildlife and environment of the area. You will need to study Figures 4 and 5 to help with this.

5 Study the different methods of oil dispersal listed in Figure 6.

a Make a note of any disadvantage associated with each method.

b Which of the methods do you think is most effective and least harmful to the environment?

6 Draw a simple cartoon, showing an official from the Exxon Oil Company meeting a local Alaskan resident just after the oil spill. Include a caption to indicate what is said!

7 Did the Alaskan oil spill have any positive results?

Dictionary

acid rain rainwater which having absorbed polluting chemicals in the atmosphere has higher levels of acidity than normal
algae single-celled organisms which live in water
by-products the subsidiary gases, liquids or solid materials which are produced as an unintended result of certain human activities
deforestation the removal of trees from a forested area
ecosystem a set of interacting interdependent living and non-living components
habitat the natural home of a plant or animal
leaching removal of soil nutrients by water passing through the soil
litter a layer of dead organic material (leaves etc.) which gathers on the land surface and gradually decomposes
logging the industry which fells trees on a commercial scale
nutrients useful minerals which provide nourishment to a living organism
queimadas a Portuguese term meaning 'burnings', used to describe the time of year when the Amazonian rainforest fires are most numerous
soil broken down rock material together with rotted vegetation and animals
submerged hidden underwater